Tongans Overseas

Published with the support of the

School of Hawaiian, Asian, and Pacific Studies,

University of Hawai'i

Tongans Overseas
Between Two Shores

Helen Morton Lee

University of Hawai'i Press
Honolulu

08 07 06 05 04 03   1 2 3 4 5 6

Library of Congress Cataloging-in-Publication Data

Lee, Helen Morton.

Tongans overseas : between two shores / Helen Morton Lee.

p.   cm.

Includes bibliographical references and index.

ISBN 0-8248-2615-9 (hardcover : alk. paper)—ISBN 0-8248-2654-X (pbk. : alk. paper)

1. Tongans—Foreign countries.   2. Tongans—Ethnic identity.   I. Title.

DU880 .L44 2003

305.89'948—dc21

2002010950

University of Hawai'i Press books are printed on acid-free
paper and meet the guidelines for permanence and durability
of the Council on Library Resources.

Designed by Cameron Poulter

Printed by The Maple-Vail Book Manufacturing Group

CONTENTS

Acknowledgments vii

"Between Two Shores" ix

1. Introduction: *Migration and Cultural Identity* / 1

2. Leaving Tonga "For Our Future" / 14

3. Life Overseas: *Community and Conflict* / 40

4. Identity in the Diaspora:
    Perspectives of the First Generation / 81
    Case Studies 1 and 2

5. Diasporic Youth: *"Stuck between Two Worlds"?* / 131
    Case Studies 3 and 4

6. Intermarriage: *"A Two-Way Life"* / 187
    Case Studies 5 and 6

7. Looking Ahead / 234

    APPENDIX A: *The Tongans of Melbourne, Australia* / 255

    APPENDIX B: *Profiles of Interviewees* / 276

    Notes / 291

    References / 305

    Index / 323

    Illustrations follow page 124

ACKNOWLEDGMENTS

FIRST AND FOREMOST MY DEEPEST GRATITUDE TO Meliame Tauali'i, who worked as my research assistant from mid-1997 to mid-1999. Her enthusiasm, commitment, and competence were invaluable. My research was funded from January 1995 to June 1996 by a University of Melbourne Women with Career Interruptions Research Fellowship, held in the Gender Studies Research Unit, Department of History. From mid-1996 to mid-1999, funding was provided by an Australian Research Council Postdoctoral Research Fellowship, held in the School of Social Sciences at La Trobe University in Melbourne.

There are many people to thank, especially the Tongans of Melbourne who contributed to the study and supported the project wholeheartedly. I am particularly grateful to Reverends James Lātū and Jason Kioa for their support and for granting me access to their files of newspaper clippings and other documents, and to Rosemary Naitoko for her assistance with piecing together the history of the Tongan settlement in Melbourne. Special thanks to Elizabeth Wood-Ellem for her consistent support and encouragement. The generous feedback from two anonymous readers and Niko Besnier helped me develop my original manuscript into the shape it now takes, and Pamela Kelley of the University of Hawai'i Press has provided valuable support and guidance.

John Mühler at the Department of Immigration and Multicultural Affairs in Australia was helpful with gathering relevant statistics. Thanks to Chris Donehue of Campus Graphics at La Trobe University for producing the diagram in figure 1 and to John Shakespeare for permission to reproduce his illustration (fig. 2). "Between Two Shores" is reproduced by kind permission of Mushroom Music Publishing and Universal Music Publishing Group. Meliame Tauali'i kindly supplied the photographs.

To my family and friends who have been there for me, especially my three wonderful children, Pauli Kavapalu and Rosie and Hannah Morton, I am forever grateful! Many others gave encouragement along the way: Marianne Franklin, Taholo Kami, 'Alopi Lātūkefu, Sam Taufa, and the scattered Tongans who have enthusiastically discussed the research with me via e-mail. These conversations, more than anything else, gave me a real sense of how complex and meaningful are the webs of connection throughout the Tongan diaspora; I hope this book gives something back to those who have given so much.

"BETWEEN TWO SHORES"

I have another place, so very far away
In dreams I'm always walking by the sea
No shoes upon my feet
Strong sun upon my back
I wake up and you're there right next to me
I left my childhood home
I came here on my own
The winter rains they chilled me through and through
And all the different ways, the very air was strange
I would have turned around if not for you
I will always be between two shores
This place is now my home
Our children here have grown
I would have turned around
If not for you.

Vika Bull, Linda Bull, and Paul Kelly (copyright © Mushroom Music Publishing and Universal Music Publishing, 1996)

1

Introduction
Migration and Cultural Identity

For the overseas Tongan, what does "being Tongan" mean?
Is knowing the Tongan language that important?
Should Tongan parents here in the United States raise their children like they do in the Islands?
How does Tongan culture adapt to American society?

THESE ARE SOME OF THE HUNDREDS OF QUESTIONS that have been asked on the Kava Bowl (KB), an Internet discussion forum with predominantly overseas Tongan participants. They are also the kinds of questions I had in mind when I began my research with Tongan migrants early in 1995. Having studied childhood in Tonga, in the South Pacific, particularly the processes through which children become "Tongan" (Morton 1996), I became interested in the impact of migration on Tongans' ideas about what it means to be Tongan. How do they negotiate cultural differences? Do they maintain, reject, or adjust their ideas about being Tongan once they are living overseas?

By following the KB discussions, interviewing some of the regular participants via e-mail, and conducting more conventional ethnographic fieldwork with Tongans in Melbourne, Australia, I was able to explore the diverse experiences of migrants and their descendants. This book is the result of those explorations, and its central theme is cultural identity in the context of migration, an issue that has been raised on numerous occasions on the KB and that is of deep concern to Tongans both at home and overseas.

Many Tongans assert that to be "really" Tongan a person must have not only Tongan ancestors, but also a knowledge of *anga fakatonga,* or the Tongan way. This concept encompasses all values, beliefs, and practices that are regarded as elements of Tongan "culture" and "tradition." As such a broadly defined concept it leaves a great deal of room for interpretation, and each person I have encountered has given a slightly different definition of *anga fakatonga* and of its many elements. Both in Tonga and in the diaspora it is also a highly contested concept, particularly across generations, and is constantly under negotiation and reconstruction. There is widespread concern that *anga fakatonga* is being lost and that the younger generations, especially those growing up overseas, will therefore lose their cultural identity. Will young Tongans overseas be "Tongan" only by virtue of their genetic inheritance, or will they continue to identify culturally as Tongan? If they do the latter, which elements of being Tongan will they consider important?

Cultural Identity and Ethnicity

My very first interview in Melbourne reminded me that "cultural identity" is as slippery a concept as "the Tongan way" and also one that cannot be assumed to be of equal significance to each individual. My first interviewee was 'Ana (thirty-eight), who left Tonga for New Zealand at the age of eighteen (see Case Study 1).[1] She then moved to Melbourne in the late 1970s, where she married another Tongan. At the time of our interview in April 1995, she was living in a modest suburban home with her husband, her two teenage children, and two adult nieces. She worked and studied part-time and was involved in a Tongan church. 'Ana was emphatic that she did not see herself primarily as Tongan; her Tongan identity was something she preferred to leave largely unexamined, taken for granted, and to be shrugged off impatiently if it got in the way of what she wanted to do in life. Yet no matter how much she was uninterested in her cultural identity, it shaped her life. It caused friction with her husband, who was self-consciously aware and proud of his own Tongan identity, and it influenced her relationship with her children, who had varying degrees of involvement with their extended family and with the members of the Tongan church they attended. Furthermore, 'Ana's identity as a member of an "ethnic" group often simply could not be discounted in her interactions with the non-Tongan population.[2]

This first interview helped to shape the research that followed, warning me not to make assumptions about how people construct their identities and alerting me to the diversity of experiences both within and between families of migrants and their descendants.[3] It revealed the importance of people's agency and decision making, and their active involvement in shaping their own lives and attempting to shape the lives of others. At the same time, the interview highlighted the kinds of structural limitations, such as socioeconomic status and the impact of ethnic stereotypes, that can impinge upon this agency. 'Ana, like many others I spoke with, also pointed out the constraints imposed from "within" by the Tongan way itself, especially on younger people.

Throughout this book the younger generations are a central concern: the children, adolescents, and young adults who have spent most or all of their lives outside Tonga. Already the overseas-born Tongans outnumber those born in Tonga, and my survey of 100 households in Melbourne showed that of 430 individuals of Tongan descent, 204 were born in Tonga and 226 were born overseas. Throughout the Tongan population worldwide there is a high proportion of young people; for example, in New Zealand just over 32 percent of Tongans were under the age of 10 in 1996 (Statistics New Zealand 1998, 11), and in Tonga itself the median age was 19.9 in the same year, with 50.2 percent of the population under 19 (*Tonga Chronicle* 1998d).

However, the published information on this critical group is meager. By focusing largely on these younger Tongans, including those from marriages between Tongans and non-Tongans, my aim is to contribute to our knowledge of their experiences, attitudes, and identities, as well as to provide a glimpse into the possible future of Tongans overseas. Of course, not all of those who were born overseas or who migrated as young children are "young," as some are now in their thirties and even forties. This group has not been excluded from this book, and it is interesting to compare their experiences with those of younger people.[4] I have included them in the cohort I refer to as "the younger generations," but by far the largest group within this cohort is under the age of twenty.

My concern with cultural and ethnic identity is with the ways they are subjectively defined, described, and experienced by individuals and how people measure their own and others' identities against an imagined norm of Tonganness. Any attempt to list and measure the criteria that define Tongan identity would be futile, as each individual has her or his own definition of that identity, shaped by her or his life experiences.[5] In later chapters it will become clear that certain elements are more widely regarded as essentially Tongan than others and that even these elements are contested and subject to transformation.

The view of cultural and ethnic identity taken here is influenced by recent work on the socially constructed nature of identity, sometimes referred to as the constructivist approach. Joanne Nagel states that in relation to ethnic identity, this approach

> stresses the fluid, situational, volitional, and dynamic character of ethnic identification, organization, and action—a model that emphasizes the socially "constructed" aspects of ethnicity, i.e., the ways in which ethnic boundaries, identities, and cultures, are negotiated, defined, and produced through social interaction inside and outside ethnic communities (1994, 152).[6]

While this view accords to a great extent with my own, a concern is that, as Gillian Bottomley argues, a "voluntarist position" neglects the fact that ethnicity can be "imposed, as well as assumed and inherited" (1992, 60). Nor is ethnicity something that can be adopted and discarded at will, particularly when there are physical markers of ethnicity and when it is linked to notions of "race" and to class structures. The argument that ethnicity is socially constructed needs to be tempered by an awareness of the specific historical and social contexts in which it is embedded and the subsequent limitations on its malleability and fluidity (Fenton 1999; Jenkins 1997). It is also important to recognize, as Arjun Appadurai points out, that ethnicity becomes "naturalized" (1996, 140) so that while it can be analyzed as a social construction, it is often experienced quite differently. While the primordialist view of ethnicity has been thoroughly critiqued (e.g., Eller and Coughlan 1993; Tilley 1997), it will become clear in this book that many Tongans perceive their cultural identities in terms of primordial attachments based on "blood" ties and inherited qualities of "Tonganness."

This "naturalized" view of ethnicity involves assumptions of authority and authenticity; the belief that there is one particular way to be "Tongan." Yet for Tongans, as for any immigrant group, in practice there is no unified or homogenous cultural identity (Gans 1997). Cultural identity, as Stuart Hall argues, is something that is constantly being produced and reproduced, with similarity and continuity coexisting with difference and rupture (1990). Herbert Gans points out: "Every immigrant family comes with its own ethnic practices, which are most likely a mix of handed-down remembered family, community and regional practices" (1997, 881). Ensuring migrants' descendants retain a sense of ethnic identity may require the reconstruction and "invention" of ethnic identity, a process Gans points out can be similar to what has been described as "acculturation" elsewhere in the literature.[7]

Thus the reconstruction of ethnic identity, or "tradition," may also be part of the process of adjusting to the host society.[8]

As well as retaining the loyalty of younger generations within the group, these processes of reconstruction also occur in response to the imposition of ethnicity onto the group by the host society. In a paper written during the early stages of my research, I argued that the term "cultural identity" is preferable to "ethnic identity" since it allows for more flexible, hybrid identities that extend beyond the imagined boundaries of "ethnic" groups (Morton 1998a, 4). Cultural identity encompasses the nonethnic, intragroup distinctions Tongans use, such as those between bush and town people, different religious denominations, and so forth. Rather than attempting to conflate culture and ethnicity, the term "cultural identity" as I use it refers to Tongans' own understandings of what it is to be Tongan and how they evaluate one another according to those understandings.

During my research it became clear that overseas Tongans are also adopting an ethnic identity, which is gradually blurring with what I have called cultural identity. In the host nations, this occurs as a response to the ideology and practices of "multiculturalism," in which ethnicity is represented in the public sphere primarily by the outward markers of cultural difference, such as food, music and dance, clothing, and so on. By accepting and working with these representations in their interactions with the wider community, "ethnic" groups can access specially allocated services and resources, and through this, groups can gain a measure of power (see Finney 1999 on Tongans in Canberra).[9] At the same time, this construction of ethnicity can begin to influence people's ideas about "cultural" identity so that over time it becomes increasingly difficult to distinguish between ethnic and cultural identity.

This blurring of ethnic and cultural identity is occurring throughout the overseas-Tongan population, and increasingly it is a response to Tongans' sense of themselves as marginalized and disempowered. "Ethnicity" may be publically constructed in terms of cultural difference, but the power relations underlying this concept (and that of "race") disadvantage nonwhite minority groups (Hage 1998; Tai and Kenyatta 1999). By accepting their positioning as an ethnic group, Tongans are asserting their difference while proclaiming their unity as a people, as well as heralding their intentions to seek ways to improve their situation. It is ironic indeed that while Tongans are intensely proud that Tonga was never formally colonized, as immigrants they have often been subjected to the "internal colonialism" faced by minority groups in Western nations (Pedraza 1994, 4). Tongans' increasing awareness of "postcolonial" issues is emerging not out of independence struggles within their own nation, but through the process of migration.

Tongan Migration

The migration of Tongans to host nations around the world, particularly since the late 1960s, has created a diasporic population that is now at least equal to that remaining in Tonga (see chap. 2). They are "diasporic" in the sense of being "multiple communities of a dispersed population" (Clifford 1994, 304; see Tedlock 1996), and while they are not exiled in the manner of the original diasporic peoples, such as Jews, we will see that even those who desire an eventual return to Tonga are unable to do so. Compared with many diasporic populations, such as the Chinese (Ong 1999), Sikhs (Barrier and Dusenbury 1989; Singh and Barrier 1996), and the "black" diaspora (Conniff 1994; Segal 1995), the overseas Tongan population is small, making them a largely invisible population in host nations such as the United States and Australia. However, they share the tendency of many diasporic and migrant populations to be positioned as part of a larger, panethnic category by the receiving nations: Tongans become "Pacific Islanders" while others are "Asians" or "Hispanics." In chapter 7 the growing tendency of young overseas Tongans to adopt a panethnic identity is examined, revealing that such imposed categories can also become internalized in the process of constructing cultural identities.

For all their new and diverse experiences as settlers in their new homes, very few Tongan migrants ever completely lose their connections—emotional, familial, economic, religious, and otherwise—to their homeland; they remain between two shores. Their children and grandchildren often have a much narrower range of such ties, although for a great many of them Tonga is still a significant symbol of their "heritage," their "roots," as well as being an often romanticized vision of another way of life. Those who retain multiple ties with Tonga can be described as "transnational," maintaining a sense of Tonga as "home" while establishing new homes elsewhere (Basch, Glick Schiller, and Szanton Blanc 1994; Kearney 1995; Mahler 1998). Their important economic contribution to Tonga, through remittances, is discussed in chapter 2; however, throughout this book it will become apparent that it is emotional and social ties that are of more concern to Tongans and that can indirectly affect even those young Tongans who have no direct connections with the islands.

Recent work on transnationalism has begun to consider the "second generation" and the extent to which ties are maintained with their parents' homeland and with members of the diasporic population (Vertovec 2001). The literature on transnationalism has also expanded from a primary focus on the global economy (see Kearney 1995; Sassen 1998) to a concern with issues of identity (e.g., see Hannerz 1996; Vertovec 2001; Westwood and Phizacklea 2000). My exploration of the construction of cultural identity by second-generation Tongans is informed by this work, and I examine the impact of new forms of transnational ties, such as those facilitated by computer-mediated communications.

Although many Tongans young and old have a sentimental view of themselves as "between two shores," the reality is that the dispersal of Tongans throughout much of the world also has led to the creation of a multitude of other ties—between family and friends in different locations overseas, within the Tongan populations concentrated in particular cities and towns, and between Tongans and others of many different nationalities. Tongans form an astonishingly complex network of connections despite the fact that large-scale international migration is a relatively recent phenomenon for them, beginning only in the 1970s.

The earliest of these connections were made long before the 1970s, although until the mid-twentieth century most Tongans traveling overseas were temporary visitors rather than migrants. One of the earliest, and certainly most well known, of these visitors was Tonga's first king, Tupou I (King George), who traveled to Sydney in 1853. His trip long has been regarded as significantly influencing his determination to keep Tonga's lands out of foreign hands.[10] Soon after that, members of Tonga's royal and chiefly families were sent to schools in Auckland and Sydney, or they traveled there for medical treatments, holidays, and official visits.[11] Commoners (nonchiefly Tongans) also had early opportunities to travel on whaling ships and other vessels and as missionaries to other parts of the Pacific. The influx of American soldiers into Tonga during World War II gave many Tongans their first experiences of wage labor and contributed to the trickle of immigration in the 1950s, which grew into a surge by the 1970s as increasing numbers

sought educational and other opportunities overseas. Some later returned to their island home, but many remained overseas and became
the first wave of settlers, later bringing family members to join them
and so beginning to weave the web of connections that continues to
grow today.

Other Pacific Islanders experienced very different historical ties to
foreign nations, particularly throughout the period of European and
American colonial expansion, but they have shared the Tongans' history of dispersing through migration and of maintaining complex ties
with one another and with their homelands. This history has led John
Connell to comment that "it is the new diaspora that extraordinarily
rapidly has come to characterize the contemporary South Pacific"
(1987, 399; see McCall and Connell 1993). Pacific Islanders have migrated in numbers that are large relative to their total populations, yet
their actual numbers are so small that they have attracted comparatively little attention in studies of migration and settlement. In his recent study of Islanders' remittance behavior Richard Brown observed,
"It is surprising how relatively little is known about the Pacific Island
migrant communities in Australia and elsewhere" (1998, 112).

This book focuses on one of the largest of the Pacific Islander populations overseas, the Tongans, particularly those in the major receiving
nations of the United States, New Zealand, and Australia. My discussion of cultural identity is contextualized within a broader examina-
tion of diasporic Tongans, looking at the ways they engage with the
wider societies in which they live, particularly in terms of their negotiations of cultural difference. Tongans throughout the diaspora combine Tongan and other elements in their daily lives in a vast variety of
ways, and my aim is to explore the impact of these multiple, sometimes conflicting, elements on individuals' perceptions of their own
and other Tongans' identities.

Tongans in Cyberspace

The KB forum and similar sites provide overseas Tongans with a means
of communicating with others like themselves throughout the world
and a chance to discuss issues and air their opinions in a context that,
because of its computer-mediated character, seems safe and somewhat
impersonal. As I have shown elsewhere (Morton 1999), an incredibly
diverse range of issues are discussed, many of which center on the con-

cerns of migrants and their descendants. When I first came across the KB I was astonished at how openly critical were many of the posts, particularly those by young Tongans, who in "real life" ideally should be respectful, obedient, and never critical of their elders or the Tongan way. To some extent this can be attributed to the anonymity afforded by Internet communications, but many posters choose to give their own names (Morton 2001b), and their messages on the KB represent an increasingly self-conscious evaluation of the Tongan way that is occurring among Tongans more generally and that is having diverse effects on both older and younger generations.

The KB is part of a larger site called Tonga Online (http://www.tongaonline.com/), established in 1995 by Taholo Kami, a Tongan and at that time a student at Vanderbilt University in Tennessee. The site was developed partly for non-Tongans who wanted to know more about Tonga and its people, but the primary impetus for the site was to provide a means for Tongans in the diaspora to communicate easily with one another.[12] Tonga Online comprises numerous different elements, from virtual postcards to travel information, as well as articles and features, news from Tonga, and so on, but the most popular is the KB forum.[13] In his mission statement for the KB, Kami stated that it aimed "[t]o provide a bridge for our island communities. Bringing people together around the KAVABOWL to discuss issues that will make a difference in the urban communities overseas and the Islands back home" (4.2.98).[14] The KB quickly became incredibly popular and was receiving over half a million "hits" per month by 1998. Originally a single discussion forum, this popularity led it to be subdivided into different forums for greetings and announcements, general discussion, poetry and creative writing, and so on. The "chat rooms" linked to the KB are also popular and unlike the main forum involve synchronous communication.

Promoted as a virtual kava-drinking circle in a virtual village, the KB became a means for Tongans around the world to communicate. Varying from short greetings to long discussions of different issues, the messages posted serve to connect friends and families, disseminate information, and facilitate the exchange of experiences and ideas. Many of the participants are located in major cities and are young and well educated (many are attending tertiary institutions or have already graduated). However, the location, age, education, and even English fluency of participants varies enormously. Their discussions have been a rich source of data for this book, and after following the forum for some time I was also able to contact regular participants directly and "interview" them via e-mail.[15]

Tongans in Melbourne

The Tongans of Melbourne are a small migrant population in the multicultural capital of the state of Victoria, with inhabitants originating in over two hundred countries. In some suburbs of Melbourne over half the population was born overseas, and while some migrant groups have congregated in particular areas, Tongans are dispersed throughout the metropolitan area with very little clustering. Appendix A discusses this population in detail, including the history of Tongan settlement in Melbourne and the results of my survey of 100 households comprising 479 individuals.[16] At this juncture, my aim is simply to give a brief overview of the population of Tongans in Melbourne by way of introduction. Interviews and informal conversations with members of this population combine with the KB material and e-mail interviews discussed previously to give voice to the views and experiences of Tongan migrants and their children.

I estimate that there are around three thousand people of Tongan descent living in Melbourne in the year 2001, many of whom can trace their migration back through chains linking them to a handful of early migrants arriving in the late 1950s and early 1960s. Most of these first migrants were young women who went to Melbourne for training, often in nursing, and who married Australians and settled permanently. Over the years they assisted family members' migration, and these new migrants then helped still more relatives, forming the chains that continue even today, as most new migrants arrive under family reunification schemes.[17] Figure 1 shows the chains of migration within one extended family in Melbourne, from the 1960s to the 1980s.[18] In total, there are now 138 members of this one family living in Australia, all of whom can trace their connections through blood or marriage back to the one original migrant who came to study, married an Australian, and eventually became an Australian citizen. Many other relatives are scattered throughout the diaspora, while some remain in Tonga.

By the late 1960s the Tongans in Melbourne had begun to develop a sense of community through social gatherings, and in 1969 they established the interdenominational Tongan Christian Fellowship. The

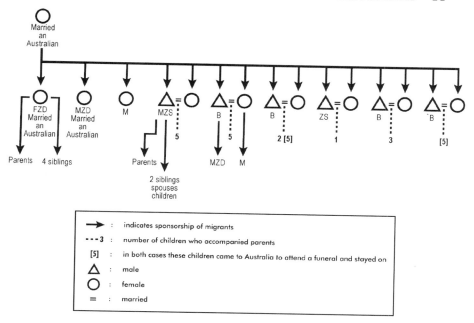

Figure 1: Chain migration within one extended family in Melbourne, 1960–1980.

group expanded and was soon having regular church services, forming dance and choir groups, sharing events such as marriages, funerals, and baptisms, and helping new migrants find accommodation and employment. Over time there were schisms in the group, with some members splitting off to form new church-based groups in different parts of Melbourne. By 2001 there were twenty-two congregations with predominantly Tongan membership in Melbourne and rural Victoria, representing twelve different religious groups.

As the number of Tongans in Melbourne has grown and the various churches have been established, the sense of a united "Tongan community" has, to a great extent, diminished. The sheer number of Tongans in Melbourne today means that they do not all know one another, as was the case in the 1960s through to the early 1980s, although Tongans who meet can usually discover some connection through ties of extended kinship. A residual sense of community does persist, encouraged in part by outsiders' perceptions of Tongans as an "ethnic group."

The Tongan-born living in Melbourne are predominantly from Tonga's capital, Nuku'alofa. They are now outnumbered by their overseas-born children, and overall it is a youthful population, with nearly 70 percent of my sample population under age thirty. Some of the children of migrants have now had children of their own, beginning the third generation of Tongans in Melbourne, and there was one child in my sample, an infant, who is of the fourth generation. Intermarriage has been common since the first wave of students arrived and married in Australia, so that many young people have one parent who is not Tongan (20.7 percent of my sample). Young people with two Tongan parents or one are differentiated throughout the book as "Tongan" and "part-Tongan" respectively, with the latter also occasionally referred to by hyphenated terms indicating their parents' nationalities.[19]

Scattered across Melbourne, people's homes vary from tiny "bedsits" (one-room apartments) to large, expensive houses. In these homes there is great variation in the extent to which Tongan elements are present. The interiors of some homes are much like those in Tonga, with pandanus mats fringed with colorful wool on the floor, handicrafts such as fans and bags on display, many framed family photographs covering the walls, and religious paintings or wall hangings. There are smells of Tongan food cooking, and within the home people wear Tongan clothing and listen to Tongan music. Other homes betray little or no Tongan influence, and household members appear thoroughly Western, preferring Western food, clothing, music, and social activities.

In terms of settlement history and socioeconomic status, the Tongan population of Melbourne can be roughly divided into two groups. The first includes the early migrants and their families and the relatives they have sponsored to join them. Many could be described as "middle class" and are employed in skilled occupations. Members of this group tend to be more geographically scattered and are more likely to own their own homes. Many mix comfortably with non-Tongans in work and social situations, especially those who have intermarried, and their homes and lifestyles are more likely to be Western influenced.

The second group is comprised of more recent migrants, who tend to live in closer proximity to each other and have fewer interactions with non-Tongans. This group is more "working class," with a high proportion of unskilled workers and lower levels of education. They are more likely to have Tongan lifestyles and home decor. Of course, these are not clear-cut categories, and there is considerable variation within each of the groups, but this distinction between them was often mentioned by Tongans themselves and is at the root of some of the tensions within the Melbourne population that will be discussed in chapter 3.

It does not follow that members of the latter group identify more strongly as Tongan than the former, and for every person I spoke with, in Melbourne and elsewhere, the issue of cultural identity was important in some way. Even 'Ana, who does not dwell on her own identity as Tongan, finds her life influenced in many ways by that identity. We will see that 'Ana is quite unusual in her lack of interest in her cultural identity and that it is far more common for this to be of considerable concern to people. As indicated by the sample of questions raised on the KB found at the beginning of this chapter, migration influences people to become more self-consciously aware of their identities. Migration entails an ongoing negotiation of cultural differences in workplaces, schools, and homes; it is a process that can entail tensions and conflict but that can also be rewarding and enriching for both migrants and their descendants.

2

Leaving Tonga "For Our Future"

TONGANS LIVING OVERSEAS HAVE SHARED the experiences of many other migrants, such as language difficulties, generational conflict, poor socioeconomic status on arrival, and so on. Like other migrants, they have found that settling in another country leads to transformations in gender relations and family organization through their interactions with the wider society from the level of individuals to the state. "Success" as a migrant can be elusive and highly variable, from international fame to poverty and marginalization.

As relatively new migrants, Tongans have also had different experiences from those of the early waves of migrants reaching nations such as the United States. The "new" immigrants, who have arrived in host nations mainly from the "Third World" since the 1960s, are less able to follow the process of rapid "assimilation" and economic advancement often experienced by earlier European immigrants (Portes 1997). New immigrants' experiences are due to factors such as discrimination against nonwhites and the changing requirements of labor markets—the earlier arrivals were a sought-after labor force while the newer migrants have arrived during times of comparatively high unemployment levels. At the same time, the very nature of migration also has changed, with advanced information and transport systems enabling multiple migrations, circular migration, reemigration (Barkan 1992), and increasing transnationalism.

While the following chapters examine in more detail the lives of Tongans who have settled overseas, here the aim is to look at the experience of migration itself. Why do people choose to leave Tonga, where do they go, and why? What has been the impact of migration on Tonga and those who remain in the islands?

Seeking "Opportunities" through Migration

One of the more poignant reminders of the dispersal of Tongan families overseas is the lists of family members, and their locations around
the world, that appear in the messages of good wishes *(pōpoaki talam-
onū)* in the weekly Tongan newspaper *Ko e Kalonikali Tonga* (English
version: *The Tonga Chronicle*). These messages mark special occasions
such as first and twenty-first birthdays, often of family members themselves living outside Tonga, and are a public statement of the continuing strength of family members' emotional ties with one another.

Scattered family members do occasionally gather to celebrate important birthdays or to attend weddings, graduations, and funerals. At a
twenty-first birthday celebration in Melbourne in 2000, for example,
many family members from interstate and overseas were among the
350 guests. Such occasions are an opportunity for dispersed sibling
groups to reunite, for young people to meet relatives from elsewhere in
the diaspora, and for other extended family members to renew their
ties. Given that kinship is centrally important to Tongans, why do
members of families move away from their homes in Tonga, and why
do they scatter to different cities and countries, often living so far away
from one another?

"Family" is in fact one of the primary motivating factors in Tongan
migration, and one of the most frequently heard explanations for migration is simply "to help the family" (see Cowling 1990, 196). The
idea of "family" encompasses the complex sets of rights and obligations of Tongan kinship as well as the deep emotional connections between kin (Morton 1996). Ideally, migration is seen as a way of improving the life chances of those who migrate and of their families
remaining in Tonga, who benefit primarily through remittances.

People frequently told me they saw migration as a way to access the
"opportunities" overseas and that their move was "for our future."
Bianca (twenty-four), a U.S.-born Mormon, explained that her parents
migrated in the 1970s "to 'start fresh' and have a better life." However,
the desire to improve the life chances of the immediate family operates
in tension with the sense of obligation to kin remaining in Tonga; as
we will see, remittances can be a significant drain on a migrant family's
income. The way some migrants lessen this tension is to assist as many
family members as possible to migrate themselves so that they can seek
their own opportunities.

In describing their reasons for migrating, Tongans speak of the perceived benefits of residence overseas compared with the disadvantages of living in Tonga—the "push and pull factors" sometimes referred to in migration studies. Although many Tongans find themselves in poorly paid factory jobs overseas, their wages are still higher than in Tonga, and they have access to a far greater range of goods and services. The low wage levels in Tonga and the increasing difficulty of access to farmland act as disincentives for many families to remain. Some migrants are further motivated by dissatisfaction with Tonga's hierarchical social system and the government, the difficulty of accessing credit (such as for starting a business), and frustration with the poor quality of services such as health care.

As we have seen, traveling overseas to attend school and tertiary institutions was a pattern established initially by the higher-ranking families in Tonga in the late nineteenth century.[1] Today, education continues to be one of the most significant reasons for moving temporarily or permanently away from Tonga, although it was not until the late 1960s that commoner families pursued education overseas in significant numbers.[2] In some cases individual students make the move overseas, and in others they accompany their parents, who may have additional motives for migrating. Those who have been educated overseas often want their own children to be similarly educated. Samuela, who settled in Australia after being sent from Tonga in the 1970s for a training course, told me proudly that all his children had attended university, adding, "That's why I'm here!"

Education in an English-speaking country is preferred, but there are also Tongan students in Japan and various European nations, as well as elsewhere throughout the world. A number of scholarship schemes are available to Tongans, funded by overseas aid, and although they usually include a requirement that the student return to Tonga to work for a certain period at the end of their studies, many either do not return or return only for that period before moving permanently away from Tonga. The two major Mormon universities, in Hawai'i and Utah, also have attracted many Tongan students, some of whom have made the United States their permanent home.[3]

Each individual and family makes the decision to leave Tonga on the basis of their own particular circumstances, and it is often difficult to pinpoint just who made the final decision and how it was reached. Many claim the decision to migrate is their own choice (see Cowling 1990; Lafitani 1992). I found that often in these cases people perceived themselves as somehow unusual or different, as not fitting in in Tonga, so they saw migration as the best option. For example, they said they had never felt happy in Tonga or that they were loners who did not get on with their peers or that they had an unusual upbringing.

Others migrate at the urging of family members already living overseas, who give positive reports of the work opportunities, quality of the education system, and so on, which further enhance the image most Tongans already have of the opportunities to be found outside Tonga. Many are more than happy to join their relatives overseas, but some are more reluctant emigrants. Families can exert considerable pressure on their members; for example, the couple I lived with during my doctoral fieldwork in Tonga in 1988 did not want to leave Tonga, as they both had reliable incomes, the husband had begun a taxi business, and they had only recently built their own home. Yet they eventually bowed to the considerable pressure brought to bear by family members of both partners to join them in Australia, and they remain there today.

Migration may be carefully planned, but it is important not to assume that this is true in all cases, and in many instances people admitted it "just happens." One person will go overseas to work and later obtain permanent residence and send for other family members, often without long-term planning. People often made comments to me such as "We just decided to stay here." 'Aisea (fifteen), whose family settled in Australia in the 1980s, said: "All I know is my father came here to visit his sister. He liked it here and brought the rest of the family over."

Women and men alike migrate either alone, with their partner, or as a nuclear family unit. One partner may stay in Tonga for a period before joining the other, who by that time has found work and accommodation. This practice has caused considerable problems, such as migrants establishing new lives overseas and neglecting their partners and children in Tonga. This occurs more often when men migrate, and women in Tonga are becoming increasingly alert to this possibility and often ensure their partners move to a destination where they can be watched over by the women's relatives. Often, the man lives with his wife's family. Another strategy is for the woman to move in with the man's family in Tonga, which helps ensure he continues to send remittances and later returns to Tonga or arranges for her to join him overseas.

This practice of one person migrating before sending for other family members is called "chain migration," and it has become one of the few ways for people to continue migrating from Tonga. Historically,

Tonga does not have the ties to former colonizing nations that many Pacific Islanders have and that have facilitated migration in the post-war period. American Samoans and Guamanians can move freely to the United States, Western Samoans enjoy concessionary migration policies in New Zealand, and Cook Islanders, Niueans, and Tokelauans are New Zealand citizens, but Tongans receive no preferential treatment as aspiring immigrants. Tongans have had to rely on regular migration channels, scholarships, and labor migration programs to leave Tonga. Since the labor migration programs have ended (see below) and immigration policies in most receiving nations have been tightened, the routes for migration have become more limited, and increasingly people have had to rely on family reunification schemes. Another practice is "step migration," in which migrants move in stages through different countries. This often includes an initial stage of rural to urban migration within Tonga (Perminow 1993). From Tonga, the migration path is then through American Samoa to the United States or, less often, through New Zealand to Australia.

Establishing the motives for Tongans' migration is a far easier task than compiling accurate statistics about their movements (see Connell, Harrison, and McCall 1991). Very limited statistics are kept in Tonga of those leaving and returning, and each receiving country has a different way of recording Tongans' arrivals and patterns of settlement. Different sets of statistics use different criteria for "Tongan," with some referring only to Tongans born in Tonga and others to anyone of Tongan ancestry. Thus when claims are made, such as Robert Franco's that there are "at least 134,000" Tongans overseas (1997, 80), they are difficult to compare with other estimations, such as Ken'ichi Sudo's of close to 98,000 (1997b, 101), or Cathy Small's of around 72,000 (1997, 220).[4] In addition, the population of Tongans overseas is growing rapidly through birth rates more than new migration. Figures thus become quickly outdated, and those that exclude overseas-born Tongans give an increasingly inaccurate indication of the size of the Tongan diaspora.

U.S. Census Bureau data seldom give statistics specifically on Tongans, and until the 2000 census Pacific Islanders were placed in the category "Asian and Pacific Islander."[5] Tongans are only a small minority group in the United States, as is the case in Australia. In New Zealand, where they are a much more significant proportion of the population, Tongans are more often recorded as a separate category in statistical data. The small numbers of Tongans in the United States and Australia compared to other migrant groups and their absence from many of the statistics on migration and minority groups has meant they are also usually absent from the literature on migration and "ethnic diversity" in these nations. In some they are not mentioned at all (e.g., Mindel, Habenstein, and White 1988) and in others only briefly.[6]

Of course, the problems do not lie entirely with the statistics collected. The fact that many Tongans settle overseas illegally makes it impossible to obtain accurate figures on migration and settlement. For many years Tongans have had one of the highest rates of overstaying per capita in Australia, with many being deported, although exact figures are not available (Connell and McCall 1989, 10; Finney 1999, 121; *Tonga Chronicle* 1999d). A recent report estimated that as of June 1999 5.3 percent of Tongans in Australia were overstayers (Maori and Pacific Islander Community Based Services 2000, 71), and according to the Department of Immigration and Multicultural Affairs, 15 percent of Tongans on visitor's visas in Australia either overstay or work illegally (*Matangi Tonga* 2000a). Of course, what must be borne in mind is that despite their high *rate* of overstaying, the actual *number* of illegal Tongan immigrants is small; in 2000 an estimated fourteen hundred Tongans were in this category in Australia (*Matangi Tonga* 2000a).

In New Zealand in the mid- to late 1970s, Tongan and other Pacific Islander overstayers were targeted by the government, and "the term 'overstayer' became synonymous with the Pacific Island communities" (Krishnan, Schoeffel, and Warren 1994, 15; see Tu'inukuafe 1990, 209). Pacific Islanders continued to be disproportionately prosecuted for overstaying; for example,

> [i]n the 1985–6 period, 86 percent of prosecutions for overstaying concerned people from the Pacific Islands, despite the fact that they represented only a third of all overstayers. In comparison, overstayers from the United States and the United Kingdom made up 31 percent of all overstayers and only five percent of prosecutions. (Krishnan et al 1994, 18)

Tongans' high rate of overstaying needs to be seen in the context of the difficulties they face migrating through the usual channels, particularly in recent years as the criteria for migration have become more stringent in all of the receiving nations. In addition, while there are undeniably cases where Tongans travel overseas with the intention of remaining illegally, there are far more cases where temporary visitors are persuaded to remain overseas by the opportunities they perceive and the urging of their families. Amnesties have enabled some of these overstayers to convert their status to that of permanent residents, but many are arrested and deported.

The most famous case in Australia of Tongans arrested as overstayers, known as the Kioa case, involved a man who came to Australia as a short-term student in 1981 and who was joined by his wife and child for his graduation.[7] He extended their visas in order to visit relatives, but during that period Cyclone Isaac struck Tonga, leaving massive destruction in its wake. His family in Tonga urged him to stay in Australia and work so he could send money home to help them, and although he applied to further extend his visa, several factors, including a delayed response to his application and the family's move to a new address, resulted in their being declared illegal immigrants. In 1983 he was arrested and held in detention for ten days before a long court battle ensued, during which neither he nor his wife was permitted to find employment.

The case was complicated by Kioa's youngest child being born in Australia, and that fact triggered a major review by the High Court of the legal principles involved in deportation cases. In December 1985 the deportation order was quashed, and the family was permitted to become permanent residents of Australia. The impact of the family's struggle continues to be felt, as it "helped to shape Australian administrative law. The details of their case are now taught to all Australia law students" (Grainger 1998, 72).

The Kioas' story had a happy ending, with the family members becoming Australian citizens and settling into their work and schooling. Overstayers sometimes find themselves in far more unhappy circumstances, as they are not only unable to access a range of government benefits and services (including free medical care), but are also limited in the kinds of work they can obtain and often become transient laborers, picking fruit for low wages and in poor conditions.[8] Overstayers may also be exploited by those who have assisted them in finding accommodations and employment and know that if they resist, they could be reported to the immigration authorities and subsequently deported. Known as *tala ova*, the reporting of overstayers by other Tongans can cause significant tensions within communities (Lafitani 1992).

Tongans' high rate of overstaying has affected immigration policy in Australia, and in 2000 a new sponsored-visitor visa policy was introduced that requires Tongans applying for a visitor's visa to be sponsored by a member of his or her family who is an Australian citizen. If there is any doubt that the person will return to Tonga, the sponsor is required to pay a security bond ranging from A$5,000 to 10,000 (*Matangi Tonga* 2000a).

New Zealand: The Largest Overseas Population

Although New Zealand now has a large Pacific Islander population, it is only in relatively recent history that Islanders have migrated there in significant numbers. Those who were given New Zealand citizenship during the colonial period (including Cook Islanders, Niueans, and Tokelauans) were the earliest migrants, but even by 1945 only around two thousand Polynesians were in New Zealand, and in 1956 around eight thousand (Bedford 1984, 118). The post–World War II period saw a rising demand for industrial labor, and while this was initially met by mainly British and European immigrants, in the 1960s assisted-immigration targets and a subsidized immigration scheme were introduced. This led to an increased intake from other areas, including the South Pacific, and by the mid-1970s many of the temporary and permanent workers in unskilled and semiskilled jobs were Pacific Islanders. Thus "[b]y 1973–4 immigration from the Cook Islands, Niue, Fiji, Tonga and Samoa accounted for six percent of immigration to New Zealand" (Krishnan, Schoeffel, and Warren 1994, 14).

Throughout the 1960s and 1970s the Tongan government encouraged temporary labor migration to New Zealand as a means of boosting Tonga's development. This aim was assisted in the mid-1970s when urban work schemes for Pacific Islanders were introduced in New Zealand, with short-term work contracts and strict provisions for their return home afterward. However, the schemes were soon discontinued, and Tongans, with no preferential access, found it more difficult to move to New Zealand.

This situation was exacerbated as economic conditions in New Zealand deteriorated in the 1980s and immigration was more tightly controlled. Then, from 1984, the immigration policies of the new Labor government emphasized personal merit as the basis for selection of new immigrants, and the number of Pacific Islander migrants increased. In late 1986 there was even a brief period of visa-free entry for Fijians, Western Samoans, and Tongans. Large numbers of individuals from these countries were granted resident status in 1988 and 1989 (Appleyard and Stahl 1995, 19). Immigration policies were again revised in 1991, making entry more difficult for unskilled migrants, which particularly affected Pacific Islanders. Unemployment and economic restructuring in New Zealand meant that between 1991 and 1994 fewer Tongans and Samoans arrived in New Zealand than left the country (Appleyard and Stahl 1995, 19). The 1990s saw a net loss of 2,515 Tongans and 1,884 Western Samoans (Brown and Walker 1995, 6). Those remaining in New Zealand suffered increasing unemployment, particularly those who had been in unskilled occupations.

By 1996, despite the tightening of immigration policies and some reversing of the migration flow from the Pacific, 6 percent of New Zealand's population was of Pacific Island descent (Statistics New Zealand 1998). Pacific Islanders are now the largest immigrant minority population in New Zealand, with numbers projected to double by 2031 (Krishnan, Schoeffel, and Warren 1994, 27).[9] The 31,389 Tongans counted in New Zealand's 1996 census were the third largest Pacific Island group, making up over 15 percent of the total, after Samoans and Cook Islanders (Statistics New Zealand 1998). This is also the largest Tongan population outside Tonga itself.

Tongans have had the highest growth rate of all the Pacific Island groups, with a rate of 11.2 percent between 1986 and 1991, compared to a growth rate of 5 percent for the total Pacific Island population in New Zealand during this period and of only 0.7 percent for the total New Zealand population (Krishnan, Schoeffel, and Warren 1994, 30). The rapid growth of the Tongan population in New Zealand is partly due to the continued immigration of young adults aged fifteen to twenty-nine (Krishnan, Schoeffel, and Warren 1994, 313). There is also a rapidly growing cohort of New Zealand-born Tongans, who in 1996 comprised 52 percent of the population of Tongans in New Zealand. Of this group, more than 70 percent were under the age of fifteen, compared with only 11 percent of Tongans born outside New Zealand (Statistics New Zealand 1998, 13). On the other hand, only 4 percent of Tongans in New Zealand were over sixty in 1991 (Statistics New Zealand 1995, 17).

Most Tongans, like other Pacific Islanders, have settled in New Zealand's urban areas, with around 80 percent of Tongans living in Auckland (Statistics New Zealand 1995, 16). The sheer number of Pacific Islanders in New Zealand and their concentration in particular locations[10] has meant that they have had an impact on government structures and policies, most notably in the establishment of the Ministry of Pacific Island Affairs.[11]

The United States: Preferred Destination

Of the three main receiving nations, the United States is seen by many Tongans as the most prestigious destination, followed by Australia, then New Zealand. In contrast to their situation in New Zealand, Tongans in the United States are only a tiny minority group. Nevertheless, their numbers are almost equal to those in New Zealand, and the much higher prestige of migrating to the United States makes this population, at least in the eyes of many Tongans, the most "important" migrant group.

Prior to the 1960s few Tongans settled in North America due to immigration policies that strongly favored European immigrants. As non-European migrants came to be accepted in growing numbers, other changes were made to immigration policies. In 1965 a quota system was replaced with a preference system, which encouraged the reunification of families, and a new visa category was introduced to allow for the reunification of siblings. The latter "allowed early Tongan migrants to bring over their sizable sibling networks" (Small 1997, 52).[12] As these changes made it easier for Tongans to enter the United States, they became part of the wave of "new immigrants." However, their numbers were still so small compared to many other groups that they have received little attention in accounts of this influx (e.g., Jensen 1989).[13]

Tongans continue to migrate to the United States mainly through sponsorship by other family members who are already settled there, and these "chains" of migration now link several generations. A few Tongans also enter via the "Green Card Lottery," or Diversity Immigrant Visa Program, which is advertised in the *Tonga Chronicle*.[14] There is some step migration through American Samoa, but most migrate directly to the United States (Ahlburg and Levin 1990). In 1984, 95.5 percent of Tongan immigrants arrived directly from Tonga, a figure that has remained fairly constant since 1974 (Barkan 1992, 100). Most settle in Hawai'i and Utah (in both cases primarily through their membership in the Mormon Church) as well as in California, although there are Tongans scattered throughout most states.

The 2000 U.S. census showed that Native Hawaiians and "Other Pacific Islanders" (identifying as one "race" or in combination with other races) made up only 0.3 percent of the total respondents (U.S. Census Bureau 2001b, 1). The total number identifying themselves as Tongan (alone or "mixed") was 36,840 (U.S. Census Bureau 2001b, 9).[15] These individuals comprised the fourth-largest group (5 percent) of the total population of Pacific Islanders, after Hawaiians, Samoans, and Guamanians. Only 13 percent of the Pacific Islanders recorded in the U.S. census of 1990 were foreign born, but this figure is distorted by the inclusion of Hawaiians. Tongans had the highest proportion of foreign-born respondents, at 60.9 percent.

Australia: The Middle Ground

By the end of the 1990s, I estimate that there were approximately fifteen thousand Tongans living in Australia—considerably less than in either New Zealand or North America. Although not regarded as prestigious a destination as the United States, Australia is generally preferred over New Zealand, primarily because of the perception that it offers more opportunities and has not suffered as badly economically in recent years. Vika, eighteen, a university student who was born in New Zealand and moved to Australia with her parents in the mid-1990s, commented, "I think to them moving to Australia was just the next level up from New Zealand kind of thing. Life was okay in New Zealand but they thought coming to Australia would be much more better."

Prior to World War II the main connection between Tonga and Australia was through the Australian Methodist Church and its continuing relationship with the Free Wesleyan Church of Tonga. Over the years the Australian Methodist Church has supported numerous Tongan students and applicants seeking permanent residence and so has played a crucial role in Tongan migration. The first significant influx of Tongans occurred in the late 1950s and early 1960s, and many who came to study went on to settle permanently, often marrying Australian citizens.

These earliest Tongan settlers arrived at a time when migrants—the vast majority of whom were British or Western European—were expected to assimilate into white Australian society (Martin 1978; Murphy 1993; Wooden et al. 1994). The predominance of Anglo-European immigrants was due to the Immigration Restriction Act of 1901, the legislative basis for what would later be known as the "White Australia" policy. The policy ended unofficially in 1966, when the federal government decided to allow skilled non-Europeans to settle in Australia. However, the policy was not formally abolished until 1973, by which time the first wave of Tongan settlers had made their permanent homes in Australia.

When formal diplomatic links between Australia and Tonga were established in 1970, after Tonga was freed from its status as a British protectorate, the Australian government began to provide aid that gave priority to the funding of scholarships for tertiary education. A new wave of students arrived, and again some remained in Australia and brought other family members to join them. Many of those who returned to Tonga helped to strengthen the links between the two countries (see Grainger 1998).

These new Tongan immigrants arrived into a very different political climate than those who came in the 1960s. In the early 1970s "ethnic" organizations began to form, as did voluntary welfare groups dedicated to the particular problems faced by migrants. These problems were also being tackled by the Australian government, which in the 1980s introduced programs to address issues of access and equal opportunity for migrants. However, the 1980s was also a time of economic recession, and the emphasis in immigration policies shifted from labor recruitment to humanitarian and family reunification programs. The 1980s saw a rapid increase in the diversity of immigrants and refugees arriving in Australia, with new settlers originating in more than one hundred countries.

The 1996 census recorded 7,068 Tongan-born individuals living in Australia. In the Melbourne sample, 205 of the 430 Tongans were born in Tonga; applying this to the census figure, we can therefore estimate that by 1999 the total population of Tongan-born and overseas-born Tongans in Australia was 14,826. Given the high rate of overstayers, the actual number could be considerably higher.

The majority of Tongans coming to Australia today are in the category of Family Stream migrants, who are sponsored by family members already in Australia. From 1986 to 1990, 63 percent of Tongan-born immigrants came to Australia directly from Tonga (Rallu 1993, 5); during the same period only 6 percent of New Zealand citizens arriving in Australia were born in Tonga. Step migration was not a common method of migrating to Australia for Tongans at that time; a 1994 study by Richard Brown and Adrian Walker showed that only between 10 and 14 percent of migrants who had left Tonga less than fifteen years earlier had step migrated (1995, 32). Step migration was more common in the past, and Brown and Walker claim it was practiced by 85 percent of those who had left Tonga more than 25 years earlier and by over 50 percent of those who had left between 20 and 25 years earlier (Brown and Walker 1995, 32).

It seems that step migration is regaining its importance today, and in the late 1990s the number of arriving Tongans who are New Zealand citizens began to rise again, due in part to the economic downturn in New Zealand as well as the increasing difficulty of migrating to Australia directly from Tonga.[16] In most cases of step migration from New Zealand, couples remain in that country long enough to have one or more children, whereas a similar pattern does not seem to occur with the few cases of migration from Australia to New Zealand; the 1991 New Zealand census showed that only 1 percent of Tongans were born outside Tonga or New Zealand (Statistics New Zealand 1995, 15).

The 1990s saw a reduction in the number of migrants accepted in Australia through family reunification programs and a toughening of the restrictions for entry in this category, and at the same time an increase in the number of skilled migrants accepted. This trend continues in the twenty-first century: the 2001–2002 Migration Program provides for a total intake of 85,000 migrants, including 37,900 places for Family Stream migrants (Department of Immigration and Multicultural Affairs 2001, 20–21). However, only 500 of these places are for the parent-visa category, in stark contrast to the 8,900 places in the program in 1995–1996 under the Labor government. This new policy will make it very difficult for Tongans to bring their parents to Australia; indeed, the Minister of Immigration, Philip Ruddock, warned that the new limit on the parent program could mean some people would wait forty years for their turn. The justification given by the federal government for this change was the claim that older migrants are a burden on health and welfare services (*The Age* 1999). This notion of migrants as burdens also influenced a new policy introduced in 1993 that imposed a six-month waiting period for a number of social security benefits, including income support, for new arrivals. In 1997 the period was extended to two years.

Throughout these various changes in policy and migrant intake, Tongans have continued to migrate to Australia in fluctuating numbers. There has been ongoing debate about whether Australia should offer Tongans, and some other Pacific Islanders, special concessions for migration. One view postulates that a practical way Australia can aid Tonga is to accept more migrants while Tonga is gradually increasing its domestic production. R. T. Appleyard and Charles Stahl conclude that since Tonga's principal export is labor services, countries such as Australia should consider concessionary migration policies: "Like any other export, in the right policy context labour export and remittances can serve as a stimulus to economic development and a change in comparative advantage" (1995, 46).

Some opponents of this view argue that aid and migration should be reduced to force the island governments to take measures that would encourage sustainable development, while others oppose such concessions on the basis of the nondiscriminatory nature of Australia's immigration policies (Cuthbertson and Cole 1995). It seems unlikely now that any concessionary policies will be introduced, but it is also clear that Tongans will continue to settle in Australia through the regular immigration channels and, in some cases, by overstaying their visas. This flow of new immigrants, their Australian-born descendants, and the descendants of the earlier migrants will result in a constant increase in the Tongan population, as is occurring across the diaspora.

Changes in Tonga

The surge of Tongans moving overseas in the 1970s was associated with a process of "internationalizing" that began when Tupou IV took the throne in 1965, following a period of relative isolation during the reign of Queen Sālote (r. 1918–1965) (Marcus 1993). Since that time, continued migration has brought a wide range of changes to Tongan society, and a recent editorial in the Tongan magazine *Matangi Tonga* claims, "The features of the country, particularly Nuku'alofa, are changing so rapidly that people who left Tonga five years ago will not recognise the place when they return" (2001a).[17]

Not all of these changes are viewed entirely positively by those remaining in the islands. There is a somewhat ambivalent attitude toward the "development" that migrants' remittances, along with international aid, have brought to the country. Many Tongans have commented to me that development in Tonga is physically evidenced by improved interisland communication and transport, electricity throughout most of the islands, more multistory buildings and more expensive houses, numerous restaurants and nightclubs, and so on. On the other hand, they also observe that there have been more negative developments, such as roads crowded with cars; increasing pollution; a higher cost of living; increasing crime, landlessness, and even homelessness; poor families squatting on land reclaimed from rubbish dumps; and the other common problems of so-called "Third World" countries (see Connell 1990; Connell and Lea 1995). International migration has helped to maintain a fairly stable population in Tonga, and with only around 0.5 percent growth since the 1980s, the population now remains at around a hundred thousand. Still, there are problems of overpopulation in the capital, Nuku'alofa, which has seen a constant influx of people from the villages of Tongatapu and the other islands of the archipelago since the late nineteenth century (Perminow 1993).

Despite these many changes, some of the basic structures of Tongan society remain much as they were before large-scale migration began; the hierarchical social order remains, with the monarch and royal family having the highest rank, followed by the nobles, and finally the commoners (see Bott 1981; James 1997a). However, migration has contributed to the emergence of a middle class in Tonga, comprised largely of well-educated commoners who have succeeded in business and other arenas (Benguigui 1989; James 1997a). Many of these middle-class families in Tonga have well-established kinship networks in the diaspora that have played important roles in facilitating their social mobility, particularly through remittances. Very few Tongans rely entirely on subsistence production today, and while many have moved into paid employment, others remaining in the agricultural sector have turned to commercial production, including vanilla and squash (James 1993; van der Grijp 1993, 1997).

Tonga's government is modeled on the British Westminster system, and in recent years the Pro-Democracy Movement, now formally renamed the Tonga Human Rights and Democracy Movement, has changed the political landscape by bringing into the open the concerns of many commoners about the government's accountability and justice issues in Tonga (Campbell 1992, 1994; James 1994, 1997a; Lawson 1994). Broader concerns about issues such as the land tenure system and problems with public services such as hospitals have been publicly raised for many years (see Tonga Council of Churches 1975), but it is only since the 1980s that concerted efforts have been made by commoners to urge the government to address them.

As well as taking up government positions as People's Representatives, commoners are also moving into leadership positions within the churches, which have retained their powerful place in Tonga since the mid-nineteenth century. Most Tongans still keep church, along with family, at the center of their lives. However, the number of different denominations of churches has grown, with Mormon, Evangelical, and Pentecostal churches drawing increasing membership.

The family has been the site of some of the most important changes in Tonga. A movement away from extended family households toward nuclear family units has had diverse impacts, from altering patterns of economic cooperation to a decline in the observance of certain *tapu,* or behavioral restrictions, such as those between fathers and children and between brothers and sisters (Morton 1996). These changes are also associated with migration, through the influence of returned migrants who have, in turn, been influenced by practices and attitudes in the host countries.

The dispersal of extended family members through migration has meant they have less involvement in one another's lives. Husbands and wives may be separated for long periods while one partner is overseas, and, as we will see, children may be left in Tonga when their parents migrate or returned to Tonga when they are older (see Cox and Low 1985; Gailey 1992; James 1993; Small 1997). Young people in Tonga often feel that their options are limited if they remain in the islands, and just like the Samoan youth Cluny Macpherson describes (1990), many yearn to move overseas. The growing frustration, "alienation and disaffection" (Macpherson 1990, 119) experienced by young Samoans can also be seen in Tonga, yet in both cases the chances for migration are becoming increasingly slim.

Remittances

A central focus of the literature on migration by Tongans and other Pacific Islanders has been on the transnational economic ties formed by remittances sent home by migrants (Morton 2002b). George Marcus described Tongan "dispersed family estates" that had developed from the migration of adult sibling groups, arguing that they had "a readily observable corporate quality" expressed in a strong sense of responsibility for one another (1974, 94). This analogy with corporations was also used in the work of Geoffrey Bertram and Ray Watters, who introduced the term "transnational corporations of kin" to describe dispersed Polynesian kin groups (Bertram and Watters 1985; Bertram 1986, 1999; Connell and McCall 1989). The use of this corporate analogy has been criticized for neglecting the conflicts and tensions that exist within kin groups, but recently Bertram has defended it as useful in the sense of a "family firm" influencing the consumption and investment patterns of scattered members (1999, 127).

Remittances are central to the concept of migration, remittances, aid, and bureaucracy (MIRAB) economies also introduced by Bertram and Watters in the mid-1980s, in relation to which they used the concept of transnational corporations of kin. MIRAB was initially used to describe Pacific states with close ties to New Zealand (Bertram 1999, 114), but it was quickly applied to other Pacific states, including Tonga, and has generated a great deal of discussion, particularly about the sustainability of MIRAB economies.

Most observers of Tonga agree that the nation's future depends on a continued flow of emigrants who will send remittances back into Tonga. It is largely taken for granted that new migrants will send remittances, as this practice has been incorporated into the concept of *fatongia,* or obligations, to kin. One of the terms most often used to refer to remittances is *kavenga,* which literally means "a burden or load" but is used to refer to this sense of obligation. Mele Fuka Vete observes that

> [t]he amount and frequency of remitting to parents are taken as measures of one's love. Loving one's parents is a highly regarded value among Tongans. Anyone who does not appear to love their parents, by remitting frequently is frowned upon and classed as *ta'e'ofa* (unloving), *mo'uingalo* (easily forgetting), and *fakavalevale* (wasteful): one has forgotten how one got to where one is and therefore has deserted one's parents. This can be absolutely humiliating and heart-rending. (1995, 62)

Remittances are most often sent to remitters' parents, then their siblings and, less often, other family members. When a man goes overseas leaving his wife and children in Tonga, he is likely to remit directly to his wife, only sending money to his parents and siblings if it is requested for particular purposes. Women, whether they migrate alone or with a partner, are the most frequent and reliable remitters. In some families migrants do not remit directly, but give money to a senior family member who sends an amount accumulated from the contributions of the junior members. While Brown and Walker claimed that Tongans' remittances are "supply driven," that is, they tend to send their money regularly rather than wait for requests (1995, 44), my own study confirms Siosiua Lafitani's finding that "the sending of remittances is not a regular activity for most migrants unless there is a *kole* (request)" (1992, 66).

The monetary remittances are used in a wide range of ways, from purchasing food and other daily needs to investment for future expenses and projects. Some of the money remitted is redirected to churches for the *misinale* (annual donation) and to schools to cover fees, and in both cases additional money may be given for building and other projects. As Kerry James suggests, these payments are effectively helping the family in Tonga by raising their social status (1997b, 7). She argues that it matters less to migrants how their remittances are used than that they have fulfilled their duty to their family by sending them, adding, "Fulfilment of this obligation represents a far more important social investment than any economically productive investment could be" (1997b, 5). However, some migrants *do* express concern about the use of their remittances. Small discusses the tensions between migrants and their kin in a village in Tonga in the mid-1990s, with migrants dissatisfied with how their money was being spent at home (1997, 197).

There is a growing tendency for individuals to remit independently rather than as part of a kin group, and James has argued that the term "transnational corporations of kin" is becoming increasingly inappropriate in Tonga's case (1993). In the Tongan village she studied, remittances "are highly individual, and many are concerned with capital accumulation" (1993, 361). In Melbourne I also found that kin groups operating in a "corporate" manner were uncommon and that the usual practice was for remitters to act individually or as nuclear family units, if remittances were sent at all. It was uncommon for remitters to be concerned with their own future return to Tonga, although as Brown and Walker found, there were some migrants who used remittances to acquire assets in Tonga, such as bank savings accounts, land, housing, machinery, and so on, in preparation for a return (1995, 39). These assets are also used to raise the returnees' social status, but unlike Samoans, whose remittances can maintain and enhance their connection to the *matai* (chiefly) system (Franco 1997), Tongan remittances are only indirectly linked to the political system—for example, by helping families meet their obligations to the noble on whose *tofi'a* (estate) they lease land.

The form remittances take varies considerably, from cash or money transfers to clothing, household goods and furniture, building materials, tools, vehicles, and other goods. There has been a decline in requests for household goods, as a wider range of items has become available in Tonga, but at the same time there has been a trend toward sending large quantities of various goods by the container load for sale at Tonga's flea markets (Brown and Connell 1993). Along with money and goods, migrants often make direct monetary payments on behalf of family and others in Tonga; for example, migrants may pay insurance premiums or purchase airline tickets for them (Brown and Walker 1995, 39). As Brown and Walker state, migrants not only pay airfares for visitors from Tonga, but also bear the other costs of their stay, which could be seen as an additional form of remittance. In-kind remittances such as these are difficult to quantify, and when combined with inadequate recording methods and unrecorded remittances, it is impossible to measure accurately the volume of remittances entering Tonga. Studies undertaken in the early 1990s with Tongan and Western Samoan households in their home countries and in Brisbane, Australia, and with traders in Tonga's flea market found that unrecorded remittances made up around 57 percent of total remittances (Brown and Foster 1995). The total annual value of remittances sent per migrant in the Tongan households surveyed in Brisbane was approximately US$2000.

To give an indication of just how significant remittances are to Tonga, from 1989 to 1990 the officially recorded remittances to Tonga totaled A$43.9 million, or 59.6 percent of Tonga's gross domestic product—and this figure represents only a portion of actual remittances (Appleyard and Stahl 1995, 33). Although there have been few studies measuring remittances received at a local level in Tonga, Sudo's study of one Tongan village showed that in 1992 remittances provided an average of 31 percent of household income, excluding in-kind remittances (1997a, 4). Richard Brown and John Foster's study in the early 1990s found that 24 percent of remittances were "in kind" (1995, 36); combined with Sudo's finding, this suggests that for many Tongan households remittances constitute a substantial portion of their income.

Some analysts have argued that remittances to Tonga, and the South Pacific more generally, create problems of dependence on this source of income and have a "disincentive effect" (Ahlburg 1991, 42) in which remittance receivers are discouraged from earning their own incomes or accumulating savings. Thus remittances are seen as discouraging individual labor and national economic development, being used for consumption rather than productive investment. It has also been observed that remittances can create inequalities between households with differential access to this money, leading to unequal access to education, agricultural and business projects, and further migration (Faeamani 1995, 152).

Other assessments of the impact of remittances are more positive; apart from their function in maintaining kinship ties, they are also seen as an important means of improving living standards in Tonga. Sione Faeamani argues, "While not denying that there are ill effects of emigration and remittance use, in the last decade Tonga has seen significant changes at the village level which have been initiated and funded from remittances, many of which have been beneficial" (1995, 140). Faeamani surveyed one hundred households in each of four villages in 1991–1992 and found a wide range of uses of remittances, from basic household expenses to capital improvements and community projects. He concludes that there has been "a change in attitude from consumerism toward investment and economic development" (1995, 152).

The assumption that remittances are used only for consumption also has been challenged by Brown and Foster, who claim instead that "remittances make an important contribution to savings and investment" (1995, 35). This more positive view of remittances is shared by Bernard Poirine, who argues that this money should be seen as an "international specialization strategy" that maximizes the efficient use of resources to the benefit of "the whole community, whatever its residence" (1998, 91). Poirine sees remittances sent from Pacific Islander migrants as "just the visible tip of an iceberg that I call the *informal family credit market*" (1998, 75, emphasis in original). He describes this credit market as a means for families to ensure the highest returns on the investments they have made in family members, particularly through education. Thus children are educated in the islands, then sent overseas to work and send remittances, initially as repayment of the "investment" made in their education and later to finance the education of other family members.

A problem with this kind of analysis is that it assumes that kin groups are involved in conscious decision-making processes about their economic futures. Referring to "optimization exercises" (Poirine 1998, 75) and even to "corporate" behavior implies purposeful planning and shared goals. Yet decision making is often far more ad hoc and much less future oriented than this, and economic factors are not always perceived as the most crucial. Of course, this is not to deny that deliberate decisions are sometimes made, but even then circumstances can subvert the most carefully made plans. Analyses such as Poirine's also assume a continuing cycle of investments and returns, but this is thrown into question by the growing tendency toward more individual decision making and prioritizing of nuclear family units.

It is important to consider the children who are brought up overseas: will they continue to remit, and do they have a role in the "informal family credit market"? Tongans and analysts of remittances share a concern that remittances may decline over time, particularly as an increasing number of overseas-born Tongans choose not to remit. For the second generation, there is general agreement in the migration literature that remittance levels have declined. Brown and Walker claim that "second-generation migrants remit, on average, about 30 percent of first-generation levels" (1995, 67). This statement conceals the fact that many of the second generation do not remit at all. Many do not have close ties to family in Tonga, often because many of their relatives have migrated or because they have never been to Tonga or had much contact with their kin there. Others simply decide that they are going to direct their income toward their own nuclear family, business, or other commitments, and they do not (or cannot) participate in supporting extended family members. Very few of the Tongans I spoke with who were under the age of thirty sent money or goods directly to Tonga, but the majority told me their parents and other older relatives living outside Tonga did send remittances at times.

Some of the children of migrants have strong opinions about the practice of sending remittances, arguing that the money may be wasted and that they should focus on supporting their own immediate families. Feleti, twenty-nine, who was born in Australia, and his wife Palu, thirty-two, who moved to Australia in the 1980s, used to argue about her family's demands for money. She admitted she found it difficult to keep sight of their own long-term goals when she felt compelled to help her kin, but Feleti resisted sending their money to Tonga. They compromised by sponsoring Palu's brother, who would study in Australia, and Feleti said,

> In my opinion it's better using your money to help him, because he will help the family as well as his own family, and it's a lot better to spend ten thousand dollars doing that than to constantly send money for food. . . . I remember getting a lot of flack from [my wife's] sisters: "Oh, you live overseas and you never send us money or clothes." But their husbands might go overseas and just send everything over, then within a week or two it's all gone.

Most older migrants told me they send money or goods but that they send their remittances infrequently and irregularly. People made qualifications such as "when we can afford it" or "when they really need it" or "on special occasions." Interestingly, many said they thought they were unusual in this regard and portrayed Tongans in general as sending remittances both frequently and regularly. For example, Jane, fifty-one, an Australian woman married to a Tongan since the early 1970s and closely involved with a Tongan church in Melbourne, said of her husband,

> He's not going to get stupid about that sort of thing. People can ask him for things and he won't give it to them. He'll say no. You know, the traditional Tongan custom is you mustn't say no; no, he doesn't do that. It's got to be something important. Yeah. He would pay a fare for his mother to come here to us and that sort of thing. No, not just for anything else.

Some studies have claimed that a remarkable number of long-term migrants continue to remit. Brown and Foster found that there was a decline in remittance levels after fifteen to twenty years but that this rose again beyond twenty years, at which point 96 percent of those they surveyed were still remitting (1995). Another study by Brown, conducted in Sydney in 1994, found that the average level of remittances increased after five years away from Tonga, that the percentage remitting never fell below 80 percent, and that this rose to 95 percent after twenty-five years (Brown 1998; see also Brown and Walker 1995).

However, the "remittance-decay hypothesis," which claims that remittances decline when a migrant has been overseas for some time (Brown and Foster 1995, 38), has been supported in other studies and certainly fits with my own research. Fuka found that after fifteen years only half of her sample of Tongan migrants in Auckland sent remittances and that after twenty years more than two-thirds sent no remittances at all (1985, cited in Connell and Brown 1995, 17). T. Tongamoa found a similar situation in Sydney and added that when permanent resident status is attained and dependents have also migrated, remittances often cease entirely (1987, cited in Connell and Brown 1995, 17).[18]

Migrants may decrease the remittances they send because they have fewer family members left to remit to or because they may have abandoned their own plans to retire to Tonga since their children and grandchildren have settled overseas. Like Jane's husband above, they also may make a conscious decision not to send money except for specific purposes. There are fluctuations in migrants' ability to remit according to their income and financial commitments in their new home, and some may be under pressure from non-Tongan spouses not to divert too much of their income away from their nuclear family. Given that many Tongans overseas are in poorly paid jobs and are living on or below the poverty line, what is remarkable is that so many *do* manage to send remittances.[19] Fluctuations in the demand for remittances also occur—for example, when migrants' parents are elderly and need more financial support, when a hurricane or other natural disaster creates a sudden need for additional assistance, or when family celebrations and crises place a demand on the resources of the extended family.[20]

Some indication of changing attitudes toward remittances can be gleaned from Kava Bowl discussions on this topic. There are always many responses to questions such as "The call of the Kaainga [extended family] in the homeland . . . do we meet 'needs' AND 'desires'?" One man asserted that

> [t]his is becoming a major conflict between those that live back in the islands and those who are struggling overseas . . . for our relatives who live in the isle, in their small minds they think that money grow out of trees, and thus expect people overseas to provide them with their need also on top of all the financial obligations of those overseas. (KB 6.4.98)

He added that he sends money only for the *misinale* and for emergencies and claimed that when families at home demand money for unnecessary items, "really it's for pure competition with the neighbor rather than to make life comfortable." Another participant listed the many kinds of expenses faced in the United States and pointed out that she has not fulfilled her own desires in order to support her family in Tonga. She argued that Tongans returning home for visits make the situation worse by exaggerating their success and wealth and creating unrealistic expectations (KB 7.4.98).

These negative views are not shared by all migrants. One participant in this discussion agreed that family "extravagances" should not be financed by migrants but said his own father had sent his family both money and goods to enable them to start their own businesses in Tonga, and it had been successful to the point that the Tongan family actually contributed financially to a down payment on a home for the writer's sister in the United States. "So you see, if applied properly, 'kaainga' can and should work both ways in helping family rather than supporting family" (KB 8.4.98).

A little-studied aspect of remittances is the "contraflows" of goods sent from Tonga to family members in the diaspora or given to migrants returning to visit Tonga (James 1997b). James argues that gifts of traditional ceremonial wealth *(koloa)* help to maintain the relationships between those at home and those overseas. She describes a *katoanga* (festive exchange) in Vava'u in 1995 in which Tongan women from the United States brought household goods and cash to exchange for fine mats.

> The degree of commoditization was masked as gift exchange. Both parties were able to perceive the transactions of goods and money as gifts stemming from affection *(me 'a 'ofa)*. The relationship between the makers and the receivers as well as the situations in which they are presented remain vital to the meaning and value of the particular mats exchanged. (1997b, 15)

James notes that demand for *koloa* from migrants and their children is increasing and that "among some sections of the migrant population, a market for *koloa* is developing along the lines of the Western market for valuable antiques or collector's items" (1997b, 18). My own study confirmed this, although this demand for *koloa* was within a small sector of the Melbourne Tongans. As well as *koloa,* many other items constituted a "contraflow," including T-shirts with Tongan motifs, handicrafts, food, and videos of events such as the annual Heilala Festival.

Contexts where *koloa* is exchanged for money and goods also occur outside Tonga; however, the money and other "gifts" given still constitute a form of remittance. One such context is the fund-raising tour, when groups from schools, brass bands, and so on travel to one or more countries to raise money from diasporic Tongans and take with them a quantity of barkcloth *(ngatu)* and woven mats *(kie)* to distribute in return.

Fund-raising further complicates the issue of measuring remittances, as the amounts raised are unlikely to be recorded in official statistics. Visiting groups from Tonga are not the only ones raising money; churches, ex-students' associations, and other groups of overseas Tongans also hold fund-raising events. The money such groups collect may be used for their own purposes (e.g., to purchase land to build a church), or it may be sent to other groups in Tonga or elsewhere. As the money raised in one fund-raising effort may be used for more than one purpose, it is very difficult to track how much goes to Tonga.

Remittances more generally are becoming complicated in this way as individuals and families send money and goods between different diasporic locations as well as to Tonga. A new twist to the issue of fund-raising and remittances occurred in July 1998, when the usual flow of money from the diaspora to Tonga was reversed. A Tongan Christian youth group from Hawai'i toured Tonga as well as Australia and New Zealand to raise funds for a youth hall. In Tonga they raised T$8,400 (*Tonga Chronicle* 1998i, 1998j).[21]

When groups from Tonga or elsewhere go on fund-raising tours they usually stay in Tongan households, with the hosts bearing the costs of accommodation, meals, transport, and other expenses. Various means of fund-raising are used, including entertainment such as concerts or dances, kava evenings, or raffles. Whatever method is employed, groups are usually able to raise considerable amounts of money. For example, a sixty-one-member group from 'Apifo'ou College, a Catholic secondary school in Tonga, spent nearly two months in Australia and New Zealand in 1998 raising approximately half a million Australian dollars (*Tonga Chronicle* 1998b).[22] At other times the fund-raising is done by Tongans overseas, and the money raised is presented in Tonga. When funds were raised by a worldwide ex-students' association for a multipurpose hall in Pangai, Ha'apai, thirteen ex-students from California went to Tonga to present the funds and also donated their labor to build the hall (*Tonga Chronicle* 1996a).

Some fund-raising can be planned for, as when an ex-students' association asks its members to contribute a set amount by a certain date, but at most fund-raising events the amount donated is left open and is often increased by competition among families wishing to display their generosity. I heard several anecdotes of people so eager to donate more money at events that they would go to the nearest automated teller machine to withdraw even more cash. Large amounts can be raised even at single events, as at the opening of a Wesleyan community centre in Sydney, where it was reported that A$122,123 was collected during the opening celebrations (*Kalonikali Tonga* 1996). The *misinale* is also a form of fund-raising, with churches overseas often donating a portion of money raised to a Tongan congregation or to a school in Tonga. The remainder may be used for various other purposes, and in some cases very little flows back into the church itself.

To get some idea of the extent of fund-raising, I examined the Tongan and English versions of the *Tonga Chronicle* for items describing fund-raising efforts in Australia. From July 1996 to the end of June

1997 a total of A$1,427,859 was reportedly raised, and of this, A$433,588 was earmarked to be sent to Tonga. The highest amount reported for any one fund-raising effort was A$261,212, raised by a group from Tupou High School in Tonga that had traveled around Australia collecting donations.[23] Since my figures only reflect what was reported in the *Tonga Chronicle*, it is likely that the actual amounts involved were much greater, as reporting from Australia was irregular and usually from one correspondent who could not be expected to know about all amounts being raised throughout Australia.

Most of these large sums of money do not get factored into the calculations of remittances to Tonga, but they clearly represent an important flow of funds into the country. Fund-raising events are a means by which second-generation overseas Tongans do contribute to remittances, albeit indirectly. Individuals who may not send cash or goods directly to their families in Tonga will nevertheless donate money at a concert or kava evening, hence in some way remaining part of the web of connections between Tongans at home and overseas. We will return to these connections in chapter 4, looking beyond the economic ties that have been a preoccupation in many previous studies of Tongan migration to the ties that are perceived as primarily emotional and social and that play a role in maintaining Tongan identity. First, though, we will look at migrants' lives overseas and their interactions with Tongans and others in the places in which they have made their new homes.

3

Life Overseas
Community and Conflict

TONGANS ARE DISPERSED AROUND THE GLOBE, yet many still invoke the concept of community, sometimes using the term *"komiunitī Tongā"* to refer to either the worldwide Tongan community or, more often, to a localized population of migrants and their children. "Community" for Tongans has two primary elements: church and family. Of these, kinship is held to be the most important—although in practice this may not always appear to be so—and migrants with members of their extended families living in the same city or town are usually closely involved in each others' daily lives, sometimes even living in the same household.

Family Ties

The composition of migrant households varies enormously, and while there are many nuclear family households, others include extended family members. It is not unusual for Tongan households to undergo numerous changes in membership as different relatives stay for varying periods. Individuals and families are usually welcome to stay in the households of their kinsfolk, and these visits may be brief or may continue for months or even years, depending on the circumstances. New migrants are often incorporated into existing households until they have settled and found employment, and it is also common for older people to live with their married children for periods of time, often moving among the households of their children in different states and countries. Aging parents usually live with one of their adult children, as most Tongans are averse to the idea of placing the elderly in retirement homes or aged-care facilities. There is growing concern among Tongans overseas about the difficulties of continuing to care for the elderly when in many households no one is at home with them during weekdays due to school and work demands.

One reason older people move between households is to help with child care, and it is common for them to stay for a year or two after the birth of a grandchild. Parents who do not have live-in relatives to assist with child care usually turn to kin in other households; formal child care is seldom used. Working couples who have no regular assistance from family or who prefer to care for their children themselves sometimes share child care by working different shifts. In her interviews with Tongan workers in Sydney in the mid-1980s, Meleane Moala found that concerns about children were the issues the workers raised most frequently, particularly the need for a Tongan child-care center, as they would not consider having their children cared for outside the family or wider Tongan community. The high cost of child care was also an issue (Moala 1986, 224). Such concerns were expressed by the participants in 'Osaiasi Faiva's study, in which only 1 out of 130 households surveyed in Sydney used a child-care center (1989, 30), and by those in the Melbourne sample, of which only 1 out of 100 households used formal child care.

Another means of dealing with the need for child care is the fostering (pusiaki) of children by family members in Tonga (Morton 1996, 56–60). Couples and single parents sometimes leave one or more of their children in Tonga with relatives when they migrate, usually with the intention of bringing the child to join them at some later stage. In other cases the child is sent back with a family member who is traveling to Tonga and cared for there by grandparents, aunts and uncles, or other kin. The practice of sending children to Tonga is examined in more detail in the following chapters.

This kind of fostering, in which children are sent across national borders, is much less common than fostering within families living in Tonga. Fostering occurs even less frequently between families living overseas, although it does still happen. Legal adoptions are increasingly popular as they make practical matters—such as access to medical and family benefits and enrollment of children in school—much simpler.

Churches

Like kinship, church membership is crucial in Tongan notions of community, and the majority of overseas Tongans devote a great deal of time, energy, and resources to their churches. During the 1960s and 1970s, when the first significant waves of migration occurred and when many migrants had no kin in their new locations, Tongan populations overseas established a sense of community primarily through their membership in religious groups, such as Bible study and prayer groups. This was commonly followed by the establishment of Tongan church congregations and a fragmentation of the initial community into smaller church groups of different denominations.

This fragmentation is partly due to the need for each denomination to have its own place of worship, but is also due to tensions that arise within congregations, disagreements over matters of doctrine and practice, the geographical spread of the population, and in some cases families' striving for higher social status by establishing their own church congregations. Some of the smaller congregations consist entirely of one extended family, usually a sibling group and their spouses and children. While some Tongans argue that the proliferation of churches undermines any sense of community in the overseas populations, others emphasize the need for people to be free to make their own choices and to act on their concerns. One of the more recent divisions to occur in Melbourne occurred when members of one church disagreed with the ideas of a new minister, leading to arguments in church and finally to most members moving to join another Tongan congregation. Such splits seem to be inevitable and also occur in other groups, such as ex-students' associations.

Church congregations vary in size, and while Siosiua Lafitani reports that some of the Tongan churches in Canberra have fewer than fifteen members (1992, 72), there are also much larger congregations. The two main churches in Melbourne claim memberships of around three hundred and four hundred respectively, although in both cases there are fewer members who maintain a regular and active involvement in the church. One of the ministers explained that there are approximately fifty "committed families," the remainder being what he called "the fringe dwellers, the fringe members who come when they feel like it."

The "Tongan churches" overseas (congregations with predominantly Tongan membership) differ in their involvement with the wider communities in which they are located. Their affiliations vary, with some attached to churches based in Tonga, such as the Free Church of Tonga, and others existing within the structures of overseas churches. Some of the Tongan churches are closely tied to their mainstream counterparts; for example, a large proportion of Tongans in Australia belong to the Uniting Church, which has been active in including Tongans in its overall organization. Most Tongan churches have Tongan ministers, either sent from Tonga or locally trained.

Tongan churches also vary in the extent to which they provide a sense of "community." In some, members' involvement is primarily religious—attending services, choir practice, and Bible study—whereas in others the church also acts as a community group and members are involved in other ways, such as social and welfare activities. In all of the churches the routine of activities can be demanding. For example, the weekly program of one of the Melbourne churches includes activities all day on Sundays and on three evenings during the week as well as some Saturdays. Special events like the Mothers' Day services or the special children's service in May *(Fakamē)* involve a lot of preparation, such as rehearsing Bible readings, songs, and drama presentations.

It is the churches, as well as extended family ties, that have helped Tongans to cope with migration.[1] However, churches also make considerable demands on people's money and time, with requests for donations not just for the *misinale* (annual donation), but for various other fund-raising purposes, as we have already seen. Often, the fund-raising events become another demand on people's time as they help prepare for and participate in concerts and other activities. The financial demands can have a serious impact on people's economic situation; in a more extreme example, members of a Melbourne church that was constructing a community hall donated up to half their salaries toward the building. In such cases, as one young woman said, "people's lives revolve around the church." Concern is frequently expressed about the impact of this on children whose parents are committing a great deal of time and money to the church, sometimes leaving the children inadequately supervised and the family with little disposable income.

Increasingly, the Tongan churches are focusing on youth, and in many cases young people represent around half of the congregation. Given that many young Tongans overseas have poor or nonexistent Tongan-language skills, an increasing number of churches are choosing to hold services in English in order to encourage their attendance. Churches may also establish youth groups and hold special services with youth presentations, and they may promote youth involvement in national church youth organizations or in some cases employ trained youth workers. Some of the youth groups provide not only religious education, but also a venue for socializing and leisure activities and sometimes more serious discussion of issues affecting young people. Activities can include lessons in Tongan dances and songs and

Tongan language, as well as concerts, talent nights, barbecues, games, camps, sleepovers, and outings.

As we will see in the next two chapters, the role of churches in the diasporic communities is a contentious issue, particularly the question of how "traditional" they should be. Some denominations are strongly criticized for their modern ways; for example, several people commented derisively to me that members of the Mormon Church "want to think they're *pālangi*." Yet people's desire for the church to be a center of Tongan culture, particularly for young people who have few opportunities to learn the Tongan language and "Tongan way," is often countered by acknowledgment that young people are often alienated by the Tongan aspects of the services and church-related activities. There are also demands for churches to be more attuned to the needs and problems of overseas Tongans by focusing on educating and informing members about issues such as legal rights, education, taxation, health, and so on, rather than simply replicating the practices of the churches in Tonga.

It is often difficult for the ministers of the churches to balance these different demands. Tongan ministers play a significant role in the lives of the church members, who turn to them for help with settlement issues and problems they encounter, as well as for interpreters, counseling, and so on. Their roles take on even greater importance than in Tonga, since they become the leaders of communities, particularly in the absence of other high-status persons. One minister, who has spent over twenty years in Australia, commented,

> I think Tongan people they seem to rely too much on their ministers. I mean, like myself, anybody who has difficulties, I think his or her minister is the first person for them to go and talk to. Whether within the church, or something to do with employment, schooling, accommodation, things like that. Yes, they seek our help, and we direct them to go where they should go.

Some ministers feel uncomfortable with the high status they are accorded. Another minister, also a long-term resident of Australia, said Tongans often spoke to him in the same respectful language used for the nobles in Tonga. He felt this was "dangerous" because the minister could forget that his role is to serve the community and "be a worker."

Ministers are also faced with the issue of whether to encourage members of the wider community to join their church, in which case many of the Tongan elements are no longer appropriate, especially use of the Tongan language. The membership of some churches is almost entirely Tongan, with some non-Tongan spouses, while others include members from the wider community. The minister of one Melbourne church actively encouraged wider membership and the involvement of the congregation in activities such as singing in local nursing homes and at community events. He asserted, "I don't like ethnic communities to build little ghettos and be on their own."

Socializing

Church activities can take up so much time, leaving few evenings or weekends free, that they put limits on the social lives of many Tongans, particularly those in the older generations. Adults who do find time for other activities tend to be involved with Tongan-oriented groups such as kava clubs (kalapu) and ex-students' associations. Other popular social activities include bingo and other forms of gambling.

Younger Tongans tend to be more involved in activities outside the church, particularly sports. Many young people have achieved considerable success in sports; for example, in Melbourne some have represented their school, district, state, and even nation in sports such as rugby and netball. In the late 1990s a new sports team, the Box Hill Fillies, an all-female rugby team, caused some controversy among Tongans in Melbourne, with some parents strongly resisting their daughters' involvement, but the team persisted and has been successful, winning the Victorian Rugby Union grand final in 2001.

Young people value sports not simply for the enjoyment, but also as a means of extending their social contacts beyond their family and church and as a temporary escape from the behavioral restrictions often demanded of them in those contexts. For the female rugby players, their training sessions, travel to matches, and postmatch celebrations are a welcome relief from the expectations placed on them by their families to behave as "proper" young Tongan women. It was amazing to witness their regular transformations from demure, modest members of their church congregation into aggressive, hard-playing, and mud-covered footballers!

There appears to be a growing trend for parents to encourage their children to be involved in activities outside the church, particularly in sports, martial arts, and music. Several parents told me their children were having piano lessons at home, and there is an element of prestige in providing expensive tuition for one's children. A minister who pays a considerable amount of money for two of his children to learn piano said he sees this as an important investment in their future. He added, "I encourage people in my church to spend money on their kids. You don't want them to be doctors? Then all right, just sit back and don't spend money."

Despite this trend of young people becoming increasingly involved in nonchurch activities, parents vary in the extent to which they allow or encourage their children to socialize more informally with non-Tongans. In part this reflects the varying social orientations of the parents, some of whom prefer to mix only with other Tongans while others socialize comfortably with non-Tongan friends and work colleagues. Parents who discourage friendships with non-Tongans worry that their children will fall prey to "bad influences." This reflects broader concerns about their children's cultural identities, making them reluctant to let their children fully participate in the wider society. These issues are discussed further in the following chapters.

Frictions within the Tongan Population

The notion of Tongan "community," which helps to create a sense of solidarity among migrants, does not prevent numerous tensions arising within and between migrant populations. Churches, as we have seen, are one source of such tensions, particularly with regard to the splitting of congregations into smaller groups and disagreements over how "traditional" the church practices should be.

Some tensions are transported with the migrants from Tonga, especially those relating to status and rank. The often unspoken tensions in Tonga between chiefs (*hou'eiki*) and commoners (*kau tu'a*) are aired more openly in the diaspora, and overseas populations that claim to have a chiefly person among them are the target of resentment by those who accuse them of using this to elevate their status. Diasporic Tongans will often eagerly attend events at which visiting Tongan-based nobles are guests of honor, displaying respect and humility in their presence and making generous presentations of food and wealth items. Yet in other contexts more negative attitudes toward *hou'eiki* are evident, and privately Tongans can be highly critical of nobles' demands on their people.

Lafitani found that *lau'eiki* (assertion of chiefly status) was a source of rivalry within the Tongan population of Canberra, adding that as commoner migrants improve their socioeconomic status, they begin to see the chiefly migrants as equals (1992, 74). In Melbourne, few tensions have arisen in this regard, simply because there are no chiefly Tongans among the population. As one resident put it, "Melbourne is quite fortunate in not taking on *hou'eiki* and *tu'a* business. . . . Although people here respect *hou'eiki*s, they are more for themselves than anything else. We also rarely get visits from high chiefs or from the king and his family, so this [tension over social rank] is hardly practised."

The quest for socioeconomic success can in itself cause rivalry as families vie for recognition for their achievements in their new country. At the same time, they have to be careful to avoid accusations of being *fie pālangi* (acting like Anglo-Europeans) or *fie mā 'olunga* (acting above oneself). This tension over status is often expressed in the distinctions made between "town" and "bush" people, determined not only by their home village in Tonga, but also by their appearance, particularly clothing, and the city and suburb in which they live. The opposition of town and bush is also used to evaluate events so that, as one woman explained, "If there is anything wrong in a wedding or birthday, often you hear someone say *'fielau: koe kau uta'* [no wonder: they come from the bush]. It is vice versa if it is good: it is seen as a town thing." In Melbourne, those who see themselves as "town" people sometimes make derogatory comments about "bush" Tongans, as in the observation that the bush people from one area of Melbourne "would invite the whole nation" to their parties. At one wedding the food was poor, and people commented that the "bush people didn't have good food in Tonga, so they didn't know how to prepare it properly." However, as a whole the population of Melbourne is regarded as "town" people by Tongans in other parts of Australia, and this is borne out by the high proportion of migrants from Nuku'alofa (73.5 percent of my sample).

Asserting one's birthplace *(laukolo tupu'anga)* draws on the distinction between town and bush people as well as that between different villages (see Lafitani 1992 for Canberra). Tongamoa found that in Sydney migrants tended to occupy suburbs where others from their village had settled and then would establish a church dominated by people from that village or even one extended family (1987, cited in Lafitani 1992, 69). Discussion on the Kava Bowl site indicates that village-based rivalries are common between groups of young Tongan men in the

United States. In Melbourne, while I occasionally heard those regarded as "bush" people referred to by the names of particular rural villages, village-based rivalry is not a major source of friction.

Tensions also can arise between established and new migrants. Newcomers are often referred to as FOBs (fresh off the boat) or Freshies. An anonymous poster on the KB complained about "crews" of young Tongan men in U.S. cities who are hostile toward newcomers, with "Tongans hating on Tongans" (KB 29.9.97). Both Frances Finney and Lafitani report such tensions in Canberra, and Finney notes that some of the earlier migrants expect the newer arrivals to defer to them "as real or perceived beneficiaries of remittances" (1999, 111). In return, the earlier migrants are blamed for *tala ova,* or reporting of overstayers, "especially if an overstayer is from a village in Tonga, a commoner background, is a new migrant and a non-member of the reporter's extended family" (Lafitani 1992, 75). *Tala ova* occurs in Melbourne only occasionally and is usually attributed to anger after some kind of dispute or jealousy of someone's success. As it is so difficult to prove, direct accusations are seldom made, but there is usually gossip about possible suspects.

In addition to their internal tensions, the different diasporic populations vie with each other for relative status; for example, Tongans in Canberra accord their community higher status than other Australian Tongan populations because they are located in the nation's capital (Finney 1999, 158). As we have already seen in chapter 2, the United States is generally regarded as a more prestigious destination than Australia, which in turn is seen as better than New Zealand. These distinctions are then relayed into tensions between settlers in the different nations. All of these tensions make it difficult to sustain a sense of community. They also can be confusing for young people struggling with identity issues and desiring a sense of belonging. A poster on the KB asks, "We do not trust each other. We mock and belittle each other. How then can we stand up and be united?" (KB 14.9.97).

Language Use

The issue of language use is another source of considerable tension within overseas populations. In the following chapter the use of Tongan within these populations is discussed, as is the growing concern about the decline in fluency among the younger generations. Here, my concern is with the use of English, which is also a contentious issue.

Many Tongans who migrated in the 1960s and 1970s deliberately chose not to teach their children Tongan, hence there are high levels of English fluency among the second generation, many of whom spoke English as their first language. Often, parents sincerely believed it was not important to teach their children Tongan, since they were settled overseas and because they wanted their children to have the language skills necessary to succeed in the host countries. Some of the parents were themselves self-conscious about their poor English and wanted their children to feel more comfortable in the wider society. Others assumed they would be overseas only temporarily, as was the case for Manu, sixty-five, who has now been in Australia for many years. His adult son, who came to Australia at the age of five, has never returned to Tonga because he is embarrassed about not speaking Tongan. Manu admitted that "it was our fault, mainly because we didn't know that we were staying here in Australia; we only came and we always felt that we would go back home. But it didn't turn out that way." As the children of the early migrants reached adolescence and in some cases adulthood, they have reacted with anger and resentment at their inability to speak Tongan.

In the Melbourne households I surveyed, I found that for people over the age of five with Tongan ancestry, 26.6 percent spoke only Tongan at home, 24.8 percent spoke only English, and the rest spoke a mixture of the two languages. English is taught in both primary and secondary schools in Tonga, and the 1996 Tongan census recorded a literacy rate of 98.5 percent, with 72.8 percent of this total literate in both Tongan and English (*Tonga Chronicle* 1998g). While literacy should not be confused with linguistic ability,[2] these figures do indicate that most Tongans are arriving overseas with at least some knowledge of English. This is not to claim that Tongan migrants do not experience language problems, as the transition from the English they learned in Tongan schools to that which they hear and need to use in their new homes certainly can be difficult. Factors such as geographic clustering and patterns of social interactions will affect the development of fluency in English, with Tongans living and working in close proximity to one another less likely to acquire English competence than more scattered populations such as the Melbourne Tongans.

Australian legislation provides newly arrived migrants with the right to 510 hours of free English tuition, or the amount of time it takes to reach a functional level of English (Department of Immigration and Multicultural Affairs 1996, 46). Yet Tongan adults who arrive in Australia with poor English skills seldom use these rights largely due to the shame associated with seeking "outside" help and the embarrassment of taking English classes with migrants of different nationalities. Adults with poor English skills get around the problem by using relatives as interpreters and by remaining insulated within the Tongan population.

Tongan children arriving in Australia are more likely to access language assistance, as there are a number of English-language schools and centers that provide intensive English programs for newly arrived school-aged children and that are organized through their schools rather than by their families. The situation today is greatly improved since the first young migrants arrived in Australia and were expected to learn English simply by being in regular classrooms. A young woman brought to Melbourne at the age of six recalled that

> I didn't know one word of English. I remember going to school and every week the teacher would say "Whose birthday is it this week?" and I would stand up every week. The children would be laughing at me and I thought "Now that's strange!" I sat down one week and a student said to me "Isn't it your birthday this week?" I said "Why?" and he said "We've realised that ever since you've come you've had a birthday every week. Is that Tongan culture, or what?" (Canterbury Uniting Church 1993)

Even Tongan children who were born overseas sometimes need assistance learning the "school English" they must use, which has more formal spoken and written forms than the English they have learned from their migrant parents (see Fabrier and Cruikshank 1993).

English-language competence does vary considerably, but many Tongans living overseas now choose to speak English to one another as well as to non-Tongans. Many of the people I spoke with preferred to be interviewed in English, saying they felt they could express themselves, particularly their emotions, better than in Tongan.

Services Available to Tongans

The shame associated with seeking help with English also tends to prevent migrants from accessing other services available to them in their host countries. Having other people know their problems and needs is embarrassing and causes anxiety that any information provided by the migrants will not be kept confidential. Tongans are often reluctant to seek assistance from government departments and welfare agencies, preferring to call on family members to help. Most people agreed that it is the practicalities of living overseas with which they need most assistance and information: filling in forms, understanding banking procedures (including taking out loans), taxation matters, insurance needs, the legalities of leases and mortgages, running small businesses, workers' rights, and so forth. Information is also needed about the kinds of government benefits and other forms of assistance available to Tongans.

When older migrants need help with the practical matters of their new lives, they turn to young Tongans with tertiary educations and familiarity with "the system." The younger generation is also called on to help older migrants in their dealings with immigration officials, lawyers, welfare officers, and the courts. For the most part young people do this without complaint, as they know it is expected of them. But it does become a burden, and one young woman I spoke with who was constantly in demand for help complained that her only reward was being the subject of gossip: "You stick your neck out and all you get is a stab in the back!"

In the smaller populations of overseas Tongans, this reluctance to seek help contributes to a situation in which they remain a largely invisible group. When they do not utilize the services available to them, they do not have ongoing access to information about changes to immigration laws and ethnic services or opportunities to seek funding for community projects. Often, information does not get translated into Tongan, and no workers with Tongan-language skills are employed by the service providers. Unless they form associations and other groups to raise their visibility and lobby for their needs to be met, both government departments and nongovernmental agencies tend to overlook them. Such is the situation in Melbourne for Tongans and other Pacific Islanders, where very few specifically targeted services exist for them.[3] The Ecumenical Migration Centre in Melbourne noted that even in the mid-1990s

> a number of government departments, service providers and other professionals . . . have voiced concern about their own lack of cultural knowledge about Pacific Islanders and the dearth of accurate statistics and programs targeting these communities. These service providers have indicated increasing contact and they acknowledge the need for positive programs and policy directions. (n.d., 3)

Another problem for the small populations of Tongans is that they are often forced to combine with other Pacific Islanders in order to be eligible for financial support. Australia's Department of Immigration and Multicultural Affairs (DIMA)[4] directs its funding in Victoria to pan-Pacific organizations such as the Pacific Island Council rather than to the different Pacific groups; consequently, organizations that are solely Tongan cannot receive DIMA funds. There are very limited alternative sources of funding, even for the combined Pacific Islander groups.

Cities with larger numbers of Pacific Islanders than Melbourne usually have more structures in place to assist these communities. In Sydney, for example, there are Pacific Islander welfare services, community workers and welfare officers, as well as the Pacific Islands Council, which is run by the Uniting Church and which acts as an umbrella body for Islanders and attempts to assess and respond to particular needs. Some government departments have employed Islanders to work specifically with their own ethnic groups, and they also provide printed information in several Pacific languages. Other even larger centers of the Pacific diaspora have more extensive structures in place. New Zealand has a Ministry of Pacific Island Affairs, and there are numerous centers, associations, and agencies, particularly in Auckland, that deal specifically with the Islander population. The situation is similar in U.S. cities with large Pacific Islander populations. As the number of Islanders in any location grows, formal associations and other groups are established and often become more vocal and active in seeking responses to the needs of migrants and their descendants. Such groups are discussed later in this chapter. Also, an increasing number of Islanders are establishing businesses and services catering specifically to those populations, from funeral directors and used car dealerships to lawyers, doctors, and other professionals.

Education

Apart from the ubiquitous "to help the family," the most commonly given reason for Tongan migration is education. Tongans as a whole believe strongly in the importance of education, and those who leave Tonga take this conviction with them to their new homes. Education and helping the family are in fact interconnected: parents help their children by taking them to a place where they can receive a good education; in turn, children help their family by becoming well educated and thus enhancing the family's status and, ultimately, its financial position, since the value of education lies in the well-paid jobs it promises to bring. At a celebration in Utah for graduating university and high school students, the Tongan director of the Utah Governor's Office of Polynesian Affairs commented that "education is what brought us here. . . . Through education you can do more good for yourself, your family, your community, and your country" (*Tonga Chronicle* 1996b).

The ideology does not always match the reality, however, and the extent to which parents support their children's education varies enormously. Some children are sent to expensive private schools or have tutors outside school hours, and some have restrictions imposed on such leisure activities as watching television in order to encourage them to study. On the other hand, there are families that place little value on education and encourage their children to leave school as soon as possible to find work and contribute financially to the family.

Some parents direct the course of their children's education even through to the tertiary level, insisting they study for degrees the parents perceive as prestigious, rather than allowing them to pursue their own preferences. Other parents are happy to leave the decisions to the children, as with 'Ana, who said of her two children's schooling, "[It is] not really that important to me to do well, as long as they're doing their best and get something, you know, if they finish school, to get a little job out of it, be educated." Similarly, Tupou, fifty-two, a father of four who has lived in Melbourne since the late 1960s, said education was important to ensure that his children could "look after themselves" as well as be "able to be worthwhile citizens of this world and this country." Tupou and his wife told their children they would like them to attend university but that they have left the decision to the children. Tupou said, "We have expressed our wish, and our hope, but I don't believe in pushing young ones really. I think the modern design of education is far too much, there is too much pressure on the young ones. All I'm saying to them is just do your best and that's all you need to do; I'm not going to put any extra pressure on them."

Children sometimes get mixed messages from parents about the importance of education. Parents impress on their children while still young how important a good education is, yet these children are also encouraged to leave school early to find work and contribute financially to their families. The problem of financial hardship precluding study at the tertiary level has been raised a number of times on the KB forum, particularly by Tongans in the United States, where tertiary education is considerably more expensive than in Australia and New Zealand. Some in the United States do benefit from their minority status in obtaining scholarships and gaining access to particular colleges and universities; others who are members of the Mormon church have access to one of the Mormon universities.

One of the major problems facing Tongan parents hoping to educate their children overseas is a lack of understanding of the foreign school system. Parents often do not understand the schools' reliance on parental support, both in the classroom and with homework. A study of Tongans in San Mateo County, California, found that parents' lack of involvement with the school and with their children's homework was due to their poor understanding of the homework material, as well as the general Tongan attitude of complete respect for the authority of teachers and school authorities, and to simply not expecting to be involved (Forté 1994). Another problem identified was parents' practice of keeping children out of school to act as interpreters for them (this was also true in some families in Melbourne); children may also miss school because parents need them to care for younger siblings or assist in other ways.

In some families children's education is further hindered by the absence of resources in the home, such as books, newspapers, and computers, and a lack of assistance with tasks such as library research. However, many of the parents I interviewed were highly involved with their children's schooling, including those who helped with homework, provided reading assistance in their children's classes (by listening to class members practice reading), or who were members of school committees.

Tongan parents often have expectations of education that diverge from that which they perceive their children are receiving. Many express dissatisfaction with the lack of discipline in schools, particularly the lack of respect for teachers. Another common complaint is the low academic expectations of schools, with parents sometimes arguing that children should receive more homework of a more difficult level (see Fabrier and Cruikshank 1993; Kalantzis, Gurney, and Cope 1992). Ironically, some of the parents who have migrated to seek a good education for their children end up believing the Tongan school system is superior. Sioeli, thirty-six, married to an Australian and with four young children, was trained as a high school teacher and expressed his disappointment with the standard of discipline and academic achievement he has encountered in Australia. He told me angrily,

I'm not happy with the school education here. Because there are basics I want my kids to know at a certain age. And they are *miles* behind! Like, simple maths, right—I get mad. See, my brother, he came here three years ago. His son is a year younger than my eldest daughter. And his maths, oh, my daughter can't compete with him! It is very sad, because when I think about it, back home, if you go to the classroom, they don't have all the fancy stuff and that, but they are doing the proper education!

Children can also face obstacles to learning within the school system itself. A study of Islander families in Auckland found that children tended to be passive students, not questioning their teachers or voluntarily contributing in class (Schoeffel and Meleisea n.d., 65). Children whose parents were raising them on the "new middle-class model"—that is, with a more Western orientation toward learning and achievement—were more educationally successful than those whose parents followed a "rural Polynesian model." Another study, also in Auckland, compared working-class Polynesian girls with middle-class *pakeha* (Anglo-European) girls and showed that the former had been influenced by their parents' emphasis on obedient attention and teacher-directed learning (Jones 1989, 1991; see also Tiatia 1998). Alison Jones describes how the Polynesian girls use various strategies to discourage discussion in the classroom and thus maintain what they perceive as the appropriate teacher-student relationship. Such strategies do not succeed in classes with very few Islander students, as is usually the case in schools in Melbourne, where those students who have been raised to be obedient and unquestioning either adapt to the dominant practices or withdraw and seldom participate.

An important influence on children's educational success is their parents' own educational background. In Melbourne, the earliest-arriving Tongans were young people who had come to Australia specifically to study, and when they had their own children, education was a priority for them. Later immigrants came for more diverse reasons, and many had low levels of education and took on unskilled work. Some of these immigrants supported their children's education, with the aim of improving that generation's employment prospects and increasing their chances of upward social mobility. Others encouraged their children to leave school young and contribute to the family. However, those less-educated parents who did support their children's education faced a range of obstacles such as financial constraints and a lack of understanding of the school system, as described previously. Richard Brown and Adrian Walker found in their 1995 study in Sydney that there is a new wave of Tongan migrants who have higher education levels. "This is indicative of greater selectivity by both Australia and New Zealand in their immigration controls, and of improved educational opportunities in the migrants' countries of origin" (1995, 29).

Overall, the Melbourne Tongans I surveyed were not highly educated (see appendix A), but 50 of the 303 individuals over the age of fifteen (16.5 percent) have postsecondary qualifications,[5] and a further 42 are studying at tertiary institutions. In addition, 15 of those who already have tertiary qualifications are continuing their studies. This rate of postsecondary qualifications is similar to the 17 percent reported for New Zealand in 1996 (Statistics New Zealand 1998, 27), but the proportion with secondary-school qualifications is higher in New Zealand than in my sample (34 and 24.5 percent, respectively). The U.S. Department of Commerce reports that in 1990, 64 percent of Tongans in the United States over the age of twenty-five had a high school diploma or higher qualification. This was the lowest rate for all Pacific Islander groups, as was the Tongans' rate of attaining university degrees, at 5.75 percent (1993, 4).

Employment

The low rates of postsecondary qualifications held by Tongan migrants are reflected in their employment patterns, with the majority in unskilled occupations, including production and processing (factory work), laboring, and cleaning, and very few in professional and managerial positions. This has certainly been the case in Australia (Connell, Harrison, and McCall 1991; Faiva 1989; Moala 1986; Price 1987), and in my own sample 60.9 percent of those employed were in unskilled positions. In New Zealand, Tongans and other Pacific Islanders are predominantly in unskilled and semiskilled occupations, and Tongans have the lowest participation rate of all Islanders in the professional and managerial areas (Krishnan, Schoeffel, and Warren 1994, 61, 65; see also Larner and Bedford 1993). Similarly, the census-based report on Pacific Islanders in the United States comments, "Tongans were more likely than all Pacific Islanders to work in service occupations and less likely to be managers or professionals" (U.S. Department of Commerce 1993, 6).

Tongans' rates of unemployment overseas vary between locations and with fluctuations in national economies. Brown and Walker showed that unemployment rates for Tongans in Sydney were lower than the national average in 1992 (1995, 25). However, in Victoria, the 1991 census recorded an unemployment rate of 29.6 percent for Tongans over the age of fifteen, which was significantly higher than the rate of unemployment for Victorians over fifteen (12 percent) and even other Pacific Islanders (20 percent) (Multicultural Affairs Unit 1996).[6] Within the Melbourne sample approximately 10 percent are unemployed, excluding students, pensioners, and those—predominantly females—doing home duties (see appendix A, table 5).

There is little incentive for Tongan migrants to prefer unemployment or other benefits over working, given the substantial demands on adults for financial assistance to family, church, and the wider Tongan community. Thus they are often willing to take on jobs with poor wages and conditions rather than not work at all. However, new arrivals are finding it increasingly difficult to maintain steady employment compared with the postwar employment boom in receiving nations, which made employment readily available.

As their employment patterns suggest, Tongans tend to occupy low socioeconomic positions in their host countries. John Connell, Graham Harrison, and Grant McCall found that, for Tongans in Sydney,

> [t]he average individual income was considerably lower than the overall figure especially when those with no income were included. There were virtually no Tonga born people in the higher income ranges. . . . When family income is considered rather than individual income, those born in Tonga still had a lower income profile than the State as a whole. (1991, 60)

In New Zealand, the structural shifts in employment associated with economic downturn have had a negative outcome for Tongans and other Polynesians. Krishnan, Schoeffel, and Warren argue: "New Zealand is drifting towards a situation of extreme racial and economic polarisation in which an ethnically visible, substantial Polynesian minority—both Pacific Islander and Tangata Whenua [Maori]—are becoming an entrenched underclass, despite the different histories and status of the two groups" (1994, 83). In 1991, 22 percent of the Tongan labor force in New Zealand was unemployed; this had improved slightly to 18 percent in 1996, compared to 8 percent for the total New Zealand population (Statistics New Zealand 1995, 1998).

In a 1990 U.S. census report, Tongans were listed at the lowest end of the income scale for the Pacific Islanders, and both Tongans and Samoans had about half the national per capita income (U.S. Department of Commerce 1993, 7). Correlated to this, both groups had high poverty rates, with Tongans at 23.1 percent and Samoans 25.8 percent. Overall, approximately 21 percent of Pacific Islanders in the United States lived below the poverty level in 1989 (Ahlburg 2000).

There are signs that this disadvantage may be somewhat alleviated for second and later generations of these Pacific Islander groups. New Zealand-born Tongans are gradually moving out of the manufacturing industry and other unskilled occupations into more service-oriented and professional occupations. Second-generation Tongans in Melbourne are in a very similar situation to that described by Samantha Maingay for second-generation Pacific Islanders in New Zealand (1995), as they are more upwardly mobile than their parents, with higher levels of formal education and occupational skills, more disposable income due to reduced expenditures on remittances and within their ethnic communities, and the benefit of knowing "the system." The Australian-born individuals in the Melbourne sample have a significantly different employment profile to that of the Tongan born. Fully 38.6 percent of the Australian-born sample who were employed were in professional or managerial positions or owned their own businesses, compared with 11 percent of the Tongan born. Unskilled occupations comprised 36.4 percent of Australian-born employment and 73 percent of Tongan born.

Simply looking at the figures for employment rates and types of occupation does not provide the whole picture of Tongan employment issues overseas. Social mobility, for example, is a complex issue that cannot be judged simply on factors such as level of education, income, and occupation. As Maingay has argued, other factors such as culturally specific aspirations, access to material resources, and so forth, can also be important. For example, Tongans (and other Pacific Islanders) may reach comparable levels of income as the wider community but may have much less disposable income due to their large families, demands from extended kin, and obligations to send remittances to their home country. There may also be different ideas about desirable occupations, with many preferring low-status jobs because they can get additional income through overtime and may have more flexible hours. Most important, status in Pacific communities is not based solely on income and occupation.

An issue Maingay does not consider is that the status of second-generation Islanders within their own communities does not necessarily rise along with their socioeconomic status in the wider society. If they have moved out of the traditional networks and are not competent in Tongan language they may be respected for their economic success but are unlikely to be regarded as of particularly high status. Some may find themselves marginalized from the Tongan community, and those who have not achieved educational and economic success are doubly marginalized. Those who have managed to achieve educational success, with its potential for upward mobility, *and* competence in Tongan language and culture are emerging as the new elite within overseas communities, despite the fact that most of them are "commoners."

Another important issue to consider is the conditions under which Tongans work. Those in unskilled and semiskilled occupations often have to work in poor conditions and may be uninformed about their rights as workers. The situation Moala found in her study of Tongan workers in Sydney in the mid-1980s has changed very little; she states that "Tongans have almost no knowledge of Australian industrial relations and have little idea of who to turn to with their problems at work" (1986, 219). She argues that "the exploitation of their ignorance is appalling," with workers having no knowledge of their rights and entitlements, safety requirements, insurance options, services available to them, and so on.

Some people I interviewed endured poor conditions, including working without appropriate safety equipment, being expected to do extra duties, and having no job security. Julie, forty-five, an Australian woman in a professional occupation and married to Samuela, thirty, a Tongan doing factory work, was angry about his work conditions. "At his work they treat him as if he's a slave or whatever. Like they wouldn't do it to Australians, but they'll do it to Tongans." Another concerned wife said her husband "has to be better than everybody else to achieve his place in the workplace. Okay, so he has to try very hard all the time, be an overachiever, and really work very hard in order to hold his place in his job."

While many Tongan migrants are happy with the work they obtain, others suffer disillusionment when they are unable to find work or when they have no job security. Some also find they cannot find work at the level of their qualifications. Sioeli described his disappointment at not having found permanent work as a teacher, and at the time of our interview he was working long hours in a factory to support his family. He complained,

I am sick of being poor and doing jobs that are not related to my field. Sometimes I wonder why I came here. . . . Australia is a great country, but it can also be a graveyard for the fainthearted. Migrants find life tougher in a new country if things do not go their way or diverts from original intention.

Sioeli explained that the only jobs he had found were temporary, so he was doing further tertiary studies while working full time in an attempt to upgrade his qualifications. "Even other jobs I've applied for, I know for sure I'm better than the others, but I never get a chance. . . . Even the degree I'm doing now, I'm not looking forward to the end of it, because I find it—the job hunting—is very difficult." At one point Sioeli obtained a temporary teaching position in a high school, but he found it frustrating because he could not convert this to a permanent position. He also found that the students mocked his accent, and he found their behavior poor compared to students in Tonga. As he observed, "I think they played up more because I'm not an Australian."

Discrimination and Racism

Sioeli's perception that his students treated him poorly because he is not Anglo-Australian raises the issue of discrimination against Tongans, much of which is based on stereotypes and ignorance. Tongan migrants have settled in many countries of the world, yet in most of these places people know little or nothing about them or their homeland. Some confuse Tongans with the African Tonga (or Thonga), and others know Tonga simply as a tiny dot in the Pacific on maps of the world. Tongans are often assumed to be the same as all Pacific Islanders, as if Samoans, Fijians, Maori, and others are all interchangeable. Those who do have a little knowledge about Tonga are often those who have visited on a cruise ship, or they may know the story of the gracious Queen Sālote attending the coronation of England's Queen Elizabeth in 1953 or of the seat specially made for the current king, Tāufaʻāhau Tupou IV, when he attended the 1981 wedding of Prince Charles and Lady Diana Spencer.

The media is one of the main sources of information (and misinformation) about Tongans, and stories of Tongans' sporting prowess have appeared since the first waves of migration occurred, creating an image of Tongans as big and strong. A number of the early stories in the Australian media focused on Tongan athletes Albert and Sanitesi Lātū, who went to Australia in 1971 and 1973, respectively, and were celebrated for their sporting abilities. One newspaper described Sanitesi as "probably the most beautifully proportioned athlete in Australia" (undated news clipping; see Davies 1978).[7] Today, as an increasing number of Tongans are achieving recognition at national and international levels for their sporting abilities, similarly celebratory stories continue to appear; think of footballer Jonah Lomu of the famous New Zealand All Blacks, sumo wrestler Musashimaru (Fiamalu Penitani), and Olympic boxing silver medalist Paea Wolfgramm.[8] Wolfgramm was described by the media in terms like "man mountain," "old fashioned warrior," and "massive hero" (Olson 1996).

Another common stereotype of Tongans is that they are all friendly, deriving in part from the name "Friendly Islands" given to Tonga by the explorer Captain James Cook. However, this image is countered by one of Tongans as violent and aggressive, which has been an element of many sports stories about them. During the 1999 World Cup final, *The Daily Telegraph* newspaper in Australia published a "report card" on the contenders, describing the Tongan team as "[m]addened killers from the friendly isles" who brought "thuggery to the tournament without producing any of the dancing skills other Pacific Islanders have. No-one will care if they never see Tonga again" (Wilson 1999, 80). Elsewhere in the several pages of articles about the World Cup, a Tongan member of the Australian Wallabies, Toutai Kefu, was promoted in more positive terms as the "Tongan Torpedo" (Tucker 1999, 78).[9] In some cities with large populations of Tongans other negative stereotypes are developing, fueled by occasional reports of Tongans involved in criminal activity such as drug dealing and violent assault, and of Tongan youth as gang members.

Many newspaper articles concerning Tongans have focused on illegal immigration. Those I have seen in Australia have dealt mainly with the detrimental impact of deportation on families. However, as we saw in chapter 2, in New Zealand in the 1970s the media contributed to the negative stereotype—still alive today—of Tongans and other Pacific Islanders as overstayers.

Tonga itself is becoming more well known through segments about Tonga on the popular holiday television programs, which tend to reinforce long-held romantic images of palm-fringed South Pacific beaches and friendly natives, but which have at least raised awareness of the existence of Tonga.[10] It is primarily these more exotic images that are presented to Western audiences, for whom "the South Pacific" represents a tropical paradise. In Australia, so geographically close to the Pacific, Tonga rarely rates a mention in the media unless something particularly sensational occurs, such as Tonga's claim to be the first country to greet the new millennium (e.g., *Canberra Times* 1999). Even then, the tone of articles is often patronizing and mildly racist, depicting Tongans as a quaint and exotic people. One 1997 article, appearing in a major daily newspaper, perpetuates this image.

> Marx would have loved Tonga: no-one can own property, no-one goes hungry and no-one is homeless, despite minuscule taxes and a lack of social welfare. Of course, the flat rate tax of 10 per cent is not quite so attractive when you see Tonga's roads or hospitals but as long as you don't drive or get sick, it's fantastic. . . . Tongans smoke almost as much as they eat (no mean feat) and pure fat appeared to be the favourite part of the meal at the feasts of rich, oily food I attended. . . . The Tongans are happy, friendly, proud—and a little weird. (Szeps 1997)

Written by a man who had participated in a cultural exchange program through Rotary International, the article was accompanied by a large cartoon (see fig. 2).

The contradictory stereotypes of Tongans as friendly, gentle, and exotic yet also big, strong, and prone to violence have created a rather ambivalent attitude toward them in their host countries, which in some areas unfortunately appears to be shifting toward an emphasis on the more negative elements. This ambivalence is not new and was evident from the first wave of migration in the 1960s, when all three of the main receiving nations still gave preference to (white) British and Western European immigrants. Tongans, like other Islanders, were regarded rather warily, and in Australia, at least, efforts had to be made to reassure the white population that the Tongan immigrants posed no threat. In 1973 an article titled "Don't Worry, They Won't Eat Us," appearing in an Australian newspaper, reported Immigration Minister Al Grassby's announcement that nonwhite New Zealanders would be able to settle as freely in Australia as white New Zealanders.

> The great-grandfathers of Maoris and other Polynesian New Zealanders might have been cannibals. But the modern Polynesian normally is gentle, good-natured, good-looking, intelligent and hard working. Except for plumpness which is liable to make many of them conspicuous (the king of Tonga weighs 21 stone), many Polynesians could pass in Australia for Mediterranean people. (Gilmore 1973, 4)

Figure 2: Artist John Shakespeare's illustration for
"Cultured? Me? Fat chance!" by Josh Szeps, *Sydney
Morning Herald,* 8 February 1997.

At this time, most industrialized nations were just beginning to promote tolerance to ethnic diversity, as immigration from many nations
brought people of different cultures to their shores. Assumptions that
immigrants would all "assimilate" were soon challenged by their maintaining at least some aspects of their cultures, and this led to increasing
support for policies of "multiculturalism" and "pluralism," which were
promoted as encouraging respect for cultural difference (Cornwall and

Stoddard 2001; Jakubowicz, Morrisey, and Palser 1984; Jupp 1996). In all the main receiving nations, government policies of cultural tolerance and attempts to combat racism and discrimination have met with mixed success. While some Tongans report that they have never encountered any difficulties because of their ethnic origins, others have suffered distressing racism.

The women and men who were among the early arrivals in Melbourne did not recount experiences of culture shock, and most described themselves as adaptable and easygoing. Seini, sixty, who married an Australian, said, "I'm a very, very easy sort of person in accepting the community and where I am. . . . I just fit in myself, just like an Australian." These early immigrants also denied experiencing significant discrimination. Seini told me she had never been exposed directly to racist comments or behavior in nearly forty years in Australia. However, she did talk about the many comments she received in her early days in Melbourne about her brown skin; at the time she made jokes in response, but now she wonders what people really thought about her. More recently, in her capacity as a volunteer worker, she became concerned that one of the people at her workplace disliked her because she was Tongan. This was not the case, however, and she exclaimed, "I thank God for that, because I thought he rejected me because I am dark!" Clearly, while she denies experiencing racism, the possibility that it could happen is not far from her mind.

Langi, seventy, who has lived in Melbourne with his Australian wife since the 1980s, also told me he has never experienced racism in Australia. "I attribute that to the fact that most of the people that I am associated with are church people; see, I haven't been involved with the outside community, where those complaints normally come from." It was a common view among those I interviewed that within church communities people are not exposed to racism. Jane told me she had not had any negative comments about her intermarriage with a Tongan: "Certainly not from my friends, because, you know, we're church people, we're Christians, and most of our friends are Christians too, so you don't get that so much." Jane and her husband attend a church with a mixed Tongan and non-Tongan congregation, and she commented, "I think a lot of Australians think that Islanders are happy, nice people, that sort of thing. Particularly in the church here. They get quite shocked if you tell them about something that's a problem and they can't believe it, because 'they're all so lovely and friendly and kind and nice'!"

The children of the early settlers are more willing to acknowledge that racism did occur and that their parents had difficulties in the context of the "White Australia" policy and associated community attitudes. Sue, thirty-two, the daughter of a Tongan mother and Australian father, described the problems her mother experienced in the workplace in the 1960s, including people who did not want to deal with a "black woman" and others who assumed she was in a junior position and refused to accept that she was in a senior role. Sue and her siblings later experienced racism as children in the 1960s and 1970s in the form of name calling, but Fusi, thirty, her younger sister, reflected that the problem declined over time: "Mum had it really badly, then Sue had it, and then I had it to a lesser degree. Because it went down. [And] they protected me."

Younger people also were more willing to recall their own experiences of racism. Mary, twenty-five, who moved to Australia in the 1970s at the age of six and was educated in a Catholic primary school, had bad memories of the nuns pinching her and teasing her about her frizzy hair. She recalled, "They'd always say to me, 'If you don't stop being naughty we're going to turn you upside down and use you as a mop!' Because I had that hair!" School was one of the main arenas for racist remarks; at a church meeting a young woman, recounting her school years, said,

> The racist remarks were unbearable at times. Australian people wanted us to be Australians and yet they never recognized us as Australians. We were still seen as Tongans—"the black Tongans." And that's something we found very difficult to understand because in Tonga we respect Australian people. When we came out here we found that we were seen as second-class people. (Canterbury Uniting Church 1993)

Some parents also mentioned problems their children had experienced. 'Ana told me her children see themselves as Australian and are hurt by racist comments. When her children complained about being called "black" at school, her husband told them to hit the children teasing them, but following his advice only got them into trouble. Soon after this 'Ana moved her children to a school with students from diverse ethnic backgrounds, and the problems ceased. Discrimination appears to be less likely in more ethnically diverse areas, and Susana, nineteen, a university student who grew up in Queensland before moving to Melbourne in the early 1990s, claimed, "I certainly haven't encountered a single strand of racism yet. I guess this is because [Tongans] are not an 'overpopulated,' unsociable group, or maybe it's because I live in a highly multicultural area. We're willing to blend in with the Australians but still retain our tradition."

Much of the overt racism in Australia is directed toward Asian immigrants and the aboriginal population (Vasta and Castles 1996). Positive stereotypes about Islanders as friendly, happy-go-lucky, generous, and so forth, tend to counter more negative images, although as "Third World-looking" people (Hage 1998) they are not unequivocally accepted either, particularly since the resurgence of conservative views in the 1990s. Discrimination and racism were reported more often by Tongans in New Zealand and the United States. Sulieta, twenty-four, a university student who grew up mainly in the United States, said, "When I am with the African Americans or Hispanics I don't feel that they treat me any different, but when I am with those who are of an ethnic background but yet they are white, they tend to look down at me because of my color. . . . Once they see the brown skin color they immediately judge us." Helenā, thirty-eight, who migrated to the United States as a child in the 1960s, observed, "Non-Tongans here in Utah have stereotypical thoughts about Tongans. I think most of them think that we are all gang members, party folks, and troublemakers."

The problem of racism is frequently raised on the KB and other Internet discussion forums, particularly by Tongans in the United States.[11] On the Tongan History Association forum a Tongan commented, "Where I live the only things Tongans are known for is their louzy attitude, their noisy big mouths, and their lack of knowledge" (KB 21.11.96).[12] A Tongan college graduate complained on the KB about discrimination by teachers and other school personnel, employers, shop owners, and police.

> My experience here in America, white people already know what they think of Tongans. The majority of white people in Utah categorized Tongans as second-class citizens. I have encountered many white people, even bishops, stake presidents and missionary presidents of the Mormon Church, who discriminated strongly because I am Tongan. Not because of my abilities and performance, BUT, because of my color and my race, a Tongan. (KB 19.2.97)

Another KB poster commented on the situation in Utah in a discussion about a program aired nationally on CBS and an article that appeared in *Newsweek* (Hamilton, Glick, and Rice 1996) about Islander gangs in Salt Lake City. The poster was angry that the media had not mentioned any positive aspects of the Tongan community in Salt Lake City and continued,

> [W]hen we first moved here from Hawaii in 1981, we faced a lot of racism here in Utah, even from the lily white Mormons. To this day, the problem is still there. It troubled me as a kid to know that the same little white shits who called us niggers on a daily basis, flatten our tires, throw rocks at us as [we] walked by, and the list goes on and on, were the same ones who were in my Sunday School class!!! When their parents were told about it, they dismissed it as child's play. Yes ladies and gentlemen, racism is alive and hell here in Zion. (KB 13.5.96)

Many Tongans in the United States are concerned that news reports of Tongans involved in criminal activities affect the reputation of the whole population. One message on the KB read, "I think that all the bad things done in the Tongan community are done by a 'few bad apples' and that gives this negative stereotype of Polynesians in general. For every Tongan kid that commits a crime there are 15 Tongan kids in college who have jobs and go to church" (KB 3.2.98). Another commented that news reports of such crimes "make it so much harder to make it in this great land of opportunity" (KB 17.1.98).[13]

Many of the stereotypes about Tongans in the United States appear to center on perceptions of Tongan youth. A Tongan woman commented on the KB that Tongan teenagers are stereotyped as "supposedly violent in nature and unruly as hell" (KB 27.9.97). The woman works with local schools and claims that when new migrants arrive, "They try to fit in so much that when they don't succeed they end up lashing against the system with the negative impulse of children vulnerable to their unknown surrounding." A young man responded to her post by writing, "As a young immigrant to this country, I felt, as they do, that everybody plays Tongan immigrant for a fools" (KB 27.9.97). He comments that he was always asked if he played football and felt that underlying the question was the assumption that he was tough and violent. "The saddest things was, when I go home and my parent has no insight or any knowledge on how to dealt with the encountered problem." There have been a number of discussions on the KB about this very issue of parents needing to understand the racism their children face at school and in the wider community.

Some messages on the KB relating to discrimination offer a different view of their experiences, as with the poster who acknowledged that negative stereotypes about Tongans exist but added that "there are also those who praise Tongan family values, who admire Tongan tradition, and who are proud of their friendship with a Tongan" (KB 29.9.97). Another volunteered, "All my places of employment people have commented how they thought Polynesian people were 'very friendly and down to earth.' They also seem very interested to hear about my background and customs. I've felt being Polynesian has been an asset" (KB 18.3.98). There are also some who argue that perceptions of racism are inaccurate. A Tongan woman wrote,

> I think that race has become a scapegoat for the low self esteem and insecurity of many of our people, blaming outsiders for our problems and overlooking the good and benefits that we have reaped through our associations with them. Sometimes we get carried away with our own sense of self righteousness that we skim over our own shortcomings as a people, and romanticize our history to justify our ire over perceived misdoings. (KB 26.11.98)

For those who do encounter negative stereotypes and racism, the experiences can affect their perceptions of their own identities and of other Islanders. In March 1998 there was a long, heated discussion on the KB generated by a message with the heading "Why I Hate Being Polynesian!!!!!!" (KB 18.3.98). The author claims Polynesians are rude, ignorant, disrespectful, dishonest, rough, and tough, then says, "It makes me mad when white people look down on me and think, 'Oh, she's as wild as they all are'" (KB 18.3.98). There was a barrage of indignant replies, some of which asserted pride in being Polynesian and accused the poster of "selling out" and being narrow-minded and ignorant or advised her to return to her islands to rediscover her heritage. One reminded her, "You have the sweat of all the pioneering tongans who have suffered to bring you to america to better your life and for you to be embarrassed about!!!! All I have to say is know where you come from and stand tall!!!!" (KB 18.3.98). Another wrote, "You shouldn't hate being polynesian, you should hate the palagis for looking down on you" (KB 20.3.98).

There also is a certain amount of stereotyping in reverse, with some Tongans holding negative ideas about *pālangi* that are in contrast to positively valued aspects of Tongan culture, such as generosity and family values. These negative ideas jostle with older, more positive views of *pālangi*, which valued whiteness more as an indication of higher rank and were not so directly associated with notions of race. Young people, particularly those raised in the United States, do see this as an issue of race and are questioning the older views. A Tongan woman on the KB wrote, "We all know that in the Tongan Culture white and fair is beautiful. No matter how ugly the face but if you have fair skin people seem to just ignore the face and focus on your fair skin. I know for a fact because I'm not fair but I have a beautiful face and yet everyone called me a nigger and it hurt my feelings. I still see the same reaction now" (KB 19.2.97).

Tongans are much less ambivalent about certain other peoples they encounter overseas.[14] Cathy Small claims that a "severe racial bias toward Mexican-Americans and African-Americans" is "typical" of Tongans in the United States. She adds,

> Many Tongan-born migrants believe that people inherit abilities and personal status in their "blood." . . . American racism, including the selective and stereotypic presentations of these minorities in the media, feeds the conception, embraced by many Tongan migrants, that Mexicans and blacks in this country are a lower "rank" of people. (1997, 225, n. 13)

A Tongan woman writing on the KB observed that Tongans have a "double standard of racism" in which they complain about racism directed at them but at the same time express racist views against others (KB 22.9.96). However, it must be added that some of the "racism" attributed to Tongans is a result of the unself-conscious use of terms such as *nika* (nigger) and *'uli'uli* (black) to refer to African Americans; these terms were used in Tonga during World War II, when many American troops were sent to Tonga (see Scarr, Gunson, and Terrell 1998). For the most part Tongans did not seem to realize the racist connotations of such terms. In chapter 6 I examine in more detail Tongan attitudes toward other groups in the context of intermarriages.

Social Problems

Migration across national borders is almost always a difficult process, even when migrants perceive their new home as offering a better life than the one they left behind. We have already encountered some of the problems Tongan migrants can face, such as low income, poor work conditions, lack of information about available services, and discrimination. Here, I examine some of the other difficulties Tongans experience, with a particular focus on youth issues.

Jane described how she perceives the main difficulties new arrivals face:

> They come here . . . thinking that they are going to be able to have untold wealth and be able to help their families at home and be well-established here themselves. And they just cannot. And they don't know how to deal with that. They have no background of dealing even with the amounts of money that they earn here, and they don't even begin to deal with it. So they live day-to-day, as far as I can observe. And I think I can observe now in our people [at their Tongan church] that they're starting to reach almost crisis point on that; the realization is sinking in and they can't cope. Getting into the gambling and that sort of thing a lot, yeah.

Jane gave as an example those who do not insure their cars; consequently, when they are involved in accidents they face enormous financial problems. She and her Tongan husband are active in the church and freely offer advice about financial management and other issues, and she is clearly embittered by people's refusal to follow their advice. "It doesn't all sink in and they don't take it all on board, partly because they think they know, and the way they've done it in the Tongan way is best." Some of the Tongan members of the same church also pointed out the problems caused by status competition, with people buying new cars or spending ostentatiously while struggling to pay their mortgages and other expenses and to provide for their children.

The fact that most Tongans are reluctant to seek assistance from mainstream agencies means that problems tend to be handled within the Tongan "community," whether it be assistance with finding accommodations and employment or support for families in crisis. Much of the burden of help falls on the church ministers, who, as we have already seen, fill a number of roles, including counselor, translator, and mediator between Tongans and outside bodies such as welfare authorities and the police. Some ministers also organize or support the provision of information through the church; for example, some churches hold information sessions on issues such as financial matters and health and produce newsletters that include articles on these kinds of topics.

Ministers are also called on to assist with more serious problems such as gambling, alcohol abuse, and domestic violence and their effects on families. Some churches approach these issues in the context of women's groups, church seminars, and so on. Domestic violence, in particular, is a difficult issue to deal with as it is so well hidden (as in most communities). The consumption of kava can also become a problem when it takes men away from their families and affects their work. An indignant message on the KB denounced the use of kava in overseas communities.

> How unfortunate that a "FORMERLY" sacred tradition has been "Prostituted" and "Degenerated" into a "Grossly Abused" form of entertainment for Polynesian men, young and old. . . . Why don't you spend the many WASTED hours spent around the Kava Bowl volunteering. There are countless numbers of young Polynesians that could use guidance, tutoring, and structure so that they can succeed within the culture here in America. . . . Lets stop trying to defend the abuse of Kava and begin working together to come up with "real solutions" to the harshly "real social problems" we are facing as Polynesians! (KB 11.3.1997)

Health Problems

There has been little research into health problems among Tongan migrants, but a number of problems related to diet, stress, and low usage of preventive measures are of concern. In Tonga itself there has been growing awareness of health issues, particularly the impact of obesity on health, but this does not appear to have greatly influenced the diasporic population. King Tupou IV, who is one of the driving forces behind the changing attitudes in Tonga, is attempting to influence his subjects overseas; on a visit to San Fransisco he urged Tongans there to take greater care of their health (*Tonga Chronicle* 1998a). A health booklet was published in early 1998 for distribution among Tongans in the United States.

In his survey of Tongans in Sydney, the main health problems Faiva reported were asthma, back pain, hypertension, arthritis, work injuries, diabetes, and alcohol-related problems (1989, iv; see also Niumeitolu 1993). Faiva also reported that dental health was poor, especially for children. Mental health problems appear to be more common for migrants than in Tonga, and Siale Foliaki has predicted that "the migrant

Tongan populations' chances of avoiding worsening mental health status seem grim" (1999, 293). He attributes migrants' mental health problems to the stresses associated with "economic hardship," domestic violence, alcohol and drug abuse, and "family fragmentation" and "social disintegration" leading to loss of cultural identity.[15]

In the larger centers of Tongan migration there are often health services specifically for Tongans, such as the Kiliniki Langimālie in Auckland, a Tongan health clinic established in 1997, and the Tongan women's health program at Sydney's Fairfield Immigrant Women's Health Services, established in 1998. In such cities it is common for Tongans to be employed by government departments to work with and educate the Tongan population on health and other issues and to disseminate information. "Traditional" Tongan healers also work within the migrant populations, tending to specialize in spirit-related illnesses (often diagnosed as mental health problems by Western physicians), but also dealing with a wide range of other conditions (Foliaki 1999; Toafa, Moata'ane, and Guthrie 1999).

Although health was not a specific focus of my own research, a number of Tongans in Melbourne expressed concern about the problem of obesity and other diet-related illnesses, including concern about overweight children whose diets are high in processed "junk" food. A social worker I spoke with reported a low rate of immunization among Tongan and other Pacific Islander families, which causes problems when enrolling the children in school, as immunization records are required. Similarly, a community health nurse working in a rural area with a significant number of Tongans told me that most did not take advantage of any preventive measures such as immunization or Pap smears and tended to use the health services only when absolutely necessary. She reported a very high incidence of diabetes and high blood pressure. In this particular area many Tongans are overstayers, a status that prevents them from accessing free medical care and further reduces the likelihood of seeking preventive health checks.

Clearly, the problems Tongans often face are compounded by a general reluctance to seek help from mainstream services and the consequent pressures on relatives, church ministers, and others within the Tongan population to provide assistance. As with many other issues affecting Tongans overseas, changes are already occurring as young people increasingly question the status quo and challenge the insularity of many older Tongans, as we will see in chapter 5. Yet many of these young people have problems of their own to deal with and can create other difficulties for their families.

Youth Issues

One of the most serious problems facing many Tongan families overseas is generational conflict, which is closely tied to parents' concerns about their children's interactions with the wider community. Many of the clashes between young people and their parents and other family members arise over fears of "bad" external influences and over restrictions on children's freedom. The kinds of behavior that concern parents range from smoking and alcohol consumption[16] to petty criminal activity such as graffiti and shoplifting to more serious criminal behavior that attracts police intervention, including gang membership (discussed in chapter 5).

Concern about young people's behavior can make parents ambivalent about their situation as migrants. As Penelope Schoeffel and Malama Meleisea (n.d.) found for Pacific Islanders in Auckland, parents often have a positive view of the opportunities and choices offered by overseas living yet are negative about the difficulties they encounter with employment, housing, finances, and, particularly, the detrimental influences on their children. The parents felt they were losing control over their children, who, they believed, were losing their cultural identities.

Divergent views on how best to raise children overseas can be a source of tension in diasporic communities. Parents who choose to be more "modern" argue that being flexible and allowing their children to fit in with their non-Tongan peers will prevent conflict in the home and thus prevent their children from getting into trouble. These parents tend to view more "traditional" parents as creating problems by insisting on keeping the Tongan way and being so strict that their children want to rebel. However, the opposite view is expressed by the more traditional parents, who claim that the children of the more "Westernized" parents are the ones exposed to bad influences and thus more likely to get involved with smoking, drinking, and petty criminal behavior. They argue that their own strict parenting will keep their children from getting into trouble.

A Tongan youth worker in Melbourne argued that the children of recent immigrants are more likely to behave in ways that concern their parents and explained this as the result of the increased freedom they have in Australia.

> It's like coming to Australia is total freedom for them, and they don't see the sense of listening to their parents anymore. Because I do experience this, I do experience the trouble that the parents are having in the church with their children among that [adolescent] age group, that they have only been here for a few years and already they're dressed in Afro-American way; and the way they talk, they can't even speak English very well, but yet they are willing to hang around with gangs and groups and they are doing graffiti . . . and it's just very, very scary. Whereas people that are born in here, children of the parents like myself, [who] are trying to teach them the best in the custom and the best in the culture, seems to be doing better among that age group.

As a youth worker, she said, she felt helpless. "I am a qualified youth worker and I can easily go through the department [of Human Services] and apply for funding and help out these parents, but I am not sure whether they are prepared to be helped, and it scares me. Because I know for a fact that if I go in as a youth worker and try to help their children, they'll see me in a different way; I am no longer a Tongan to them. They see you totally different. It would be very, very hard."

The final issue she raises is important, as it relates to the reluctance of Tongans to accept "outside" support. A Pacific Islander (not Tongan) social worker dealing with numerous Maori and Pacific Islander cases referred by the Department of Human Services in Victoria commented to me that working with Tongan families was particularly difficult as they "hide behind their culture" and "have barriers up." The social worker spoke of the "closed network" of Tongans who wanted to deal with their problems within their own extended families rather than have outside involvement.

Some schools across the diaspora have social workers to support Pacific Islander students, but most cities with Islander populations have few qualified professionals or funded programs to deal with the problems facing young people, and much of the work is done on a voluntary basis. A social worker in Melbourne expressed concern that many Islander children and adolescents were "getting lost in the system" and received no culturally sensitive support. Yet there is disagreement about the need for Tongan professionals such as youth workers and counselors, and while some overseas Tongans feel it is important to have people familiar with the language and culture working with young people, others argue that there are problems involved in having "insiders" involved in such capacities. There are also differences of opinion as to whether youth centers and other community venues are needed. Young people often said they felt such things were needed, but some parents claim there are already enough services provided but that the young people choose not to use them. 'Ana commented, "I think there is enough there, but I think they are just too lazy to go to those things." Clearly, there is no consensus about how best to tackle youth problems, but in Tongan populations overseas a number of initiatives have been put into place, particularly in recent years.[17]

As stated earlier, some churches are now attempting to focus on youth issues. In centers with larger Tongan populations churches sometimes organize major events targeted at youth, such as the Tongan Methodist youth rally held in Auckland in 1996. Over fifteen hundred youth attended and were addressed by motivational speakers, all successful Tongans who were selected as role models. Youth groups from New Zealand presented items, and the rally was filmed for television and broadcast on radio (*Tonga Chronicle* 1996c).

There are also some Tongans working more independently with youth; for example, in Melbourne a small group of young men regularly visits Tongan boys being held in detention centers.[18] Some Tongan families are involved in fostering programs, caring for young Tongans who have been removed from their families for various reasons. Young people are also beginning to organize informal support groups for themselves, such as the group of Melbourne young people who meet regularly at a park on Saturdays to have barbeques, play rugby, and just spend time together.

An issue of growing concern is young people's encounters with the legal system. Cultural conflicts within families and lack of support systems within the wider community for these young people often underlie the problem (Wilkins and Yaman 1994), but it is exacerbated by the discrimination, harassment, and racism Islander youth often encounter in their interactions with police (Cunneen 1995, 394; Francis 1995). Other problems they face include the lack of information available to them regarding the law and the neglect of their specific needs and problems by legal and correctional institutions. Tongans, like other "ethnic" youth, are more likely to be searched, arrested, and injured in their contact with police than other youth. Some attempts are being made to address these issues, such as the establishment of committees to advise police on multicultural issues, but the problems are by no means resolved (Chan 1996; Cunneen 1995).

Formal Associations

Concerns about youth and the apparent inability (or unwillingness) of the wider society to deal with those problems can provide an impetus for Tongans to establish formal associations. These are often seen as a way of creating a greater sense of community and of dealing with more general social and health problems. In part, they are also the result of Tongans' growing awareness of their minority status and their designation by the wider society as an "ethnic" group. A new rhetoric of empowerment through unity appears to be gathering force among some Tongans who are coming to recognize the need to work together. A post on the KB captured this well.

> We, the Tongans, my people, my people I love, must stand together, holding hands together, to reaffirm each and every one of us, and to empower one another within our ethnic group, the Tongans in America. We must work together, in little things, in little ways, so we can overcome. I see the black people and the latinos are more united than us. We must be together, we must be united, we must have one agenda, and we must raise our voices together, for our voice to be heard here in America. (KB 19.2.97)

The process of forming associations can be difficult, however, partly because many people do not know the procedures involved or even how to begin the process. Many people I spoke with said they would like to be involved in an organization, particularly with the goal of establishing a cultural center for young people to learn Tongan language, dance, and "traditions," but would then shrug and say they did not know how to go about making this a reality. There is also considerable skepticism about formal organizations, as many people assume there will be factionalism, tensions, corruption, and a lack of direction. Their skepticism is not unfounded, as these are the problems that have dogged many efforts to establish formal associations and that foil attempts at gaining a sense of unity. Gareth Grainger notes that the result of these problems has been the fragmentation of the Tongan population in Australia

> into smaller and smaller independent Church communities largely focussed on single extended families and their retinues. . . . Whilst the Tongan community in Australia is very large in terms of Tonga's population it has less voice in Australia's multicultural policy processes than it might have through the difficulties of achieving reasonable consensus and representation through a single and strong national ethnic organisation. (1997, 17)

When formal associations are formed, they are often weakened by small groups breaking away to start separate associations, and internal conflicts arise that slow down the process of conducting all the formalities of registration, constitution writing, committee selection, and so forth. Some people even argue against setting up formal associations at all, claiming they encourage Tongans to isolate themselves from the wider society. One man told me he disagrees with "the nationalistic stuff" because he believes it makes Tongans "form little ghettos." Instead, he argued, it would be better for them "to be more cross-cultural, not just the Tongan mentality all the time."

Notwithstanding these obstacles, many formal Tongan organizations have been established and operate with varying degrees of success. The majority can be found in the centers of larger Tongan and Islander populations, and in both New Zealand and the United States numerous groups have been established, from large national organizations such as the National Tongan-American Society to smaller local associations. The Tongan groups have diverse functions that include offering courses on various skills; fund-raising; credit associations; assisting with employment, accommodations, and immigration procedures; and even leasing land and encouraging the production and marketing of Tongan foods.[19] Informal outreach groups have also been established by Tongan parents in some areas to teach Tongan language, dance, and culture and to work with schools to assist Tongan students (M. Fonua 1996; *Tonga Chronicle* 1997a).

Not all associations are exclusively Tongan, with many identifying themselves as "Pacific Islander" or "Polynesian." This is often the case when funding is directed at pan-Pacific groups rather than the smaller, individual populations of Islanders, as in Melbourne. Given their diverse cultural backgrounds, histories of migration, and settlement experiences, it is not surprising that difficulties arise when the Pacific groups are forced together simply because they have been designated by the government as one cultural group. In Melbourne there have been several pan-Pacific associations formed, such as the Pacific Island Council of Victoria, but Tongans have had little involvement with such groups. There are numerous examples of pan-Pacific associations in other parts of the Pacific diaspora, with varying levels of involvement by Tongans. Such associations include those based at universities (such as the University of Utah's Pacific Islander Students' Association); those established to work with the government, such as the Polynesian Advisory Council of Utah; and those run through churches, such as the Uniting Church's Pacific Islands Council in Sydney (a separate organization from the Pacific Island Council of Victoria). Others focus on "cultural heritage" and the arts, including the Polynesia Polynesia Cultural Heritage Society.[20]

Throughout the diaspora there are now numerous events and festivals centered on the Pacific populations, such as the annual Pasifika Festival in Auckland. A growing number of conferences and other meetings on the Pacific diaspora are being held, some of which are organized by and for Islanders themselves, often through student associations. Some of these community events and meetings specifically involve Tongans, such as the annual "Tongan Day" in Sydney. The Tongan History Association Conference at the University of Utah in Salt Lake City in April 2001 was an academic conference organized by Tongans and with predominantly Tongan participants and audience.[21] Sponsored by the Pacific Islander Students Association and the National Tongan American Society, it was part of the Fifth Annual Pacific Islander Awareness Week.

Diasporic Media

A number of formal associations, both Tongan and pan-Pacific, produce newsletters or magazines or have radio programs or Internet sites that publicize their activities and include discussion of relevant topics. The many forms of Tongan media in the diaspora and at home all serve the overarching function of disseminating information to the scattered worldwide population by keeping migrants and their descendants informed about events in Tonga and overseas. As such, they serve a vital function in creating a sense of "community," both locally and internationally, and in helping maintain the emotional attachment of those in the diaspora to Tonga itself.

Most of the larger overseas populations have access to locally produced publications such as the *Taimi 'o Tonga* (Times of Tonga), published in New Zealand, and the *Tongan Herald,* produced in Sydney. *Tonga Abroad* is published at the Brigham Young University-Hawai'i campus, and other Pacific publications from the United States include *Polynesian Lifestyles, USA,* a monthly magazine launched in 1997 and based in Utah; *Polynesian Times,* from California; and a student publication from the University of Utah, *Moana,* which features articles, poetry, and artwork by Polynesians. The Tongan editor of *Moana* described the publication as an "attempt to bridge the gap between working class Polynesian communities in Utah and academia, making the university accessible to our youth, which would encourage the recruitment and retention of Polynesian students and faculty to this university" (Niumeitolu 1997, 1). There are also numerous radio programs; for example, in Sydney in the late 1990s there were eight separate Tongan programs.

Another important form of media for many Tongans in the diaspora is publications from Tonga. Many subscribe to *Ko e Kalonikali Tonga,* the government newspaper that until recently was published in briefer form in English as *The Tonga Chronicle* (they have now been combined). Tongans living overseas often contribute letters to the editor of the *Kalonikali* and other popular publications such as the *Tohi Fanongonongo,* published monthly by the Free Wesleyan Church of Tonga, and *Taumu'alelei,* another monthly, published by the Catholic Church in Tonga. The English-language magazine *Matangi Tonga* includes detailed and often critical articles on Tongan affairs. Like most of the Tongan publications, it also includes stories of Tongans who have been successful overseas, as well as issues concerning migrants.

The newest form of communication between Tongans is the Internet, and we have already seen that sites such as the KB rapidly have become popular, particularly with younger Tongans. The number of Tongan and other Pacific Islander sites is astounding, and they continue to proliferate as more and more people acquire the skills to access and construct such sites.[22] Along with such sites that provide news and information, discussion forums, and chat rooms, there are now numerous "home pages" set up by individual Tongans living overseas who present information about themselves and their families, often with accompanying photographs, stories, and other items. One of the more recent sites to be established is Planet Tonga (http://www.planet-tonga.com), which includes no less than twenty-four discussion forums and was established by Tongan university students in the United States. Another recently established site is the Tongan Youth Forum (http://www.voy.com/17898/). The welcome to the forum states: "Tongan Youth recognizes the difficulties that our younger generation encounter at school and their current environments. Therefore, in an attempt to alleviate these difficulties, we provide this forum to enable discussions and hopefully bring resolution for these problems." Although both these new sites are more sophisticated in design than the KB, the subject headings and messages show that the concerns the participants want to discuss are unchanged.

Many Tongans have enthusiastically embraced this new technology, and even in Tonga itself an increasing number of people are accessing the Internet and contributing to discussions on forums such as the KB. Some sites are now based in Tonga, including Tonga on the Internet (http://www.tongatapu.net.to) and Kalianet (http://www.candw.to), both of which provide an array of information about Tonga.[23] In future years it will be fascinating to see what changes computer technologies bring; in chapter 7 the possibilities and problems are explored, including the vision articulated by some Tongans of using these new forms of communication to link all Tongans throughout the world and even through time.

4

Identity in the Diaspora
Perspectives of the First Generation

FOR TONGANS WHO HAVE MIGRATED AND NOW LIVE OVERSEAS, cultural identity is inevitably tied to their experiences in Tonga. Yet cultural identity is far from static and unitary for these migrants; rather, it is something that is constantly in flux, sometimes taken for granted and at other times self-consciously asserted or reshaped and adjusted. Furthermore, settlement in another country does not just involve negotiations between two identities—for example, Tongan and American— but also making choices *within* those complex categories and in different social contexts.

Ties to Tonga

There is considerable variation in the extent to which Tongan migrants continue to see Tonga as "home" or hope to return in the future. Even so, many do maintain multiple ties with Tonga while establishing social networks in their new location. These transnational connections are not simply between Tonga and their host society, but also across the diaspora, and while they are predominantly kin based, they can also involve churches, ex-students' associations, and other kinds of links, as we will see in this chapter.

Very few people I encountered during my research expressed regret at migrating. The majority were generally satisfied that they had made the right decision and had, overall, bettered their own lives and the lives of their children and improved the circumstances of family remaining in Tonga. When I asked what, if anything, people missed about Tonga they were often vague and nominated things like family, friends, the food, the more relaxed lifestyle. It is the deeply seated emotional and sentimental ties, often difficult to articulate, that appear to be most important when people reminisce.

If we think of migrants' views of Tonga as forming a continuum, from highly positive to highly negative, there is clearly a clustering at the more positive end, diminishing considerably by the more negative end. Tonga is, in many migrants' memories, a beautiful, peaceful homeland rich in tradition and with a unique history as an independent Pacific kingdom (see Morton 2001a). The fact of migrating can greatly increase people's ties to their island "home"; Sitiveni, thirty-four, who lives in a European city where there are no other Tongans, told me, "I think about my culture more deeply than when I was in Tonga. I sing the Tongan songs with more emotions and feelings. I am proud to be a Tongan, which I took for granted while I was at home." Many retain a deep emotional attachment to the idea of Tonga as a homeland and as an intangible essence that can live in one's heart. Messages posted on the Kava Bowl by young and old alike frequently allude to this vision of Tonga. One poster asserted, "We may have left the island but Tonga, we took it with us in our hearts" (KB 24.3.98). Another wrote, "Someday we will all move back to that beautiful king-dom in the south pacific, and we want to move back and be able to contribute our talents and knowledge to our country" (KB 21.11.96).

Often, this vision of Tonga includes the idea that it has none of the problems found overseas, and there is a genre of letters written by mi-grants to the editor of Tonga's government newspaper, *The Tonga Chronicle,* reminding those at home of Tonga's advantages. On the KB, too, Tonga is sometimes portrayed in this way.

> Whenever I go to Tonga I appreciate it for the way it is, that there is no beggars or homeless people on the streets which you can find in London, New York and elsewhere. You also appreciate that there are no major Law and order problems, that you can still leave your door unlocked when you go out, that you can still leave your car with doors unlocked in the main street of Nukualofa, that women can walk alone late at night on the streets. (KB 13.9.97)

For some, the idyllic vision of Tonga is something of the past, and they view it today as less than perfect. Concerns are expressed about a range of issues, including poor medical facilities, overcrowding on the roads, difficulties of gaining leases to land, and the generally poor liv-ing conditions. Some migrants are particularly concerned about the political situation in Tonga, and their letters to the Tongan newspapers published at home and overseas expressing concern about perceived corruption and greed within the monarchy and government stand in contrast to those that extol the country.

Those who maintain ties to Tonga do so mainly through their kin, forming the kind of "kinship bridge" Evelyn Kallen described for Samoan migrants (1982). The extent of contact with family in Tonga varies enormously, and while some families are in contact by telephone several times a week, others get in touch only during emergencies and family crises. Families with a majority of members living overseas are more likely to have frequent contact between the dispersed members than with those remaining in Tonga. Older people often become the hub of contacts between their scattered adult children and extended family, since family members tend to maintain frequent contact with the household in which the older persons live, in Tonga or overseas, to make sure they are well and to discuss family matters. Many of these older Tongans are the most obviously "transnational," and some move between households and nations surprisingly frequently, actively working to maintain the ties between their dispersed family members. Younger people are the least likely to have frequent or regular contact with family in Tonga, and many have no such contact. I spoke with a few young people who did make an effort to maintain direct ties with family at home, and they all stated intentions of returning to Tonga at some point or of establishing businesses in partnership with family in Tonga.

Phone calls are the most common means of keeping in touch with family, although letters, faxes, and even e-mails are also used. Photographs and videos of family members and important events are circulated, often by the older members as they move between households in Tonga and the diaspora. As we have seen, remittances sent to Tonga and the "contraflow" of goods from Tonga are another important means of maintaining contact. Ties are also maintained with institutions in Tonga, particularly churches and schools, the latter through the active ex-students' associations. News from Tonga is circulated via the many forms of media discussed in chapter 3, and stories and letters from the diaspora help to maintain a mutual flow of information and ideas. It also is common for families in the diaspora to pay for kin in Tonga to visit for important occasions such as weddings, funerals, and graduations.

Members of the Tongan royal family are frequent overseas travelers, and their visits help to maintain loyalty to the monarchy and emotional ties to Tonga. Wherever they visit, enormous efforts are made to celebrate their presence with feasts, dance performances, talent shows, plays, and other events. The king's children and grandchildren also have spent periods of time living overseas, as when Princess Pilolevu lived with her husband in San Francisco while he was consular general of Tonga, and when Prince Lavaka Ata 'Ulukalala lived first in Auckland, then moved to Canberra to study for his degrees in defense studies. The presence of the prince and his wife, Princess Nanasipau'u Tuku'aho, also led to other visits by the royal family, especially on the occasion of the prince's graduation in December 1997.[1]

Returning Home

Migrants also retain their ties with Tonga through return visits. For many, such visits are too expensive to contemplate, and people often made wistful predictions to me that they would return "if we win Tatslotto" or "if we get rich." Some families save for years and sell expensive items such as cars to raise money for a return visit, but many interviewees had not returned to Tonga at all since migrating, in some cases for over thirty years. Others could afford to visit only occasionally, usually for a special family event or national celebration, while others managed to visit every two or three years. Very few visited more often than that, and those were usually older persons whose adult children funded their frequent travel between family in Tonga and overseas.[2] Nevertheless, Tongans returning for visits constitute the majority of visitors to Tonga, given that the tourism industry remains small.

When asked to imagine where they might choose to go if they won a free holiday anywhere in the world, most Tongan migrants I spoke with chose Tonga, as did their non-Tongan partners. Respondents who said they would prefer to go elsewhere tended to be those who had been able to visit Tonga occasionally since they migrated, those who enjoyed overseas travel and wanted to explore other parts of the world, and those who had negative views of Tonga and no wish to return.

Events such as weddings and funerals are the most common reason for returning, closely followed by national events such as the king's birthday celebrations and the annual Heilala Festival. Some Tongans return at intervals to attend church conferences, and other conferences—such as those on constitutional reform held in the late 1990s—also attract visiting migrants. Tongans who have found success overseas, including sports stars and entertainers, often return for visits.

Christine Gailey found that migrants returned to Tonga for a variety of reasons: "saving or acquiring the funds or targeted items that spurred the migration in the first place, visa problems, layoffs or failure to get a steady job, job dissatisfaction, sudden and compelling kin obligations (e.g., funerals to attend), intolerable living conditions, or homesickness" (1992, 55). As her statement indicates, some return to Tonga more permanently. The following message by a Tongan woman on the KB reveals how intentions to return are often closely tied to the nostalgic sentiments described earlier:

> I had a great life in Tonga. I did not go hungry nor slept in the cold. But, my parents (having 5 girls at the time) decided to seek a better future with possibilities for their girls as to not confine them to having to marry for survival. So, I left Tonga at the very young age of 6 and came to the states. The life we endured was a HARD one and I learnt how it feels to be hungry and cold. I learned how it feels not to have a mother at home (she had to work). And many times, my parents wanted to give up and return to the simple life that they had in Tonga. But, they struggled on for their girls and SUCCEEDED in their mission.
>
> My parents now want to return to THE GREAT ISLAND OF TONGA to live out the rest of their days and eventually, so will their girls. The roots of Tonga are deep in my heart because I left the island, but took Tonga with me. You can place a small group of Tongans on any Island and it will be GREAT, because its NOT the island that makes Tonga great but the people who were born in it, descended from it, reside in it or having roots from it. THAT'S WHAT MAKES TONGA GREAT!!!!!! (KB 24.3.98)

Recent migrants often have firm intentions of returning at some point, but as people settle in their new homes and establish kinship and other social networks there, the likelihood of return diminishes.[3] Many older migrants express a desire to return to Tonga but feel they are tied to the country in which their adult children are settled. On the other hand, they often fear growing old overseas and perhaps ending their lives in an "old age home."

In a discussion on the KB about whether overseas Tongans should return to Tonga, one young man posted a message that captures the dilemma facing many older migrants. He explained how his parents had met as students in Hawai'i.

They always had a desire to return to Tonga after they graduated to
help their families who sacrificed for them to go to school in America
and to help their fellow countrymen. But when they met, married,
and had me their perspective changed. This is the land of opportunity
and they wanted the best for each other and their children. They
helped get first mom's brothers and sisters to the States and then
dad's. I think it was to help ease their conscience about not going
back to stay. But in the back of their minds there was the dreams of
youth they had given up for a land they barely knew. My dad still
talks about going back to retire, but even that may be wishful thinking. His wife is buried here, his mother and family are here, his children are here. All he has are desires, stories, and memories of Tonga.
. . . He visits Tonga every other year but he feels like a stranger in the
land he grew up in. (KB 22.7.97)

Some migrants who attempt to return find it difficult, particularly
facing lower wages, problems in establishing businesses, and a lower
standard of living. A Tongan minister in Melbourne estimated that six
or seven families from his congregation returned to Tonga each year,
all of whom returned to Australia when the move was unsuccessful for
various reasons. He added that when people announce their intentions
to return to Tonga, members of the congregation now joke, "When
will you be back?!" One man who attempted to return in the late 1980s
after living in numerous countries over a period of more than twenty
years commented, "I felt that during those years, I was alienated from
Tongan culture simply because of lack of contact and being encultured
with my host culture, of wherever I lived. Since returning to Tonga . . .
I went through the worst culture shock of my entire life."

Sending Children to Tonga

One of the primary motivations for migrants to return to Tonga, temporarily or permanently, is to ensure that their children learn *anga
fakatonga*. More common, however, is the practice of sending children
back to live with relatives or attend a boarding school while the parents remain overseas. The motivations are the same: ensuring the children learn Tongan ways and the Tongan language and removing them
from perceived negative influences.[4] In Australia, the idea that children are free to leave home at the age of sixteen worries many Tongan
parents and can precipitate a decision to send an adolescent to Tonga.

The lack of Tongan-language skills of many young people is a further concern. The mother of three teenagers wrote on the KB that

> [a]s much as we (parents) try to speak the language at home, it was no use. Reason being, they spend 90% of their time with English speaking people at school, at play time, at church, that's right, only 10% or less was spend with us Tongan speaking people. . . . I sent them to Tonga for 2 whole years and man, not only they learned the culture, they were able to know more of their people, and yes they came back fluent and can read, write and speak the language. (KB 16.4.97)

In one Melbourne family, three sons in their early teens were sent to Tonga for three years. The main concern of the parents was that they were mixing with *pālangi*s, "getting the *pālangi* ways," and had begun to skip school. A visiting relative convinced the parents that it would be best to send the boys to school in Tonga. When they first arrived, they stayed with relatives on their father's side; after a number of conflicts with them, the boys moved in with some of their mother's family for the remainder of their stay. The boys had mixed experiences, but all returned with improved language skills and a desire to adhere more closely to Tongan ways. For example, before they left Australia their relationships with their sisters had been quite relaxed, but on their return they insisted on observing the *faka'apa'apa* (respect and avoidance) between brothers and sisters. Their younger brother, who was not sent to Tonga, is now trying to convince his parents to allow him to spend time there too.

Losa, forty, and her late husband were also influenced by a visiting relative and decided to send their eldest son, in his early teens, back to Tonga. "Both my husband and I decided for him to go. It's just that we wanted him to have a touch of, or have a feel of the background of all the way that we have been brought up, because we realized there's too much, too many things here that they can grab and take it, whereas back home it was limited amount." Later in our interview she added that she had known her son was beginning to be strongly influenced by his non-Tongan peer group, which she felt would make him rebel and possibly try to leave home. According to Losa the final decision was the son's: "We didn't want to force him." Her son had visited Tonga several times before, so he knew what to expect and knew his family there. When the son returned to Australia briefly after a year away, he chose to return to Tonga. His mother commented, "I think he knew that he had something back there." His time in Tonga has made him, his mother believes, "a different person altogether . . . different because my sister and my brother-in-law have been saying marvelous things about him, even his studies too; he's coping all right; he's a big boy now."

Sometimes it is older Tongans who pressure their adult children to send their own children to Tonga. A minister in Melbourne urged his son to send his two children to Tonga because he felt they had "started to ignore most of our Tongan ways" and had begun mixing with "Aussie kids" and committing minor crimes. They were sent to live with their uncle, and their grandfather reported that they were "a bit more peaceful" when they returned to Australia and more willing to listen to their parents. However, he added that some children who return to Tonga are not helped, usually because they are sent to live with elderly grandparents who "spoil" them.

This minister's generally positive attitude toward sending children to Tonga contrasted with the views of several other ministers. One commented that "the answer is not in Tonga, not in Australia, but with the parents." He said parents were blaming Australian society, claiming their children were being badly influenced by their peers, when the parents themselves should be taking responsibility for teaching their children "how to live." He believes the children who are returned to Tonga see it as a punishment and claims they often suffer because the relatives they are sent to live with are already busy and cannot supervise them properly, hence they are free to behave in the very ways that had concerned their parents in the first place. Later in life, he argues, these young people will suffer psychological problems because of their distress about being sent away from their parents.

Another minister also expressed concern about the long-term effects of sending children to Tonga. He spoke of "the psychological effect on the children" and added,

> I don't think many Tongans realize how much damage is done. Secondly, when you try to teach them Tongan—they're not going to live in Tonga; I think your Tongan in your own household will be enough to maintain the young ones. And thirdly, those who send children to Tonga to try to educate them for better behavior—I mean, if you can't discipline your children, who else can? And I don't believe you should allow other people to discipline your own children; you should be responsible for that.

The minister claimed that even when children appeared willing to return to Tonga it was more because they wanted to get away from their parents, "not [because] they are interested in anything Tongan."

A third minister decided to discuss the matter with his children.

> See, when I asked my children where their future would be, and they told me in Australia, I see no point in sending them to Tonga and then bring them back here and they have to suffer in trying to reorientate . . . because their expectation changes when they go to Tonga; they live there for one year and their whole system thing is changed, and then when they come here they have to be confronted with another culture shock. . . . If it's just to have a feel for the culture, you could do that when you go on holiday.

He added that if the purpose of sending the children back was to discipline them, it did not help and instead could cause problems in that the children would lose time from their studies in Australia. Many Tongans share these ministers' views and are adamant that they will not send their children to Tonga. Seini said, "*Never!* I will never, ever do that. Put it this way, Helen, if I can't solve [my children's] problems, who else will solve them? . . . We are very, very close, you know, they are very dear and I thank God that we didn't do that."

In the cases described thus far the children sent to Tonga have been young teenagers, but much younger children are also sent for various reasons. Informal adoption is very common in Tonga, and today this sometimes involves sending children to or from Tonga to live with other family members. Mele, forty, told me her father in Tonga had asked for her eldest daughter, born in New Zealand, but she refused because she was worried her daughter would not know her or would be "spoiled rotten" by her family in Tonga. In other cases parents send young children, even babies, to Tonga to enable the parents to work. Often these parents send for the children when they are more financially secure or when the child is old enough to cope with the parents' working hours. At times this strategy has unhappy results: a minister in Melbourne recounted the story of one child who had been sent back to Tonga as a baby to so that her parents could work and was brought back to Australia at the age of nine. The child's teacher reported suspected abuse to the authorities, who asked the minister to assist them. He discovered that the mother felt the child had been spoiled by her grandparents in Tonga and was harshly "disciplining" her; the daughter was allowed to remain at home, with the minister overseeing the case for several months.

Kerry James argues that sending children back to Tonga acts as a means of securing their loyalties to their kin network

> and also [provides] a form of social security for the foreign-born children by allowing them to build on their kinship networks in Tonga. Some of these fostering relations are so unstable, however . . . that I have doubts that the socialisation of the young into a web of kinship duty and obligation will be as successful or compelling for the younger generations who have been born away as it is for older people and those young adults who have been born and raised in Tonga. (1993, 361; see also 1991, 17)

It is clear there are divergent views about the value of sending children to Tonga, with many expressing concern about the issues James raises. There are growing fears about the effects of this practice in Tonga, partly because of the burden their care places on the relatives in Tonga and partly because of the *"pālangi* influences" they bring with them. There is a widespread perception in Tonga that these visiting young people are causing trouble and negatively influencing their peers who have grown up in Tonga. For example, when large-scale fighting erupted between two boys' schools in 1997, there were many in Tonga eager to blame the influence of boys who had been sent to the schools from overseas.

Such concerns about the influence of young people sent to Tonga by overseas parents are part of a rather ambivalent relationship between Tongans at home and in the diaspora. Although migrants are often eager to maintain ties with Tonga and retain an emotional attachment to their homeland, they sometimes find when they visit that they are not unequivocally welcomed. Central to this ambivalence is the perceived threat overseas Tongans pose to the "true" Tongan way, since they are seen as bringing with them all kinds of foreign influences. A number of posts on the KB have concerned the need for visiting migrants to "be real" and remember their Tongan identities and values. One message about visiting Tongans who showed off by dressing up and portraying themselves as successful received a response from a poster in Tonga that said, "Yes, we locals in Tonga always laugh when we see those coconut-Amerikanas trying to look so American! The more they try, the less American they look" (KB 6.11.96).[5]

Visiting migrants report that they are often derided as *fie pālangi* (acting like Anglo-Europeans) or *pālangi loi* (fake or phony Anglo-Europeans), and this can be particularly devastating for young, overseas-raised Tongans visiting Tonga for the first time to explore their cultural identities, as we will see in the next chapter. Migrants may also be accused of being *fie ma'olunga* (trying to appear high in status) if they are thought to be too ostentatious in their gift giving, clothing, or spending in Tonga. At times, the tension operates in the other direction, with visiting migrants claiming these accusations are based on jealousy. As we have seen, remittances can also be a point of conflict, when migrants are unhappy with the way the money and goods they send home are being used.

Maintaining Identity Overseas

Maintaining ties with "home" is clearly a complicated matter for many migrants. Increasingly, it is within the diasporic populations themselves that the main work of identity construction and reconstruction is carried out as those populations grow and become interconnected by an intricate net of relationships that cross state and national borders. I have often heard Tongans in Melbourne (and Sydney, and Auckland, and elsewhere) claim that they are "more Tongan than the Tongans in Tonga," as they lay claim to a more authentic Tongan identity than those at home (Morton 1998b). Such a claim obviously contradicts the reasoning for sending young people back to Tonga to learn the Tongan way, and it also contradicts the often-stated fears of migrant parents that their children are losing their Tongan identities. There are no simple explanations for such contradictions; they need to be understood in the context of the seemingly infinite variety of ways in which migrants and their children deal with their experiences overseas and how these experiences impact on their identities as Tongans.

The most obvious way Tongans maintain their cultural identity overseas is through their interactions with immediate and extended family. Within populations of Tongans overseas, it is common for people to frequently visit one another's homes, particularly those of relatives, and to closely interact with other Tongans through church membership and participation in groups such as kava clubs, ex-students' associations, and sports teams. Tongans living in isolation from other Tongans often express terrible loneliness and a strong desire to be with other Tongans or to return to Tonga. It was this need to have contact with other Tongans that inspired Taholo Kami to establish

Tonga Online and the KB, and many of the participants in the KB have expressed their gratitude for the links with other Tongans the site facilitates. When I asked migrants whether they would try to find other Tongans if they had to move to a new location, most asserted that this would be important to them and claimed they would be most unhappy without any other Tongans nearby, although this was less often the case for their children.

Many Tongans overseas expend considerable time and energy maintaining ties with family members and other Tongans: young married couples will drive across the city almost daily to visit their parents, or families will travel for over an hour each way to attend a Tongan church. Most of the ties they form will be within the same city, but traveling between cities is also common. One such frequent interstate traveler was Sela, a twenty-six-year-old single woman. She lived with her family in Melbourne and frequently visited relatives and friends in Sydney. She usually drove—a trip that takes around fourteen or fifteen hours, allowing for meal breaks. In a period of six months she visited Sydney on at least ten separate occasions, accompanied by various family members. The trips were made in order to attend birthday parties, weddings, funerals, and court cases; to meet groups such as rugby teams visiting from Tonga; to assist relatives with immigration and legal procedures and filling in official forms; to attend special church services; or just to visit relatives. Her visits lasted from several days to a month. While in Sydney Sela also drove relatives to and from work and many different church and social functions, attended fund-raising concerts and dances, and went to nightclubs with her cousins. Not all young people move around as frequently; in this case the combination of her high status within her family (as the oldest daughter), her tertiary education, and her car made her the ideal person to help and advise extended family members, and she accepted this role due to her own strong sense of family obligations, her community spirit, and her gregarious nature.

Most parents encourage their children to establish ties with other Tongans. As we have already seen in chapter 3, they may also actively discourage them from associating with non-Tongans on the grounds that they will be a negative influence. However, it should be added that a minority of parents do discourage ties with Tongans. In some cases this is because the parents have made a conscious decision to distance themselves from other Tongans for reasons such as family conflict or intermarriage. In others cases it is a desire on the parents' part to ensure that their children are as successful as possible in their new country, sometimes accompanied by an attempt to prevent their children from being negatively stereotyped; this will be discussed further in the next chapter.

Identity and Citizenship

Many of the early Tongan settlers in Melbourne who married Australians and decided to settle in that country permanently applied to become Australian citizens themselves. This was not an easy task in the 1960s, under the cloud of the "White Australia" policy, and some were interviewed intensively before being accepted as citizens. As immigration from Tonga continued, with an increasing number of couples and family groups settling in Australia, there migrants were less concerned with taking out citizenship.

Whether or not they intend to return to Tonga to live, many migrants are reluctant to take out foreign citizenship, since this would automatically invalidate their Tongan citizenship. Apart from the emotional impact of losing Tongan citizenship, there are practical implications such as loss of land rights and voting rights. Those who take out foreign citizenship usually do not intend to return to Tonga and feel their primary ties are with their new "home." As one woman said, she had spent her childhood in Australia and had most of her family living with her here, and she decided to apply for citizenship to "prove her bonds" with the country.

Taking out citizenship thus becomes a statement of identity, although seldom a complete rejection of Tongan identity. A poster on the KB wrote,

> When I became an American citizen, I became an American, not a hyphenated American, although we hyphenate ourselves for identification. That does not mean however that I have to forget all those Tongan values that I learned as a kid growing up in Tonga. I have added American values to my bag of values since then. (KB 12.3.98)

The links between citizenship and identity can also be confusing. Sosefa, forty-four, who migrated in the early 1980s and is now an Australian citizen, commented that

> I think like an Australian . . . [but] when people start talking about Australians as white people, I feel alienated . . . [and] when people understand "Australian" as anybody who becomes a citizen, then I feel

included. So I think I think like a white Australian, but I'm, every now and then I'm aware that I'm not Australian! . . . You know, sometimes I forget that I am different, until somebody draws my attention to it. You know how you walk in shopping centers and you thought you are all white like them?

In Melbourne, I found some uncertainty among Tongans about just what it meant to be "Australian." It was variously defined as having an Australian parent, having Australian citizenship, being born in Australia, and being a permanent resident. In the household questionnaire I administered, one question asked for people's ethnicity, using the category "Tongan Australian" to indicate those with one Tongan and one Australian parent. This caused confusion as some assumed it meant Tongans born in Australia. Discussing this with them made it apparent that the categories of "blood," birth, citizenship, and residence are used in fluid and changeable ways in the construction of identity. Feleti, born in Australia to Tongan parents, said, "Crazy as it may seem, it probably took me twenty years to decide that I was an 'Australian' with a very Tongan upbringing and with a deep understanding of the 'Tongan' way of life."

Tongan-born Kalo, who lives in Sydney, recounted a lovely story about her young daughter's assertion of identity. When Kalo, her Tongan husband, and their children visited the Polynesian Cultural Center in Hawai'i, her seven-year-old daughter spontaneously performed a hula as a band played a Hawaiian song. On being asked by the lead singer where she was from, the little girl replied, "I am from Tonga." Her mother said to me,

> I nearly flipped when she said, "I am from Tonga." Just the same, I was proud, but I was hoping that she'd have said, "I am from Australia." I guess I wanted these Hawaiians to know that we Aussies can do the hula just as good. Afterwards, I asked her why she said Tonga instead of Australia; after all, we are from Australia. She promptly answered, "Because we *are* Tongans, Mummy!" I dared not ask further questions for fear that I might confuse her, so I left it at that. I think I'm the confused one here!

The parents I interviewed in Melbourne varied in their perceptions of their children's identities. A constellation of factors influenced their perceptions, including the family's level of involvement with other Tongans, the languages used in the home, the children's school peer group, their involvement in extracurricular activities such as sports, and so on. The most frequent description parents gave of their children's identities was "both" (i.e., Tongan and Australian) or "half and half," whether or not both parents were Tongan. Very few said their children were solely Tongan or Australian, and when they claimed their children were "mostly Australian," they often qualified this by saying something like "with a Tongan heritage." Parents are often unsure how to identify themselves, let alone their children, particularly when they have been overseas for many years. Lu'isa, a woman in her late forties and married to an Australian, told me that "even though I do know that I'm different I sometimes forget until someone asks, 'So where are you from?' I've spent more of my lifetime here than in Tonga, having spent the second half of my high school years here. I guess I've become somewhat acculturated to the Australian way of life."

The question of what defines "true Tongans" or "real Tongans" is a common concern, particularly for young people uncertain of their own identities. As I have shown elsewhere, "Tonganness" is a highly contested and complex concept (Morton 1998b). While authentic identity is most often associated with Tongan "blood," language, and knowledge of the Tongan way, it is also defined as something in the heart, an essential quality that can, according to some, even be acquired by a person with no Tongan "blood" at all. Individuals' Tonganness is often measured against an imagined norm, with people defining themselves and others as more or less Tongan, as "not really" Tongan, or as "purely" Tongan, and so forth. A minister in Melbourne described himself as "a genuine Tongan but not a typical one. I think how I define a genuine Tongan would be different from someone who is very narrow-minded and haven't had the experience of mixing and being with other people in other countries." Central to this imagined norm is *anga fakatonga*, and the remainder of this chapter examines the impact of migration on people's ideas about "the Tongan way," especially from the perspective of family relationships and child socialization.

Transforming Kinship

An overwhelming majority of Tongans identify respect, *faka'apa'apa*, as the core of *anga fakatonga* and as the most crucial aspect to be retained and passed down to future generations. The primary context in

which respect is important is within the family, although it is also recognized as a more overarching value that is central to the strictly hierarchical social ordering in Tonga. On the KB respect is frequently in-
voked as a defining feature of Tongan social relations. Sensitivity to the
importance of respect strongly influences the site administrators' edit-
ing policy, although not always sufficiently for all participants, as the
following indicates:

> Why is there so much profanity on the Kava Bowl? The center of our
> Polynesian culture is God. Next to that is our respect for others. We
> are taught to respect our elders and give a more formal respect to the
> women of our race. On the KB we should have a respect for those who
> are on, or around the screen. That respect is what makes us who we
> are. Respecting others will keep us humble and remind us that we are
> not of the world but of Polynesia. "Keep it real." KEEP YOUR CULTURE
> AND DON'T BREAK IT. (KB 7.5.97)

Respect is associated with particular kinds of interactions within
families (see below), but it is also a rather vague and malleable concept
that people adjust to their own beliefs and circumstances. There is an
element of practicality in people's attitudes to respect, and where they
see that it is going to cause difficulties they will find ways to redefine or
even ignore it—as can be said for *anga fakatonga* itself. For example,
Tupou, a man of considerable standing among the Tongans in Melbourne, explained that when his mother was ill he often had to enter
her bedroom to help her, despite this being very disrespectful in the
Tongan way. But, he said, "Mum's need is more important than this
culture business."

As a concept structuring wider social relations, *faka'apa'apa* was criticized by some for being used to exploit those of lower status. Langi
feels strongly that in Western societies children are not taught to respect their elders. He tried to ensure that his own children would appreciate this value, which he sees as both Tongan and Christian. Yet he
strongly opposes many aspects of the Tongan way and so did not teach
them respect as a Tongan value but as a Christian one. He explained
that he didn't want to teach them "the Tongan way of *faka'apa'apa*.
Faka'apa'apa to those above you and ignore those under you. . . . That's
why I say Tongan custom is not Christian practice."

Some parents acknowledged that "Tongan respect" was too often
won through fear, and while they did not abandon the concept of respect, they redefined it as a general form of "good manners" and deem-

phasized the particular practices associated with *faka'apa'apa*. As Losa put it, "Respecting, well, it's not really a Tongan way of life; it's supposed to be all over the world." The non-Tongan partners I interviewed tended to identify respect as one of the "best" things about Tongan culture, but in the sense Losa describes rather than in its particularities.

One of these particular aspects is the *faka'apa'apa* children should show for their fathers, including not touching his head, sharing his food or drink, or being overly familiar with him. In Melbourne there was a fairly even split between the Tongan families who maintained these *tapu* and those who did not.[6] In all but one family where the parents had intermarried the *tapu* were not observed; the one exception was a household with a Tongan father who had spent his late teens in Tonga and returned wanting to uphold Tongan traditions. Even in his case, his Australian wife said she thought they would only uphold it "a bit."

In some of the Tongan households couples had divergent views on the way children should interact with their fathers. For example, a minister explained that he resisted his wife's attempts to stop their children from touching his head, eating his food, and so on, because he believed the Bible emphasizes sharing and equality, and, like Langi, he wished to teach his children these values rather than the Tongan values associated with hierarchy. Different opinions are also apparent across generations; Tupou explained that his elderly mother has "struggled" with his refusal to make his children observe any *tapu* with him. Of his relationship with his children, he said, "It's great as far as I'm concerned because I think it brings us together closer." In other households a compromise is reached, and parents are flexible about when the *tapu* must be observed. Mele encourages her five children to observe the *tapu* but is prepared to be flexible. "Sometimes their father wants to play with them, oh, and they'll climb all over him, and, you know, sometimes I just let them. I think there are times when the father would like to play with his children."

Another relationship involving *faka'apa'apa* is that between children and their father's sisters, particularly the eldest, their *mehekitanga*. Ideally, this relationship is a formal and somewhat distant one in which the *mehekitanga* has higher status and considerable authority over her brothers' children (Morton 1996, 128–129). As with *tapu* associated with fathers, families vary in the extent to which this is observed. Often, the father's sisters live in another state or country, so contact is limited, which can mean their role is diminished, but some families attempt to maintain a more traditional relationship between their children and the father's sisters despite this distance. For example, Paula's wife, Siu (see Case Study 2), told me she had sent the top tier of her daughter's first birthday cake to the girl's *mehekitanga* in Tonga, who sends the couple's oldest son a *ta'ovala* (waist mat) for each *fakamē* (children's Sunday).

As is often the case in Tonga today, *mehekitanga,* and the associated role of *fahu,*[7] become significant to young people only on ceremonial occasions, particularly funerals. Otherwise the children's relationships with their father's sisters and their children may be much the same as with other relatives and depends largely on the individuals involved. Some *mehekitanga* establish very close and affectionate relationships with their brothers' children. Many parents and children reported that the children's *mehekitanga* "spoiled" them, bringing them candy, cakes, clothes, and other gifts. This was sometimes described as being more "in the Australian way," as was the development of a close emotional relationship between children and their *mehekitanga*. Nevertheless, there are families in the diaspora who value the more traditional relationship as a symbol of Tongan culture. Sione, thirty-eight, who migrated to Australia with his wife in the early 1980s and now has four children, encourages a more traditional relationship between his children and his sisters because he sees it as such a unique cultural practice. "Not many country in the world can do it. That's why I want to do it, and I want to see it, and that's good identity, to be a Tongan, like that."

Of all the respect relationships, the most important is that between brothers and sisters and involves a range of behaviors centered on avoidance between opposite-sex siblings and the higher status of sisters. Again, I found a fairly even division between families who kept this *faka'apa'apa* relationship and those who did not, with a slight majority keeping to it. In some families cross-siblings are allowed to do things that would be shocking in the Tongan way, such as watching television together in their pajamas. Usually there are some restrictions, such as not entering a room when the sibling is getting dressed, but otherwise many families allow free contact between them. Sometimes this is simply a matter of not following the *tapu,* and in others it is a deliberate attempt to foster a close relationship between the siblings. Tupou said he resisted his wife's attempts to restrict the interactions between their sons and daughters, saying, "Don't worry about it, it's good to see that they get on well." The practicalities of living overseas can also make it difficult to keep the *tapu*. In the Melbourne households there tended to be a correlation between the observance of *tapu* between brothers and sisters and between children and fathers, but in some families only one or the other category was maintained, with no clear pattern emerging of either one being more likely to be kept.

Whether or not the various respect relationships are taught to children, the great majority of Tongan children do learn the importance of kinship, especially the ideals of closeness and togetherness *(feohi)*. As we will see in chapter 5, *feohi* is an aspect of being Tongan that is usually highly valued by young people. For adults, this centrality of kinship poses the dilemma, both in Tonga and in the diaspora, of how to balance the needs of the nuclear family versus that of the extended family. For migrants, there are demands from extended family in the same location as well as elsewhere in the diaspora and in Tonga that must be juggled with the living costs of the immediate family. This can cause tension within the family, especially between spouses who have different ideas about where their money should be directed. For example, wives sometimes resist the attempts of their husbands' sisters to exert their rights and demand material possessions, food, money, and services from the brothers. Family members in higher-status positions also can exert considerable pressure on lower-status members to provide various kinds of support, creating further tensions.

Families with low incomes are in a particularly difficult position. As Craig Janes points out in his study of Samoans in urban California, the catch is that while being poor creates problems in meeting familial obligations, it also makes it all the more important to meet those obligations as they are the only way to ensure help will be available if it is really needed (1990, 117). Yet over time, obligations to kin can become too burdensome, and many Tongan families, like American Samoan migrants (Mamak 1993), develop more self-reliant strategies in order to cope financially.

The centrality of family can also cause difficulties for family members who have a more "Western" attitude to privacy and who find the constant demands of the extended family draining. This is especially true of non-Tongan spouses, but it also affects Tongans, such as the minister who declared, "Sometimes you would appreciate a little bit of quietness and alone, so you won't like to be in a system that is so communal." Mele, who grew up in a small household and spent most of her spare time doing homework or reading, is now married to a "traditional" Tongan and finds it difficult when his extended family visits. "At times I need my privacy, okay, because I grew up being private. I need my privacy, I need to lie down and think about something, but I can't, because the relatives are there. If I disappear into the bedroom and lie down, then [they think] 'oh, maybe she doesn't want us in her house!' "

Tension between the needs and demands of immediate and extended family are particularly likely to erupt during events such as weddings and funerals, where gifts are exchanged, large quantities of food prepared and distributed, and familial obligations met. Some individuals and families attempt to keep such events as traditional as possible, sometimes going to great expense to purchase the fine mats and *ngatu* (barkcloth) required as gifts. At times this practice is done on a grand scale. As Cathy Small notes, "Tongan-Americans regularly boast about the outlay of food and traditional wealth that occurs in the United States as opposed to Tonga. . . . [T]here is no doubt that Tongan tradition in the United States is more elaborate and embellished than parallel commoner events in Tonga" (1997, 71). Thus a commoner wedding in the United States, New Zealand, or Australia can resemble a chiefly wedding in Tonga, with numerous guests, extravagant food, and the display and exchange of quantities of *koloa* (wealth items such as fine mats and barkcloth).

Others continue to stress the importance of gift giving but substitute cash and other goods for the traditional wealth items. Gift giving can also follow the prestige-seeking pattern of "ostentatious presentation" Janes observed of Samoans in California (1990, 164), but at other times a deliberate attempt is made to avoid such overgenerous gifting by having more Western-style events.[8] Frances Finney reports that while living in Canberra in the mid-1990s, Princess Nanasipau'u encouraged women "to reduce the cultural burden placed upon them by adopting alternative, simpler practices on formal occasions," leading by her own example (Finney 1999, 179).

Other such changes are beginning to occur at life-crisis events, such as new categories of people to be presented with gifts, changes to usual procedures, and so on. Not suprisingly, these changes can cause significant tensions within the community. At a funeral held at a Tongan church in Melbourne, for example, the body was left in the church after the funeral service on Sunday until the following morning, when it was taken for burial. When two friends of the dead woman arrived at church early that morning to begin preparing food for the mourners, they were shocked to find the casket closed and unattended, so they opened it and spent the morning talking to the dead woman, crying and carefully arranging lace cloth over her. When one of the women recounted the story some months later, she was still angry that her friend had been left alone, against the usual mourning practices.

Such changes to Tongan practices occasionally may be deliberate, but for some people it is not a matter of choosing to keep or reject the Tongan way—they simply do not know correct practices. Seini told me she did not know the Tongan way to behave at events such as weddings and funerals, as she had never learned in Tonga. Her relatives laugh at her when she gives sympathy cards and money at funerals rather than giving *koloa,* but she also defends her way as being of more practical help to the bereaved family.

Parenting Overseas

Familiarity with the practices associated with ceremonial events is just one aspect of traditional Tongan culture that some adult migrants do not have. Parents of the current generation of young people also often have not learned many of the Tongan skills such as mat weaving, tapa production, and so on, and thus cannot teach their own children. There is a gendered aspect to this, with female-associated skills much less likely to be taught than male skills such as preparing the *'umu* (underground oven), spit-roasting pigs, and cultivating taro and other root crops. The source of this difference lies in the characteristics of the activities themselves: the male skills can be learned in suburban backyards and the materials needed are readily accessible, plus they are activities done only on particular occasions or intermittently, whereas the female skills require more specialized materials and involve an ongoing labor input. Thus a teenage boy can prepare an *'umu* on a Sunday and have his family enjoy the fruits of his labor immediately, whereas to produce a mat or piece of *ngatu* a girl would have to put in many evenings and weekends of intensive labor using materials not easily found overseas. In addition, the male tasks are more readily learned by observation than are the complicated processes of weaving and tapa making. Tupou expressed his pride when his youngest son, born in Australia, was able to roast a pig on his own for Christmas one year, having watched his male relatives perform the task many times.

One of the few skills that is widely taught to both sexes in the diaspora is Tongan dancing. Children are often taught by extended family members known to be particularly good dancers, and many of the churches also teach dance, some through their youth groups. As we will see in the next chapter, young people have differing views of this, with some valuing the ability to dance and others performing only reluctantly.

When children are taught to dance they may or may not be told the meanings of the songs accompanying the dances or of the different movements they use. Much depends on their own grasp of the Tongan language and on the teachers' own understanding of the dances. Very few young people these days are told the *fananga,* or mythical stories of ancient Tonga; those who are told tend to hear them from older relatives rather than their own parents. It seems more common for *fananga* to be told in households with intermarried parents, primarily because these parents tended to consciously attempt to teach their children about their Tongan "heritage." In some cases it is the non-Tongan spouse who seeks out these stories to tell their children because the Tongan partner does not know them.

On the other hand, most children hear many other stories about Tonga, particularly of their parents' childhood experiences. These stories are often told as humorous or moral tales that stand in stark contrast to the children's comparatively luxurious lives. Parents often delight in telling their children about growing up taking cold showers, having to grow their own food and catch fish to eat, eating off of banana leaves instead of plates, and the like. Parents' and grandparents' memories often evoke for children an image of Tonga as it was many years ago, and the much more modern Tonga they encounter if they are able to visit thus comes as quite a surprise.

The sexual division of labor commonly found in Tonga, with males going outside to do "dirty" work and females working indoors on "clean" tasks, is seldom strictly upheld in the migrant households. In those homes where the division is upheld, it is done as a conscious assertion of the Tongan way, but even the more conservative parents I met tended to be flexible in this regard. A more common gender-based distinction is the practice of what Tongans often refer to as "boys go and girls stay." In other words, girls are expected to stay close to home while boys are given considerably more freedom. I found that once again there was a roughly even split between those families who maintain this aspect of the Tongan way and those who give girls some degree of the freedom enjoyed by their non-Tongan peers. Some parents find compromises that enable daughters to have a little more freedom—for example, girls will be allowed to go on outings, but only if the parents drive them there and pick them up at an arranged time. Teenage girls may be allowed to attend events only if they are chaperoned by an older relative.

Other parents encourage girls to see themselves as boys' equals and do not restrict their freedom. Mele commented, "I think they have the idea of equal, of everyone is equal. . . . I would rather they would go out and find out for themselves, you know, rather then just keeping them here and tell them 'This is wrong' [or] 'You shouldn't do this.' . . . How on earth is she going to know?" Sosefa has four children, including two adolescent daughters, and expressed similar sentiments. "I'm one of those who believe in the full freedom for young ones. We have given them what we thought we should give them, and there's a stage in their journey when they should decide for themselves. It's not good telling them 'This is bad' [or] 'This is good.' . . . I think they have to learn for themselves." He said he had endured critical comments from other Tongans but added, "I say, 'So what? They haven't done anything wrong.' "

Families with intermarried parents who adopt a largely Western lifestyle tend not to restrict girls more than boys. Those who attempt to blend Tongan and non-Tongan practices can experience some disagreement between the parents on this issue, but it is not always the Tongan parent who attempts to impose restrictions. I encountered a few cases where the non-Tongan partner was from a cultural background that imposed similar limitations on girls' freedom, and they thus wished to maintain the practice, whereas their Tongan partner wanted their daughters to have more freedom.

Despite the willingness of some parents to allow their daughters the freedom to go out unchaperoned, very few approve of any of their children leaving home before marriage. Concern about the possibility of a child leaving home and the shame it would bring to the family makes some parents try even harder to restrict their children's freedom and force their obedience. Others claim they are lenient with their children because they feel this will encourage them to stay at home.

A formal debate on this issue was held by a Tongan Uniting Church congregation in Melbourne in 1995. Those arguing that children should be forced to return home if they leave claimed that it was "Tongan culture" for them to remain at home before marriage and that if they were allowed to leave, they would only get into trouble—for example, girls might become pregnant before marriage. There was time allotted for discussion from the floor, and one Tongan woman, a qualified teacher, talked about the need to let children explore the world, have experiences, and make their own mistakes. She advised parents to let their children leave but to tell them they were always welcome to return home. She also encouraged the parents to stay in contact with children who left home and to offer support when needed.

Another contentious aspect of parenting is whether children should be made to conform to Tongan standards of dress and "proper" appearance, such as long, braided hair for girls. As with so many practices associated with "the Tongan way," approximately half of the parents I spoke with pressured their children to conform to these ideals and half allowed their children more freedom of choice. Siu told me her adolescent daughter often pleaded to be allowed to cut her long hair, but she insisted the girl had to wait until she was twenty-one. Here again, many families reach a compromise in which the children are allowed to dress "*pālangi* style" in daily life but must wear Tongan clothes to church and formal Tongan functions.

Going to church can itself be a source of family conflict, as parents can place a great deal of pressure on children to attend services regularly with them, to dress appropriately, and to participate in the various children's and youth services. Christianity is nowadays seen as integral to the Tongan way, and we have seen that in the diaspora as in Tonga it takes a central role in many Tongans' lives. This applies to young people as well, and at certain times of the year they can be expected to devote considerable time to church-related activities. For example, in many churches the celebration of *fakamē* (children's Sunday) involves young children from Sunday school and teenagers from youth groups presenting memorized quotations from the Bible, as well as songs and dramas in both English and Tongan. *Fakamē* involves a lot more than the service itself, with frequent classes and practices held in the preceding months. Many families hold classes, "*ako fakamē*," at their homes for groups of children from their extended families to practice their presentations.

Sundays ideally are set aside for worship and rest, so conflicts often develop when young people want to do other activities, particularly sports, on Sundays. Paula explained that when his oldest son began playing rugby he made him promise never to play on Sundays. When the boy was chosen for his state team, Paula relented, and the son worked out a happy compromise where he attended church and taught Sunday school before heading off to his matches. In other families it is more difficult to reach a compromise, and parents may even use force to make their children attend church and keep Sundays free of other activities.

Underlying many of the parental demands for conformity with the Tongan way is the ideal of children's unquestioning obedience and respect. This ideal requires that children not challenge or criticize their parents' decisions and orders and not freely express their own opinions. This issue is often the most difficult for migrant parents, whose children are exposed to schooling, non-Tongan peers, and other influences that give a different message about adult-child relationships. Many parents strongly resist their children's attempts to argue and question, sometimes using violence to assert their authority.

Parents who want to allow their children more freedom to speak up and argue find this difficult when their own parents live with them, and they may feel torn between wanting to please their parents and wanting to have a close relationship with their children. It can be hard for them to defend their chosen style of parenting, as this would be disrespectful to their parents. Nevertheless, there are many who make the choice to raise their children with more open communication. Losa stressed how important it is to "try your best to explain to your children, be honest with them, be open with them and let them come out of their shells, you know, try and listen." Similarly, in a church newsletter the mother of three teenagers advised parents to improve communication with their children by listening to them more, avoiding confrontations and "emotional abuse," and giving supportive feedback (Tu'inauvai 1995, 2).

In many couples one partner is more willing to adopt Western attitudes toward child rearing, and this can be a source of conflict between the parents and confusion for the children. Usually this issue is kept within families, but there have been attempts in some of the churches to discuss the topic more openly. An Australian youth worker told me that at a Uniting Church camp for Tongan families one couple talked openly about their different attitudes, with the mother wishing to enforce obedience and respect and the father wanting more open dialogue with the children. The father, in this case, feared that the children would leave home if they were unhappy with their relationship with the parents. This discussion led another woman to admit that she and her husband had a similar difference of opinion.

Another highly contentious topic—closely tied to that of obedience and respect—for Tongans at home and overseas is the physical punish-

ment of children. Church ministers, who are regarded as community
leaders, have divergent views on the issue. Some ministers I spoke with
strongly disapproved of physical punishment, with one claiming that,
rather than being a form of discipline, it was often the result of parents
having difficulties in their own lives and then taking out these frustra-
tions on their children. Others support parents' right to hit their children and as parents themselves use this form of disciple. One minister
told me that he once had been called by police to assist with a case in
which another minister had beaten his teenage daughter because he
was concerned she was mixing with friends of whom he disapproved.
The first minister had to explain to the other the legal implications in
Australia of such severe punishment. Another minister I spoke with
was opposed to legal restrictions on parents' use of punishment.

> Well, I reckon it depends on how it is applied. When it is out of anger,
> to me it is totally wrong, just to satisfy my anger at the child. But if
> the motive [is] because you love your child and you don't want your
> child to go on that particular path and end up somewhere he doesn't
> know yet, well I would encourage parents to do that. Not out of anger
> but out of love. And I disagree with the government here interfering,
> because I reckon that all those people that promote that supposedly
> on behalf of the children, they do not love their children more than
> the parents.

Parents' level of education and awareness of cultural differences
often influence their acceptance or rejection of physical punishment.
Sitiveni, who is the father of two young children, said, "When I went
to the university, I started to change my attitude toward our 'Tongan
way' of raising children. Basically I thought there were other ways of
doing things. I also realized that the parents have limited ways of
doing things. . . . They went through it and they are doing it themselves. . . . I was a teacher before I went to the [university], and I remember defending our Tongan way of punishment in those days. Considering my background, I think I would not have changed my
attitudes if I had not gone to the uni."

However, there is no clear division between parents who are more
"traditional" and those who have adopted more *pālangi* child-rearing
styles when it comes to physical punishment. Although the more traditional parents tend to use punishment more readily, there are also

"modern" parents who encourage their children to communicate with them and have a close relationship but who also choose to punish "in the Tongan way." It is common for Tongan parents to argue that *pālangi* methods of discipline are worse than their own; for example, on the KB a Tongan man who said he was born and raised in the United States stated that he regards the Western practice of "time out" as demonstrating a lack of love for the child (KB 29.7.97). Mele explained that she felt the *pālangi* practice of sending children to their rooms is crueler than physical punishment.

> They are, emotionally, in a little prison of their room for about one hour, okay. But for the Tongan children, no, we do not send our children off to their room and lock themselves in there; no, we don't, we whack them a little, you know, just psshh [gesture of a smack] and that's it. And the children, you know, the hurt is only for a few seconds and it will go away.

Through her involvement with her children's school, Mele had observed non-Tongan parents swearing at their children and calling them names and found this far worse than smacking.

Mele also mentioned the concern of many Tongan parents about Australian laws prohibiting parents from punishing their children in the way they feel is appropriate. She commented, "I think they often cross the boundary of the law, because they wanted their children to be brought up in the Tongan way." She explained that although many parents want to bring their children up in the Tongan way, they are unable to spend much time with the children due to their heavy workloads. Then, when they do interact with the children, the parents expect them to know how to behave and punish them if they do not, leaving the child confused. "If in their mind they wanted their child to be brought up in the Tongan way but the child does not understand, how on earth is the child going to behave in the Tongan way?" Mele stressed that while she supports the use of some physical discipline, she believes parents should make time to talk to their children, play with them, explain the Tongan way, and reassure them that they are loved. She worries that Tongan parents tend not to praise their children when they do well, which she believes causes them to "think they're not good enough." This, she argued, carries over into adulthood and leads to lower self-esteem and lack of motivation.

While some parents resort to harsh punishment, others realize such actions can backfire. An Australian youth worker commented,

> I shudder sometimes when you see the parents go whack [gesturing hitting] and you see the parents telling the kids off in front of everyone, you know, just total humiliation. I mean, I think that will always be an issue, but I think most of the parents here, well, they all know that if they hit their kids, their kids are off to the police and they're the ones in trouble!

The issue of child punishment is raised repeatedly in the churches and at other venues and has been a recurring topic for discussion on the KB. Proponents of physical punishment argue that it is the norm in Tonga (and, it is often argued, Polynesia), is needed to instill obedience and respect for authority, and is a sign of parents' love. The perceived problems and bad behavior of *pālangi* youth often are blamed on the Western child-rearing methods of recent times, and the threat of state interference in parental discipline is regarded with anxiety and resentment. In a KB message supporting "traditional child discipline" a Tongan man argued that "[t]he courts have invaded family life in America until the family is practically destroyed as a result. If the polynesian people follow the U.S. example, their family life as they now know it will also disappear" (KB 11.8.98). Another Tongan man wrote,

> I think US law has overreacted to the extremes of abuse and taken away the responsibility we have to discipline. . . . The problem with the Tongan way is that discipline is sometimes excessive and some parents literally beat up the kid with fists and other things. I am for discipline and grew up on the end of my father's "leta" [leather] belt. I know we would not be here today without the strong guiding hand. . . . Discipline with love is the best combination and the proverb still holds true—"spare the rod, spoil the child." . . . I'm taking my kid home to Tonga. I think I will do a better job bringing them up than the US Government telling me how I should discipline. (KB 7.11.96)

Some of the messages on the KB advocated a more moderate approach to discipline. A Tongan counselor working in a middle school did not disagree with all use of physical punishment, but wrote, "We, as polynesians, need to open our minds to other ways of punishment. Maybe, punishment is not what is needed, but some talking and find-

ing out what is really going on in their minds. . . . We must elevate ourselves into finding better resolutions to our conflicts, rather than just
beating a child" (KB 3.3.97). She added in a follow-up post that "[m]ost
polynesian parents go a little beyond the necessary physical punishment and across the line into child abuse" (KB 3.3.97). Opponents of
harsh physical punishment express concern about the possible physical, emotional, and developmental harm to children, or they argue
that changing child-rearing methods are a necessary part of changing
with the times or, more pragmatically, that it is against the law in
many Western countries.

The decisions parents make about raising their children overseas
sometimes result in a complete rejection of attitudes and practices
seen as "the Tongan way," but more often they are melded with what
is seen as "the *pālangi* way" to give children "the best of both cultures." Mele, for example, teaches her children what she describes as a
modified version of the Tongan way. She tells her children, "In the
Tongan custom this is what we do, okay, so I expect you to do that, because in our family we regard ourselves as Tongans, so I think if we are
Tongan then we should be able to behave in the Tongan custom."
However, she also wants her children to be bicultural and has put a
great deal of thought into how to achieve this. She describes her
method as emphasizing to her children the similarities in Tongan and
Australian cultural values and practices. When they encounter differences between the cultures, she hopes they will understand why those
differences occur.

A long message on the KB from a Tongan living in New Zealand
beautifully illustrates the depth of thought many parents put into raising their children.

> I try to live as a self respecting westerner, firmly believing and dedicat-
> ing my life to a slightly different set of values (collected overseas and
> mixed with some good old ones from Tonga). . . . For myself being
> overseas it doesn't matter so much who I am or who my parents are,
> or what station in life I am at etc, just that I am. And I want this for
> my children and for theirs. . . . For my own children I have raised
> them to recognize goodness wherever it occurs, not as Tongans, or Eu-
> ropeans etc, but as fun loving and honorable human beings, who nei-
> ther consider themselves superior nor inferior to anyone, but as
> equals. . . . I have been ridiculed as if I have denied my children their
> cultural heritage. I don't think I have. They have Tongan features,

some speak the language, others aren't that interested but they understand it, and they know how and where I grew up in Tonga etc. They
have Tongan in them whether they like it or not. They also have the
freedom to do with that whatever they want. But I have made sure
they know that they are not special or different in any way because
they are Tongan. (KB 1.5.99)

Parents' decisions about child rearing are influenced in part by their
children's own attitudes and concerns, and parents often reported that
their children strongly resisted attempts to impose the Tongan way on
them. One mother said her children argue that "if you want to stick to
anga fakatonga, why don't we all go back to Tonga?" As in many societies around the world, children also urge their parents to be aware of
the changing times. Manu described a confrontation with his adolescent son over some misbehavior.

And we just said we want to talk to you, and we talked about the way
we were brought up, Mum and Dad, told him the good things about
Tonga, and he kept quiet . . . and because we were so serious, we
thought that he would come up with something, so he said, "Thanks
very much, Mum and Dad, and I can understand what you are talking
about, but that"—and I'll never forget this!—"but that was then, and
this is now!" Yeah, I think he was right. And he said, "You try to take
me to there, those years; I just can't." And he was right . . . and I said
to my wife, "Oh, I think [he] has taught us a very good thing."

Language Dilemmas

One of the most emotional issues confronting parents and children in
the diaspora is language use. Many Tongans see language as so much
the heart of Tongan culture that young people's poor language skills
are perceived as indicative of their loss of "culture" in general. This
concern about language does not occur solely in the diaspora; since the
1980s there has been growing awareness in Tonga that English is becoming the preferred language in many contexts. The former director
of primary education in Tonga, linguist Dr. 'Ana Taufe'ulungaki,
worked to introduce bilingualism into the school curriculum with an
emphasis on teaching in Tongan in the early years of school to give
children a strong foundation in Tongan. In an interview she asserted
that

[l]anguage is what makes a person a complete being, it makes you what you are, it makes a Tongan a Tongan. If a Tongan does not know how to speak Tongan then I do not think he or she is a Tongan. To speak in Tongan you have to think like a Tongan, and that is something that is installed in your sub-consciousness, it is your culture and heritage, and it is something which you can't express in any other language. (P. Fonua 1991, 10; also see *Tonga Today* 1988)

This question of whether a person can be a "real" Tongan without the language is a sensitive and divisive one for many Tongans. It is frequently raised on the KB, where some participants choose to post messages only in Tongan.[9] There have been many arguments about this: some claim it excludes young Tongans who no longer speak the language, or they argue that the KB should be accessible as widely as possible beyond the Tongan community, while others assert the value of participation in the KB by older Tongans with minimal English or of Tongan language use for those trying to learn the language or improve poor skills.[10] Some of the comments relate directly back to the issue of language as an essential element of culture: "Why can't all you non-Tongan speaking TONGANS learn how to speak Tongan?? Our language is the backbone of our culture, not English—the coloniser's language. Learn to be bilingual. . . . [I]t's a shame you don't know your own language" (KB 10.2.98). We will see in the next chapter that while some younger Tongans uphold this view, others are more flexible.

As discussed in chapter 3, the first wave of migrants often deliberately did not teach their children Tongan. Yet even parents who *do* want to teach their children Tongan face an uphill battle, given that the children are exposed to English in so many contexts. Sosefa has tried to encourage his children to speak Tongan by talking to them in both Tongan and English, but he admits their Tongan is "funny Tongan, broken Tongan," and they prefer to speak in English. When the children were younger he and his wife tried to teach them Bible verses in Tongan for the *fakamē* celebrations, but "it was a lot of pain, you know, we went through too much pain trying to do that, but not anymore."

Mele, who strongly believes being bilingual and bicultural will help her children succeed in Australia, reflected,

> I remember when our children grew up, at first my husband wanted them to speak English. And I told him not to, I told him *not to!* Because his English is not that good. I told him, "Your English is not

good and I don't want the children to pick up wrong pronunciation, wrong grammar, wrong English from you. Why don't you leave English to the experts? The children will go to school, in three months the children will be able to speak English. Why don't you keep talking to them in Tongan? If they can speak Tongan from zero to age five, they'll never forget it. Never, ever forget it!"

Mele's husband then instituted a new rule for the family: only Tongan was to be spoken within the boundaries of their property, and the only English to be heard in the home was to be from the television, which the children were allowed to watch only at certain times. Today, the children all speak Tongan fluently, but they prefer English and resist their parents' rule by whispering in English when they think they are out of earshot.

Without external support it is difficult for all but the most determined parents to succeed in teaching their children Tongan. In diasporic locations with larger Tongan populations there are a growing number of centers for language learning, many of which are aimed specifically at younger Tongans. In New Zealand there has been a Tongan kindergarten movement since the early 1980s, modeled on the *kohanga reo* (language nests) set up for Maori children. The children attending the kindergartens are taught in Tongan and learn Tongan dances and songs. In Sydney there are several primary schools that now include Tongan-language classes, with the first of these programs beginning in 1996. At one of the schools a quarter of the students are Tongan, and most of the Tongan students now study Tongan while the rest study Italian (*Tonga Chronicle* 1996d). When this school's program began, more than half the Tongan students were more fluent in English than Tongan, while others used a mixture of Tongan and English vocabulary and were having difficulties in most subjects. The Tongan teacher who initiated the program has encountered some resistance to her program from the Tongans themselves, stating, "Some [students] have been told by their parents that they are Australian now, not Tongan. Others want to attend Italian studies with their mates rather than the Tongan class." For those who do attend, the program appears to be helping with academic and behavioral skills as well as boosting their self-esteem.

These kinds of programs also tend to be established where there are active Tongan organizations, thus even in Canberra, with its small Tongan population but active association, a Tongan kindergarten was set up in 1995. In Melbourne, where until recently there were no formal associations for some years, there are no kindergartens or funded school programs. One of the Tongan churches in Melbourne has twice attempted to set up Tongan-language lessons, but since they have to be run on a voluntary basis they have not been able to continue. The minister also noted that the classes tended to attract the *pālangi* spouses of Tongan church members rather than the youth for whom they were targeted. This is not necessarily because of a lack of interest by the younger people, as factors such as their reliance on parents for transport to and from the church and their already high level of commitment to other church activities may have made it difficult for them to attend.

Dealing with Change

In this chapter we have seen many differences both in the way *anga fakatonga* is conceptualized and in the changes people are prepared to make in relation to it in the context of migration. There appear to be gendered differences in people's willingness to change, and when I asked Tongans whether they thought men or women were holding on more strongly to *anga fakatonga*, the great majority said they believed men were more "traditional" and "conservative."

Sioeli's response was typical: "Maybe the men are more conservative than women; I think it is easier for women to give it up." According to Jane, "The women are more flexible than the men, generally speaking, in this [church] community. I think the women are way ahead of the men." And Sālote observed, "From my experiences among the Tongans that I know and among the church and stuff like that, I tend to think that men are the ones that are trying to hang on to the best of the Tongan cultures and the customs at the moment. Women are just letting go."

It is understandable that men are trying to hold on to their roles as Tongan husbands and fathers, as, after all, these roles are not too dissimilar to the still patriarchal norms of Western societies. To a great extent their attitudes and behavior would be reinforced rather than rejected by the wider society in which they now live. As one minister pointed out, Tongan men often resist change that threatens to undermine their power within their immediate family. "He's the boss of the place, and here I think they feel their power is diminishing, and that's why I think they feel there's something lost."

It is more difficult to understand women's willingness to change, because although change could in some respects improve their situation as wives and daughters, they stand to lose the higher status accorded to them as sisters. However, Tongan women living overseas often cannot gain much in their role as sisters (and this is increasingly true in Tonga as well). Most adult migrants are working hard to support their families both here and in Tonga, hence this is a leveling process where brothers and sisters become more equal. As we saw previously, women's role as *mehekitanga* is losing its importance, and while they may still claim their roles at ceremonial events, these events are themselves undergoing transformations that can diminish the advantages sisters would traditionally enjoy. For younger women, the role of sister is often perceived simply as the source of restrictions on their freedom and seldom brings direct benefits.

In practical terms, therefore, it is easy to understand why women are not holding as firmly to tradition, since they can gain new freedoms as well as less restrained relationships with various kin, including fathers, brothers, nieces, and nephews. When I asked Vika whether men or women were trying harder to hold on to the Tongan way, she replied, "I would like to say the women. I can't. I don't feel like they are hanging on. More men are trying to keep it, while the women, who have been kept quiet for such a long time, they're like a flower that's just opened up, and they're going to soak up all the sun before they think they're going to die too! [Laughs.] So, I think the men are the ones who are keeping it."

Another practical reason for the changes in women's behavior and attitudes is that they are more likely than men to be the primary caregivers and therefore have more to do with their children on a daily basis. As their children undergo the process of negotiating cultural difference, some mothers are willing to make changes in their parenting to accommodate influences from the wider society. Women are often under more pressure from their children to change than are men, although there are certainly women who resist this pressure and retain a more consciously "Tongan" parenting style.

When people talk about change, whether in Tonga or the populations overseas, it is often women's freer behavior that is discussed—women now drinking alcohol or smoking, wearing nontraditional clothing (jeans, shorts, miniskirts), attending nightclubs and other social venues, going out unchaperoned (referring to young women), and so on. Because formerly there were so many restrictions on women's behavior, especially before marriage, these changes are very noticeable. But despite these changes at the behavioral level, much of the *ideology* of sisters as having higher status remains, and this gives young women a strong sense of their own identity as Tongan women. They can embrace change without having this sense of self threatened, whereas for men change can mean the loss of their power and self-identity as "chiefly" husbands and fathers.

Different attitudes to change can also be observed in long-term and more recent migrants. In Melbourne, the earlier settlers often married Australians, and in any case much of their time was spent working and socializing with non-Tongans, given that few Tongans were present at that time. As parents, many were willing to be flexible and open to "the Australian way" as part of their commitment to settling permanently in that country. On the other hand, some of the more recent migrants have been able to move into a larger Tongan population and work and socialize with other Tongans. Their contact with the wider society is primarily through their children, and there is a tendency for these parents to try harder to hold on to the Tongan way partly through fear of losing their children to outside influences.

These more "traditional" parents can meet with criticism for not attempting to adapt to "Western" ways. Sioeli sees it as an issue related to level of education.

> There are some Tongans that come here, they still, they live here as if they are living back home, so it is so difficult for them to integrate into this society. . . . You will find that the Tongans that have education, they are easily more adaptable than the Tongans who haven't. Because I've got a cousin here . . . he didn't go to school, and he is a real Tongan in the sense that the things he does here, he does the same here as back home, whereas myself I can be, I can act like an Australian, I can act like a Tongan, I can easily adapt; [I am] more flexible in that way.

Despite the differing degrees to which people are willing to "adapt," overall there is a strong tendency for people to have a pragmatic attitude towards *anga fakatonga*. Tupou said,

> I will maintain [*anga fakatonga*] as long as it keeps the harmony in our [family] relationship. I have trouble when the *anga fakatonga* comes up and is a cause of tension in our household. . . . I will respect it as far as it serves the purpose, and if it's a source of tension and will do

any damage to a relationship or any other; if it's got any side effect that will damage the relationship, then I'm not going for it.

Although Christianity and the Tongan way are often seen as interrelated and inseparable, they can also be portrayed as being in tension with each other, as we saw in relation to the value of respect. Disassociating Christianity from *anga fakatonga* can be a means of criticizing the latter from the safe moral ground of the former. At the church seminar on "Tongan-Australian Families," mentioned earlier, one participant, a Tongan mother of five, commented, "I'm afraid that we have come to worship our culture. I don't mind if we lose the Australian or Tongan culture as long as we are still Christians." The minister who helped organize the conference said, "I use my culture as a way of building up a relationship with my neighbor. If my culture stands in the way of my relationship with my fellow Christians, then I would rather have my fellow Christians than my culture." This separation of religion and culture can occur across all denominations. Many Tongans claim that Mormons are most likely to use their religious beliefs to challenge Tongan beliefs and practices, but Tamar Gordon (1990) has shown that Mormons can also find ways to maintain aspects of *anga fakatonga* they regard as important, such as the *faka'apa'apa* relationship between brothers and sisters.

Tongan behavior is often stereotyped by Tongans themselves, with criticism leveled at that behavior seen as not only against Christian morals but more general Western values as well. The most common criticism I heard was about gossip, from old and new migrants and from their children. Gossip is seen as the downside of the closeness of social networks. As one minister put it, "The network that has helped you in good times becomes a handicap for you in bad times." Anxiety about gossip leads to a tendency to cover one's opinions and emotions in order to present a "good face," but this is also subject to criticism. Sioeli observed that "there are some they hide their true feelings. Right? For example, sometimes the Tongans, they don't tell the truth because their fear of offending other people."

Criticism is also directed at what people describe as "laziness." Tongans sometimes accuse other Tongans of being lazy and of not striving for success overseas, not seeking better jobs, and not supervizing their children properly, especially at church, where, I was often told, they let their children "run wild" outside during the service. As in any population such criticisms and accusations can lead to tensions and ruptures,

while at other times they are used humorously and even self-deprecat-
ingly.

The way Tongans talk about *anga fakatonga* often shifts, portraying
it on one hand as a unitary, unchanging concept and acknowledging
on the other that it is in fact constantly undergoing transformation
and redefinition. This transformation is occurring in Tonga and to a
much greater extent in the overseas populations. A Tongan poster on
the KB described the constant transformation of the Tongan way using
the analogy of evolution.

> The Tongan way is being put to the test in the great social laboratory
> of life every day and wherever we've chosen to live. The resulting
> strains therein make being Tongan an interesting phenomenon to de-
> scribe, define and contain! An ebonic gangsta wannabe in the Bay
> Area who was born in Tonga but was brought up in the Housing proj-
> ects has similarities to a similar strain in the State Housing areas of
> South Auckland in New Zealand. Yet in the same street, there's a
> church going, ta'ovala wearing Sunday school teacher of the same age
> and of similar background. (KB 4.9.99)

The idea that the Tongan way is undergoing continual change is a
topic that has been addressed by members of Tonga's royal family. The
king's daughter, Princess Pilolevu, actively advocated adaptation and
change during the four years she lived in the United States. In an interview in 1996 she said,

> I keep speaking to Tongans in San Francisco, saying to them you know
> you came from Tonga 20 years ago with your ideas about Tongan cul-
> ture very intact, but you must accept that your children born here are
> of a different calibre. There will be certain aspects of our culture which
> will prove useful to being in America but there will be other aspects of
> it which are the exact opposite of what they are taught at school,
> what their friends believe. (M. Fonua 1996, 17)

Speaking more generally, she argued that "Tongan culture is constantly undergoing change. I ask myself why has the Tongan culture
been the longest surviving in the Pacific? It is because we have the ability to change the Tongan culture to suit us and the times, that's the
key, and this is why we have to try and maintain it overseas" (M. Fonua
1996, 18). Her brother, the crown prince, is also encouraging the acceptance of change. On attitudes to clothing among Tongans, he commented, "A lot of people set great store by dressing in the Tongan fash-

ion, because they are afraid that people may criticize them for not wanting to be Tongan, that is a ridiculous attitude, really. There is a lot more to being Tongan than dressing" (P. Fonua 1998).

At the forefront of transformation and change are Tongan artists, musicians, and others involved with the arts. Tongans have long created uniquely Tongan music forms from outside influences as diverse as brass bands and reggae. Young musicians and singers today are continuing to meld Western and Tongan music and lyrics. To give just one example, the album *Princess Tabu* by Tongan Australian singers Vika and Linda Bull incorporates Tongan elements in the lyrics, music, and cover art (Bull and Bull 1996). It includes a beautiful Tongan love song, "'Akilotoa," with background vocals sung by the men of a Tongan kava club. With its cover art of *ngatu* designs, Tongan fans, and featherwork, it draws on their the Bulls' Tongan heritage while the music shifts between Tongan and contemporary Western elements.

Music and other arts can also be a site of controversy, where the changes to "tradition" are both embraced and resisted. A debate on the KB about whether or not a Tongan music program on New Zealand radio should play a modern Tongan song with lyrics that might be offensive to "traditional" Tongans illustrates such controversies. The Tongan representative of the radio program, who posted the initial message raising the issue, concluded after some discussion that

> the easiest option would be to let it pass. That is to say: Don't try to rationalise it or you'd be forced to examine this and perhaps our 'ulungaanga faka-Tonga [Tongan way] in its entirety. Stay in the comfort zone and don't question these long held beliefs. Which is fine except that perhaps many in the community we serve, including the author of Fefine Vava'u [the song], may have already rationalised it and made their own difficult decisions. (KB 19.2.97)

In another incident the station manager of the New Zealand radio station where the Tongan program is based wrote to the Tongan magazine *Matangi Tonga* in response to an article mentioning complaints about the use of allegedly offensive Tongan language on the program. He pointed out the particular context in which the words were used and added,

> Part of our role is to reflect what and where our community is at. . . . Compared to Tongans in Tonga, our community in Auckland are probably better informed, more open, more cosmopolitan and accepting of

new ideas and new ways of doing things. Some are still uncomfortable with the prevailing attitudes in their new environment, but my experience is that most no longer accept some of the hypocrisy and the pretences of *"tō'onga faka-Tonga"* as practised in Tonga. I believe that *"tō'onga faka-Tonga"* is currently being redefined by our community so that it's more appropriate to an Auckland setting. (Hao'uli 1995)[11]

The visual arts are another arena for the negotiation of change. Seven Tongan artists in New Zealand created an exhibition titled *Fanguna 'e he Manatu Ki Tonga* (Awoken by memories of Tonga) in 1994, in which they displayed their work, much of which incorporates traditional Tongan motifs and materials (*Matangi Tonga* 1994). Similarly, the artists exhibiting in the *Tiritiri O Te Moana* Pacific Islander fine art exhibit, held in Utah in 1998, combined modern and "traditional elements" in order to "define and redefine a contemporary Pacific Islander identity . . . which will serve to contest the monolithic and many times negative depictions of Pacific Islanders within the predominant culture" (KB 19.3.98).[12] Tongan stone sculptor Filipe Tohi, based in New Zealand, combines Tongan, other Pacific, and Western influences in his work. He said in an interview, "It is our history and our culture—and the onus is on us to try to revive and preserve it. . . . Our culture and traditional way of doing things need to be taught to our people, and we have to maintain the teaching as treasure, otherwise, one day we will all be just *pālangi* with brown skin" (Tāmo'ua 1998).[13]

This need to retain a sense of cultural identity while participating in a Western society is important to many Tongans and other Pacific Islanders. The organizer of the Pasifika Festival in Auckland described the "Pacific Island New Zealanders who have a traditional heritage combined with a New Zealand upbringing. . . . They have a new way of design, of music and of looking at the world. . . . We are moving forward in a global culture, while retaining threads back to our own cultures" (cited in Anae 1997, 131). The young Tongans who are negotiating their identities through art, music, and other forms of performance are the public face of a process the younger generations of Tongans in the diaspora are undergoing, as we will see in the following chapter.

CASE STUDIES

1. 'Ana

'Ana, thirty-eight, lives in a rented three-bedroom house in a working-class suburb of Melbourne with her husband, Peni, thirty-eight, and two teenage children, a girl (Lopini, fifteen) and a boy (Filipe, thirteen). Two of her nieces, both young adults, have been living with her since a dispute with their own parents more than a year ago. All members of the household except 'Ana's children were born in Tonga. 'Ana was raised by her father's sister in Tonga, then went to New Zealand at the age of eighteen and stayed several years before migrating to Australia in the late 1970s, where she married Peni, who had migrated from Tonga at about the same time. 'Ana remembers Tonga as "really nice and clean, even in Nuku'alofa itself," and she blames the government for what she sees as the "dirty," poor state of Tonga today.

'Ana works part time and is studying to upgrade her existing qualifications. Her children are in high school, one niece is studying at a tertiary institution, and the other is unemployed. Peni provides the main income, working full-time during the day and part-time doing security work at night and on weekends. This necessarily limits his involvement with the rest of the household, and thus the bulk of the responsibility for parenting and running the home falls on 'Ana.

The family exemplifies a pattern common to many migrant households in which different members have varying degrees of involvement with other Tongans. All belong to the Uniting Church, but 'Ana, her son, and her youngest niece tend to limit their involvement to attending Sunday services only. They socialize mainly with non-Tongans. The others are more heavily involved with the church and prefer to socialize with Tongans. Only Peni and the oldest niece speak Tongan well, and Peni's English is poor. The most obvious difference within the family is 'Ana's cynical regard for much of the Tongan way and the ease with which she interacts with non-Tongans, compared with Peni's staunchly Tongan outlook.

'Ana argues that as a migrant "you have to do exactly what people do here. I mean, you don't really *have* to do it, but . . . it helps you fit in. . . . The society here is so different to Tonga, I mean if you want to live the Tongan way, go back to Tonga and stay there." When asked if anything about *anga fakatonga* remains important to her, she replies, "The manners. Not the culture. I don't really believe in some of the Tongan culture. Some [aspects] are good, and some I don't believe because [they are] irrelevant. . . . I don't really care about the culture, not really." By "manners" she refers to respect not just according to the ideal of *faka 'apa'apa*, but respect more generally, to all other people. 'Ana believes that living overseas has an inevitable impact. "I think we're losing the *anga fakatonga*. We do lose it, because our kids go to school here in Australia, and they see things, and they learn other things too, so there's a big difference there. I think it's changing."

'Ana's attitudes affect her parenting: "I thought the Tongan way was wrong. I just think the Tongan way of bringing up kids was wrong." Instead, she emphasizes communication with her children and encourages them to stop and think about what is right and wrong and to make their own choices. Of her children, 'Ana says, "If they want to say something they will say it. They're given a choice and chance to say what they think as children. When I was brought up I was never allowed to say anything, you know; just shut up and do whatever you're told, and that was it. But these kids are lucky because they have the choice to speak up." She disagrees with the use of physical punishment, although it was part of her own upbringing.

She also is adamantly opposed to the practice of sending children back to Tonga, which she says is done so they "learn to be Tongan, and the customs, and the manners; they don't learn manners here, they don't really like learning them here, because when they go out there they mix with Australians too, and they seem to follow the Australian ways." As far as her own children are concerned, she says emphatically, "No way! No way, I wouldn't do that! I believe that while they are young that's the only way to learn—with your own parents. Because if I send them to Tonga, when they come back they won't listen to me, so I believe in that very strongly not to send them away." As with many parents, she says that if the children were to go to Tonga, she would want to accompany them.

As a parent, 'Ana does not keep strictly to the usual Tongan gendered division of labor, the various behavioral restrictions between brothers and sisters, and so on. She has made sure both her children can do any household chores, gives them an equal amount of freedom to go out, and encourages them to have a close relationship. She doesn't like the idea of her children growing up "separated from each other," so they are allowed to go in each other's rooms, Filipe even sleeping on a mattress on the floor in Lopini's room at times.

She does expect them to keep to the *tapu* in relation to their father, that is, not drinking from his glass, eating his food, or touching his head. Yet she explains this to them not as the Tongan way but just as respect for Peni. "I don't relate it back to Tonga." The children have been told about the important role of their father's sisters, but their own *mehekitanga* "don't really care about those things; it's not really that important."

The children see themselves mainly as Australian. They have been encouraged to get to know their extended family, but 'Ana doesn't regard it as important that they stay involved with Tongans outside the family. As they were growing up they were not told Tongan stories, either myths or memories from their parents' childhoods. They also have not been taught any Tongan skills by their parents, although a relative visiting from Tonga taught Lopini to dance, which she then continued to learn through the church.

'Ana comments of Lopini, "I don't think she's really interested in it; she likes it, but I think it was my husband that really talked her into it. And we have to pay her fifty dollars to go and do a dance, just to suck up to her to go and do a Tongan dance! And sometimes she just says she's sick of it and the costume, it hurts her arms, and things like that, but she's a very good dancer, very good."

Lopini is very positive about her relationship with her parents, and she appreciates that they trust her, are honest with her, work hard, and do not hit her. However, she is struggling with her identity as a Tongan, particularly the fact that her spoken Tongan is poor. When asked how she would define *anga fakatonga*, she replies, "I don't really understand it. *Kavenga*, that's gifts and stuff isn't it?" As for the importance of *anga fakatonga* to her, she says, "In a way it is—I don't know, very confusing. I think it's from being brought up here." Part of her confusion may well derive from her parents' very different degrees of "Tonganness," yet the open and communicative relationship she has with them is likely to make her identity struggles somewhat easier than those of young people who feel unable to discuss such issues with their parents.

2. Paula

Both Paula, fifty-one, and his wife, Siu, forty, are more like Peni than 'Ana; both are what could be called "traditional" Tongan parents. They rent a modest three-bedroom house in a working-class suburb, but since Paula lost his job as a laborer some months before our interview, they have relied on unemployment benefits to support their family of four children. Paula migrated to Australia after the birth of their oldest child, now twenty years old, and Siu and their son joined him once he had permanent residence. Their youngest child is six years old. With Paula out of work, both parents are very involved with the children's lives.

Like 'Ana, Paula is opposed to sending children back to Tonga, asserting, "Well, I don't like it. I don't like to separate any of my children from me, from us. I don't trust anyone, even if she is my mother or my grandmother, grandpa, I don't trust them to look after any one of my children. And I just like them to stay all the time with me and their mother." Paula also expresses the sentiments of many parents when he says he is reluctant to separate his children, wishing instead for them to grow up together.

All members of the family speak both Tongan and English; in the home the parents tend to speak Tongan and the children English. They are strongly religious, having nightly family prayers and frequent religious talks from Paula, and they regularly attend the Uniting Church. Their social lives revolve around church activities, although some of the children also play sports. Apart from the friends they mix with at school, the children, like their parents, tend to socialize primarily with other Tongans.

Like many Tongan parents Paula and Siu try to impress on their children the value of education. Paula said,

> I want them, I force them to go to school. I think our oldest son, eld-est one, if I did not force him to go to school, I don't know where is he now. . . . I've told them, "I want you, all of you, to go to school . . . if you want a good job, if you want to live in a good house, if you want anything good, just depends on what qualifications you get." I like them to go to school, all of them.

However, when his oldest son said he wanted to go to university and that it would take several years to get a degree, Paula replied, "Too long, three or four years! I want you to get a job to help me!" He worries he won't be able to afford to send any of his children to university and that they will have to work to support their own studies.

The children are allowed to have non-Tongan friends, but only if they bring them to the home where they can be supervised. Both parents fear the negative influences of such friends. Paula refused to allow his adolescent son to attend a birthday party, saying,

> If he [was] going to the birthday party of a Tongan, I would let him go, but if he's going to the birthday party of his friend who is an Aus-tralian, and if I allow him to go, probably he will get drunk, he will drink, or smoking, or you know. . . . If he ask to go with the Tongan people in the church, the youth, go watch a movie or go to a party, it's all right, because we know everyone who will go and we know their parents. We go in the car there and then we know everything from there. But if he want to go to the nightclub or the snooker house, we don't know what he's doing there.

Their restrictions on their children's behavior lead to occasional clashes within the family. The oldest son left home briefly in his late teens after a conflict about his parents' refusal to let him go out with his non-Tongan friends. Paula described how during an argument about this issue he punched his son in the head, then, when the son threatened to leave home, angrily told him to go. The son returned home after four days, having stayed with relatives, and, according to his parents, he stopped asking if he could go out with anyone but Tongan friends from their church. From Paula's point of view, his son's capitulation justified his actions as a father imposing control over a wayward child.

As is apparent, Paula and Siu are strict with their children and see themselves as raising them in the Tongan way. Both admit this is a struggle, as the children tend to argue with them and question them in a way they were never permitted as children themselves. Yet they hold on to their belief that *anga fakatonga* is important, emphasizing the need for the children to be respectful and obedient. Siu says of her desire for her children to be unquestioningly obedient, "Sometimes I feel I really want to stick in the Tongan culture, and I always told them, if you are a Tongan you have to listen and do what we tell you in the Tongan culture." Thus far, the younger children have not rebelled against their parents, although there are signs of resistance (for example, the oldest daughter shaved her legs against her parents' wishes and tried to keep it secret from them). Whether or not they will later rebel more openly and whether or not they retain their strong identification as Tongan remains to be seen.

The couple are particularly insistent that their children observe the *tapu* between brothers and sisters. Paula would like to be able to build a little house in his backyard for his sons to sleep in, as is common in Tonga, but the cost and building regulations prohibit this course of action. They also observe *tapu* in relation to Paula, who says he tells the children all about the Tongan way. The girls are expected to keep to Tongan ideals of appropriate appearance, with long hair worn in braids and modest clothing, until they are twenty-one. The children all know Tongan dancing, and the boys have been taught to make an *'umu,* roast a pig, grow taro, and so on.

The children identify themselves primarily as Tongan, telling their friends they are "Tongan, from Tonga," although all but the eldest have never been to Tonga. They are keen to go there, but as Paula observes sadly, "Oh, I'd love to take them one day, we wish to, I wish to take them to Tonga, but how much money I got?" The children eagerly watch anything on television about their parents' homeland and ask their parents many questions about Tonga. With most of their extended family in Tonga and scattered across the diaspora, the church enables them to remain involved with other Tongans. Paula and Siu hope their children will marry Tongans so that they might hold on to *anga fakatonga,* but they acknowledge that already it is a struggle keeping their children tied to the Tongan way. As Paula says, "Oh, hard, it's hard!"

A mother and her three young children not long before migrating to Australia in the late 1970s.

Young Tongan woman in *puleta-ha* and *kiekie* holding her Tongan Australian niece outside church.

Tongan woman wrapped in mats for mourning, after the funeral of her father's cousin in Sydney, 1997.

The funeral of a Tongan minister's mother, Melbourne, 1999. Some of the women are relatives, others are members of the minister's congregation.

Young women in a mixture of Tongan and Australian clothes (note *ngatu* print cloth) outside a Tongan church in Melbourne.

Tongan-style wedding at a Uniting Church in Melbourne, 2000.

Tongan wedding at a Uniting Church in Melbourne, 2000: a mixture of Tongan and *pālangi* elements (see chap. 7).

Tongan wedding, 2000: The bride's uncle dances at the wedding reception (see chap. 7).

Women's rugby union team, the Box Hill Fillies, Melbourne.

President of the National Tongan American Society (Ma'utof'ia, Kaisa Lui) with a plaque commemorating the Tongan History Association conference in Salt Lake City, Utah, in April 2001.

5

Diasporic Youth

"Stuck between Two Worlds"?

YOUNG TONGANS IN THE DIASPORA gradually are beginning to find ways to describe their experiences, voice their concerns, and otherwise speak out. In creative writing, art, Internet discussions, youth forums and rallies, and in many other contexts, they are exploring their identities, questioning the Tongan way, and negotiating ways to balance Tongan and other influences in their lives. The experiences and views of young people are the focus of this chapter, and it will become clear that they can be both candid and highly articulate. Yet most of the words we will hear were spoken in interviews or written on Internet forums, where the speakers can choose to remain anonymous. It needs to be borne in mind that speaking out in these ways is very difficult for most young Tongans in "real life" situations with other, older Tongans present. Many of the issues discussed here are seldom discussed openly, and when they are, they can be the cause of generational conflicts that leave young people feeling alienated, confused, and angry.

It has long been assumed in the literature on migration that the children of migrants tend to turn away from their parents' culture, but that the "third generation" have a renewed interest in their cultural heritage (Reitz 1980). It was assumed that migrants and their children would experience "cultural clashes" as the children were influenced by their new environment. This has been challenged by later research showing that while conflict often does occur, particularly over issues such as autonomy, sexual behavior, and family honor, it does not necessarily mean young people will completely reject their ethnic identities, nor do all migrant parents hold inflexibly to their original culture (Holton 1994, 191).

The early work was also challenged when it was found that the children of migrants can feel differently about their ethnic identities at different stages of their lives, with the strength of identification often declining in adolescence and strengthening in young adulthood (Peltz 1995, 45; Vasta 1995). Thus rather than rejecting their parents' culture only to have their own children return to it, these changes can occur in individuals over time. This is often the case with young Tongans, who experience renewed interest in all things Tongan once they have gone through a period of identity conflict in their teens.

Whether or not they reject their parents' culture, the children of migrants often form a "crucial bridge" between their parents and their own children (Peltz 1995, 45) and become what Georgina Tsolidis has called "the sandwich generation" (1995, 140). As we will see, some Tongans are more comfortable than others in this role, and many have struggled with their relationships not only with their parents and other relatives, but also with other Tongans and with members of the wider society in which they live.

Growing Up Overseas

Young people's explanations of Tongans' motives for migrating echo their parents', emphasizing the opportunities available overseas to improve the lives of immediate and extended family. They also acknowledge that often migration was not a carefully planned strategy. As Veisinia, nineteen, who was born in Australia, explained, "Dad came out for a holiday, liked it, and brought the rest of the family." Surprisingly, many young people did not know why their parents had migrated and were vague even about when migration had occurred and in what circumstances; apparently in some families such topics are not discussed.

Most young people had a positive view of migration, although they were clearly aware of the many problems Tongans can face when they arrive overseas. Foremost among the problems they identified was "money," a shorthand for the various financial problems migrants have to deal with. Other problems they identified were finding employment, dealing with racism, understanding a new culture, learning English, and "waiting for their papers" (waiting for permanent residency applications to be processed).

Young Tongans living in Melbourne mostly said they were happy to be in Melbourne and often compared it favorably to cities with "too many Islanders." Yet the larger Tongan population of cities like Los Angeles, Sydney, and Auckland appeals to some young people, and for others just about anywhere would seem appealing if it meant escaping the restrictions imposed by their parents. Lesieli, sixteen, who lives in a large, very "Tongan" household, dreams of going to Sydney, which she associates with holidays away from her strict parents, and where she imagines being able to go out at night and having a level of freedom she does not have in Melbourne.

Many young Tongans live in nuclear family households. Those, like Lesieli, whose households include extended family members, tend to speak positively of their interactions with them. Many especially valued their close relationships with their grandparents, turning to them to learn about their family history, Tongan language, and the Tongan way. None of the young people I encountered had a completely Tongan lifestyle; for example, they eat a mixture of Tongan and other food even at home, and very few said they eat Tongan food daily. In so many other respects their lives are a blend of different elements: the clothes they wear, the music they listen to, the entertainment they choose—for each individual that blend is unique, shaped by life experiences and personal taste, as well as the demands made on them by parents and other older relatives to hold on to their Tongan "roots." It is common for youth to have a growing appreciation of elements of Tongan culture as they move into their late teens. For example, young people who had resisted wearing Tongan clothes in their early teens began to feel pride in wearing them to church and social functions; this seemed to symbolize a general relaxing of their resistance to the Tongan way once it became more a matter of choice rather than one of parental force.

The friendship groups of young people in Melbourne varied from all Tongan to all Australian, with many having friends from different ethnic backgrounds. Many agreed that they were able to relate to other migrants more easily than to "the Aussies." Some who had Australian friends said they did not relate to them in the same way as their Tongan friends. Lesieli explained, "Like the way we joke is kind of the Tongan way. Which Aussies wouldn't understand. Like you kind of joke in an Aussie way for an Aussie to understand it." Vika, eighteen, claimed that "having a Tongan friend is so different from a white friend. A white friend you get along pretty well, but you feel there's always a limit. With a Tongan friend you can do whatever you want with them. Everything is fifty-fifty."

Although many young Tongans in the United States said they had friends from different ethnic groups, not all found it easy to fit in with non-Tongans. Lucy, nineteen, said that at her college

you can't be with the African-American students because you're definitely not "black." You can't be with the Hispanic-Americans because
you sure can't converse with them. You can't be with the Asian-Ameri-
cans because you don't look anything like them. The list goes on and
on, but I suppose it depends on the individuals you're interacting
with and the environment you're in.

Cultural differences between Tongan and non-Tongan friends can
interfere with otherwise close friendships. Susana feels she can't complain to her *pālangi* friends about the restrictions her parents place on
her freedom to go out, as they don't understand. "When it comes to
Tongan tradition I enjoy talking to Tongans because it saves me the
time of having to explain everything. But for other things such as boys
and stuff I'd talk to my *pālangi* friends for they consider it a casual
topic," whereas, she said, Tongan friends may be judgmental or spread
gossip about her. With her Tongan friends, "even though we converse
normally and are good friends, I still feel a bit uncomfortable. When
I'm with them I feel several years younger, I don't know why." Of
course, in some cases young people do not have much say in their
friendships outside school hours, as their parents do not allow them to
socialize with anyone but other Tongans for fear of negative influences.

Whether or not their friends are Tongan, many young people felt
strongly that they needed ties to other Tongans, and they saw relatives
and friends frequently. When asked how important it would be to find
other Tongans if they moved to a new place, some said it would be crucial. Susana replied, "To me it's extremely important to see other Tongans. I don't want to lose any of the Tongan that remains in me." Others were not so concerned, and a minority said they would welcome
moving away from any Tongans.

The extent to which their own families are involved with other Tongans varies. Some parents choose to keep their children away from
Tongan church and other social activities. Vika said her parents had
been closely involved with other Tongans in New Zealand, but when
they moved to Australia they did not develop such close ties. Vika followed their lead and stayed away from many events, but she said it was
still important to her to see other Tongans, "because in New Zealand I
took it for granted. Because I saw Tongans everywhere and I took that
for granted. When I first came here I was just—like my first impression,
trying to contact. . . . I just needed a Tongan contact to make me realize that I am Tongan. To keep reminding me that I'm Tongan." When I

asked if she does sometimes forget that she is Tongan, she said, "Yeah, sometimes I feel like that; I forget it. I need to step back and say, 'Hey, that's not me.' I have to remember who I am."

Many young Tongans have encountered racism and discrimination, often based on negative stereotypes about Islanders. Lose, sixteen, who was born in Australia and asserts her pride in being Tongan, complained of "just being stereotyped sometimes because I am an Islander. I am therefore seen as rough and tough and with a tough, maybe abusive, background." More often, racist remarks are directed at them simply because they are "colored" and "different." Being different can also be an asset, however. Malia, twenty, whose parents migrated in the late 1960s, observed that "being a Tongan living in Australia is something so interesting to Aussies that have grown up here all their lives. Our nature is something so amazing to them and as time passes the younger generation make Tongan customs into something so trendy." Differences that are observed by non-Tongans can become a source of pride for some young people. A Tongan Australian man in Melbourne commented on how there were always extended family members living in his home. "My friends often said 'My goodness! How many cousins do you have? I've never seen so many cousins in my life!' And that's something that I find an asset—having all these relatives" (Canterbury Uniting Church 1993).

In Melbourne, with its small population of Tongans, young people can feel their difference is particularly noticeable. Vika said that in New Zealand, where she was born, "I was just another Tongan girl at school and in the shopping malls. Here [in Melbourne] it's different. There are more European people here and it's just, it's like the only person in the—you know if you are in a crowed room? You're like the only person there. You've been isolated from everyone else. Yeah, that's what I feel like." Others do not experience this; 'Aisea lives in a large and strongly "traditional" household and yet said of growing up Tongan, "Oh, it wasn't much different. I just saw myself as the same as everybody else and they treated me like everyone else." Even in the United States, where racism was reported more often in interviews, some young people had not found it a problem. Solomone, thirty-one, who as a child migrated to the United States with his family in the early 1970s, commented, "Growing up in an all-white neighborhood, I did not really experience any racism. In fact, I sometimes forgot I was a minority because it just did not matter. . . . Even now, I sometimes forget I am not white."

Creating Identities

What children make of the many different elements that influence their cultural identities is unpredictable. Where it was once assumed that children were passive receptors of cultural knowledge, learning to internalize the values and norms of their parents and thus conforming to a shared and unified "culture," more recent models of child development see children as actively engaged in their own socialization (Wentworth 1980). As we will see, young people make choices, have opinions, challenge the status quo, and are otherwise involved in the construction of their own identities. As became clear in the previous chapter, this is a process that continues over the entire lifespan.

The importance of the relationship between parents (and other caregivers) and children in the process of acquiring cultural identities cannot be denied. It is partly in the interactions between them that the work of constructing and reconstructing cultural identities occurs, a process that has been called "ethnic socialization" (Phinney and Rotheram 1987).[1] However, there has been little detailed research into these processes: how parents attempt to transmit cultural identity to their children, what are the children's own subjective experiences, and how these relate to their "adaptation" to the society in which they live (Bernal and Knight 1993; Rumbaut 1994). There are a great many variables to take into account in any individual's case, including whether they were born overseas or migrated as children, their gender, and their parents' level of education, social status, and parenting practices, for example. Much of the research on young people in ethnic groups has been problem focused, which has been valuable, particularly in the area of policy-making, but which tends to ignore the fact that problems are not inevitable (Rosenthal and Cichello 1986). Many Tongan young people do experience a range of problems, yet there are positive aspects of their experiences that are also important to acknowledge.

While "ethnic socialization" within families is an important influence on young people's cultural identities, it is by no means the only influence. Recent studies of ethnic youth reveal a whole range of important factors, from the influence of peers, degree of interaction with the ethnic and wider community, and perceived discrimination, to the physical appearance and personal qualities of the individual (Amit-Talai and Wulff 1995; Maher and Caldow 1997; Rosenthal and Feldman 1992).[2] Awareness of oneself as a member of an "ethnic" group and designation as such by others also can be important in creating a more self-conscious sense of identity. As we saw, youth who had experienced racism had a keener sense of ethnic identity.

There has also been increasing recognition of the ability of young people to shift *between* identities in different contexts (Rosenthal and Hrynevich 1985; Rotheram-Borus 1993). This ability is evident among young overseas Tongans, and these shifts often can involve significant transformations in appearance (clothing, hairstyle, etc.) and behavior according to whether they are at home, church, or school, or socializing with peers. They also blend their identities at times; for example, Vika wears a *puletaha* (Tongan women's-style, knee-length dress worn over a long skirt) to church but has shortened the dress to create what she calls a "Westernized Tongan outfit." Shifting between contexts is not always easy, as a post on the KB points out: "[I]t is not easy to 'be a Tongan' in [the United States]. It's like playing 'roles.' One minute you're a Tongan and the other, you are stepping out of that circle to join the rest of society" (KB 26.11.96).

Young Tongans who have moved between different parts of the diaspora are most likely to experience confusion about their identities or to perceive themselves as "stuck between two worlds" or "torn between two cultures." For example, 'Ofa, nineteen, now living with paternal relatives in Melbourne, has lived in Australia, Tonga, and the United States. When I spoke with her she described herself as "one hundred percent Tongan," partly because she spent most of her first seven years living in Tonga, but also because she has moved around and maintained a sense of Tonga as "home." Later in the same interview, however, she described herself and others in her household as "like real Aussies. . . . We never speak Tongan." Vika, who moved from New Zealand to Melbourne, said, "I'm sort of going off my culture at the moment. Which is sad, I know." She later added, "I'm a pathetic kind of Tongan!" and still later, "There's some of the culture that I don't agree with, but it doesn't mean I have to abandon my culture. . . . I think even if I was born in New Zealand I still am a Tongan. Deep down I know I am one." Adding to her confusion is the fact that many people assume she is Maori. "I like to explain to them that there's a difference between being a Maori and coming from New Zealand." Vika did not identify as Australian, and toward the end of the interview she offered this: "I don't think I could handle being a white person. Their life is too mucked up. . . . Oh, I feel sorry for them; they're lost."

Even those who appear to move comfortably between identities and contexts in their daily lives sometimes find that on a more abstract level it is difficult to describe their identities. Sela, who has lived in Melbourne since she was a young girl, commented, "Sometimes I wonder if I'm too *pālangi!*" And a young woman living in Australia posted this message on the KB: "Being unique and proud of one's heritage is not the same thing as one's identity. My Tongan identity seems to have been watered down by my assimilation with the Australian society and my quest for an Australian identity. But then, what is a Tongan identity? What is an Australian identity? I think that perhaps there is no such thing as identity—we only share time and space, that's all" (KB 30.10.97). The way many young Tongans described their identities was to distinguish between their non-Tongan "ways" and their essential core of Tonganness, something that often was not important in their daily lives but that they saw as an inescapable part of them.

Joe, thirty, said that going to live in New Zealand at sixteen to attend boarding school had a profound effect on his sense of identity.

> I remember that I missed Tonga very much then. But somehow between then and now I have lost a lot of the bonds I felt with Tonga. I used to feel as if I belonged to Tonga. I am amazed that this feeling has somehow disappeared. Never really thought of it until now. All of a sudden I am aware that I feel as though I don't need to have a national identity to be a complete person. . . . New Zealand is becoming such an international place, and I like it. I feel I can pick up whatever good behavior I want regardless of what culture it is from.

Later in the interview, however, when he spoke of his growing interest in genealogical research, he commented, "Maybe I'm more Tongan than I think." Another New Zealand-born Tongan, Thomas, forty, said, "I feel myself to be Tongan, [but] when I was growing up I felt myself to be a New Zealander. As I became aware of myself, I felt different and found myself being a Tongan. This 'Tongan' is different to those in Tonga."

The definitions of "Tongan" given by those born overseas are similar to the views of the older generations to a great extent, with a focus on *anga fakatonga,* "blood," language, and "heart." The major difference is that young people are more willing to allow for lack of language, poor knowledge of the Tongan way, and even lack of Tongan blood. Thomas said, "I think to be Tongan is a feeling more than anything. You can have the blood, but you need more. I think it is an insightful thing."

When I asked 'Ofa about the possibility of non-Tongans claiming to be Tongan, she asserted, "If they want to be Tongan, hey, all right. Somebody can accept and look and love our culture the way that our own people does, and I think, oh, that's great, more power to them." Similarly, Anapesi, fifteen, who has lived in Australia since 1985, said, "I don't think it's in the blood, I think it's in the thinking, and in the actions."

At times young people can find their sense of identity clashing with context: they feel Tongan when they are with non-Tongans, but then do not feel Tongan when with other Tongans. They are left with a sense of not really belonging to either group and therefore uncertain about their own sense of self. Despite the confusion that can surround their search for identity, few young people said they would choose to be anything but Tongan (or part-Tongan). Despite the fact that many were openly critical of aspects of the Tongan way or of Tongans' behavior overseas, most expressed pride in their Tongan background. When they described what they thought were the best things about Tongans they frequently identified the same things as their parents: respect and the closeness and togetherness of families. Many also said they liked Tongans' friendliness, Tongan food, and, for those with Tongan-language skills, the ability to speak a language other than English.

Many of the KB posts assert young people's pride in their Tongan upbringing. In response to a question about how Tongan parents should raise their children in the United States, one participant wrote, "I was raised straight TONGAN style and I'm grateful. Yes, the whole 9 yards, the FAKA'APA'APA, the LANGUAGE, the CULTURE, all that! And the SHOE when you had it coming! We have a big family and we are way INTO all that Tongan stuff. I think it'll be hard for our generation to keep it strong in our families unless we keep practising it today" (KB 18.3.97).

There also are those who admit to being ashamed as children of their Tongan background, most commonly those young Tongans in the United States. Some said they had "despised" or "hated" being Tongan, often due to the racism they experienced, although as they matured they felt far more positive, even proud. Lucy said, "It was not until recently that I accepted the culture and wanted to preserve it for other 'Americanized' Tongans to be a part of. . . . It was difficult, at the age of ten, to try to explain to another ten-year-old what ethnic background you were from, where it was located, and why you were in America. Therefore, I hated being Tongan because it caused 'complications.'"

Anasela, nineteen, who was born in Melbourne, was highly critical of most aspects of the Tongan way and gave the strongest statement of rejection of her Tongan background that I encountered.

> If I had to be born again I wish I was never Tongan, because you're taught to be someone that you're not. It's hard to live up to. Because emotionally I don't think I'm built to be a Tongan, I mean I can't—all the criticism, people criticize you for what you try to do and to be, so if you make a mistake, it's 'no you're meant to be this person.' . . . It's like [being] a robot.

Even so, being Tongan holds meaning for Anasela, and she recalled that as a teenager "I became a rebel, but just remembering who I was and where I came from helped me to get through it."

Many young Tongans described going through a period of rebellion in their teens, and whether or not they shared Anasela's view that their Tongan identities helped them through it, most stated that they subsequently developed a new appreciation for being Tongan. One poster on the KB, a nineteen-year-old woman whose parents had migrated to the United States in the 1970s, described her experience.

> My father used to say: "Kids, if only you knew, me and your mother were like the blacks to America." This never hit me till now. All through high school I did my own thing, never went to class, got high, hung out with frienz and never took to hear what my parents had to say. This is just a quick reminder to us as youth growing up in the main land. Our parents came so far to get us here. Don't take it for granted. . . . Tongan youth stay up and proud!!" (KB 4.10.97, original all capitalized for emphasis)

'Ofa admitted, "Actually, my dad tried to bring me up in the Tongan way, and halfway through it I didn't like it, so I rebelled from it and decided that it was all good for him but there was no benefits for me. So I felt that I had to rebel. But now, being my own choice, I do choose some things to be Tongan, I do choose some things to be in English, and you just mix up."

The most positive descriptions of parents came from young people who had been allowed to have this "mix" of Tongan and other ways, and this certainly appears to be the key to avoiding (or at least minimizing) rebellion and generational conflicts. One young Tongan on the KB described the hardships her parents encountered when they migrated to the United States in the 1960s and said she felt they had given her "the best of both worlds. . . . While my parents struggled with the American Ways that seem so TABU to our TONGAN CULTURE and TRADITIONS, they learned quickly that they had to integrate the two. . . . [M]y siblings and I often sit and reminisce of the blessings we have enjoyed because my parents were somewhat willing to adjust and accept some of the American ways of life" (KB 17.8.98). Another U.S.-born Tongan made a similar statement: "My parents brought our family here to give us a chance at a brighter future and they have exceeded that. Not only have they educated, clothed, and provided [for] us, they have loved us unconditionally. Meaning when we choose to do things the American way, they don't necessarily agree with us, but they accept it" (KB 19.11.97). Achieving a balance between Tongan and *pālangi* ways is not easy, and the best intentions of parents are not always appreciated. Veisinia said of her parents that "the Aussie way dominated their influence towards us more than the Tongan way. At first I thought it was an unfortunate and naive type of upbringing, but I'm just thankful that *now* we (the children) *want* to learn about our culture and it was never something that we turned away." The idea that young people are more likely to be interested in their Tongan background if it is not forced upon them recurred in interviews and on the KB.

Sometimes, when parents are unwilling to adjust to new circumstances, it is up to the individual to seek some kind of balance. One young man compared being in the United States with walking a tightrope.

> In order to successfully walk the rope of life, the new-age Tongan must balance what is good in the Tongan culture with what is good in the American culture. If he/she concentrates too much on one or the other, then they will lose balance and not be able to survive in both environments. . . . At home, my parents were very strict and imposed a Spartan, rough life style that demanded complete obedience and respect for elders. Then I would go to school where they taught me to question authority and be an individual that can stand alone in the

world. What I finally realized as being important was that I had to
find some sort of balance between the two cultures. I had to be like a
chameleon and change my mind frame to fit the environment I was
in. (KB 27.4.96)

Another young man suggested how to blend two cultures: "Keep
what benefits you and your identity, subject to it not being detrimental
to society as a whole, discard anything that doesn't fit the above, adopt
anything that does, and ignore the rest. Happy blending!!" (KB
23.6.97, original capitalized).

Identity and the Homeland

Given their deep sense of pride in being Tongan, many young people
are anxious about whether they count as "real Tongans" if they have
grown up overseas. As 'Ofa said, "You know the Tongan way but you
don't *really* know the Tongan way." On the KB, a young man wrote, "I
cannot say that I am a Tongan. . . . I would [be] more comfortable with
Tongan-American. The Tongans in Tonga are the true Tongans, because
they live the 'culture'. We, who were born or raised in the States, cannot possibly believe that we are culturally aware as our brothers and
sisters back home. We are constantly bombarded with Western influences that will definitely alter our identity" (KB 19.4.96).

As with adults, young people have different opinions about the
value of taking or sending children home to Tonga. Some view the
practice positively, as did one young poster on the KB who grew up in
the United States but at the age of nine returned to Tonga with his parents for six months.

> The best way for a Tongan youth to gain discipline is to go back to
> Tonga and live there for a period of time. My experience in Tonga
> taught me things that I still use today. Before going back to Tonga in
> 1984 I was one of those "fie kovi" [badly behaved] kids that always
> caused trouble in school. While in Tonga, I learned quickly that that
> sort of attitude got you nowhere. (KB 27.4.96)

He went on to explain that the most important lessons he learned were
humility and not taking for granted the opportunities he had in the
United States.

The more common practice of being sent by parents to Tonga to live

with relatives is difficult for many young people, who have had varying experiences in Tonga. Australian-born Lusi, twenty-four, said,

> There are some that have enjoyed the idea. They get there and they
> enjoy themselves and come back. There is one of the girls I know who
> went there, well, she didn't want to get on the plane. She was crying,
> she wouldn't let go of her parents because she didn't want to get on
> the plane. And then it was the same thing when she was coming back
> from Tonga. She wasn't going to come back at all. . . . She enjoyed it
> that much and she ended up returning to Tonga and getting married,
> and she lives there now with her kids and everything. Changed her
> life.

In chapter 4 I mentioned a family that had sent three sons to Tonga
as teenagers. Each had different experiences, which affected the way
they reacted when they returned to Australia. The second-oldest son
found it very difficult and was adamant that he would not send his
own children to Tonga, but his older brother is very keen to send his
own children there and proudly asserts his Tongan identity. He said of
his experience, "I felt good about it. It made me aware of myself culturally and what I have in Australia." 'Aisea, their youngest sibling, explained why he thought Tongan parents send their children to Tonga:
"For discipline. Because some of the kids here get too out of hand, so
you send them back and hopefully they straighten up. . . . [My broth-
ers] were sent back because they were getting a bit out of line." 'Aisea
wishes he could go to Tonga as well, "because I'd like to learn a bit
more about the Tongan customs." He also says he will send his own
children back to Tonga, "because I don't want them to be too much
Westernized." Lusi agrees sending children to Tonga can be beneficial,
"because a lot of them come back here a lot more calm and a lot more
kind of reserved." She wanted to go to Tonga herself to do a year of
high school: "I even begged my parents the last time I was in Tonga [on
holiday]. But my dad told me no because the standard of living over
there is just too poor." She is determined that when she has children
she will send them back to Tonga or go to live there with them for a
year or so.

Young people who are unhappy about their lack of understanding of
the Tongan way and language are often most supportive of the idea of
sending their children to Tonga. When I asked Malia what she wants to
teach her children about being Tongan, she responded, "I wouldn't

know what to teach them, that's why I would definitely send them to Tonga to learn the hard-core way." But a much more common view was expressed by Vika, who said of parents who send children to Tonga, "They think because they can't handle kids here, sending them back to Tonga a Tongan would handle them for them. I think it's so, so weird!" She claims the parents' attitude is "If they're in Tonga I can do whatever I want now and Tonga can deal with that problem. Which is stupid. . . . Tonga's a country, not a salvation for them." As for the children being sent away, she said, "I think some kids are scared to death because they're so used to the life here and they feel like if they go back they might not adapt because they think the Tongans would not accept them because they're Tongan kids from Australia, they're Tongan kids from New Zealand, or whatever country." Vika would not send her own children back to Tonga. "They're my kids. If I can't look after them, who can? It's just stupid. I should be able to raise my own children." Of course, much depends on the age of the child and the reasons for sending him or her to Tonga. Susana was sent back to Tonga as a baby, then returned to live with her parents in Australia when she was five years old. She said, "At this age, I couldn't say there was any effect at all. I think it's fine when Tongan parents do it and then have the child back at an early age. It's a problem when the child they're sending back is a teenage rebel. I think it's wrong; that child won't, I think, learn a thing because of their anger."

Just the fact of being separated from one's parents can be traumatic, and this is also true for children moved between relatives in the diaspora. 'Ofa was born in Australia, and her parents took her with them to Tonga as a baby. They visited Australia again when 'Ofa was six and left her with relatives when they returned to Tonga. She told me,

> I think it was cruel. Because a lot of people never explained to me . . . imagine you're six years old, you've been with your mother and father all those six years of your life, and then to be left with people that you just met for two weeks, and then you're supposed to live with them. I think people did not have an understanding of where I was coming from. And even I didn't have any understanding of what I went through. But now, much older, now I understand.

'Ofa stayed in Melbourne until she was thirteen, then went to join her parents and siblings who had migrated to the United States. At seventeen, when her parents detected signs of rebellion, they decided to send her to Tonga, but when her father's mother in Australia became ill, they sent her there instead. She recalled that "they sent me here to Australia to calm down." When I asked how she felt about the move, she replied, "First year I cried every night, and then the next year I calmed down for a little while. Then now I don't mind it so much." Later in our interview she said, "I used to blame my parents for sending me here. I hated it, this and that. Now in the long run I'm very fortunate that they did send me here because I'm very close to my grandmother." She named many other relatives she had come to know in Melbourne, then continued, "So in the long run I've grown out of that hatred against my parents for sending me here so young. That I know now what good came out of it." Despite her attempt to portray the positive aspects of her moves, 'Ofa was clearly an unhappy person, with considerable bitterness about her experiences. At one point she sighed and remarked, "I think my whole life is a problem."

I asked 'Ofa her views on children being sent to Tonga, to which she replied, "I think if they get sent to Tonga against their will, I think it doesn't do them any good, especially if they don't want to change. I think they become worse. Unless you suddenly have this interest about your background or learning about everything because you are in Tonga and everything, you end up loving it. But it can work both ways. It depends on that person that's getting sent down there." When she has children of her own, she says she will take them to Tonga for a year in their mid-teens, staying with them and giving them the opportunity to "learn where they came from, everything, you know—respect, everything."

Some young people do choose to return to Tonga without their parents, usually because they want to know what Tonga is like and to resolve identity conflicts they are experiencing. It can be a positive experience, but Anasela, who had chosen to go back on her own ("I wanted to know a bit more about my culture and see what it was like") had an unhappy one when she lived in Tonga for three years in her early teens. She said she felt at home there but did not enjoy the experience "because people try to tell you what they want; you're not allowed to think for yourself, and you have to follow what they think. It's like a prison. I'm forced to do what they expect me to do." The experience had its benefits, she says, but she remains ambivalent. "It's changed me in a lot of ways in that I'm not so stubborn. I used to be really stubborn, but now I'm just nice to everyone, but the thing is I hated that people take advantage of when you're nice to them." Anasela is determined never to send her own children back. "I just don't want them to be influenced by the past. If they want to go I'll let them go, but I'm not going to force them to go."

Parents who disagree with the practice of sending children to live with relatives in Tonga and who, for various reasons, do not want to move back there often compromise by taking their children for holidays to Tonga whenever they can afford it.[3] These holidays are often much more pleasant experiences for overseas-born children, as they do not have to deal with the daily realities of going to school, contributing labor to the household, and so on, and they are often treated as special guests. Even a short trip can give young people a stronger sense of their Tongan identity. One young woman writing on the KB said, "I was born and raised in Australia . . . but had the morals of a Tongan. . . . [F]irst it was hard to understand, meaning trying to understand the Tongan and Palangi ways of life . . . and one year I was lucky enough to take a trip to Tonga, and believe me that really helped. . . . I'm proud of my culture and its morals" (KB 17.2.98). Numerous other posts by young people on the KB include enthusiastic descriptions of visiting Tonga for the first time and having the opportunity to meet members of their extended family and learn about "Tongan culture."

When I asked young people where they would go if they won a free holiday, most said they would go to Tonga. Vika said, "I think if you want to explore life, explore the world, I think you should start where your roots are from and then work yourself up. Start from there. So I would like to go to Tonga." Veisina replied, "I don't know how I feel about Tonga now, but I know I'd love to visit Tonga. I heard the night life is great, the good-looking guys are still on the island, and just to visit family." Those who said they would choose a holiday elsewhere did not necessarily reject the idea of going to Tonga; they wanted to see the world, and as they said, "Tonga's always going to be there!" The image young people have of Tonga influences their feelings about visiting or living there. Some take on the nostalgic and nationalistic sentiments of their parents or have their own memories from early childhood and see Tonga as a place where they would be happier, freer, and more relaxed. Lesieli told me, "In Tonga you don't really need to work, you have a farm for food."

Holidays, like longer stays, can involve both positive and negative experiences, and some find that even on short trips they encounter problems, such as less than welcoming attitudes from some Tongans they meet (see below), not understanding much of what happens, not being able to communicate adequately in Tongan, not liking the food, and so on. Lopini, fifteen, daughter of 'Ana (see Case Study 1), did not enjoy a holiday in Tonga with her family in her early teens, when they stayed with her mother's parents. "I felt a bit trapped. I wasn't really allowed to do anything, I wasn't allowed to go anywhere, and I wasn't allowed to hang out with my boy cousins, you know that *faka'apa'apa* crap? I got told off because I didn't know the stuff." On their first day in Tonga her grandfather told her to help with the cleaning, and she felt throughout the visit that he was "bullying" her.

Holidays can also provide quite a culture shock for young people raised overseas. Lucy visited Tonga at the age of nine and said, "I *despised* things. I thought of things there as 'Third World' or 'old-fashioned,' yet I still felt at home." Similarly, Bianca said of her trip to Tonga, "I felt like an outsider because I felt things weren't 'cool' enough, and I thought everyone was backwards. I wanted to be back home with the TV, radio, and telephone and the fast pace of city life." She added, "As I grow older I realize what a peaceful place it was," and she even contemplates living there for a while at some stage.

Some who have never been to Tonga are wary of what to expect. Susana commented that her parents hoped to return to Tonga when they retired but said she had no plans to visit them. "I already know that I wouldn't be able to handle cold showers nor the smallness of the islands and many other things that Tonga lacks compared to that of Australia." As for moving more permanently, many are anxious about the lack of "opportunities" in Tonga and say they would live there only if they could get a good job and "help" in some way. Richard, twenty-five, the son of a Tongan father and Australian mother, commented that "I don't know what sort of work I'd do, and it wouldn't be much [of] a future if I brought my family up there."

Tongans raised overseas who choose to go to Tonga to live when they are young adults tend to do so out of a desire to offer something back to their parents' homeland or as a way of finding their identities. Lupe, now in her thirties, moved to Australia with her parents as a nine-year-old and returned to Tonga after her university studies with the intention of "[doing] the cultural bit" for a year. She ended up staying for twelve years, moving through the ranks of a government department. When she left it was because she felt the cost of living in Tonga was too high compared to her wages, but she still expressed the hope that she would return in the future.

Young Tongan visitors to Tonga are sometimes shocked by negative attitudes toward them. Some put this down to envy: "I feel that because I was born and raised here in the States, often times I am looked down on because I have had that opportunity" (KB 14.2.99). Others see it as a cruel response to their lack of language skills and poor understanding of the Tongan way. A young woman wrote on the KB, "I (a 100% true blue tongan) myself, grew up in South Carolina, where there ain't no other Tongans. When I first went to Tonga about 3 years ago ALL the girls even some of my cousins were calling me names and talking shit about me because like you, i didn't know jack bout tongan language . . . tongan culture . . . nothing" (KB 25.8.97). A young man who posted a message titled "Love to be Tongan, hate to be Tongan!!" asked, "Why is it that Tongans are the very same people that put you down, for trying your best!! . . . I spoke English when I was in Tonga, and all they did was laugh behind my back and make little comments in Tongan . . . and when I tried speaking Tongan they would laugh in my face instead of behind my back! . . . Geez you can never win in a situation like that, and I'm proud to be Tongan but not when I see my own people look down on me!!" (KB 5.2.98). Being derided as *fie pālangi* or *pālangi loi* can be distressing and confusing, especially for those who are still trying to secure their Tongan identities. The same young people who go to Tonga seeking their "roots" can find themselves dismissed as "fake" Tongans.[4]

Language and Identity

Critical to young people's sense of cultural identity is their attitude toward language. While some defiantly claim to fully identify as Tongan without Tongan language fluency, others believe they are somehow not "real" Tongans without language skills. Those who are fluent can tend to be somewhat intolerant of those who are not. Vika, for example, said angrily, "The language is really important. What's the use of being Tongan and can't speak their own language? It's so ridiculous, it's so stupid to call yourself Tongan and don't know how to speak the language." Such intolerance often disappears when they have children of their own and realize how difficult it can be to teach them Tongan while living overseas. Not only are children constantly exposed to English, but they are often uninterested in learning Tongan. Only when they are older do they regret not making more effort. Some do attempt to learn but are put off by the teasing and joking that meets their mistakes; as one girl said, "Tongans don't let you live down something like that!"

Language issues are a popular topic on the Kava Bowl, with many posters describing the frustration and embarrassment of not speaking Tongan. One wrote,

> I was raised here in the States, unfortunately my parents stressed the importance of English, thus I can understand and barely speak Tongan. Now at the young age of 30, I'm trying to teach myself. Not easy because my family lives in another state. There are very few Tongans around. I get frustrated and embarrassed when I do try to speak and people mimic my Western accent and mock my ignorance. Give me a break, I am trying to educate myself. . . . Yes I am full Tongan, I am embarrassed (especially when trying to speak to my elders) at my ignorance. (KB 16.4.97)

Another poster complained of being ridiculed by Tongan speakers, saying, "[I]t hurts when Tongans treat you as though I am less Tongan than they simply because I don't speak anymore. Tongan is my first language but my tongue has forgotten how to use it. . . . People's attitudes hurt me because I am VERY Tongan in the truest sense" (KB 16.4.97).

Some young people even turn to the KB as a way of improving their Tongan.[5] "Thanx to the KB I can read and write Tongan better than I speak. (Believe me, that isn't saying much!). I would never dream of making fun of anyone's English. Yet some Tongans get off on making me feel inferior for my ignorance. I'm embarrassed enuff, trust me" (KB 16.4.97). Solomone, who has been trying to relearn Tongan partly through participating on the KB, said, "I once knew how to speak Tongan but have since lost the ability. I feel terrible about such a loss because to lose one's language is to come dangerously close to losing one's culture and identity within that culture."

In an article titled "Can We Become Tongan without Speaking Tongan?" in the Polynesian student magazine *Moana*, David and 'Anapesi Ka'ili voice their concerns about the decline in Tongan-language ability both in Tonga and the diaspora (1999). They explain the decline as a result of "European language imperialism" and claim that "Tongans have been indoctrinated into believing that the English language is the only language in which they can obtain power, prestige, and economic well-being. In consequence of such indoctrinations, many Tongans have come to perceive the Tongan language as an impediment or an obstacle to their academic and economic progression" (1999, 15). They strongly advocate bilingualism and assert that by speaking Tongan "we are endowed with a sense of connection, commonality, and bond toward our cultural community. It is through these associations that we begin to completely identify with our native culture. This identification cements a sense of cultural dignity and validation. It also delineates a distinct Tongan cultural group."

The authors are involved with the Planet Tonga web site, which includes a Tongan-language journal *(Tohi Fatu'anga Lea)* where participants can post poems, songs, stories, essays, and so on, in Tongan "for the purpose of vitalizing and enriching the Tongan language" (T. Ka'ili, e-mail 4.6.01).[6] Far more Tongan is used in Planet Tonga forums than in KB forums, which may be of further help to those seeking to improve their Tongan—but which may also deter those with poor Tongan skills from participating (Morton 2002a).

Apart from the Internet, other ways young people seek to improve their skills in Tongan without risking ridicule include attending Tongan churches, listening to Tongan songs, and reading Tongan newspapers. One young woman even made a deal with her cousins to pay them a fine if she spoke English. 'Ofa reads aloud to her grandmother, who is patient with her mistakes. "If my grandmother wants me to kill her ears with my Tongan, then she tells me to read out the newspaper for her. Takes me about a whole day. . . . I know how to read it, but the pronunciation for me is really hard." Embarrassment about poor pronunciation, "wrong" accent, and inadequate grasp of Tongan grammar often means that many young people understand much more Tongan than they are willing to use in their own speech, which can mean they overhear all sorts of conversations between Tongan speakers who are unaware they understand! Some speak Tongan only when they feel safe or uninhibited; I know of one young woman in Melbourne who speaks Tongan when she is affected by alcohol but at other times denies knowing any of the language. It is also common for those with some knowledge of Tongan to combine it with English to speak what is sometimes referred to as "Tonglish." Even inserting some Tongan words or phrases into their speech gives them, at least among themselves, some claim to "authentic" Tonganness.

Yet those who are trying to learn or improve their Tongan through the KB, church services, and newspapers are gaining only a partial knowledge of the language. It may help them in conversations or understand more of what is being said in church, and so on, but it does not give them full command of the complexities of the Tongan language as used in formal situations where nobles or royalty are present or in oratory, sermons, or song lyrics and poetry, where specialized and often archaic language is used. Thus these fledgling speakers still remain toward the bottom of an implicit scale of authenticity, opposite those with greater command of the language. Those who are not "full speakers" may try to use what Tongan they know to create a sense of belonging, but they have to struggle against what Bonnie Urciuoli refers to as "border marking," in which those who do not "have" the language are assigned "opposing places" to those who do (1995, 539). There are signs that this opposition may not be as stark in the future, as the number of Tongans with poor Tongan-language skills increases.[7] As we have seen, already there is considerable confusion about the relationship between language and culture, as indicated by the following post on the Tongan Youth Forum:

> i fear that this rapidly growing generation of tongans will have no connection to the culture through the avenue we know as language (in this case, the tongan language). what then? will they still be tongan because their roots are embedded in tonga? most definitely, in my perspective, but it will not be the same, no? because if the language is not understood or easily transmittable to them, then what else within the tongan culture is lacking in their life? (TYF 20.6.01)

For Tongans growing up in the diaspora, the struggle to secure an identity in childhood and adolescence obviously involves more than acquiring language skills, although language is often portrayed as the "key" to identity. Jemaima Tiatia describes the ideal image of a "true" Islander held by many Islanders in New Zealand as follows:

> To qualify one must be a competent speaker of the native language, have learnt to prioritize the extended family and cultural commitments of the church, to observe the Pacific Island doctrine of respect in the presence of elders, and to have mastered an unquestioning obedience. Failure to fulfil these requirements will instinctively mean one's identity will be in question by those who already "know" or have already attained this knowledge. (1998, 7)

For young people it is important that their identities are acknowledged by others, yet as we have seen, many find that this acknowledgment is not forthcoming, leaving them without any clear sense of who they are. In another New Zealand study, Melani Anae has found that overseas-born Samoans are regarded with considerable ambivalence, even antagonism, in Samoa and among older migrants—particularly young people with poor Samoan-language skills who are involved in the New Zealand way of life. They often feel rejected by both the white New Zealand and the Samoan communities, and while some manage to feel secure in their identities, many others "experience identity confusion" (1997, 133).

Many young Tongans share these experiences, and one Tongan woman living in the United States posted a message on the KB that captures the dilemma they face.

> I constantly get criticized for not speaking 'MY' language and I'm full Tongan. . . . I get criticized from the whites and the Tongans. . . . From Tongans I always get the crap of I don't act Tongan enough. . . . It makes me real sick and sad because I have to Prove myself to the whites—speaking English the best, trying to get a white collar job so they don't judge me on my clothes, trying to get with white society, and then proving myself to the Tongans—trying to speak Tongan fluently, trying to be the generous Polynesian by just giving money to just any TONGAN and figuring out later that they are just using me, trying to make Tongan food and so on. (KB 25.8.97)

Critically Tongan

Only a minority of overseas-raised youth are able to successfully navigate a path to acceptance by both Tongans and non-Tongans: those who have achieved educational success and social mobility (or at least the potential for mobility) while also acquiring the language skills and cultural competence necessary to be acknowledged as authentically Tongan. Whether they belong to this minority or have taken a different path through Tongan and non-Tongan social worlds, most young people are critical of some aspects of "the Tongan way."

The KB provides a forum for the expression of such criticisms and opinions about historical and contemporary issues in Tonga itself. Many young Tongans have strong feelings about a land they may never even have seen, and one theme of their posts is a revision of Tongan history, a challenging of the "official" memories of Tonga's past. One young woman wrote, "I suppose the greatest pity of all is the Loss of an entire Civilisation because we 'Tongans' have no idea about what motivated our ancestors, what were their goals, their fears, how they really felt and lived their lives, the whys of their beliefs and convictions. . . . [N]othing is left but a few rarely told legends of what Was . . .

and even less thought of what Could have been" (KB 3.2.98). Her post referred to the impact of Christianity, one of the central pillars of contemporary Tongan society. Similarly, a Tongan man argued that "Christianity has encroached too much on our culture and traditions that we don't have anything of our own anymore. Everything is controlled by the churches (salvation for example) and money. Tongan culture and traditions are slowly being sacrificed" (KB 27.4.97). A reply from a Tongan man in Australia agrees that "the missionaries did destroy a big part of our Culture," but he adds, "I am thankful that although 'some' of our culture and tradition was destroyed, I'm glad that we got something much better and greater, which is really at the heart of culture and tradition anyway, and that is I believe the Good News about Jesus Christ" (KB 1.5.97).

Along with Christianity, the history of Tonga's "independence" has also been subject to rethinking (Morton 2001a). A young woman studying overseas argued that although not formally colonized, "Tonga experienced all other aspects of colonisation." She added that when she thinks over Tonga's history, "I ask myself where did freedom go?" At a later point she writes, "I'll definitely wean my grandchildren on this side of Tongan history . . . one day!" (KB 30.10.97).

Eclipsing these historical topics, however, are the posts discussing Tonga today. There have been numerous posts criticizing or supporting the monarchy and government, often sparking long, heated debates. A Tongan man born in New Zealand described his father as "essentially a slave of the local noble" while still in Tonga. "As a young Tongan professional raised in palangi-land, by parents who ensured that my sibs and I were aware of the world we live in, I look at Tonga and see a country that really needs to get rid of its bad traditions" KB (7.5.97). He identifies Christianity, the monarchy, and "exploiting nobles" as Tonga's main problems and adds, "I still have Tongan roots, and it hurts me when my people continue to live in this backward, dirty mess. It could be such a beautiful country."

A young woman wrote a long post criticizing the current political situation in Tonga, concluding, "Anyways, I love tonga because it is my heritage, I want my children to be proud of Tonga—but as I witness first hand the great unfairness and widening of the haves and have nots—I want to speak in behalf of my heritage" (KB 21.11.96). One of the many who responded to her post argued that Tongans living overseas should not interfere, saying, "[A]lthough we see a lot of poverty in Tonga and the fine line between rich and poor, they need a Monarchy, and won't last without it. Nothings going to change Tonga, I don't think. We can't try and change Tonga to better suit us who do not live there. . . . It's sad to see the division between rich and poor, but if they don't think its broke then I don't think we should try to fix it" (KB 22.11.96). Others who have contributed to similar discussions proudly defend Tonga and the monarchy, dismissing the criticisms as Western influenced and ill informed. These different standpoints can be seen in discussions of many other topics concerning Tonga, with some of the overseas Tongans enthusiastically proclaiming their intentions to return to Tonga to "help out."

The Tongan Way

The interest of young Tongans overseas in issues relating to Tonga is outweighed by their concern with diasporic issues—those that affect them in their daily lives. A central issue is "the Tongan way," that all-encompassing and multiply defined concept that most of them have struggled with from an early age. Many young people are well aware of the fluidity of the concept, and those with some knowledge of contemporary Tonga know that *anga fakatonga* is being transformed there through constant social change. In interviews and discussion forums they often related with amusement the shock their own parents had on returning to Tonga after long absences and discovering that "the Tongan way" they had attempted to maintain overseas had been altered in ways they never imagined possible.

Whether they are aware of its transformations or view it as a static and unchanging concept, few express a desire to lose *anga fakatonga*; indeed, most defend it proudly. 'Ofa said that for young Tongans in Australia, "some [of the Tongan way] is lost, but it's kind of mixed up now. It's very flexible. . . . I think it's very important that we don't lose it. We've got to still keep it, but to an extent. But, yeah, it's very important to keep it. It's where we came from. It's where our roots are. It kind of says who we are." 'Aisea described all the elements of the Tongan way that he saw as important and argued that it should be kept "because if we weren't all that Tongan we probably would be disrespectful to others. Including our family members, brothers and sisters. And we'd be too much *pālangi*."

Yet Tongans who are unwilling to make any adjustments to their host society are frequently criticized by young people. Vika's criticism was typical: "They come over from Tonga with their culture, and some of them don't want to change. In a country like Australia you need to change a bit. Not a whole lot; you just need to compromise. For you to survive in this country. You can't be the same. You have to change a little bit." Similarly, Tavake, twenty-six, who was born and raised in the United States, commented,

> The one thing I notice is that Tongans settle and are at ease where they are at. Rather than to better themselves. I know that most Tongans have a hard time to assimilate to society here. Therefore they try to bring the life that they once lived in Tonga and bring that same attitude here to the States. When in doubt they learn the hard way and they find out too late. That America is not all that it's cracked up to be. I mean you realize that it's hard here in America, especially if you have no education background and if you have a big family. You are going to just barely make it.

In Melbourne, the children of the earlier migrants are aware of the differences between the Tongans they associate with and the more recent arrivals, who tend to cling more closely to the Tongan way. Feleti observed that his parents' generation, which has been in Australia for over thirty years, has gone through various problems but has basically adjusted to life in Australia. The newer arrivals, he said, are "trying to create a little Tonga" and are insulating themselves from the wider society. Feleti believes their children will have difficulties as teenagers, when they "have to go out into the real world" where they feel they do not belong, which will hinder them from "progressing and succeeding."

This concern with "success," particularly economic success, means many young people are keen to see a reduction in the demands on families for remittances and contributions at events such as funerals and weddings, and through fund-raising. These young people often argue that it is important to meet the needs of the immediate family before others, and while they uphold the importance of respect and of ties to the extended family, many believe that obligations to extended family create unwarranted demands on families already struggling to make ends meet. Two young men wrote a joint critique on the KB of overgenerous gifting, arguing that money is often given "in amounts that are way beyond a family's ability to be self-sustaining. . . . In short, you must help yourself before you can help others. Take it easy on the kavenga [obligations] if you can't afford it" (KB 17.1.97). They added that demands on young people to contribute to family income in order to meet such obligations were a factor in preventing many of them

from continuing their education beyond high school. One young
woman wrote, "I believe that our lives in the U.S. would be less stress-
ful, especially for the women, if we left the Koloa [wealth items such as
pandanus mats and *ngatu*] back in Tonga. Of course, we all have our
own opinions, but the mats are materialistic, expensive to buy and export, and the way I be seeing some relatives fight over the stuff, it's
messed up!!" (KB 3.3.98).

In response to a KB post asking if a balance can be found between
Tongan and *pālangi* culture a Tongan university student wrote,

> In order for the Tongan family to survive in America, we sometimes
> have to sacrifice some aspects of our culture. My house payment,
> other bills, and other financial obligations and the well-being of my
> family will come first before extended family obligations. Unfor-
> tunately, many Tongan families don't understand this, and so a circle
> of poverty develops that passes on to the kids and so on. The cycle
> needs to stop. Tongan people need to have bank accounts—even more
> important . . . get an education and a good job so you have the
> money to dish out to extended family without hurting you and your
> family. (KB 14.3.97)

He complained about his cousin using the Tongan notions of hierarchy
to help herself to his possessions. "I'm sorry to say, but to me, unless
you are immediate family that tu'unga [hierarchy] shit don't fly with
me because this is America, home of the free!" Such challenges to the
privileges of high status are also being made in relation to the Tongan
nobles, with a growing reluctance to meet the demands of nobles for
money and services.

Other aspects of Tongan behavior overseas that are often criticized
by young Tongans include the consumption of kava and alcohol, gambling, and "laziness." Gossip was also an issue that concerned many of
the young people I spoke with, as they were often the targets of gossip
and felt they were being watched and judged no matter what they were
doing. Veisinia said of Tongans, "They can be the biggest gossipers;
don't get on their bad side, look out for whom you're making friends
with, they may just turn around and stab you in the back." On the KB,
gossip is also criticized.

> I was (am) always told that I should watch myself from Tongans be-
> cause they can be very vicious, emotionally. Many Tongans are ngutu
> lau (gossipers), most times in a bad way. I don't think that they really

mean it though, I think that's just the way it is! No matter what you do, someone is watching you, even if your not doing anything wrong they will still find something to talk about to put you or your famili down. I definitely don't think this is right! So many Tongans have sep- arated from the Tongan community due to this reason! . . . Tongan culture is a great, strong and loving culture when it wants to be. But there are times that I am so ashamed to see what some people are like. (KB 19.3.98)

A young man living in the United States wrote, "[A]s much as I love being Tongan, there are characteristics about Tongan people that annoy me. They love to tear each other down, and anyone that makes it to the top, they try even harder to tear that person down" (KB 28.9.96).

Gender Relations

Some older migrants have been prepared to initiate changes in what they regard as "proper" gender relations, but many in the younger gen- erations are pushing for even further relaxation of some of the stric- tures on their behavior.

As we have seen, one area that appears to have changed consider- ably in many families is the relationship between children and their fa- ther's sisters, their *mehekitanga*. Young people nowadays often have close and affectionate relationships with these women, sometimes against the wishes of their own parents. 'Ofa said that for her, "that *mehekitanga* stuff is out," and she confides in her father's eldest sister, plays with her hair, asks her for favors, and generally acts in ways that would be inappropriate in the more conventional relationship. 'Aisea described his aunts as "like our second mothers," although he added that they take on a more traditional role on important occasions. Some of the young people I asked about this relationship said they had not even realized it was supposed to be any different from their relation- ships with other kin. Only occasionally did I hear of instances of *mehekitanga* expecting their brother's children to be respectful and sub- servient to them. Even this can be resisted: a young woman from Mel- bourne went to Sydney to bring her cousin to live with her after dis- covering that the girl's *mehekitanga,* with whom she had been staying, was "treating her like a slave."

Unlike the relationship with *mehekitanga,* it has proved much more difficult for young Tongans to convince their parents to relax their rules about restrictions on young women. Susana reacted emotionally when I asked her how she had felt about being Tongan growing up in Australia. "It majorly sucked when I was growing up. Not being able to go out casually with my friends was my problem." Susana noted that her younger siblings had been given much more freedom and feels that the oldest daughter bears the brunt of the restrictions on girls. As a young girl, she said, "I would always have to sit by my mum's side and behave, no matter how desperate I was to run outside and play, like my brother." Malia exclaimed, "You're not allowed a date till you're twenty-one, and thank God, I'll be twenty-one in September and I'm there!"

These restrictions on young women often cause family conflicts; according to Lesieli, "I've seen lots of Tongan girls run away because they're left like prisoners." Even when women have reached twenty-one and are given more freedom, their families often keep a close eye on their activities until they are married. At twenty-six, one young woman in Melbourne was given considerable freedom to do as she pleased, but she was still secretive with her family about any romantic involvements and at the time of our interview was planning to elope with a boyfriend her family did not know she was seeing.

Lucy, who was raised in a "traditional" household, was critical of restrictions on unmarried females and said, "The 'Tongan girl,' according to my mother, stays home and has no knowledge of the term 'a date.' The respectable and 'common' thing to do is have the gentleman come to your home, ask permission to converse with the girl and that's it— converse with the girl, at home, while the mother or father is in the same room. While on the other hand, I grew up in America and think this custom is outlandish, ridiculous and uncalled for." The issue has been the topic of many lively discussions on the KB, and the forum has also proved to be a social outlet for some of these young women. One asked,

> Why are tongan parents so strict??? My parents are always telling me to stay home on the weekends, not to have any guys call the house, can't bring any american friends over because I'm tongan and that's not the 'anga' faka tonga. I'm a proud person to represent my culture and take pride in who I am but I still don't understand if they want to bring us up in the tongan traditional ways and the way the culture is run here in america. And if that was the case then why don't they just send us back to the island and raise me there??? (KB 22.7.97)

A young man responded by telling her that as a Tongan woman she is "the cornerstone," "revered," and "holy ground" and that she should listen to her parents (KB 25.8.97). Several other responses were from young women who shared the original poster's predicament but who were more accepting of the restrictions on their freedom. A young woman wrote,

> My parents never let me leave the house without a male chauffer even now (I am 23!). And sometimes I am escorted by younger teenage brothers! I hated it when I was younger, but I now I know better. Sex, crime, and drugs can approach you whether you consent to it or not. Having family members around all the time can sometimes be of help in sticky situations. . . . I do agree that Tongan parents should SOME-TIMES ease the grip on our leashes, but I'd rather them worry about me than not. Even at this age, it's nice to know someone still cares. (KB 25.8.97)

Another poster was more ambivalent.

> We should always remember that our parents love us and that we love them. We will always respect our parents and everything we do will be out of our love and growth as Tongan children growing up in America. . . . You also have to remember that Tongan Parents are always more strict with their daughters than their sons because the Tongan Culture teaches a double standard; the Tongan culture is a very sexist culture although the families are headed by women. (KB 25.8.97)

A young woman living in Australia was also frustrated by this "double standard."

> One issue that needs to be addressed and should be taken into consideration is many teenage Tongans are stuck in two cultures that are contrary to each other. An extract from my experiences is my parents do not allow me to be associated/socialize with my chosen friends outside school hours. As a result of this rule is I feel isolated and feel that I no longer have anything in common with them as I cannot participate in the conversation they are conducting amongst ourselves, the reason being is I was absent from their social activities during the weekend. But this rule does not apply to the male species. Talk about sexist attitudes. Another example is when I want to attend uni functions and when I want to go to the library to do some research/study, it's a must that I have a chaperone present. (KB 12.5.96)

Women who have experienced these restrictions usually claimed they would not expect the same of their own daughters. Of course, many migrant parents have relaxed these restrictions and give their daughters considerable freedom, particularly once they are in their late teens. This has occurred more often in the past few years, and the women I spoke with who were in their early twenties and had waited until they were twenty-one to gain their freedom often expressed surprise that so many younger girls could now be seen at nightclubs and other social venues. Like Susana, many commented that their younger sisters had more freedom than was given to them. Often this greater independence is introduced only gradually, and Vika, at eighteen, said she was not yet able to make her own life decisions. "That's sort of half-and-half. They have given me some independence, but they've still got one rein just to me and the other one they're still holding to. So I haven't got the full control yet."

Other aspects of gender relations are also changing, partly through parents' decisions to accept change but also through young people's resistance to practices they see as "old-fashioned." Brothers and sisters often form close relationships whether or not their parents encourage this; many young women resist the expectation that they will keep their virginity until married; and even parents' attempts to teach children the Tongan division of household labor meets with resistance. As well as being critical of aspects of gender relations, there is an element of cynicism about "tradition" in some young people's views. Lopini observed that there are males who abuse the ideal of respect between male and female relations of the same generation. "Like, the *faka'apa'apa* thing, with guys and that, they're like, 'Yeah, we're *faka'apa'apa*,' and the next minute they try something on you. They abuse the trust, that's why I sometimes get shitty with the Tongan traditions. Like, what's the use if no one's going to abide by it?"

Churches

Church membership can be important to young people for the opportunities it provides to socialize with other Tongans, but for many there is also a deeply religious commitment. When I asked young people if they would still attend church if there was not a Tongan church accessible to them, the majority answered in the affirmative, adding that they would still prefer a Tongan church. This contrasts with the findings of Tiatia for New Zealand-born Islander youth who, she says, often only attended church because they were pressured to do so by their parents, sometimes with the use of physical force. "Not one of the participants mentioned their church attendance to be a voluntary decision, or that the church was adequately meeting their needs enough for them to desire it for themselves" (1998, 75).

Some of the young people I spoke with fitted this picture, saying they would not attend church if their parents did not force them to do so, but they were a minority. However, the commitment of others to their churches does not mean they are uncritical; there are many aspects of the different Tongan churches with which they express dissatisfaction. Some of the young people cited corruption, particularly the misuse of members' donations; the high expectations placed on members, such as not drinking or smoking, dress conventions, and so on; and the issue of language, with many young people not understanding services conducted in Tongan.

Another common criticism of churches is their role in placing obligations on people for commitments of time and money. Tiatia says of the situation for New Zealand-born Islanders: "This onerous expectation 'hammered' into them since birth can cause a rift in the New Zealand-borns' perception of the church. If the church demands of them an unfettered allegiance, on top of the external pressures of educational and occupational success, it seems inevitable that some will leave the church as a means of escaping the pressures associated with the church, or to do well academically and occupationally" (1998, 8). This seems to be a problem throughout the diaspora and has been raised occasionally on the KB. One young woman wrote of her difficulties growing up and of how her mother "spends most of her time and money on the Tongan Stake here in Utah, but hardly has time for us. I think that its more than just us kids that are the problem" (KB 12.3.98). Similarly, Susana complained that her parents "always volunteer to feed the whole church and for the next week we are near starving."

Churches are also criticized for not acknowledging young people and their particular needs and concerns. In New Zealand, Tiatia found that youth feel powerless within the churches and that "the youth voice has been suppressed to such an extent that Island born church members subjugate, ignore and belittle the significance of the ideas and values the New Zealand born wish to implement in order to cater for their own needs" (1998, 9). Yet an increasing number of churches do pay some attention to youth, as we have seen, with some churches making special efforts by hiring youth workers, running youth programs, and encouraging youth participation in special services. One church in Melbourne has run a number of very successful camps, which have a strong focus on youth and give them opportunities to share their experiences and feelings. Haloti (see Case Study 3) commented, "It's easier that way for us to bring it up, open up more that way, than it is for us to sit around in a big group, the whole church." However, he added that some other activities aimed at acknowledging youth and family problems were not as successful; for example, he admitted that at the formal debates organized by the same church young people tend not to stay and listen to the proceedings.

Young people who do feel dissatisfied with their churches sometimes leave, often to join charismatic churches that stress the individual's relationship with God. Here, they find escape from the expectations placed on them by the Tongan churches and the gossipping that occurs among their congregations. Usually older adolescents make this choice independently, but occasionally groups of young people make a joint decision to leave the church. At one church in Melbourne some years ago a serious rift developed between the youth group and the older members of the congregation. There are so many versions of this conflict now that it is impossible to know exactly what happened, and as one of the youth involved commented, "It was never over one incident, it really was something that had been boiling for a long time." One of the broad issues involved was the resistance of the youth group to having little say in how the group was run and the tensions this caused. What is clear is that the entire youth group left the church. It was a very difficult time for the youth and their parents, and even today it is an emotional subject for them. Several of the young people who were involved were visibly upset when they recounted the event. One told me she had "gone off the rails" for a while afterward; another has attended a charismatic church since that time; and another said she has never returned to any church. A young man who was involved said, "I had to rebuild my whole life. Clean the slate completely and all the pain and everything associated with it."

Leaving the church can also be an act of rebellion by adolescents, who may return as young adults. One sixteen-year-old girl I met had not left the church her family attended, but had also been attending a Mormon temple without their knowledge. When I asked her why, she explained that it was partly because "the guys there are nondrinkers, nonsmokers; I'd like to find a husband that doesn't do [those things]." She paused, then admitted, "No, it's just 'cos everybody talks about the

Mormons and they hate them and all this and I went out, I don't know whether I did it to be rebellious."

Parents

Leaving a church or experimenting with other religious groups are serious forms of rebellion given that church is regarded as such an important part of life. Other ways in which young people rebel are many and varied, and as we saw in chapter 4, there is considerable concern among Tongans about "youth problems." From young people's point of view, the problem actually lies with the older generations, particularly their parents. Many argue that generational conflicts would be minimized if only parents would be prepared to be flexible and make some adjustments to their host society. 'Ofa observed that "it's hard to live in Australia for some of the kids if their parents try to teach them the Tongan way and to follow it." She feels the answer lies in "educating older people, that it's all right if your daughter or your son does this. It's natural, you live in Australia. . . . There's certain expectations that they put on you that are not really necessary."

That parents do not listen to their children or give them time and attention is a common complaint, and many young people react by sharing little about their lives with their parents. Although the ideal is for families to be close and to have "togetherness" *(feohi)*, the reality is different in many cases. Anasela observed that for many Tongans, "you don't really get to know your family. People may think that you are close with your family, but in a deeper level it's not." Lucy said, "I don't communicate with my parents unless I have to—I mean, I don't inform them of what's going on in my life. . . . We hold conversations, but it's rarely about me. I find it easier to communicate with my siblings because they would better understand my perspectives." On the KB a young woman wrote, "Ice skating, football etc is great and is second nature for a palangi parent to involve their kids but does not appeal to our Tongan parents to make time for these activities. I had great parents but they would not drive me to a movie or any other extra curricular activity (seldom) it just does not count in our culture as important" (KB 30.10.96). Another young woman said of her family, "It was one way communication thing and my brothers and I never learned to communicate our thoughts and opinions on what we thought was right or wrong because we had to obey them and shut up! Don't get me wrong, I was brought up in a great environment with loving parents who were devoted christians and am very grateful for it. I just wish there was an open relationship between my parents and us children" (KB 29.4.96). She explained that she could not discuss personal problems with her parents or brothers and regrets not having had the courage to say "I love you" to her mother before she passed away. "I just wanted to say that the Tongan way is great if we balance it with the 'palangi way' of doing things also."

Many young people insisted they would have more open communication with their own children. Veisinia said, "I'd like to be very open with my kids, i.e., if they smoke or drink, they do it in front of me. I also want the boys to be able to talk to their sisters or vice versa." She added, "Sitting the children down properly and discuss problems instead of yelling is what is wanted." Those who have been brought up to communicate openly with their parents expressed gratitude for this. Tavake said, "I am very thankful that my parents have an understanding that most Tongan parents lack. Which is communication, and I owe that to my folks. My parents never tried to bring me up in the Tongan way here in America." He added that they did teach their children about Tongan culture—so they felt comfortable attending Tongan functions and associating with Tongans—without enforcing the behavioral rules and restrictions associated with *anga fakatonga*.

The lack of time many parents have for their children and the poor communication between them frequently has been cited as a factor in children's learning problems, since they may not be getting help or encouragement with schoolwork or adequate time to do their homework due to other expectations placed on them in the home; additionally, parents may not be aware of problems their children are experiencing at school. Furthermore, children often are strongly discouraged from being *fie poto* (trying to be clever), and when coupled with the expectations of unquestioning obedience and respect, the result is children who are hampered from learning the independent, critical thinking skills needed in formal schooling.

Another parenting issue that concerns young people is the use of physical punishment, although just as with adults, they have differing views on the subject. Many associate punishment with the lack of communication between adults and children, saying that if their parents thought they had done something wrong, they would hit rather than "[listen] properly" to their explanations. Many felt strongly that harsh physical punishment—which they often referred to as "abuse"—should not be used. Lusi, who was not physically punished herself, believes it has long-term effects "because a lot of them carry it on until they're adults. And then you know kind of aggressive behavior becomes part of their being. And it becomes a part of the life of that person. They've been hit all their life and then that person kind of hits other people, you know, aggression kind of comes in." 'Ofa referred to the physical punishment often meted out as "cruel" and claimed that Tongans do not know how to manage their anger and aggression as a result. "I think that's the thing that needs to be changed is how you discipline your kids and the difference between violence and difference between teaching your kid. . . . I think that is a big issue that needs to be taught for us generation coming up." Like many others who were opposed to harsh punishment, she still says she will "spank" her children as well as use other forms of discipline such as "grounding" them.

A similar view was posted on the KB: "[T]he problem with some parents is that too much anger and rage comes out when they beat the kids. Not all of the anger that goes into beating the kid is necessarily a reaction to what the kid did, a lot of it is personal anger that is inside the adult. . . . Kids begin to harbor terrible feelings of injustice and these feelings do not go away. They will inevitably resurface in some form or another" (KB 4.3.97). The writer notes that her own father was beaten a great deal as a child and vowed he would not beat his children and that he had kept that vow. She now feels very strongly against beating but still supports "slapping" and "spanking."

Paradoxically, some young people find that being "told off" rather than beaten can be more distressing. Lusi commented, "Like my dad— if you get told off by my dad that's just the end of the world." Vika's parents "always lectured us, oh, well, me. I think if I got a hiding I preferred that than—because when they lecture me it really goes straight to my heart. It really hurts me more than them hitting me. So I prefer them to hit me than to lecture me. . . . They mostly do that [lecture], and it really does help. It makes me think."

To some extent young people share older Tongans' fear that without physical discipline Tongan children will be more likely to stray from "the Tongan way." Vika argued, "I mean, if Tongan parents don't discipline their children then we'll all be like white kids. Won't be able to control the kids . . . so, yeah, there has to be an appropriate time to be hitting a child," Similarly, 'Aisea claimed that "the Australian way's a bit too soft and not enough discipline. Whereas in the Tongan way there's always discipline and respect. . . . If you have discipline you have respect." Asked how he felt about the physical punishment he received, he replied, "Oh, it's good because now it shows that I respect:

I've grown up respecting everyone and I listen to what my parents say, and I always abide by their rules." About Tongans' use of physical punishment he said, "I think in some ways it's good and some ways it's not because sometimes the Tongan parents just hit their kids because [the parents] are lazy and they won't let their kids run around and play. And in the good ways it is good for—just, like, they're disciplined."

Some youth who defend punishment as a means of keeping the Tongan way also argue that it is done "out of love." Another young man, in a message on the KB, described being beaten frequently as a child and expressed his gratitude, saying he and his siblings have "all gone on and made a good life on this earth and I would lay a lot of this on the discipline administered to us by our parents" (KB 23.6.97). He argues that "[t]his seems to fly in the face of modern western thinking but as far as I'm concerned it worked on me and if it ain't broke why fix it? After all those of us that have embraced western society whole heartedly are often those that have the most family problems. . . . Western society in my view has nothing to teach us about how to raise a family and in particular children properly and positively." He concludes by saying that he plans to "use the strap" when he has children of his own.

Overall, however, young people are less likely than their parents to see physical punishment as acceptable, and many have been influenced by Western definitions of "abuse." Yet they have divergent views about parenting more generally, and, just as we saw with adults, those who support a more Western upbringing blame the "traditional" parents for creating youth problems, while those who see themselves as upholding the Tongan way blame the more Westernized parents for allowing their children to be exposed to "bad" outside influences.

Gangs

Harsh physical punishment, as well as parents' strictness and lack of communication with their children, are commonly blamed for some young Tongans' involvement with gangs. Parenting practices that lead to family conflicts are seen as compounding young people's sense of alienation and thus leading them to turn to each other for a sense of belonging. In response to a KB post asking why young people join gangs, a young Tongan man wrote that the gang fulfills a need for love and respect, adding, "I think a lot of this trouble goes back to their identity . . . loss of cultural identity. I think a lot goes back to the family" (KB 23.10.97). Cultural identity certainly seems to be an issue, and the names of the gangs often indicate a strong identification as Tongan: Tongan Crip Gang, Tongan Style Gang, Tongan Bad Boys, Tongan Mafia. Yet membership in the gang can involve rejection of the Tongan extended family and the Tongan way, suggesting that gang members are experiencing considerable identity confusion.

When "Concerned Parent" wrote to the KB asking for advice after her fifteen-year-old son joined a gang (KB 13.3.98), the responses unanimously argued that opening up the lines of communication with him was most important, combined with honesty and understanding, and that hitting him was not the answer. One poster did suggest sending him back to Tonga, but another responded by saying, "[D]on't send your gang son to auntie in Tonga. Too many gang wannabes there who will just make your son think he is the king. Don't send your son to Utah either. All the worst gang kids have already been sent there." (KB 13.3.98). One young man who spent time in Tonga as a boy but grew up in the United States explained gang membership in terms of other Tongan characteristics.

> The most important thing I learned while in Tonga though was that there is a certain desire in all Tongans to be the best, to punish the other guy, to beat him down into a pulp and prove to the world that you are better. This is why I think we are naturally pointed towards sports, especially the violent ones. The problem is that sometimes this inner desire manifests in activities that are gang related because being in a gang epitomizes and brings out the most in this special desire. This desire which I like to refer to as "fie lahi" is not necessarily a bad thing. On the contrary, I think of it as a source of strength and pride. The problem comes in how Tongans use this strength. (KB 27.4.96)

Involvement with gangs appears to be most common in New Zealand and the United States, where Tongan youth are members of both Tongan-only gangs and those with "mixed" membership. The increasing criminality of these gangs is of tremendous concern to many Tongans, including other youth. A report on gangs in Utah claimed that more than 10 percent of gang members are Pacific Islanders, with the dominant gang being the Utah Tongan Crip Gangsters (Hamilton, Glick, and Rice 1996). A police study cited in the report found that these gangs in Utah are becoming increasingly involved in violent crimes. In 1997 a fifteen-year-old Tongan boy wrote of his anxieties about Tongan gangs to an e-mail discussion list (Kau Ta'e'iloa 10.3.97). When I replied, asking him what motivated him to write to the list, he explained, "I'm concerned about this cuz I haven't even met half of my cousins, and family. And I don't want to meet them when I go to their funeral. With gangs like these, they pit family against family. All my cousins are in a gang, and I don't want to be. Ya see, cousins on my mom's side are rivals w/my cousins on my dad's side" (Kau Taʻeʻiloa 14.3.97).

Recent research in Melbourne concluded that gangs such as those found in the United States associated with violence and criminal behavior are uncommon in that city (White et al. 1999a).[8] "Gangs" in Melbourne tend to engage in minor offenses such as graffiti, vandalism, substance abuse, and shoplifting, and the violence is usually confined to fights with other "gangs" in schoolyards or on the streets as part of the tension between different groups of ethnic youth and the racism they exhibit toward each other.[9] They do share some of the characteristics of American gangs, however, such as a predominance of male members, particular identity markers (e.g., clothes, shoes), and connection to a "territory," or particular social space.

Many of the young people who "hang out" in groups perceived as gangs are not involved in crime and are instead spending time together more for "social activity, peer support, personal identity and self-esteem, and friendship networks (White et al. 1999b, 11). Such youth commonly experience conflict with their families, so these groups provide an alternative support base. These "street-frequenting" youth (Pe Pua 1996) usually congregate in public settings such as shopping malls, parks, and streets.[10] However, their high visibility and the impact of stereotypes about youth "gangs" often lead police and other authorities, as well as the general public, to regard them with suspicion and hostility, as discussed in chapter 3.[11] As Steven Francis reports,

> Inspired by the physical appearance and bad behaviour of a small minority, many young Islanders are branded as thugs and, when in a group, deemed to be part of a gang. . . . Rather than understanding the sense of community and support engendered by congregating and socializing with other young people of the same culture, assumptions are made about the clothes worn, the colour of the skin and the activity of congregating in a public space. (1995, 189)

Young Tongans' typically boisterous behavior when with their peers may contribute to the assumptions made about them, as they tend to laugh loudly and to be physically exuberant, pushing, slapping, and hitting each other in fun. Their body language when interacting with people of higher status is very different, and when questioned by police and other authorities they may show respect, as would be expected in their homes, by lowering their eyes and not speaking unless spoken to, and then only in a low voice and uttering few words. This can be misinterpreted as sullenness and refusal to cooperate, and Francis notes that it "can increase the chances of prosecution and harassment" (1995, 191).

To a large extent, the relatively small Islander population in Melbourne has meant that young people have tended to form interethnic friendship groups. As the various Islander populations grow this could change, and broader factors could also have an effect. Rob White et al. warn that "the pre-conditions for more serious types of gang formation are beginning to emerge in the Australian context" (1999a, 13).[12] These preconditions include unemployment, social marginalization, and polarization. Cuts in funding to youth services and a lack of community resources for youth also are part of this wider problem. In addition, media stereotyping and harassment by police and others such as security guards in shops exacerbate the situation and can actually encourage the young people to move from simply forming groups to more ganglike activities.

Taking Action

Joining a gang, rejecting their Tongan identity, or cutting ties with their families may be the responses of some young Tongans to the family problems and cultural alienation they experience, but those who want to retain their involvement with Tongans, and their identification as such, seek other ways to deal with these issues. Many desire changes that will reduce some of the confusion and difficulties they experience.

Increasingly, young Tongans' critical evaluations of the Tongan way and of Tongans' behavior overseas are leading them to speak out and become actively involved in dealing with the issues concerning them. Through forums such as church newsletters, national and international newspapers and magazines, radio programs, and the Internet, young Tongans are sharing their views and analyzing the problems their generation is facing. These analyses are becoming increasingly sophisticated as youth reflect on their positions as members of marginal-ized populations and on the history of Tonga's relationships with world powers. As more young people study at tertiary levels they are beginning to draw on postcolonial theories to articulate their concerns. To give just one example, an article in the student magazine *Moana* written by a young male university student discusses the impact of colonization in the Pacific and the "internalized colonization" and "institutionalized racism" facing migrants in the United States, arguing that this has led many parents to socialize their children in the American, not Tongan, way (Ka'ili 1997, 7). Tevita Ka'ili says,

> I am proposing that we deconstruct and decolonize the child rearing philosophies of our colonizers in order to expose its negative impacts on our children. With the high percentage of school drop outs, gangs, criminal activities, and low academic performance among Pacific Islanders, it is possible that these behaviors are children's way of reminding us and the dominant White society that they adamantly and resolutely oppose being deprived of their native cultural heritage. (1997, 7)

On the KB there also have been frequent discussions about how young people could help one another in practical ways, particularly through mentoring programs, big brother/big sister programs, fundraising for scholarships, and the like. The site owner, Taholo Kami, encouraged these discussions and urged participants to turn them into action.

> I honestly believe that we can begin to make a difference—I hope we can use the KB to focus on some solid ideas on how to begin programmes that will restore self esteem to our young people from an early age, make them feel proud to identify as islanders but to attach that identity to positive development. . . . Why don't we determine solutions for our own youth—We seem [to] come up with so many good ideas, lets act!! (KB 11.9.97)

However, the various ideas have not resulted in action, which Kami explained as due to the relative youth of many KB participants, who "doubt their ability to affect their community" because they have been socialized not to have opinions and to simply follow orders (e-mail 8.8.97).

The fact that issues and problems are being openly and seriously discussed on the KB and other forums is important in itself. Discussions on topics such as "Pro-active methods, techniques and approaches to helping Poly youths succeed" (November 1997) and "How best to encourage Poly kids studying in western schools" (October 1997) encourage participants to share ideas and experiences. The Internet forums also enable youth to participate in discussions on topics that are extremely difficult to talk about openly in "real-life" Tongan conversations, such as homosexuality, abortion, domestic violence, child sexual abuse, and so on, as well as on other topics of concern to them as young people, such as friendship, love, school, and sports. As one participant wrote,

> The kavabowl helps gives us cultural identity and unity; especially to the second generation students outside of Tonga. We learn from each other and seek for those examples to emulate within our own culture. We have an opportunity to have open communication for some of the things we are too afraid to discuss with our parents or leaders. The kavabowl has been the means for our finding answers and reflecting on very important decisions for our lives. (KB 12.1.98)

With the KB receiving around twenty thousand "hits" a day in late 1998, it seems that many others also find such sites a valuable resource.

Initiatives in working with youth in the diaspora are increasing as many of the "second generation" reach adulthood. With their understanding of the issues faced by young Tongans overseas, they are promoting youth-oriented programs. One example is the Tongan Youth Council (TYC), set up through the Tongan Association of New South Wales in 1998 out of concern that many youth in Sydney are not attending church and are experiencing family conflicts. The council, run by young adults and teenagers, deliberately avoids the emphasis on hierarchy found in Tongan social life in order to encourage youth participation. The TYC's aim was to address issues as varied as substance abuse, teenage pregnancy, unemployment, education, cultural identity, and Christian values. In a full-page article on the TYC in the *Tongan Herald,* the message to Tongan youth was this:

> Let us help you. Let us help each other. Let's strengthen each other that as Tongans living in Australia, we can take up the opportunities in this great land for which our fathers have wisely moved here for.

We need to take the good from our mother country, and learn to live in this great land. But the only power we can have is through education and meaningful employment. Better jobs will bring satisfaction and a smile to our faces. More money will bring satisfaction as we are ABLE to meet financial commitments to society, to our family, and to ourselves. (*Tongan Herald* 1998)

Reclaiming Identity

The aim of youth organizations such as the TYC is not only to help young people deal with the problems they face, but also to help them appreciate and understand their Tongan background. As Malia said, "Even though the customs are not as strongly stressed, younger Tongans today are becoming more curious about the culture and wanting to express the culture more and more often." This was obvious among the youth of Melbourne, where negative stereotypes are not as prevalent as in some cities with larger Tongan populations, and where being an Islander is "cool." Although they often also identify at least in part as Australian, they (and their parents) frequently commented that Australians and other *pālangi* "don't have a culture," so they felt being Tongan offered, as one father put it, "something to hang on to."

Young Tongans overseas are well aware of the widespread concerns of adults that "Tongan culture" is being lost, or at least diluted. While they often go through a period of rebellion and rejection of "the Tongan way" in adolescence, many older teenagers and young adults emerge from a period of ambivalence about their Tongan identities to embrace their Tonganness. For some, the process of reclaiming "culture" primarily involves "emblematic ethnicity" (De Vos 1990, 212): the outward demonstrations of ethnicity such as clothing and other elements of appearance, music, dance, and food. But the majority of young Tongans are well aware that *anga fakatonga* is much more than this, even when they find it difficult to articulate just what the concept means. Hence many are keen to demonstrate the valued behaviors such as respect and humility; they want to know Tongan myths and history; and they want to understand the meanings underlying the song lyrics and dance moves they learn. Some become what I have called "born-again Tongans" (Morton 1998a), enthusiastically behaving and appearing as Tongan as possible, while others find this difficult and settle for incorporating some elements of the Tongan way into their lives. A young man on the KB wrote, "[A]s a Tongan living overseas, I am grasping for anything Tongan to ensure the survival of my native culture within me so I can hopefully pass it on to my children" (KB 25.11.97).

Tongan music is gaining in popularity, and as the population expands, there are an increasing number of events at which youth can celebrate their identity through performances in dance groups, bands, and choirs. Of course, definitions of "Tongan music" and evaluations of its authenticity are highly varied, and the Tongan music that appeals to many young people (particularly that influenced by reggae) may not be seen as "real" Tongan music by their elders. However, music regarded as more authentic, such as kava songs, is also reaching this younger audience—for example, an overseas-born young man in Melbourne has recorded albums of Tongan music that have gained wide popularity among diasporic youth. He explained, "I was hoping to perhaps re-present music that I love in its original form, to a younger generation that closed its ears to our Tongan heritage" (Tongan History Association forum 12.9.99).

One church youth group whose members were resistant to displaying their Tongan identity underwent a transformation after they met a Tongan youth group from Sydney. The members of the latter group were very keen to express their Tongan identity through dance and song and influenced the Melbourne group to take more interest. As group member Haloti explained, "We requested that we knew what the dances were about. When they started to show us and tell us, it meant more to actually know what you were doing while you were doing those actions." The group members became increasingly interested in other ways of expressing their Tonganness, and when they wore Tongan clothing to a special church service and sang hymns in Tongan to the congregation, their parents were thrilled. As their youth worker commented, "The difference was that they were doing it because they wanted to, whereas two or three years ago it was the parents telling them they had to do it."

The reassertion of Tongan identity can even occur when young people have the opportunity to interact through organized activities such as sports. A Tongan rugby club has become an important focus for some of the young Tongans of Melbourne, both male and female. One minister discussing the club mentioned that "the name 'Tongan' is very important to them." Although the young women involved are actually bucking Tongan notions of ideal feminine behavior, they are nevertheless choosing to associate with other Tongans, and members of the club are beginning to take a wider interest in Tongan culture, playing Tongan music, saying prayers before each game, and trying to speak Tongan to each other. Their matches are well attended by proud family members and other Tongan spectators, which helps give these young people a sense of membership in a larger "community."

Clearly, young people are engaging with their "Tonganness" in many different ways. The construction of a secure identity is usually easier for the children of parents willing to seek a "balance" or "mix" between the Tongan way and the ways of their host society. One of the crucial elements of finding this balance is the opening of communication between adults and children so that together they can negotiate their way through this process. Yet this in itself contradicts a fundamental element of *anga fakatonga:* the hierarchical social structure that positions parents as authority figures and children as unquestioningly obedient.

Each family deals with this contradiction in its own way, and in many cases a satisfactory resolution is never found, particularly when parents disagree with each other and there is an ongoing tension between the desire of one to hold on to *anga fakatonga* and of the other to let go, or at least make some concessions. The presence of extended family members such as grandparents can further exacerbate such tensions. Some families experience significant intergenerational conflict, and many young people do have difficulties establishing secure identities and feel highly critical of many aspects of Tongan values and behavior. Yet as we will see in the following case studies, this does not mean that the experience of growing up overseas should be viewed only in negative terms. In addition, both individuals and families change over time, in the process of constantly reassessing and reconstructing cultural identities.

CASE STUDIES

3. Haloti

Nineteen-year-old Haloti and his family are, by all outward appearances, a migrant success story: settled in a middle-class lifestyle in Australia, well educated, and comfortable in both Tongan and non-Tongan circles. Yet their lives overseas have not been easy. Apart from both parents working very hard over the years to support their family, the main area of difficulty for them is the clash between the Tongan and Australian ways of life and the generational conflicts that resulted from it. As the youngest child, Haloti has benefited most from his parents' willingness to compromise, whereas his three older siblings, particularly the oldest son, have found it harder to be the children of migrants.

Like many of the Tongans going overseas in the 1970s, Haloti's parents saw their move as temporary while his father, Tupou, studied for a tertiary degree. Then, as did many others, they stayed on, applying for permanent residence and then citizenship and raising their children in Australia. Now they live in a large house in a leafy suburb of Melbourne with Haloti and his two sisters, who are both in their twenties. Their oldest child, a son, married and moved out several years ago. Also living in the house are Tupou's mother and his sister and her two adolescent children, all of whom are Tongan born and all from Nuku'alofa.

All but Haloti's grandmother speak English well, and while the older generation is still fluent in Tongan, the younger ones speak only a little. The family is well educated: Haloti's father has a tertiary degree and his mother a diploma, his two sisters are at university, and the others all completed high school. Haloti recently finished high school and is working as a "bouncer" (security) in a nightclub while deciding on which course of study to pursue. All members of the family are actively involved in the Uniting Church, and they have a large extended family living in Melbourne with whom they are in close contact. Over the years Haloti's parents have gradually decreased the amount of money and goods they send to kin in Tonga, but they still communicate with them once or twice a month, usually by telephone.

Haloti is aware that his family has benefited from his parents' decision to stay in Australia and says that if he had grown up in Tonga he "wouldn't have had a lot of the things I've had here, the opportunities. . . . I just couldn't imagine life back in Tonga." He visited Tonga in his early teens but did not really enjoy it. He remembers being teased for his lack of Tongan-language skills and being called *pālangi loi*. The language issue is a sore point with him; he and his siblings were encouraged, as were many of the migrants' children, to speak only English as a way of ensuring their academic success. He says,

> When we go to big Tongan functions and people start speaking to you in Tongan, and you're just standing there and you have to explain that you really can't speak Tongan, and you just think to yourself, well, what am I doing, as a Tongan, you know? . . . My brother speaks Tongan and me and my sisters don't, but it's funny when we go out to dos [functions] and that, usually we sit in the corner and he's the one talking to everyone; it's just that we can't basically because of the lan-

guage barrier. A lot of the time it hurts, it hurts. . . . I also find with Tongans, you slip up with your language, they kill themselves laughing, and to them it's a big joke and you don't ever want to try it again. . . . That's what we found a lot, especially when we were younger, when me and my sisters were younger, we would really try to learn how to speak Tongan, but every time we made just a little mistake, everyone in the house would just laugh—we just gave up, it's not worth it.

Several years ago the family visited Tonga, where the siblings found themselves unable to communicate adequately with many of their relatives. When they returned to Australia their father encouraged them to speak Tongan. Haloti's sister, Lusi, remembers, "I think my dad realized then how hard it was for us being over there." However, they were feeling angry with their father and did not respond well, so he returned to speaking English with them. Lusi says Feleti, her oldest brother, "ended up teaching himself how to speak Tongan. Just tortured himself. It tortured him that much because I guess in the Tongan way you know he was expected to do a lot. There was a lot he couldn't do because he couldn't speak Tongan." After a second visit to Tonga, Lusi determined that she, too, would teach herself Tongan.

Ever since the second time I went to Tonga I've been reading as much as I could [in Tongan]. Hymns, newspapers, anything in Tongan, I read it and try to understand it. And if I don't then I'll look up the words in the dictionary. I even try to memorize the dictionary. Yeah, I've tried everything. We've had Tongan lessons at church. I like to talk Tongan to my grandmother because she'll point out what I'm saying wrong and she won't laugh at me.

Lusi wants to ensure that any children she has will speak Tongan. "I want them to speak Tongan because I know what it feels like not to be able to speak Tongan."

Despite his own lack of Tongan-language skills, when he is asked the frequent question "Where are you from?" Haloti identifies himself as Tongan. "I say, well, I'm Tongan, basically. It's hard to say, 'cause you're born in Melbourne, brought up in Melbourne, bred Australian, but people still ask 'Where you from? Where you from?' all the time. Basically you got to say that you are Tongan for that reason." Still, he sees himself as mainly Australian, as do his siblings. Feleti, his brother, experienced more difficulties securing an identity than his siblings, in all likelihood due to the much greater split he experienced between his home life and wider Australian society. It was not until he revisited Tonga at the age of twenty that he "managed to find myself as an Australian with a very strong Tongan background." He explains,

> The way we were brought up was very Tongan, but growing up with all your school friends being Australian. . . . I find everyone in my age group, we always said we had two lives. . . . We had our home life and Tongan life and church life; that's one life, home and church. And then you had your school life and that was your Australian life. . . . I think you'll find a lot of my generation are stuck in between, whether they had two lives or whether they were stuck somewhere in between.

Feleti argues that it is easier today for young Tongans to move between their Tongan and Australian identities because there is less racism than even ten years ago. Overt racism may have diminished, but negative stereotypes are still present, and Haloti says the most common one he encounters is that of "drunken Tongans." He asserts that "because just one or two are just going to pubs [bars], they give them the reputation, the stereotype that everybody sees, or most of the people see. Which isn't too helpful to the rest of us!" At times he even feels embarrassed to be Tongan, saying, "When bad things happen and it's caused by a Tongan, you just feel really ashamed about your race."

The more positive stereotype he commonly hears is that Tongans are "the real sporty types," which, he says, helped him at school to form a good relationship with his sports coach. Haloti is also aware that being an Islander has become "the in thing" in Melbourne and comments that "you walk around the city and a lot of people are wearing Islander shirts, things like that, bone necklaces, it's just weird. . . . Everyone just wants to be an Islander." He attributes this to the popularity of Islander entertainers and sportspeople like Jonah Lomu.

He likes being identified as a Pacific Islander and feels it gives him "a sense of community" with other Islanders. He has not encountered the rivalry between different Islander groups that is common is some other cities. "I think because there's not as many Islanders over here, the Polynesians are trying to stick together and hold their ground. Not against everyone else, but just as a community. Hold together as a community, rather than fighting against each other." His parents have encouraged this, and he has a lot of Islander friends, met through sports and through "just meeting on the street and seeing that we are both Islanders."

Like many young Tongans, Haloti is critical of many aspects of the Tongan way and of Tongans' adjustment to settlement overseas. He feels many do not try hard enough to succeed in their new homes, settling for poor wages, not striving "to achieve the top goal," and not using their money wisely. In part, he acknowledges, this is due to familial obligations draining their incomes, but he also believes "it's laziness, just couldn't be bothered going out and trying hard." He admits, "I use the Tongans in Melbourne, the Tongans here as role models not to be like. I can look around a lot of times and go, I can't be like that, I can't be like that!" He also dislikes gossip. "Oh, big mouths! A lot of gossip . . . one small things starts and it just gets bigger and bigger and it just never dies, it never dies, it just keeps going."

Generational conflicts are another issue on which he has strong opinions, and he blames them on the reluctance of many older Tongans to adapt to the Australian way.

> The younger generation likes to mix it up with the Australian culture so that it's more acceptable to them, and to a lot of Australians around who can see, but the older Tongans it's just a tabooed subject: it's the way it is, leave it, it's been like that for I don't know how long . . . especially in our church there's been, not a lot of attempts, but a lot of ideas go up, just to change little things which the elders just won't have a bar of it, they wouldn't want anything to change, but there's been a lot of influences; we want to change little things, change a bit of our lifestyle. . . . Well, I know it's happened in our family, we're just a mix of cultures. When we were growing up as young kids, boys aren't allowed to go into the girls' bedroom, not even open the girls' door or nothing, now it's just basically down the Australian culture where you just knock—we were brought up not to watch TV in the same room as the girls, now its just everybody jumps into the room, beds and all, everyone watches TV. We've mixed up a lot of the culture.

Haloti's family has evolved from a more traditional Tongan household to the kind of "mix" he describes. Feleti remembers feeling ashamed when his Tongan mother met him at school in her *puletaha* and *kiekie* (Tongan dress and waist decoration). He closely relates to "Grandpa's Song" on the album *Princess Tabu* (Bull and Bull 1996), which describes a young girl's shame when her Tongan-clothed grandfather comes to take her home from school. He also recalls representing Tonga on a float in an international festival as a child and being angry when his mother told him he should be proud to be Tongan when he knew he did not identify as such.

The changes that occurred in the family developed through the children's resistance to their strictly Tongan upbringing. Haloti recalls, "We were brought up firstly mainly in the strict Tongan way, which I think was hard for us, but then slowly, slowly mix, where they mix the cultures between the two cultures. . . . I think it was because we were resisting, they saw that, they saw the resistance that we had against it and the last thing they wanted us to do was leave because of the way we had been brought up at home." As he observes, "It was hard for them to put up with four rebelling teenagers, that was just enough for them!" An example he gave was his parents' attempts to make their daughters do the indoor chores and their sons the outdoors tasks. When they reached adolescence they actively subverted this—for example, if they were all outside kicking a ball around and the parents demanded that the girls go inside to wash the dishes, they all went in and helped clean up, then all returned to their game.

Haloti is highly critical of "traditional" Tongan parenting.

> Basically the Tongan way of bringing up children is just rules, rules, rules. You know, it just never ends. Just, there's a Tongan way of upbringing that's a very, I feel very cold, basically no relationship between the child and the parent. It's a relationship where it seems the parent is the commander and whatever they say has to be done by the child. I've seen it a lot where I go to a Tongan person's house, and the child would have never ever spoken to their parents about anything, about anything. They've never sat down with the parents and had a conversation about anything, which I find really sad, because it's the Tongans like that, that end up moving out, moving away, just to be rebellious. They just rebel and take off because they've got no one else to turn to.

Of his own parents, Haloti says, "The values they've given me are so important. I could never imagine myself growing up in another family, with other parents. . . . They've taught me to believe in myself, one thing is strongly they've taught me to believe in myself, to always work hard to achieve goals, which has stuck in my mind." The only changes he would make in bringing up his own children would be "to try and be their best friend" and to "always be there for them." Because both of his parents worked, he felt as a child that they had little time for him, but now, he says, the family is "pretty much a tight-knit group."

Another reason his parents were willing to make some changes in their parenting was their experience seeing teenagers running away from their families due to ongoing conflicts. Two of Haloti's own siblings moved out for some time, and he recalls, "I think that hurt my parents so much that they had to open up and had to view different grounds to see why, why it happened." At around that time their church held a meeting with other Islander churches about the problem of generational conflict, which he feels also influenced his parents. One of the main topics was "expressing yourself, you couldn't express yourself to your parents because of the obedience and respect so a lot of things had to be expressed to other people, which the parents found was disturbing, but they couldn't understand why [their children] were expressing their feelings to other people because they couldn't express them to their own parents." Since then, he says, "we've had a lot of meetings down at the church where a lot of parents have been taught about how to listen, to forget about the obedience, the discipline, everything, and just listen. A lot of them found it hard." One of the changes his parents made was to significantly decrease their use of physical punishment; consequently, the younger siblings have few memories of being hit, unlike their older brother.

The practice of sending children back to Tonga is something Haloti regards with ambivalence. Seven of his friends have been sent back to Tonga at various times: "they've been sent over there to be disciplined, but they've just come back not having changed, just basically gotten worse." Most of them rebelled against the strict discipline in Tongan schools and caused so many problems for their families in Tonga that they were returned to Australia. In one case, the friend was sent to Tonga not because of any trouble in Australia, but so he could attend the school his father and grandfather had attended. "He was a really good guy. But when he came back, you could start to see things change; he used to hang around with the wrong crowd over there, and I think it's changed him for the worst." Another friend of Haloti's who chose to go to Tonga for three months to "rediscover his roots and all that" returned to Australia behaving in a more Tongan way, but "once he got back into the system over here, he just changed back to the way he was before." Despite the mixed effects on his friends, Haloti says he would send his children to Tonga so they can have what he feels he missed out on: "to learn to be Tongan, just to know where they were from, where they are coming from."

Feleti, who struggled more with his identity, would like his children to go to Tonga in their early teens for a year "not for an education but for an education in life, that you've got to remember that this is where your grandparents grew up, this is how they grew up; understand what a feat it is to be here [in Australia] and grow up here, and how lucky you are; I would send them for that reason." When the family visited Tonga when he was a teenager, Feleti wanted to stay on for a year, but his father was concerned about the effect it would have on his education.

See, for Dad, he was saying, "You're going to be behind in your schoolwork and I've fought so hard to get over here to give you a good education, so you're going to finish it," and yet on my side of things I was saying, "Well, this is my last opportunity to go to high school in Tonga, and I'll miss that experience, I'll never be part of the Tongan thing if I don't do this at least, and it's already too late." It took me ages to get over that.

As a young adult Feleti returned and stayed for five months, coming to terms with his identity and getting to know his relatives. "It was something that just closed a gap in my life. I could just move on."

Haloti has not returned to Tonga for more than a brief holiday, but as he gets older, he is becoming more comfortable with being Tongan, feeling he can pick and choose which elements of the culture he will take on. He likes Tongan food but eats "a good mix of both. Every time I go to one of my mates' houses it's always a good mix of both; we just grab what we like out of the Tongan food, then it's always up to McDonalds after that!" He now wears Tongan clothes to church functions, whereas even a few years ago he refused to wear them at all; he is learning to appreciate Tongan music and avidly watches any videos sent from Tonga. He has learned Tongan dance and is in a youth group that performs at functions. About the dancing, he comments, "In a way it's good to keep that culture side with us, the culture." When some cousins from Tonga visited, they taught him how to make an 'umu and roast a pig, skills of which he is very proud. He socializes with Tongans and other Islanders and admits it is important to have other Tongans around. He says if he had to move to a place where no Tongans lived, "I just wouldn't be able to find it easy spending my whole life with others. . . . It's just something that you just need, you need to know is there."

Haloti has received advice from his family about marriage.

> Every time we talk about it, I just tease my mum [and] say, "Mum, how come you didn't come to the wedding yesterday?" She just laughs, but she'll say, "Is it a Tongan girl?" and my grandmother will say, "No, no, if it's a Tongan girl I don't want to know about it!" My grandparents are the ones that have urged me away from Tongan [women]. Which I've found surprising, I found really surprising. I thought they would be the ones who would be straight down the line for Tongan. But my grandmother says that she wants me to marry an Italian or something like that, and my grandfather said he wanted me to marry a Greek. . . . I was shocked, I was speechless, I couldn't say

anything! Well, my grandmother told me to stay away from the Tongans because there's a lot of hassles; family, family this and family
that. Yeah, I'm not too sure, it just depends.

Haloti and his family are indeed a "tight-knit group," although Feleti is
somewhat outside that close circle, having clashed with his parents
throughout his teens. The experiences of this sibling group are similar to
those of many young Tongans throughout the diaspora: they have grown up
with Tongan parents and other kin and been immersed in the life of a Tongan church since infancy, yet they grew up speaking little Tongan, observing
few of the behaviors associated with the Tongan way, and feeling unsure of
their cultural identities. Each child has struggled in his or her own way to secure an identity, and clearly this struggle has been easier for Haloti than for
Feleti. As the youngest child Haloti has benefited from his siblings' resistance and rebellion and the consequent concessions made by his parents as
the family sought the "mix" of cultures with which Haloti seems so comfortable today.

4. Makalesi

At twenty-nine, Makalesi is older than most of the "youth" whose experiences were discussed in chapter 5, but having grown up overseas, her reflections provide important insights into the changes that can occur throughout
childhood and adolescence. In contrast to Haloti's case, her family has remained strongly traditional, and to this day her parents speak little English
and are primarily involved with other Tongans in their daily lives.

Makalesi's maternal grandfather, from the remote Tongan island of Ni-
uafo'ou, was the first in their extended family to migrate. He moved to California in the early 1960s through American Samoa and Hawai'i and subsequently helped all seven of his children migrate to the United States with
their own children. Makalesi's family migrated to the United States via American Samoa. Her father went to the United States first, for a year, then
arranged for the family to join him from Samoa. When they left Tonga,
Makalesi was four years old and had three younger sisters. Another sister was
born during their two-year stay in Samoa, and an adopted son completed the
family. She explains their migration as a means to "strive for betterment for
everything and anything" and believes it has enabled them to reach a higher
standard of education, find better jobs, and enjoy a more comfortable
lifestyle than they could have hoped for in Tonga.

Her parents had it tough as migrants, she recalls. "I could cry thinking of
what Mom and Dad had to go through for a better life here in the States. . . .
I am bawling right now because it is much for me to think about and realize

that I constantly have to make up for this journey that [my parents] went through." The family did not return to Tonga until the 1990s, when Makalesi completed her master's degree and her parents felt "they have accomplished a lot and it was time to show us off to Dad and Mom's family." She thoroughly enjoyed the visit and has since returned four times for holidays, and she would like to work there some time in the future. Throughout their time overseas her parents have sent remittances to Tonga, both money and goods, and Makalesi is continuing that herself, as well as keeping in contact by letter and e-mail. She also keeps up-to-date with events in Tonga by reading Tongan newspapers published in Tonga and overseas, searching for information on the Internet, and watching videos sent by relatives.

Makalesi found it difficult growing up overseas and says that as a child in the United States she "hated anything that had to do with Tonga or being identified as a Tongan. . . . I did not feel welcome anywhere because everyone looked down on me because I am dark brown." Now, her views have changed, and she proclaims, "I am Tongan and that is who I am and I will never be able to undo that fact. I have never described myself as an American Tongan. In my book there is no such thing. I am proud to be a Tongan! It doesn't hurt to live like a *pālangi* as long as you do not forget who you are or where you are from." She says she has tried hard to make sure it is not so difficult for her younger siblings, trying to "make them see that they too are equally important and it makes no difference what skin or country they are from."

When Makalesi's family first settled in California, there were only five other Tongan families in the area. From her grandfather's initial migration, Makalesi calculates that there are now 234 members of their *kāinga* (extended family) living in California; many thousands more from other families have also settled in that state. Makalesi sees members of her extended family and Tongan friends almost daily. Her immediate family is Roman Catholic, and although most of them are still actively involved in the church, Makalesi has ceased attending the Tongan services or any Tongan functions. She explains,

> I am upset because after twenty years, nothing has changed or no new things are added. People are still looking around and gossiping about others and how they look or what they are driving or who they are or who is dating who and so much bullshit. I have no patience and no time for it anymore because I am getting too old and have too much on my plate to deal with these uppity Tongans. I dislike it so much because they do everything for show.

Having been "forced to attend" church throughout her life, she is now "taking a stand": she remains a devout Catholic and so still goes to church, but she chooses to attend the English services.

Being forced to attend church was just one aspect of her strict upbringing. Her mother was particularly keen that the children be brought up in the Tongan way, whereas her father was more willing to make adjustments to living overseas. Makalesi's parents also disagreed about the use of punishment.

> [They] fought all the time because Mom was not happy with Dad's way. But Dad did not believe in disciplining and did not hit or hurt us. He believed in talking things out and also allowing the kids to have a mind and express themselves because they too have opinions. My Dad was very liberal. . . . We would have to be really bad for Dad to punish us. Mom, on the other hand, would slash us at any time because we were girls, so if we looked bad, she would be blamed. Mom punished us a lot. We were always good kids because we know that Mom is there to hand down punishment. That was a big problem for me.

Today, Makalesi defends Tongan parents' use of physical punishment. She describes her relationship with her parents as good, saying she loves and respects them and feels that as the oldest daughter "I am their idol!"

The children were all taught "the Tongan way" in regard to the sexual division of labor, the restrictions on girls' behavior, respect between brothers and sisters, and so on. Makalesi's parents restricted her freedom "until I was out of college and [then] Mom and Dad was a little easy, but still kept me like a prisoner." Of their other expectations of her she says, "They have always taught me in [the Tongan] way and have asked me and all of my sisters to be Tongans. It means that we need to watch what we wear, who we go out with, watch what we say and be strong about our heritage and history." When she was younger, she had difficulty accepting the many demands on her, but this changed as she got older and came to terms with her identity. "*Anga fakatonga* used to be a big problem for me, but now I really enjoy it and love it because it makes me feel strong and proud of my culture, heritage, and my identity." In fact, Makalesi is highly critical of Tongans who do not follow the Tongan way, accusing them of forgetting their values and selling out to the *pālangi* way.

None of the children in Makalesi's family were sent back to Tonga, and her parents disagreed with the practice. "Their thinking is that we came to search for something better for our children, and why would we send them back? . . . They want us to learn and enjoy the new world, the *pālangis'* world and learn and gain what we can from it." Makalesi feels it can be good "for troubled kids because they need to get into the Tongan culture and really identify with it," but she is adamant that she would never send her own children to Tonga. Rather than send Makalesi and her siblings to Tonga, their parents told them many stories of Tongan history and of their own childhoods "every day of my life! . . . It is an everyday word in our household: Tonga this, Tonga that!"

Although Makalesi's parents raised their children to identify strongly as Tongan, she and her siblings are equally comfortable in Tongan and non-Tongan contexts. They are fluent in Tongan and English, speaking Tongan with their parents and older relatives and English with each other and outside the home. In their constant shifts between contexts they eat both Tongan and non-Tongan food, wear both Western and Tongan clothes, have friends from many different ethnic backgrounds, and enjoy a wide variety of music. The ease with which they shift between Tongan and American contexts is largely because of their involvement with the latter through school, sports, work, and other activities such as after-school clubs and choir. When she was younger, Makalesi's parents were unhappy with the idea of her being involved in extracurricular activities such as sports, believing she should concentrate only on her schoolwork. She persisted, however, and at the age of fourteen also worked part-time in order to contribute financially to the family. Her parents' emphasis on education nevertheless did have an effect, as she is now studying for her doctorate. She told me with pride that she is the first of sixty-three grandchildren to attend college and obtain a degree.

Makalesi's education, the disagreements between her parents about how much to adjust to the American way, and her own experiences within the Tongan community in her local area have all contributed to her rather critical view of other Tongans. She believes overseas Tongans are "greedy and money hungry," unwilling to ask for help when they need it due to pride and shyness, and says they have "lost all meaning of their identity."

While she is certain she will teach her own children what she sees as "traditional" Tongan values and behavior, since she regards these so highly herself, she plans to temper this with other values she has acquired, such as imagination, self-motivation, and gender equality. These values, combined with having "every right to decide for themselves," are actually the opposite of what children are taught in "traditional" Tongan families, but Makalesi is convinced she can find a balance and help her children to succeed in the United States while holding on to their Tongan identities.

As for marriage, she says, "I have thought about this day and night for the last five years. It hurts sometimes, but I have learned to overcome my dislikes about Tongan men and deal with the fact that I will be married to one some-day. It has to be a Tongan man because Mom and Dad are still alive. . . . I am always considering my parents because they have literally gone through a lot for me and all of us." As the oldest child, she feels she has to follow their wishes but also admits that "only a Tongan man can relate and understand me and my ways of doing things, but not a *pālangi*." For now, she remains single and, after her years of struggle, lives comfortably in both Tongan and American contexts, devoting herself to her studies and enjoying her hard-won pride in being Tongan.

6

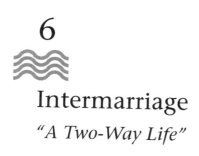

Intermarriage
"A Two-Way Life"

WHEREVER TONGANS SETTLE, IN CITIES AND TOWNS throughout the diaspora, they are never entirely isolated from the wider society in which they live, and they interact with people from a range of backgrounds in many contexts, such as school, church, work, and at social venues. Sometimes these interactions lead to marriage, and today there are intermarriages between Tongans and people of many different nationalities.[1] An increasing number of these marriages include non-European partners. In Japan, for example, a small community is emerging of Tongans married to Japanese. This diversity of relationships is further complicated by the fact that in many cases *both* partners are living in a country to which they, or their parents, have migrated.

Research into patterns of intermarriage has identified a range of factors influencing individuals' marriage choices. Paul Spickard found that structural factors are important, such as the size of the ethnic community and the sex ratio within it (1989, 344). But cultural factors are also important, and "a group's own perception of its relative social status, the general society's toleration of intergroup relationships, and different ethnic groups' images of each other all seem to have played parts in determining how high the rate of intermarriage would be and who would marry whom" (Spickard 1989, 344). Spickard notes that additional factors, such as "community supervision" also have to be looked at—the informal social controls like gossip and harassment that act as deterrents to intermarriage (1989, 362). As we will see, all of these factors operate in the case of marriages between Tongans and others.

Janet Penny and Siew-Ean Khoo argue that the proportion of intraethnic marriages—those within one ethnic group—rises as the pool of potential partners within that group increases and as ethnic "self-awareness" increases among the younger generations (1996, 33). However, the opposite trend, toward an increasing number of intermarriages, can also be identified, due to a lessening of ethnic tensions and the greater "assimilation" of second and subsequent generations. Both trends can be observed among the Tongans of Melbourne, with those in the more insular group of recent migrants tending to prefer intramarriage, whereas the children of the first wave of migrants and the kin who followed them seem to have a greater acceptance of intermarriage. Of course, ethnicity is only one of many factors—others include age, education, and social background—that can influence marriage choices (Roy and Hamilton 1997).

Since the 1980s the rate of intermarriage has increased in many of the Western nations with high rates of immigration, and subsequently there is a rapidly growing population of children with "mixed" ancestry. In the United States fully three-quarters of all marriages now occur between people of different ethnic backgrounds (Small 1997, 233, n. 44; see Alba 2000; Root 1992; Zack 1995). In Australia, at least 60 percent of the population is now ethnically mixed: "For the next generation of these unions, the children will not so much be blends, or blends of blends, but the nation's new demographic core, forging a new Australian identity (Clark 2000, 4). This trend is making "multicultural" a less appropriate way to describe the Australian population, since the concept is centered on the idea of maintaining distinct ethnic groups. The gradual merging of these groups through intermarriage is creating the hybridity that increasingly characterizes the population not just of Australia but of many Western nations.

Pacific Islanders throughout the diaspora tend to have relatively high rates of intermarriage. The rates were especially high during the early waves of migration, when marriage partners of the same ethnicity were difficult to find and intermarriage was a means of settling permanently overseas. For marriages occurring in Australia in 1975–1979, intermarriage rates for women born in Fiji were 81 percent, for other commonwealth Pacific countries (including Tonga) 69.4 percent, and for other Pacific countries 94.9 percent (Price 1987, 196). Elsewhere similar patterns were found; for example, Cluny Macpherson reports that by the early 1970s one in three Samoans in New Zealand was marrying a non-Samoan, and by 1991 approximately 32 percent of Samoans born in New Zealand had one non-Samoan parent (1997, 93). For Tongans in New Zealand, 1996 census data indicate that over a third of marriages are with non-Tongans, and 25 percent of individuals of Tongan descent recorded two ethnic backgrounds, while a further

12 percent recorded three (Statistics New Zealand 1998, 12). The 2000 U.S. census showed Pacific Islanders had the highest proportion of all "races" reporting more than one race,[2] and some 25 percent of those who identified themselves as Tongan also reported one or more other races or Pacific Islander groups (U.S. Census Bureau 2001b, 9). The U.S. census shows that 27,713 individuals reported being solely Tongan, while 2,227 also had ancestry from one or more other Pacific Islander groups and 6,900 were Tongan in combination with other races.

Obtaining accurate statistics for Tongan intermarriages in Australia is impossible, given the problems of statistical collection and the categorization of Tongans simply as "Other" in so many data sets. Few studies of Tongans in Australia have considered the issue of intermarriage, but Frances Finney found that of a hundred married couples (including de facto relationships and separated partners) in Canberra, 52 percent had intermarried (1999, 172). This is slightly higher than in my sample in Melbourne, in which 47.8 percent (or 54 out of 113) of marriages and former marriages were intermarriages.[3]

Within the Melbourne sample, there were forty-two currently intermarried couples living in the households. Of these, sixteen were Tongan men married to Australian women (including one Tongan Australian man), and ten were Tongan women married to Australian men (with one Tongan Australian woman). Marriages between Tongans and partners other than Australians (six Tongan men and four Tongan women) included individuals from a range of nationalities: English, German, Greek German, Greek, Indian, Maltese, New Zealander, and Samoan. The higher rate of Tongan men in my sample intermarrying was also found in Finney's study (1999, 172). The intermarried adults' ages range from eighteen to seventy, and they had a total of forty-eight children, ranging in age from under a year to twenty-seven. Eleven of the couples had no children.

Tongan Attitudes toward Intermarriage

Even before Europeans found their way to Tonga, intermarriages had taken place between Tongans and others, particularly Samoans and Fijians (Kaeppler 1978). When Europeans began to arrive, as traders, missionaries, beachcombers, and so on, some of them formed relationships with Tongans—nearly always Tongan women—and sometimes children were born to these unions. Even today in Tonga there are a number of large extended families bearing the surnames of some of these early European visitors and settlers. From the beginning of European contact, many Tongans viewed the *papālangi* (now usually shortened to *pālangi*) as high-status persons, and such unions were seen as prestigious, much in the way that unions between commoner women and chiefly men were advantageous to the women's families.

Given Tonga's unique history in the Pacific, with an absence of formal colonization and large-scale European settlement, Tongans generally have little or no sense of resentment toward Europeans for past wrongs. Combined with the central importance of Christianity to most Tongans and a general appreciation of the missionaries who brought it to their land, this has meant that intermarriage with *pālangi* is still viewed positively by many in Tonga. The children of such marriages may be treated as somewhat special by their extended Tongan families, particularly if they have the fair skin that is typically regarded as more beautiful than dark skin. This preference for fair skin is, of course, another reason for the popularity of intermarriage, particularly in the case of Tongan men marrying *pālangi* women. Yet another reason for the acceptance of intermarriage is that it is often seen as a means of migrating from Tonga, so that while many intermarriages are clearly based on love and the desire of both partners to spend their lives together, there are some in which the non-Tongan partner is simply a "passport" out of Tonga for his or her spouse. Some of the non-Tongan partners accept this; Gillian, thirty-nine, still happily married to her Tongan husband of many years, commented of their marriage, "Husband basically was looking for a green-card marriage—wife was looking for love and adventure."

Decisions to marry non-Tongans are influenced to some extent by the attitudes of the wider society. In different places and at different times, attitudes to intermarriage can vary greatly, and while they may be tolerated, even celebrated, by some, others will strongly disapprove. In Australia, as in many other Western nations, there was a long period when intermarriage was frowned upon. Seini, who arrived in Australia while the "White Australia" policy was in place, commented, "I remember the minister who spoke at our wedding said about ten years ago this wouldn't be happening, because of the white policy." Even at one time, and within one country, different attitudes can be found to coexist: Jane says she has rarely experienced any negative comments about her "mixed marriage," yet her own grandfather refused to have Christmas with the family after her marriage "because he wasn't going to have Christmas with that black man!"

Some non-Tongans intending to marry Tongans find that well-meaning friends and relatives will warn them of the problems they will face. Julie received such advice when she was planning to marry Samuela. "I knew a few friends that told me all the bad things about the Tongans and all the good things, and I sort of weighed them all up and wondered whether I could, if I could you know put up with those bad things, so to speak." Her friends were also "quite shocked" that Julie, employed at a professional level, "married a Tongan who's got no qualifications, who works in [a factory] and everything." One of the "bad things" Julie's friends referred to is domestic violence—the stereotype that Islander men bash their wives. Before Viliami, twenty-six, married Jenny, twenty-nine, his Australian wife, her mother's friends warned her that Tongan men had a reputation for beating their wives. Kerry found that when the movie *Once Were Warriors* was released, people assumed her Tongan partner, Lopeti, must also be violent toward her, like the Maori men the film portrayed.

Kerry and Lopeti have encountered racism, as when people have made comments to them "referring to my partner as a black, you know, so and so, and to go back to his own country and stuff." When I asked Julie if she had ever been treated unfairly because she was married to a Tongan, she replied, "Well, as soon as you tell them you're married to a Tongan you can just see the face drop, you know. And sort of—I know when I'm with my husband sometimes I don't get the service that I normally would if I was on my own or with another *pālangi*."

Interestingly, the same claims about the problems of marrying Tongans are made by some Tongans themselves in urging their children or other young family members to marry an "outsider." The most common argument given to Tongan women against marrying a Tongan man is that their husbands could be violent toward them. Some are also warned that their husbands will expect them to do all the housework. In a similar vein, Tongan women are warned that Tongan husbands will be "lazy" and not strive for success in their jobs, hence a non-Tongan partner is seen as more likely to be a good provider for the family. Both males and females are also warned that they will be "marrying the whole family" and therefore be subjected to many demands for financial and other assistance. Some young people come to this conclusion for themselves; for example, Lopini said she would like to marry a Tongan but was concerned about the *kavenga* (obligations) to his family. "Once you marry him, you're marrying the whole family;

they're constantly annoying you, or they'll be asking for money or dumping their kids at you or [expecting] their family to come [and stay]."

Even the children of intermarriages are sometimes warned by their Tongan relatives not to marry Tongans, although their own parents tend to be less concerned about their choice of partner. When I asked Jane whether she would like her children to marry Tongans or non-Tongans, she replied,

> I honestly don't mind. I know the Tongan side, and [the Tongan] grandma was very strong on this; she used to repeatedly say to the children, "You must not marry Tongans." She was a thinking person, though, she was a character, she really was. Because she believed it was too much of a burden. Okay? And she wanted them to be free of it. But no, it doesn't worry me, I think there are good and bad in all societies and its just whatever the individual is like; it doesn't worry me at all. Chinese or anything, I don't care. I mean I think the common, shared beliefs and the shared values and things are more important than what race you're from.

Intermarriage can be seen as a way of avoiding the "burdens" of familial obligations or as a way of coping with them, depending on the individual's perspective. As Macpherson found for Samoans in New Zealand,

> Some explained their decisions as a means of ensuring that they could continue to support their families because their spouses were sympathetic to Samoan culture and because their incomes were not subject to claims from spouses' families as would have been the case if they had taken Samoan partners. Others explained their decisions as a means of reducing their commitments to their own families, by arguing that their non-Samoan partners were unsympathetic to the requests of kin. (1997, 94, n. 20)

The idea that a non-Tongan partner may not comply with the demands of the extended family is one reason that some Tongan parents *do* urge their children to marry Tongans. Also, just as "a few bad apples" have contributed to negative stereotypes about Tongans, some *pālangi* spouses have created a negative view of *pālangi* more generally.

An American woman expressed her concerns on the Kava Bowl forum that her daughter's plans to marry a Tongan had met with some resistance from other Tongans. A *pālangi* man married to a Tongan woman replied sympathetically, "It's a sad thing, to hit that anti-palangi feeling in your intended in-laws. But having seen many mixed marriages start (and some fail) and to see the . . . well . . . the quality of palangi that the Tongans seem to marry, there's no wonder there is apprehension in the family. It took much time and many experiences (good and bad), not to mention trips to Tonga, to bring my family (my in-laws if you like) around to the fact that I was in for the long haul" (KB 14.9.96). This "anti-palangi feeling" also can be understood in terms of fears that *pālangi* partners will have a detrimental influence on their Tongan spouses. As Lucy, a Tongan who has observed intermarriages in her family, claimed, "It seems like the non-Tongan drains the Tongan culture from the Tongan."

Other Tongans recognize that each marriage is different and that intermarriages can work or not depending on the people involved. A Tongan minister in Melbourne who has had considerable experience dealing with intermarried couples said,

> Some people think of mixed marriages as a bad thing. It can be bad, but it can be a beautiful thing, I think, depending on the makeup; if it clicks, it's a beautiful thing because you can choose the best of both worlds. But if it doesn't, it highlights the problems. . . . I think it's a richer makeup of parents, but if one becomes a pain, then it's not worth having. . . . Like I said before, when the mixed marriages click, it's beautiful, it's much better than a marriage with just one culture, because you can pick, you can walk into two different worlds with no problems, but if it doesn't work, you know, it's almost—the other becomes an enemy, so it's like entering an enemy territory, and that's sad because it shouldn't be like that. That's why I feel if it can be maintained and encouraged, then those children of mixed marriages can be proud of both cultures, and you say to them, look, you are better off than someone who just grew up in one culture.

In his study of intermarriage in the United States, Spickard found that there were "hierarchies of preferences," with some groups regarded as acceptable sources of marriage partners, others as conceivable but unlikely, and others as nearly inconceivable (1989, 364). He showed that this has changed over time, through generations and through the course of U.S. history.

> [E]ach group has a discernible and relatively stable hierarchy of preferences, determined by the group's historical ideas about itself and others, and by its evolving position on the American ethnic scene. . . .
> How far down the hierarchy an individual is willing to go depends on a variety of other social circumstances, such as generation removed from the Old Country in the case of immigrant, the degree to which other groups are perceived as being compatible in culture and status, and external restraints placed by the dominant ethnic group. (1989, 364)

Many Tongans have the kind of hierarchy of preference Spickard describes. In most cases *pālangi* are considered most acceptable and people with dark skin, such as African Americans and Australian Aborigines as least acceptable. Between those two extremes fall other groups: for example, in the United States Mexicans are considered to be somewhere in the middle of the spectrum of preferences.

A young Tongan woman who dates African American men wrote on the KB, "From the reactions I've encountered upon the Tongan Elders, they look up to the 'Whites/Mexican' or anything that's lighter than the normal Tongan skin (color) than they do the Afro-American. I can't believe the racism that goes on within polynesian cultures" (KB 21.12.96). 'Ofa, who lives in Melbourne but has spent some time living with her parents in the United States, commented that her mother does not want her to marry an African American. When I asked why, she replied, "I think most Tongans are prejudiced. Not prejudiced, but very—like, if your skin's light then you're this beautiful girl, and if you're dark you're this mongrel!"

These attitudes mean that intermarriages can be adversely affected by the negative reaction of the Tongan family. A Tongan woman married to an African described her marriage as "a rocky and hellish road" because "I have been trying to force my family and culture to accept me and my marriage" (KB 20.2.97). She said she now focuses on the marriage and believes that if her family really loves her they will "see beyond color lines and culture differences." In her post she describes her feelings of guilt: "I was so caught up in everyone else seeing that he was a real human being like me, but I degraded him by making him try to be accepted by my people. . . . What makes my culture more important that he must jump through hoops so they can see his color of skin is not a defect of humanity?" She now avoids "the constant hum of rumors and degrading comments" and seldom sees her family. "Now, I have a beautiful little girl. And I will not subject her to the pain of trying to be accepted by my family because her skin has a tint of black." She feels that choosing to stay married

> has cost me my culture and my family. This is a choice I have made, only because my family and culture has made me choose between the family I have made, and the family I am from. My daughter will KNOW of the Tongan culture, but I will of course leave this "black thing" out. Instead, I will stress teaching her the culture that loves her and accepts her: her father's. And in doing so, I also understand that the only tie she will have with the Tongan culture will be knowing that "her mother is from there" and occasional family gatherings. . . . It took a lot of beating by the ones I love to finally come to this point, but I love my husband and daughter too much to make them feel like outcasts by my family. I just hope by her generation things would have changed and she would be able to be one with her Polynesian heritage. (KB 20.2.97)

Young Tongans who identify with African Americans as marginalized and disempowered often have a completely different perspective from that of their parents' generation. A young woman living in an area with no other Polynesians and who has been dating an African American man expressed this view simply: "I've finally found another culture other than Palangi, the culture of Blacks . . . Uli uli's. . . . Their race is different from ours, I realize this, but I find it comforting to know that I share a similar trait with them, which is, being OF COLOR!!!!" (KB 8.3.97).

In her study of the attitudes and beliefs about intermarriage of second-generation middle-class Chinese and Koreans in the United States, Nazli Kibria suggests that "collective identity shifts" can occur over time, affecting the way intermarriages are evaluated (1997, 525). Her study shows that the second generation is developing a pan-Asian American identity, based partly on the notion of "Asian values" (respect for elders, emphasis on education) that are seen as shared by all Asian American groups. Intermarriage between these groups is increasingly acceptable to them, whereas they were frowned upon by their parents and grandparents. This pan-Asian American identity is also based on a shared sense of exclusion from mainstream society and limited opportunities for integration, as well as a sense of difference from the "morally decaying" white American society.

Conflicting with these attitudes is the ideal of retaining racial and even lineage purity, complicated by romantic ideals. Kibria explains, "[T]he ideology of romantic love, intermingled with the ideas of individual choice and freedom, served as a constant backdrop to the second-generation's ruminations on the 'boundary dilemmas' of outmarriage, even among those who expressed a strong and conscious commitment to limiting their choice of partner along racial and/or ethnic lines" (1997, 527). Kibria's findings are relevant to second-generation Tongans, for whom a Polynesian or Islander identity is in tension with the desire of some to maintain the "purity" of Tongan "blood" and be true to their Tongan heritage, and with the preference of yet others for intermarriage with *pālangi*. Complicating all of these attitudes are ideals of romantic love and happiness, freedom, and a desire for social mobility.

Some second-generation Tongans also have a growing awareness of the power relations that can underlie Tongan-*pālangi* relationships, particularly in the United States. One aspect of these power relations is the way *pālangi* women are (usually unwittingly) helping perpetuate a sexual double standard where young Tongan women are expected to remain virtuous but where Tongan men's promiscuity is tacitly accepted. A young woman on the KB complained about this, adding, "What I'm trying to say is, they can go around and date those palangi girls, and with this day and age you know they will do anything for a Tongan man, but when they want to settle down that's when they look for a 'Tongan' girl with expectations of an angel? I honestly don't think it's fair and that the 'Tongan' woman deserves the same RESPECT!!!" (KB 18.2.98).

The KB has been the site of many complaints by Tongan women about Tongan men forming relationships with *pālangi* women. One young woman wrote,

> It's sad to see the Tongan brothas look to white women instead of the sistas for love. Because no one can love another Tongan like a Tongan—we all know where we've been and where it is our future needs to take us. It's a hard thing to love another Tongan because this culture teaches us to hate ourselves. To all the Tongans out there—good luck and stay true, and to all the Tongan sisters who are betrayed by the brothas—remember if you can't find them here, go back to the

Motherland. The boys in Tonga know who they are that's why they are not afraid of our beauty! (KB 22.1.97)

Some KB participants have argued that Tongans who marry *pālangi* are influenced by dominant ideologies that value "whiteness." A Tongan woman, speaking of intermarriages between Tongans and *pālangi,* said,

> For me this brings up questions of aesthetics, desire and one's positionality within power stratifications. What are the ramifications behind a Pacific person, desiring a Caucasian? For a Pacific Islander to state reasons such as, "I am more compatible with a Caucasian", or "skin color doesn't matter in love", is very idealistic and negates the power disparities within issues such as race, gender and class. (KB 22.10.98)

Another woman argued along similar lines, saying Tongan men choose *pālangi* women because they are taught "white is right" and that intermarriage will help them succeed. She added,

> From what I've heard from Tongan males is that we Tongan and "colored girls" have attitudes and our personalities are not as complying or subservient like that of a white girl. So in this sense can we also add that perhaps our so called "brothers" are seduced by the lure of complacency without responsibility and in a different sense lured by the "cultureless" and shifting allegiance of the West? Are our males believing the "hype", and buying into the Western beauty paradigms, thus neglecting themselves and in reality all of us both male and female alike? (KB 30.12.96)

She further asks in relation to Tongan women involved with black men: "[B]ecause image is a tool used to sustain a dominating politics I wonder if black males' desire for us over their black sisters is because of the same reason our Tongan brothers desire white women?"

Some male participants on the KB have reacted strongly to accusations that they prefer *pālangi* women, and one took the opportunity to vent his feelings when a post appeared, apparently written by a *pālangi* woman expressing her attraction to Polynesian men (KB 14.9.97). His reply, with the heading "no thanks white girls try some white boys," read,

> White girl, its funny how your only credentials is being white. Did you think that we as brown men would just fall all over your feet like

we have been taught? Check again babe. A real Tongan girl is all that. She is spiritual, kind and physically beautiful. She is strong and is smart. Her strength is what keeps our families alive. Yes we Tongan men may go to white girls every now and then but its not for love. (KB 15.9.97)

Those who argue against "mixed" relationships often claim Tongan couples have a better understanding of one another, with some qualifications. For example, a young Tongan American woman wrote on the Tongan History Association forum that

I have witnessed firsthand the cultural problems encountered by my parents and I have no wish to repeat these in my own marriage. While cultural compatibility is just a part of a successful marriage, to me it is an integral part. Racial congruence, however, does not necessarily equate cultural similarity. There are definite differences between a Tongan man raised exclusively in Tonga and a Tongan woman raised solely in the United States. Significant differences also exist between Tongan individuals raised in the same country. (THA 19.10.98)

She adds that she is in a relationship with a Tongan man, saying, "While I used to think we'd be more compatible with our racial equivalents, that is not the case—at least for me. Cultural equivalency has greater impact. Our relationship is far from perfect but my ability to communicate with him is at a level I haven't been able to duplicate with anyone else. . . . I attribute this to shared values, experiences, race, and a similar upbringing."

The young Tongans I interviewed had similarly divergent views about intermarriage. There was a noticeable gender difference, with more females stating they would prefer to marry Tongans, a pattern reflected in the lower rate of intermarriages for females in the Melbourne sample.[4] Veisinia stated, "I'd love to marry a cute Tongan or half-caste Tongan. Because they already know the Tongan way or can adapt to it easier." Lesieli said, "I'd like to find a Tongan husband. I don't know, I guess they can just communicate better with my parents—that's what I think now." Lusi also said she would prefer to marry a Tongan. "I guess they give you that kind of, you know, like you've got so much in common with them, so you can kind of understand each other a lot more easier than trying to make a *pālangi* comprehend the Tongan way. Not so much—I'm not too Tongan, but I've always admired the Tongan way. So that's why I'd like to marry a Tongan." She added that she would prefer a Tongan who has been in Australia only for a short time, who would be very familiar with the Tongan way. 'Ofa wants to marry a Tongan as well, but one who is "not too Tongan!" Her ideal man would have grown up in Australia, "but still know his Tongan side at the same time and know how to mix it up. You know, we can't follow the Tongan rule in every way. Like tradition and stuff like that . . . and everything has to be really equal. Because I find that most marriages, especially Tongan couples, the men dominate the women. And it's sad, but that's what I do *not* want to happen to me." Susana wanted to find a partner who would "know the best of the two cultures." One of the males who said he would choose a Tongan woman echoed the others' views when he explained it was because "Tongan women are better . . . because they understand the Tongan ways."

Ideas about whether or not to marry a Tongan can change over time. American-born Bianca said,

> Growing up I dated mostly *pālangi* guys—not because I didn't like Tongan guys, but because at my school that's all that was available. Most of the Tongan guys at my school or in my community were either related to me or I didn't like them. As I grow older I tend to be more strongly attracted to Tongans, not that I don't like other nationalities, but I feel more comfortable with a Tongan male. It didn't really matter before if I married a non-Tongan, but as I get older I think more and more strongly about marrying within my race. Not only would they understand more about Tongan culture, but I would like to grow old together with someone who might want to go back to Tonga and retire.

Some who said they would prefer to marry a Tongan were still ambivalent about it, mainly because they are aware of some of the more negative views of family obligations. Vika, who has struggled with the issue of her Tongan identity, said, "Marrying a Tongan, he will help me understand where I come from. And some issues. While a white person wouldn't. You'd have to go very deep with a white person to make them understand." However, later in our interview, when talking about family problems Tongans experience, she said, "When someone is married to a guy or girl, they are not only marrying that person, they're marrying the whole family. I think that's the worst thing." Ambivalence can also be due to a sense of obligation to meet parents' wishes. While most young people declared they would be free to make their own choice of marriage partner, there were some who felt their parents would expect them to marry a Tongan and that they should comply, as we saw with Makalesi (Case Study 4).

Experiences of Intermarriage

A few of the couples I interviewed who had intermarried had met in Tonga, when the non-Tongan spouse was working or visiting there, but most had met overseas, through work, church, or at social functions. Most said that they had not set out to find a "different" partner but rather fell in love and, with more or less support from their respective families, decided to marry. Once they were married, they had to deal with their cultural differences, not only in their own relationship, but with their families and friends as well. The following post on the KB aptly captures the difficulties posed by some extended families:

> I have noticed with some mixed marriages, it is the influences of the families and in-laws more than anything that creates the most problem, and they strike at the heart of the couples' insecurity by harping on the "you're just too different!! . . . it will never work . . . he/she is not like you . . . he/she doesn't understand us/you . . ." This creates a most unfortunate situation where the trust gradually erodes and the differences become greater and the gap between the married couple becomes wider as they both polarize with their particular families for support when they should be in the middle holding each other up. These problems are not confined to just mixed marriages but there are more differences for the outsiders to pick on. (KB 26.11.98)

Family members may not actively disapprove of the union but can make things difficult by withdrawing from the couple. Viliami and Jenny told me that soon after their marriage they organized a barbeque and invited some of their relatives, but none of Viliami's family came except a male relative also married to an Australian. This latter couple told them that they, too, had found a reluctance on the part of many Tongans to become involved "in the *pālangi* things" because of anxiety about not being sure what to bring, what to wear, how to behave, and so on. Friends of one or both partners can also withdraw if they are unsure how to deal with the "mixed" relationship, leaving the couple feeling isolated.

Intermarriage has been described as "an intimate performance of juggling identities and the ideologies associated with them" (Breger and Hill 1998b, 28), which aptly describes the situation for Tongan intermarriages, each of which is a unique "performance." Within their own relationships, and with their children, the couples I interviewed had dealt with cultural difference in many different ways and formed a kind of continuum between an Australian and a Tongan orientation. Some of the couples remained happy together because one partner had effectively surrendered his or her culture within the marriage. Such was the case with Seini, whose adjustment to her marriage was made easier by her initial experiences in Australia in the 1960s. "I lived with a *pālangi* family, and it gave me the idea of how to cook the dinner and cakes, and [they] went on with their daily routine and it sort of gave me an idea about it." Once she was married, Seini was determined to fit into her husband's society. "I made up my mind the day I got married that I would make my life here, this is my life; whatever happens to me, I'll be buried here, and this is home." After a long wait to be granted citizenship, she was finally able to attend a citizenship ceremony. "And since that day, I never regretted it, because I feel that's my choice to marry an Australian and this is my home, you know. It, wherever I go, it's funny, even [when I] go to Tonga, but every time I come back here I feel, oh, gee, I'm home." Later she added, "I don't want to forget that I am Tongan, but I want to be happy the way I am."

Seini has always cooked Australian food for her husband and children, and within their home their lives are very Australian. Her husband has never visited Tonga or learned any Tongan language and is only marginally involved with her Tongan relatives. Seini is fiercely protective of his Australianness, getting angry when Tongans speak Tongan around him and thus exclude him from the conversation. Her own Tongan-language ability has declined during her life in Australia, and she now prefers to speak in English. She admitted that "I have to do my writing in English and then I sit down and try to translate it into Tongan. . . . With English I can whip it up so fast and so quick, but with my Tongan—but I've got no choice, I have to speak English in this household, all the time."

Although her lifestyle is primarily Australian, Seini does retain her involvement with other Tongans, particularly through her extended family, and over the years she has had various relatives stay in her home, either new immigrants or young people experiencing family problems. She is also active in a Tongan church but admits to feeling awkward at occasions such as funerals because she is unsure of the proper etiquette. She has also come to dislike some of the food popular with Tongans and admitted that when she is given tins of corned beef (a common gift at important events) she feeds it to her dog. Seini described her ability to fit into both the Tongan and Australian circles with which she is involved as "a two way life. . . . When I go to the Tongans I just make myself to suit with what they are doing." This ability to move between the two "worlds" is common; another woman explained that in different situations, "I have to think which hat to put on."

Seini's husband is not unusual in his lack of knowledge about Tonga and the Tongan way. Julie, married for several years to Samuela, admitted, "I think I've got a romantic view of Tonga. I think I just see coconut trees and white sand and beach and everything, and lots of fruit, fresh fruit and fish. And that's about all. So I don't know very much about Tonga." Julie has now turned to the Internet to find out more and says of this source of information,

> I think it's great. It's an avenue that the *pālangi* can understand. Because they can get different views and from Tongans who, you know, understand their own culture, and *pālangis* who have been through it. And you just get so much feedback, and I just thought it was a real eye-opener, and I was, you know, I couldn't wait to get on it every time just to find out more about the Tongan people, and just out of interest. Not just because my husband's Tongan, but out of interest, really.

A few who marry Tongans have some knowledge about Tonga and the Tongan way already, having visited or worked in Tonga. Others visit Tonga after their marriage and actively seek out other information. The extent to which the non-Tongan partners attempt to learn to speak Tongan varies considerably. In two of the Melbourne couples the Australian wife spoke fluent Tongan as a result of living in Tonga, but most of the other non-Tongan spouses spoke no more than a few words. Some partners admitted they understood quite a bit of Tongan but were reluctant to try speaking Tongan themselves.

Finding ways to remain Tongan and maintain a marriage with a non-Tongan can be difficult. There is a widespread perception that intermarried Tongans tend to drift away from their Tongan "roots." This is true to some extent, as intermarried couples are far more likely than Tongan couples to disengage from other Tongans, even moving to locations where there are no Tongans. Intermarried couples are also more likely to buy a home rather than rent and to focus on saving and meeting the needs of their nuclear family unit. In some cases the non-Tongan partner is from an ethnic group that places a similar emphasis on family obligations, hence they are sympathetic to the concept of *kavenga*. I also found that many of the non-Tongan spouses insisted their partner was not a "typical" Tongan, which they believed made it easier for them to negotiate cultural differences. For example, when I asked one woman how she and her husband dealt with different ideas about gender relations, she claimed he was "not a typical Tongan chauvinist."

In contrast to Seini's marriage, Kerry and Lopeti have adopted a more Tongan orientation, partly due to Lopeti's strong ties to his Tongan family. Kerry feels Lopeti "pulls" her toward the Tongan way, and as the child of migrants herself, with no strong attachment to her parents' cultural background, she is happy for her to children "to have something to follow. . . . I think it's good for them to go to the Tongan culture." At first, Kerry found interactions with her affines difficult, particularly because of the restrictions placed on the brother-sister relationship. She found it hard to understand why she could joke and swear with Lopeti's sisters except if he or his brothers were present. "And it astounds me, like when I was first with him it astounded me how the sisters could just change completely. Not say 'shit' and nothing to slip out, it would astound me. But now that I've been around so long I do it myself. So I can change roles straightaway because I've learnt along the way."

Kerry has also been trying hard to learn Tongan and is now finding she uses common Tongan phrases with her daughter. "Because I'm with the Tongans so much and I hear it so much it just automatically comes out without me even realizing." Increasingly, she is identifying with her Tongan affines, and she told me,

> I know that I don't have any Tongan blood, but in some ways I consider myself a Tongan because I associate with the Tongans so much and I mean I even speak a little bit. . . . I think I'd be considered as a Tongan by some people. Maybe others wouldn't think that. The people that don't know me real well or the Tongans that don't know me real well. But by my partner's family they'd probably consider me Tongan. . . . I am not a full Tongan, even though I do consider myself a part-Tongan.

Julie also went through a stage early in her marriage when she tried to identify as Tongan.

> I remember I really enjoyed Tongan, really wanted to be a Tongan, and I used to call myself a white Tongan. And I used to wear the, at special occasions like the *misinale* or whatever, I used to wear a *ta'ovala* and things like that because I was very interested in Tongan culture and that, but, yeah, I don't really want to be Tongan because I know I'll never be a Tongan because I've noticed that you know Tongans will always see you as a *pālangi* trying to be a Tongan. They would never accept you as a Tongan.

Julie and her husband are still involved with his family and a Tongan church, but their daily lifestyle is predominantly Australian. When I visited their newly bought home, there were no traces of Tongan influence apart from some taro and yam served with our meal.

Sioeli's wife, Kylie, thirty-one, said he had changed over the course of their marriage, becoming increasingly focused on their own nuclear family rather than his extended family. She laughed, "Oh, I remember if I ever said anything bad about his family he used to go off his brain, but now, maybe he's used to it, he doesn't worry about it." Like Kerry's initial difficulty understanding the brother-sister relationship, Kylie found some aspects of the Tongan way difficult to deal with. She told me of her shock when Sioeli's brother asked for her fourth child soon after she was born. Sioeli wanted to accede to the request, but she refused. She was telling me her brother-in-law thought they would not want the child, since it was their fourth girl, when her husband interjected, saying, "No, he didn't mean we wouldn't want her! No, he's got two boys and no daughter." Kylie and Sioeli have very little involvement with Tongans other than a few of his relatives, and like Julie and Samuela, their home shows no Tongan influences.

There are many aspects of "the Tongan way" that can cause difficulties for couples. Not only is the avoidance between brothers and sisters sometimes hard for partners to understand, but the higher status of the sisters (and father's sisters) and their ability to make demands on their brothers (or nephews) for time, money, and services can also be the source of considerable resentment. Many of the non-Tongan spouses expressed concern about the general level of support expected from them, particularly financial demands. Julie said, "I don't mind sending money home to the mother and father particularly. But all the rest can go and do some work. But I don't mind helping out for education. I think that's important. And for clothing. But I just don't like sending it just for it to be wasted on food. But health or anything I don't mind either." Like several others, Julie complained about the amount of money spent on phone calls to Tonga and the general differences in priorities for the use of their income.

The issue of Tongan family members borrowing items and not returning them also cropped up in several interviews, as did the problems that can arise when Tongan relatives actually live with the couple. There were also many humorous stories of cross-cultural misunderstandings and incidents that highlighted the couple's different backgrounds. Jane related a number of stories about her mother-in-law visiting from Tonga and their mixed communications and cultural differences, such as her mother-in-law's insistence on rearranging the living room furniture to sit around the perimeter of the room, as in homes in Tonga, or her frequent sweeping of the front lawn, which killed the carefully nurtured grass.

Most of the non-Tongan partners I spoke with had both positive and negative views of Tongans. Jane admires Tongans' support of one another within families, their generosity, and their gregariousness. However, she is also quite critical of Tongans, saying,

> In this society they are sort of incapable of organizing themselves financially, most of them I think, because that generous side to their nature; they never get ahead and they're sort of in trouble in that way. Oh, and their lack of reliability. They're very, very hard to work with. And their lack of consideration for others in terms of that sort of thing. They just take you for granted.

Others also mentioned financial problems caused by fund-raising and the Tongan refusal to ask for help outside their own community, but at the same time they valued Tongan generosity and friendliness.

Julie, who saw gossip as the only negative quality of Tongans, expressed many other spouses' views when she said,

> I think they're just very friendly, very open. Your house is open to anybody. I think family. Family plays an important part. It can be good or it can be bad. But from what I've gathered, from what my experience has been, it's been pretty good. If I'm ever sick or whatever the sisters sort of come over and look after me. Or send somebody and they stay with me for a week and do all my cooking sort of thing. So I'm pretty lucky that way. . . . I feel very happy around Tongans, you

know, like it's just that contagious sort of laughter and then the singing. I really enjoy that. And I love the humor. With some Tongan men they've got a wonderful sense of humor and I really enjoy that. And I think that they're just willing to do anything for their families. They'll sacrifice anything for their families, the Tongans.

Parenting Issues

Intermarriage often causes couples to be more self-consciously aware of the issues surrounding "cultural identity," particularly when they have children. This concern with identity can make them more aware of parenting issues more generally, and Penny and Khoo found this awareness can be a significant benefit of intermarriage (1996; Kibria 1997, 524).

Sometimes, little negotiation about cultural issues is needed between the couples, because the Tongan partner makes a decision to live a "Western" lifestyle and to bring their children up that way. Seini, for example, exclaimed, "I won't dare bring them up in the Tongan way; that's very unfair, I feel, it's unfair to my husband, it's unfair to my children. And even my grandchildren now, [when] they come here, we speak in English. . . . I feel it's unfair, because we are living in a country that I will die in one day . . . and they will go on, they'll go on with their lives, in living in this country." Later she added, "That's one thing about my children, they are typical Australians."

For others, drawing on both parents' backgrounds in child rearing is valued and regarded as an "exciting challenge." A Tongan woman married to Australian man wrote on the KB,

> I am married to a palangi and sure it is difficult at times to make him see and understand my cultural point of view. But this is where communication skills, such as articulation and negotiation, come to the fore. By simply talking about the issue, we can come to understand each other's perspective. . . . Mixed marriages can be a blessing—think of your own children having the best of both cultures. Hopefully their mixed cultural heritage will enrich their lives and others whom they will interact with in their lives. (KB 22.10.98)

The importance of communication was also stressed by a Tongan woman, married for many years to an Australian, when she spoke at a church seminar.

I found from the beginning that it is very important to communicate with your partner—to find out about his culture and upbringing, his life in general and his involvement in the church—and for him to know about you. Because there are differences—you look at things in different ways and have different attitudes about things. For example, with my husband, family is his priority—church and extended family are second. I was brought up in the Tongan culture—your family, church and the extended family are of equal priority. And that is very important, because it will cause a lot of friction if you're not careful. Also, I was brought up to listen and obey without question. My husband was brought up to listen and ask questions. It is important to understand this when dealing with your children. (Canterbury Uniting Church 1993)

This woman also stressed the importance of Tongan parents taking an interest in their children's activities and understanding the Australian society in which they are living.

We parents who have been born in Tonga also need to realise that we are no longer in Tonga—we are now in a very different society—and to understand that our children will grow up and think very differently from us because of the influence of the society they are living in. So if we are to prepare our children for this society we may have to accept that we cannot bring them up exactly the same as we were brought up. (Canterbury Uniting Church 1993)

In her own parenting she admitted she had experienced difficulties "trying to balance up my experience as a Tongan and what I learned from watching and talking to other parents."

Finding a Balance

Some intermarried Tongans believe it is not important to teach children Tongan language or "culture" because the children are undeniably Tongan. Sitiveni, who is raising his children in Europe, insisted, "I think they will always be Tongans no matter whether they know the Tongan culture or not." Those couples who do want to raise their children to identify strongly as Tongan experience many of the same difficulties as the Tongan parents discussed in chapter 4. Sioeli wants to try to raise his children "in the Tongan way" but admits he is not having much success, particularly since they do not speak Tongan. "I'm trying to, but they're not, because even though I try to stress the way I want them to behave, they still behave in a different way. Because they go and mix with kids at school, so they tend to follow what they are doing. So as much as I would like them to grow up as I did, they are not 100 percent on that. I mean, I'll be happy if about . . . 60 percent, but that's really pushing it!"

Intermarried Tongan parents who are keen for their children to know what it means to be Tongan also tend to want their children to be *seen* as Tongan. As such, they may insist that their children wear Tongan clothing to church, learn Tongan language and dance, and otherwise demonstrate their Tongan identities. The parents may also insist on having Tongan celebrations for important events in their children's lives, such as birthdays, weddings, and graduations, despite the fact that sometimes the children themselves resist this. For example, a Tongan Australian woman wanted to alter some of the Tongan elements of her twenty-first birthday celebrations—in one case by asking if some of her gifts could be redistributed to her godmother instead of to her *fahu* (a Tongan relative of high status to her). Her Tongan mother refused to allow this and was determined that the event be as "Tongan" as possible.

Some of the issues intermarried couples have to deal with crop up only occasionally, as with this birthday celebration, and even when the partners have different expectations, it is often possible to reach compromises. When Kerry's first child was born, she was surprised to discover that in the Tongan way the baby is named not by the parents but by a relative, often the father's sister. She found a compromise. "Being very close with my partner's family I didn't believe in that tradition, but I wanted to respect them, and with no hurt to them I decided to name my daughter a different name and put what they chose as a second name."

Other issues surround daily activities in the household, such as the division of household labor. Julie and Samuela have already had disputes about their own division of labor, since Julie insists on doing tasks like gardening and other outdoor work, as well as redecorating work such as painting. Samuela has capitulated and now also does indoor tasks that he once argued were women's work, such as cleaning and clothes washing. However, Julie worries that when they have children he will revert to his former ideas about household labor.

The non-Tongan spouses' commonly held belief, described previously, that the Tongan partner is not typically "Tongan" is often raised in relation to parenting. When I asked Jane about her now adult children's experiences of growing up, she replied, "I don't think they've found it very difficult. I think because my husband is pretty intelligent and pretty *au fait* with the way things are done here, so he's pretty much an in-between person; he's not really traditional Tongan at all, and he understands, you know, and so he doesn't drag them into, you know, there's not a lot of conflict about things at home." As for the influence of *anga fakatonga* on their parenting, she said that

> there's probably a bit of it in the way we do things, but no, we don't have an absolute "you've got to do that that way because that's the Tongan way." Not in our home. Except for things like customs about visiting people and taking them gifts of food or whatever, when new people come from Tonga and things, some of the things we kind of do, but no . . . there's not a thing, "Oh, you've got to do it that way because that's the correct way, that's the Tongan way". Because my husband's not like that.

Jane clearly sees her own family as different from the Tongan families they know through their church, and she is disparaging of Tongan parenting.

> There's a lot of differences. . . . I mean, the Tongans think they've got a great way of bringing up children; I think they're hopeless. The traditional Tongan way. The way of treating children when they're small, up to teenager, when they're younger is, children are seen and not heard, children will do as they are told; children are belted if they don't do what the parents require of them. There's very little communication with children, with the traditional Tongan parents. Children are fed and clothed, but their other needs are not really met very well. They're kind of neglected. For example, the children in the church round here, the parents will be having all their programs and doing things and the children just run riot. You know, no one's supervising. They're not trained well in how to behave in various environments at all. They're just left. They're fed, and they're not taught much else. They're just smacked if they're naughty. Then when they get older you get this funny thing when they get into teenage and the boys and girls are getting older, there's a great discrepancy between the way the girls are treated and the boys are treated. The boys are just let go. It's as though they cannot be controlled or supervised or anything, they just do what they like. And that's why you find a lot of inadequate

Tongan men. Truly, truly! . . . And the women, the girls on the other hand, are controlled, confined, held close to the family, held close to the mother and not allowed to do this, not allowed to do that, and closely supervised. And that's got its—you can't do that here in the same way.

In contrast, the views of an Australian man, also married to a Tongan for many years, were more positive. He said at a church seminar,

> To me one of the most positive aspects is the socializing that the children get, right from babyhood. By being involved in the church and the Tongan community our children get this very valuable social skill and I think it stands them in very good stead. . . . One beautiful thing about being in the Tongan community is that if your child does something wrong—goes somewhere or something like that—there's always someone who's seen you! . . . One of the things that happens when a non-Tongan man marries a Tongan lady is that he may feel in the early stages of the marriage that he doesn't see his wife enough. She seems to be spending most of her married life at the church. This can cause a bit of stress at times. But the men that I know who are married to Tongans have found that when they look back over the years they have found how valuable it's been for their wives to be taking the children along to the church and to be mixing and feeling part of a great brotherhood or sisterhood. (Canterbury Uniting Church 1993)

One of the problems this man did admit parents faced was deciding how much freedom to give their children. Sioeli is beginning to face this very problem as his oldest daughter approaches her teens. He worries that if he is too strict she will run away from home or that it will in some other way "backfire" on him. Kylie supports his strict discipline to a large extent but is also keen for her children, all girls, to have more freedom than Tongan girls are often allowed. I asked if this caused problems between them and she replied, "Oh, it's already started. My oldest daughter, she's eleven, and she wants to go and sleep over at a friend's house, and I always let her and he whinges [complains] that she should be home, that she shouldn't be out."

Sioeli said that he was so appalled by the poor behavior of young people in Australia that he has considered sending his children back to Tonga to grow up there, but he is unsure that this will work. He told me of the son of an Australian father and Tongan mother who had been sent to school in Tonga because he was getting into trouble in

Australia. "It's much harder with mixed. So they sent him back home, then they really disciplined him, but it was a bit too late, he was, he was about fourteen I think, because when they sent him from here he was into drugs and all that. But he said towards the end he was okay. But the thing is, he has to come back here, so he will probably revert back to his old habits!" Kylie said she would be willing to let her children go to Tonga for a period if they were willing, not as a form of discipline, but to learn about Tongan culture. The children would have to be "old enough to look after themselves," she said.

Megan, thirty-nine, who was married to a Tongan in the United States for many years, said she has told her youngest son that "if he gets into any more trouble with the law, then I will send him to live there [Tonga] until he is eighteen. I meant this with all my heart. I would rather see him learn what hard work is, and I know the family would welcome him because he is his father's son." She spoke of other young people she has known who were sent back and "have been very thankful to their parents for doing it."

Many of the non-Tongan partners said they would like their children to have an opportunity to visit Tonga to meet other relatives and learn more about the country and culture, but few were as willing to entertain the thought of sending them unaccompanied to live with relatives as Megan was. Kerry told me she was already having disagreements with her husband on this issue. Lopeti was sent to Tonga for the last two years of high school after rebelling against his very traditional parents. He now views that experience positively, as a means of helping him to understand the Tongan way and, as Kerry put it, "become a man," and he feels any sons he has should also have that experience. According to Kerry,

> we've talked about if we ever have a son, and my partner always says he wants to send the sons to Tonga when they are thirteen, fourteen, so they can go to school there. And I'm like, "No way! Our kids aren't going to Tonga!" So we're disagreeing about that already and we still haven't had a son. But I don't know who would end up making the final decision on that. Like I think if my boys wanted to, I mean ultimately the decision would lie with them, and I'd have to learn to let go, and I know that that's the Tongan way. But at the moment I could never see myself doing that because I'd just miss them too much.

Jane, who has seen many of the Tongan children from her church sent home, said she is "distressed" by the practice and sees it as "a lack of understanding about the needs of children." She added that although many parents send the children back to attend a particular school, "I think it depends very much who's caring for them in Tonga, supervising the rest of their lives, apart from what's happening at school." As for children being sent home as a form of discipline, she argued,

> I think it's because the parents are unable to cope with the sort of things that the children are exposed to in this society, and they have no strategies for dealing with it. I mean, it's not easy, it's not easy for any parents, of any society, oh, you know, it's not easy for Australian parents. But the Tongans have no strategies at all for dealing with it. Their only strategies are physically beat them or kick them out of the home. They don't seem to have any other strategies. Most of them, you know, not all. I mean, we've got some . . . and that's their option, they're sent to Tonga, that's the implications that keeps them out of trouble.

Physical Punishment

Forms of discipline apart from sending children back to Tonga also cause significant tension in many of the intermarriages. Sometimes this tension is caused by the Tongan partner's family; for example, a visit from Sioeli's parents from Tonga created difficulties when the grandparents chastised the children for things they were normally allowed to do, and since the children spoke no Tongan and the grandparents no English, Sioeli and Kylie found themselves mediating between them. Usually, however, tension arises due to the partners' different attitudes toward discipline, particularly the Tongan parents' acceptance and use of physical punishment. For Kerry and Lopeti, this looms as a potential problem, and she said, "I know that if my partner was to hit one of our children in that way, I'd be quite devastated and I wouldn't accept it at all." As for Kylie:

> When they smack their kids they go a bit overboard, they hit them too much. I don't know if you've ever seen a Tongan kid being hit; they just don't stop. . . . But [Sioeli] thinks that it's good, but it's not, because, you see the Tongans now when they grow up, they're out of hand now, they're wild. See, and he can't see it, but I can see it. The men, when they come here, they just go wild. They don't have any self-discipline at all. And I think that's because they lacked in it. You

know, they didn't experience anything in their childhood, so they're experiencing it once they get married, you know.

Julie expressed a similar dislike of physical punishment.

I think discipline has been the hardest for me. Well, it's really . . . not shocked me, but more sort of really stunned by it all because I just can't understand how they can hit the child so hard and really escape with its life or whatever. And then the child just loves their parents to pieces. And I'm thinking, gee, in a *pālangi* kid you'd just run away from home and that would be it. And I just can't understand how this attachment is with that, with the people who have beat them to a near pulp, you know. You know sort of, that's not my way of discipline. I think there's more effective ways, but I've been told that mixed marriages, they have the worst kids. They're the ones that have to be beaten more, they're really hard to handle. . . . It concerns me because I think of how much love they normally show, and but just during that one beating you know, and I'm thinking, you know, if the kids are taken away, you know they would just suffer so much. But it's just part of their natural way they've been brought up. You know, that's the way they show discipline, and it's probably, you know, a hard thing for them to stop. It's just something that I really don't like that much at all about it. I tend to stay away from it if I hear anybody scream, you know.

Conflicts over issues such as discipline and other aspects of the Tongan way can contribute to the breakdown of marriages. One Australian man I spoke with had recently divorced his Tongan wife after many years of marriage and told me bitterly that he did not want to "spend another twenty or more years being frustrated by Tongans." He said he feels alienated from his adult daughters, whom he sees as more Tongan than Australian because they were brought up predominantly by their mother while he worked long hours. Sitiveni, divorced from his European wife, said, "I think there was a lack of understanding between us especially on my ex-wife's side toward my culture. I got the feeling that she thought that her culture was superior to my culture."

As in the wider Australian society, among the Tongans of Melbourne it is more common for women to retain custody of children following a separation or divorce, and this is also the case for intermarriages. In cases where the non-Tongan partner is female, the children often have little or no further contact with their Tongan relatives unless they decide, as older teenagers or young adults, to seek them out as part of a process of coming to terms with their Tongan identities. However, I did encounter one case in which the mother had allowed her two children by a Tongan man to be adopted by his relatives, and there were two single male parents, both Tongan, who had been married to non-Tongans.

The Children of Intermarriages: "Not One or the Other"?

The experiences and identities of the children of intermarriages have been found to be highly diverse. Parents and other caregivers are important influences on children's identities, yet they vary in the ways in which they deal with their children's "mixed" ancestry. Some parents actively encourage their children to be proud of their identities and dual or multiple cultural backgrounds; others are concerned more with helping their children deal with racism and discrimination; and some may even choose to ignore the question of "culture" (Benson 1981; Rosenblatt, Karis, and Powell 1995; Tizard and Phoenix 1993). Susan Benson found that when parents disagreed about how their children should identify, it became difficult for children to "come to terms with their ambiguous ethnicity" (1981, 139).

Issues of identity are not always overtly addressed within families, and often young people's struggles to secure their identities are intensely private or discussed with peers rather than family members. Penny and Khoo (1996) found that while the "happy" couples were those who had agreed to raise their children primarily as Australian, the adult children of these marriages still professed a strong sentimental loyalty to the non-Australian parent's culture, although most of the parents were unaware of these attachments.

Other factors influence the construction of cultural identity for the children of intermarriage, many of which are the same as those for any children of migrant parents. Wider societal attitudes, including racism, are significant, as are the family's social class, their local neighborhood, the school the children attend, and even individual differences in the children, including their physical appearance. There is likely to be a close interrelationship between their cultural identities and the ethnic identities imposed by the wider society, and despite the increasing "hybridization" of societies (Cornwall and Stoddard 2001), the policies and practices of host nations force people to choose from a narrow range of racial and ethnic categories. These categories are associated with the kinds of stereotypes I have discussed, which can feed back into young people's identities. Ultimately, the children of intermarriage make their own choices, guided by these multiple influences, and while some relish the "mix" of heritages they embody, others struggle long and hard to secure their identities.

Many of the couples I spoke with had a positive view of the impact of their intermarriage on their children and made comments about them having "the best of both worlds" or having "all the good bits" from both cultures. Some are also aware of the difficulties the children experience, but many do not acknowledge such problems. One of the most frequent positive comments I heard, in the Tongan Australian families, was that having one Tongan parent would give their children a sense of cultural identity, which Anglo-Australian children were seen to lack. However, even parents who have a positive view are sometimes concerned that their children will never be regarded by other Tongans as "real Tongans." Jane, for example, adamantly believed that "the Tongans don't think anyone is a Tongan unless they are a full Tongan."

Julie had no children at the time of our interview but was planning a family and was thinking about how her children would identify.

> I think they come from two backgrounds but living in one country, and I'd like them to assimilate into the Australian way of life, but also remember their Tongan heritage and appreciate it and sort of get to know their families from both sides, and if they're interested, you know, to learn more about that culture. But as for now I think we're in Australia and I think Australians are mixed, there's a multicultural thing, with Tongans and Australians, but we're all sort of one. But I think that they should always remember the culture from where they come from.

Julie believes her children will benefit from having parents of different cultures. "I think they learn that there's more than one right. . . . Just because something's different doesn't mean to say it's wrong. And they can see different ways of doing things. So I think it would broaden their way of thinking. They would get more ideas, I think." When she has children, she would like them to learn about their Tongan ancestry but worries that her husband will be unable to teach this. "My husband doesn't know the old stories. I keep getting him to try and tell me. I'm the one that gets on the Internet to try and find the old stories. I'm the one that tells him. He doesn't know his own culture. I keep teaching him his culture."

Some non-Tongan partners attempt to give their children an under-standing of Tongan culture through close involvement with their Tongan partner's extended family and by attending a Tongan church or taking them for holidays to Tonga. Sue's Australian father took his family to Tonga while the children were young. "Dad wanted us to learn the language while we were young. So we went to Tonga when we were about ten, and he wanted us to appreciate the customs and I think have respect for them. So that was really important, like he wanted us to have that. Even though we were brought up as Australians. But he still wanted us to know where our mother came from." Fusi, Sue's sister, added that their parents had given them "a strong grounding. So we know where we're from, we're not guessing. . . . We know our family, we have been brought up equally on both sides." Although their parents wanted them to know both cultures, their daily lives were Australian. Sue explained, "Mum made a conscious decision to bring us up the Australian way. When she came here and married an Australian, she decided she would speak English and raise her children that way." There were still difficulties for the girls as they grew up in Australia, as Sue pointed out. "I thought that I was like everyone else, but everyone else told me that I wasn't. Because you know, we grew up in like a white suburb. And so we got teased a lot. So sometimes I [would] think, 'Oh, I wish I had blonde hair.' When I was little. It changes, of course. And that's because it's changing now. It's so multicultural in this country now."

The question of how others identify children is important, as it forces the children to be constantly aware of their "differences" and to question their identities. For some, this awareness involves being exposed to racism and discrimination, while for others it is a more general sense of being "in between" or "outside" their parents' ethnic groups. At a church seminar, a young man born in Melbourne, with an Australian mother and Tongan father, said,

> Ethnically I see myself as both Australian and Tongan. I'm not one or the other—I'm just sort of in-between. When I go out people look at my dark skin and they think: "Hey, man! You're black!" but I am part Australian and part Tongan and for me there's no real distinction. . . . The positive aspects about being that way is that I find that I get the best of both worlds. It has helped me to grow as a person to see both the Tongan side and the Australian side. I can choose which side I go by in any situation—whatever suits me best! And it also means that I

can get a lot of varying experiences that a lot of Australian kids won't get—with the Tongans I feel as though we're all family. . . . I also feel that a strong point about the Tongans is that because they're such a minority there's a very strong bond. I feel that, although I don't see a lot of Tongans so much any more, they're still very close to me and they'll always be friends for life. Whereas sometimes you feel that you can't feel that way with the Australians. Another thing about having Tongan and Australian parents is that you can play them off against each other! (Canterbury Uniting Church 1993)

Nevertheless, this young man also experienced the problem of being seen as Tongan by Australians and as Australian by Tongans and thus feeling "separate from both groups at the same time." When asked if he would have preferred to be in a fully Tongan or Australian family, he replied, "I prefer to be as I am. I feel that with all-Australian parents or all-Tongan parents it's almost one-dimensional. Whereas my sphere of family and friends and connections all through the Australian side and the Tongan side is such a wide array—I feel really lucky that I've got all those different inputs."

The problem of not feeling fully accepted by either Tongans or non-Tongans was shared by many young people. At the same church seminar, a young woman, also with an Australian father and Tongan mother, commented,

A difficulty I found with the culture was identification as to who I was. With the full Tongan people I was a *"pālangi"* and I was different from them, whereas with the *pālangi* I was classified as being a Tongan. So I was not a part of either. It was only with other half-caste friends that I felt part of a group and could relate properly, because they had been through the same experiences that I had been through. (Canterbury Uniting Church 1993)

This young woman had found it difficult at school because few of her peers even knew where Tonga was. She added,

I also found it difficult to identify with the "Tongan way." There was a difference with what was expected from Mum regarding Tongan things and what was considered Australian and what we were growing up with in our society. . . . I suppose I did go through a bit of an identity crisis with being a half-caste. Through my teen years I probably went through more trying to find myself than normal teenagers do, in the sense that culturally I didn't feel a part. I did that just through trying things and trying to find myself through other people—and finally filling that void with the Christian faith. (Canterbury Uniting Church 1993)

Even within their own extended families, the children of intermarriage can experience difficulties. In some cases relatives may feel uneasy about these children's identities or may frequently raise the issue of their mixed parentage. Children of intermarriages who grow up in predominantly Tongan households may find they often need to assert their Tonganness and may be teased about their parentage. Sela told me how her brother's son, born to a *pakeha* New Zealander and growing up in the Tongan grandparents' household, was frequently teased about his identity from an early age. "We used to say to him, 'You're a *pālangi!*' because his mother's a Kiwi, 'a *pālangi*,' or 'You're a Maori Kiwi!' or something like that, and he said, 'No, I'm not, I'm Tongan.' So even to his grandparents he says, 'I'm Tongan.'"

Some children of intermarriages grow up knowing few Tongans apart from some of their Tongan parent's relatives, and as teenagers and young adults they often they seek to understand more of their Tongan "side." The children of one of the early Tongan settlers in Melbourne had little involvement with other Tongans, as their mother gradually stopped attending a Tongan church and even ceased sending remittances to family in Tonga. The children, all boys, did not learn Tongan and had little contact with their Tongan family. Later they all became interested in knowing more about being Tongan. At different times they have all visited Tonga and to varying degrees maintain connections with other Tongans in both Tonga and Melbourne.

This process of rediscovering a Tongan identity can occur much later in life as well. Alice, now in her fifties, was born in New Zealand to a part-Tongan mother and non-Tongan father, but because she was taken away from her mother at a young age, she never learned anything of what it meant to be Tongan.[5] She married a non-Tongan, and it was not until one of her own adult daughters decided she wanted to know more about being Tongan and persuaded her mother to accompany her to a Tongan church that she began her own search for her Tongan identity. Alice found her search very difficult, however, and claims it took five years to be fully accepted by the Tongans at the church; only after word spread about her Tongan kinship connections was she seen as "really" Tongan. Despite this, she still feels that identifying as Tongan has meaning for her, and she talked of finding her "core" of Tonganness.

Alice's children are examples of the increasing number of children whose intermarried parents were themselves offspring of intermarriages. Such children have not two, but three or more different potential cultural identities on which to draw. As Spickard has pointed out, these multiple identities can increase the opportunities for young people to make choices about how they identify themselves. "One could not choose to identify oneself as something for which one's gene pool did not qualify, and the choice one made had enormous social and psychological implications, but if one came from multiple ethnic strains, increasingly one had the option of access to them all" (Spickard 1989, 367). In a fascinating doctoral dissertation on multiple identities, Robert Wolfgramm, who has Tongan, Fijian, German, and other European ancestry, describes his own search for identity, sparked by the promotion of multiculturalism in Australia in the 1970s (1994). Raised for eleven years in Fiji by maternal grandparents, then living in Australia with "Australians of Anglo-Celtic background," he has spent only ten days in Tonga. Wolfgramm argues that "[d]efinitions and conceptualisations of ethnic identity become variable, problematic and even confusing when applied to a self. . . . [T]hese difficulties are highlighted and compounded when applied to someone whose ethnic composition is highly hybridised" (1994, 47–48). He concludes that he identifies mainly as Fijian but adds, "Sometimes I am one ethnic self; sometimes I am many; sometimes I am none" (1994, 287). Children with two, three, or more potential identities on which to draw in constructing their identities can have considerable scope to move between identities and develop what has been called a "new multiracial consciousness" (Daniel 1992). Young people can learn to play on their "mixed" identities, and some even use their "Tongan side" or "*pālangi* side" to excuse or explain aspects of their personalities. For example, among the young people I spoke with, some claimed their chronic lateness was due to their Tongan side, while others attributed their desire for privacy to their Australian side. Of course, they can also experience considerable confusion and ambivalence about their identities, as we have seen.

This confusion can be exacerbated if the children of intermarriages go to Tonga and are confronted with negative attitudes about their backgrounds. In a message to the KB with the heading "Hard to be Half," a Tongan Greek young woman, brought up in Australia, explained that she had grown up in her Greek extended family and "with a Greek identity, even though I was always proud of my Tongan blood"

(KB 24.8.97). She went to Tonga for a holiday, on her own, "as I wanted to learn more of my Tongan side," and recalled that

> I have always been so proud to be Tongan and have always loved Tongan people as well as the culture, yet my experience in Tonga turned out to be a rather discouraging one, to put it mildly. I was constantly judged and stereotyped by fellow girls, often hearing the expression "fea palangi" (or however you spell it), said behind my back, as well as being constantly criticized by everyone from my own relatives to the local shop owner, just for not being able to speak Tongan. So much for the "friendly islands". Is speaking the language going to prove to them that I love being Tongan more than I already did?? And why are half casts given more of a hard time about it then full Tongans?? I'd really like to know!! (KB 24.8.97)

Her message received sympathetic responses from others with similar experiences. One response was from a young Tongan Italian woman who had been mainly influenced by her Italian family yet was proud of her Tongan identity as well. She went to Tonga at nineteen to enter the Miss Heilala beauty contest and found that some Tongans "blatantly categorised me and verbally attacked me because they assumed by the way I looked that I was 'fie palangi', when if anything, I was the biggest 'fie Tongan' on the island" (KB 25.8.97). She then went to university in Auckland wanting to "study with and learn more of Polynesians and the culture" and spent a year attending all the Tongan functions she could "in an attempt to 'fit in.'" But she ended up with "more of an identity crisis and one big headache." The advice she gives is this: "[I]t doesn't matter what they think, it's how you feel inside, and if you feel you are a Tongan, you are! Don't feel you have to prove it!" Another poster wrote encouragingly, "[I]f you've got tongan blood in you then your a tongan you don't have to speak the language to become a real Tongan. If the blood is there then your a tongan no matter what other people says" (KB 25.8.97).

Not all young people who visit Tonga report negative experiences, and some find it can be a valuable, identity-affirming time spent getting to know relatives and the Tongan lifestyle. Fonua, eighteen, had little contact with his Tongan family from the age of two, apart from several visits to Tonga as a child. He visited again with his Australian mother at the age of sixteen, and at first he was excited to be in Tonga, exclaiming at the airport, "I'm home!" However, this was followed by a crisis; he said he did not know where he belonged and was thinking, "I don't know who I am!" Then, members of his extended family began to welcome him into their households, and he spent his two-week holiday visiting relatives, spending time with his cousins, talking and joking, and learning how to spit-roast pigs, grate coconut, and other skills. During this short visit he underwent a transformation, taking on the characteristics of young Tongan males, wearing T-shirts that proclaimed his Tongan identity, and avidly reading anything he could find, from the Tongan-English dictionary to tourist brochures. He drank in the stories his aunts told him of his family history and cherished the *tupenu* and *ta'ovala* (men's skirt and waist mat) he was given as gifts. Fonua decided he wanted to live in Tonga and attend school there and vowed he would marry a Tongan woman and ensure his own children had what he felt he had missed out on. Sadly, on his return to Australia he found it difficult to become involved with other Tongans, due to family issues concerning his "mixed" parentage, and he set aside his dreams of returning to Tonga and resumed his life as an Australian.

Tongans themselves often feel confused about how to identify the children of intermarriages. Vika said of young people with mixed ancestry, "I think they're stuck in this place where they don't know who they really are; they're not complete. I mean, I'm only guessing here. I think they're sort of in the middle, in between someplace, but they're not sure what their identity is. I mean, if your father's white or your mother's white and your other part is Tongan. But just one of the parts will overrule them and they will lean to one part more than to the other. And I feel sorry for them because they lose from the other part." I asked her which "part" she felt usually overrules, and she replied, "In Australia, their white part. Their blood's too strong." When I asked Vika later in our interview what it means to be a "real" Tongan, she returned to the topic of mixed ancestry. "If they were half but they knew how to speak Tongan, ate Tongan, had the heart of a Tongan person, then that's a true Tongan. But if they said they were full Tongan but don't act like a Tongan person and doesn't have the heart, doesn't speak the language, and so on, are they less of a Tongan than the half-caste? I don't know."

Language Issues

The relationship of language to concepts of cultural authenticity was discussed in chapter 5; for the children of intermarriages, who are often struggling to secure their identities, language can assume a criti-

cal role. If migrant couples who are both Tongan find it difficult to ensure their children speak the language, it is even harder when one parent is not Tongan and he or she speaks Tongan poorly or not at all, so
that the parents do not speak Tongan to each other.

In most of the intermarried Melbourne families, the parents had not
succeeded in teaching their children Tongan. In some cases this was a
deliberate choice; for example, although Kylie says she encourages her
husband to speak in Tongan to their children, Sioeli is repeating the
pattern of many of the first wave of migrants (whose children are now
young adults) who deliberately did not teach their children Tongan in
order to enhance their chances of success in the Australian school system. The Tongan Greek woman who wrote to the KB about her identity
problems also commented on language, saying, "My Tongan mother
never tried to discourage our Tongan identity, she merely did not see
learning the Tongan language as important as our school education,
personal growth and Christian development. Frankly I don't blame
her" (KB 24.8.97). The Tongan Italian woman who responded to her
post commented, "[M]y mother too did not feel that learning the Tongan language was as important as our education and Christian development. She always believed that we are Christians before we are Tongan, Italian or Australian for that matter. Although my mother felt she
was doing what was best, little did she know the implications this
would have on us in later years" (KB 25.8.97). These implications included the children's regrets about not speaking Tongan and the negative attitudes they encounter from other Tongans, who often regard
them as *fie pālangi*.

In a few cases Tongan parents had not encouraged their children to
speak Tongan or identify as Tongan because of their own ambivalence
about being Tongan; these parents had chosen to leave Tonga because
of issues such as family conflict or dissatisfaction with aspects of Tongan life. More often, however, the Tongan parent simply did not make
any special effort to speak to the children in Tongan. Jane said of her
children,

> I think it's a shame that they can't speak the language. But it's not my
> responsibility; I mean, I don't see it as my responsibility, I can't teach
> them Tongan. It was my husband's, and I don't think we understood,
> or he understood when they were small, which is the time to do it,
> that if he'd conscientiously spoken Tongan to them when they were
> small then they would have had it. But they don't. . . . There's noth-

ing much the Australian parent can do about it. If the Tongan parent doesn't want to do it, or doesn't bother to do it, well, it doesn't happen.

Thomas, whose father is Tongan, claimed, "I never heard Tongan spoken until I was about fifteen or sixteen." His father worked long hours and the family did not associate with other Tongans, so he simply had no exposure to the Tongan language.

Like some of the non-Tongan spouses, young people who are not actively taught to speak Tongan often understand a great deal of what is said, having picked up a basic understanding through their contact with other Tongans. Some make an effort to improve their language skills when they are older, as part of their more general attempts to understand what it means to be Tongan and to establish contacts with other Tongans beyond their families. Others, who have been unable to master the language, enlist the help of relatives who are fluent in Tongan to help their own children learn Tongan. This strategy is also used at times by non-Tongan spouses; Kerry, for example, has ensured that her young daughter speaks Tongan by having her spend a lot of time with her father's family, all of whom speak Tongan at home. "I think that if my daughter didn't know Tongan, maybe she would feel like she didn't fully belong. Because, I don't know, maybe because she's got a *pālangi* mum, and then if she didn't know the language that would just hinder her even further, because she wouldn't fit in. And because we as a family associate with the Tongans so much it's just vital for her to know Tongan."

The issue of language highlights the diverse experiences of the children of intermarriage. Some grow up speaking no Tongan, while others are fluent; some who are not taught Tongan as children later attempt to learn the language, while others never try. Those who do not speak Tongan fluently may not feel accepted as "real" Tongans, and in any case their "mixed" parentage means they can encounter ambivalent, if not outright negative, attitudes toward them from other Tongans. Given the high rate of Tongan intermarriage, there is an ever-growing cohort of "part-Tongans," so this lack of acceptance by Tongans is a critical issue confronting Tongan populations overseas and in Tonga. While it is being discussed openly in certain contexts such as Internet discussion forums, in other contexts it is avoided or only reluctantly addressed. The risk that many of these young people will be alienated from their Tongan identities is very real, and only when their voices are heard and their views taken seriously will this perhaps be avoided.

CASE STUDIES

5. Sālote and Mike

Sālote, thirty, was sent to live with her father's sister and her *pālangi* husband in New Zealand at the age of seven. They arranged for her to have twice-weekly language lessons from a Tongan teacher living nearby, and she also visited the woman's home on weekends to further her lessons; now Sālote is proud of her fluency in Tongan. Although many of her father's relatives lived in New Zealand, most of her mother's siblings moved to Australia. In 1984, while she was in high school, Sālote visited her mother's relatives in Sydney and decided she would prefer to live with them. Now, she says, "I am Tongan but I live in Australia; Australia is my home. I am proud to be Tongan, but I am an Australian citizen and I am also proud to live in Australia." At a later point in our interview she also described herself as "part Australian."

After high school, Sālote undertook tertiary studies and began working in a professional position. At work she met Mike, thirty-one, born in Australia to Maltese parents and also with a university degree. When they decided to marry they encountered enormous resistance from Sālote's family. She recalls,

> Oh, you couldn't believe the problems that I had, being that I was the first grandchild in my father's side, and I was the first grandchild in my mother's side; you must have some understanding of how big that would be, the position that I was in. That I have got to be the best role model for the rest of my brothers and sisters behind me. And that was, like, really a heavy burden to carry on your shoulders. . . . But we had a lot of problems, especially with my mother. . . . I don't think she hated [Mike], but she was so scared of not knowing what he is, not knowing his background, not knowing what the other *pālangi* will bring into the family; she was scared that if I married the *pālangi*, the *pālangi* would take away what I had. You know, what I can give them. I think that's mostly part of it. They were scared that if I get married to him I would certainly forget them and not be able to keep on giving the help and giving them what I normally would give when they asked me, or when I give them what I wanted to, if I married the *pālangi*. It was very, very difficult. But we decided that we wanted to fight them on it, so we won, and we are quite happy about that. But I

think they sort of see the sense in it, you know, and I think it makes it easier for the rest of my brothers and sisters behind me, because it opens the door that has been closed to my family for a long, long time.

Despite their ambivalence about her husband, Sālote's family gladly welcomed the birth of their son.

I think that most Tongans, they seems to be proud to have a mixed Tongan, to be a mixed blood. I don't know, for some reason, you know, like in Tonga my mother used to say to me that when the *pālangi* were coming to Tonga when she was little, they used to look at them very highly. Whereas nowadays, if your daughter is going out with a *pālangi*, they look at that *pālangi* in total different way, like very low. And they seems to think that that *pālangi* is not good enough.

Mike believes that part of her family's resistance to him was due to his Maltese background. He asserts that Tongans have mainly encountered "lower-class Maltese" and had formed a "low opinion" of them; as a member of "the upper middle class" he is sympathetic to their views and says he understands their resistance to him. Mike grew up associating with other Pacific Islanders, particularly Maori and Samoan, and feels quite at ease with his Tongan affines, since he sees similarities between Maltese and Polynesian cultures, particularly in terms of the importance of obligations to the family, including those "back home." He is sympathetic to demands from Sālote's family on their time and money.

You are basically a well of funds for family back home, or even family here, if somebody dies and they're, depending how close they are, they could be committing thousands of dollars, and that's the biggest fright I think for a lot of the *pālangi* that mix with Tongans. I mean, if it's another Islander they have a bit more of an understanding, but that's, I think that's the biggest fright. The, also the centrality of the church to anything, to social outings, to everything, it can be very church based. The importance of family . . . for my European background family is very important, but I know for a lot of Australians they used to find it a bit of a shock that you do get on so well and see so many of your family so regularly.

Sālote worries that the demands of her extended family will cause problems.

> I always ask him [Mike], I always say to him, if you tend to think that
> I am doing too much, tell me. Because I would appreciate somebody
> telling me that, you know, instead of me overdoing something and
> going short at home. I'd rather see that my son is clothed and stuff
> like that before I go along helping somebody else. I don't mind help-
> ing anybody if they needed a help, but I tend to think that sometimes
> they overdo the *kavenga* and they don't sit down properly and think
> about what should be done and think about the priorities that how
> things should be done; they just, you know, I don't know whether its
> Polynesian, whether its Tongan.

Sālote is anxious for her husband to have her family's approval and often
points out his mistakes after they have attended a family or community
function.

> But he is very willing and it makes it much, much easier because he is
> wanting to understand, you know. He's very persistent with things
> like that. Sometimes with me it's difficult because I think in Tongan
> and then I've got to explain that in English and it makes it hard and I
> just had enough of it sometimes and [I think] "Oh, forget it, I'm not
> going to talk about it anymore," but then he is very persistent because
> he wanted to know, and I said, "Oh, I think its only fair that I explain
> to him."

Due to her high-status position within her extended family, Sālote is used
to making decisions for the family and making demands on other family
members, so she has had to make adjustments since her marriage.

> I have a lot of help from my husband in dealing with things like that.
> If I sort of find myself in trouble with not being able to work out what
> I should do or whether I should think Tongan or whether I should
> think Australian, or, you know, should I do it the Tongan way, should
> I do it the Australian way, and I always ask his help, you know. Some-
> times I tend to think that's my Tongan thinking coming along, I tend
> to just do things and not realize that I have my husband, that I
> needed to tell him, I needed to ask his opinion of things.

Sālote and Mike stay in close contact with her relatives in Tonga and send
money and in-kind remittances several times a year. They keep up with Tongan news, mainly via the Internet, and enjoy watching videos of events in
Tonga, sent by Sālote's mother. They have even talked about going to work
there, but only if they could earn the same wages they earn now or "if we

won Tatslotto!" They have visited Tonga together twice and on the second trip took Mike's parents. He recalls, "They loved it there. I think it reminded them a lot about Malta." However, much of daily life for Mike and Sālote is more Australian than Tongan. They own their own home, the decor of which shows no Tongan influence, they both work, and they have a social life with non-Tongan friends. They eat mainly European-influenced food, wear Western clothes except for special Tongan functions, and speak English with each other.

Mike, like many non-Tongan partners, can understand a great deal of what is being said in Tongan but tends to speak in English, as his spoken Tongan is poor. Sālote and Mike are unable to have conversations in Tongan, and she sorely misses being able to use her first language. "I get very lonely, and I need to speak my native tongue from time to time, I need to have somebody even just to say hello and have a chat. I need to speak it. Because I find if I speak English for a couple of months and not speak Tongan, once I go home I tend to sort of, you know, my mind sort of geared up towards English speaking and I am slow with my Tongan. So I tend to sort of—oh, I long for it, you know, I miss it."

Sālote has reflected on the situation of Tongan migrants and how their children blend Tongan and non-Tongan practices. "We tend to take on the good in both customs." She is critical of the first generation of migrants for their reluctance to let go of the Tongan way. "They live in Australia and they want to be sort of modernized, but they still bring the old ways with them, and it's very, very difficult sometimes to explain to them what's going on." She says of the older members of her family,

> Some things in the customs they tend to think, this is the Tongan way, this is the way that we do it, it's the right way. And I always argue with them and I said to them, "No, the Tongan way is not always the right way!" In Australia there are things done the right way and I do that; it's my opinion that it's the right way. So I choose to do it that way. I think, once they see somebody doing, taking a step forward and doing that, they seem to [say] "Oh, maybe we'll do it." And they sort of give it a go. But I think it is just up to an individual like myself; I tend to fight about it and I tend to want to educate my family about it.

Sālote is also highly critical of Tongans who continue to see Tonga as "home" and says her adoptive mother (her mother's sister) often talks about wanting to go home to Tonga.

And I said to her, "Then what are you doing here, Mum? Why did you want to come to Australia, what did you want from Australia?" And I keep telling them that they can't sort of come in here and take Australian money and send it to Tonga and not give something back to Australia. I said that I think it is only fair that if I work in Australia and I get money out of it and I am able to help feed my family and help them look after their needs, provide for their needs, I tend to feel that I should give something back to the custom and to the culture of Australia. But they don't seem to understand this. They always talk about "I want to go home, my home is in Tonga, that's where my house is."

Although she is close with her own family, with other Tongans Sālote sometimes feels like an outsider. She would like to be involved with the women's group at the Free Wesleyan Church she attends but feels they would not want to listen to her views. She complained, "I don't know whether they look at people like me, that grew up here and grew up in New Zealand, and sort of, I don't know whether I would carry a lot of weight in a group like that. But that's what I mean, they won't budge. They don't seem to think that I can bring good into a group like that. They don't seem to welcome that."

Sālote and Mike have a young son, and they are keen to ensure that he benefits from their intermarriage by being exposed to "all the good bits" from the Tongan, Maltese, and Australian cultures. They share similar values and do not see their cultural differences as causing any conflicts with regards to parenting. They agree that they will both be strict by Australian standards and will impress upon their son the value of education. Sālote doesn't believe it is imperative for him to speak Tongan in order to identify as Tongan, although she would like him to be bilingual. She argues, "I don't really think that not being able to speak the language doesn't make you a Tongan. . . . It doesn't matter whether you speak the language, whether you do what you are supposed to be doing; you are already part Tongan, you are already part of the custom."

Like many other Tongan parents, Sālote believes respect is the most important value to teach her children and says, "If he can't have anything else from the Tongan culture I would like him to have that." However, her views about the Tongan concept of respect have been affected by her own experiences growing up overseas. She would like her son to respect his parents and elders because they have more experience, but she also wants him to make his own decisions. Open communication with her son is also important to her, and she believes that "you've just got to be very open-minded about children and you've got to allow them room to grow."

Sālote supports the idea of sending children back to Tonga, although she admits that it is not a successful strategy in all cases. Of her own son she says, "If [my son] is sort of getting into trouble and I can't seem to handle him, you know, it gets out of hand in here, I would certainly send him to my father and my mother in Tonga. And I would get that sort of support and help from them. I wouldn't send him anywhere else in here." Mike, on the other hand, argues that they should be able to cope with any problems with their son themselves, but he supports the idea of sending him to Tonga "for a nice few weeks' stint" to let him learn more about Tonga.

As for the use of physical punishment, Sālote and Mike agree that it is acceptable within limits. Sālote says, "I certainly got disciplined physically, and I believe in it to some extent. I would smack [my son], but I'm not going to go in there and just, you know, like some people that you see they just go and hit their kids; to me, I can't do that. I don't believe in overdoing it. . . . If I can avoid it I would like to avoid it!" She believes that living in New Zealand and Australia has influenced her views on punishment. "I tend to see that there are other ways of having to cope with having to discipline your child than having to give them the stick." Mike shares her views and feels it is important to be strict and to have an active role as a parent in order to prevent their son from "running wild."

They intend to make sure their son understands both Tongan and Maltese cultural values and practices, but they are also prepared to make adjustments to the norms of Australian society. For example, in relation to the ideal, common to both Tongan and Maltese cultures, that daughters remain close to home and have limited freedom, Sālote says, "I would like to think that if I have a daughter I would still like my daughter to experience what the outside world is like, what the world is like. Not grow up and married and not know what a nightclub looks like, and you know, people talk about it and she is sitting there not knowing what it really is. I'd like her to experience that sort of thing."

Most important to them is that their son develop a secure identity. Mike comments, "I can see one of the greatest things lacking in Australian youth is that they don't know who they—they're nothing, they have nothing, they owe nothing to anybody, they have nothing to call on. Whereas [our son] will always have family, he will never be alone." He also worries about Tongan youth who do not speak Tongan or know *anga fakatonga*, saying, "That's a sad thing to see. That they're as lost as any other *pālangi* out there. And they've got such a rich culture sitting behind them."

6. Sulia

At the age of twenty-eight, Sulia is still struggling with her Tongan Australian identity, and in our interview she articulated many of the issues facing the children of intermarriages. Now living alone in Melbourne, she grew up in rural Victoria with her Tongan mother, Australian father, three siblings, and an adopted brother (a nephew of her mother's). Her mother, who migrated in the 1960s when in her early twenties, told the children she had left Tonga because she opposed the injustices of the hierarchical social system, and in Australia she had little to do with other Tongans after the first few years of her marriage. Reflecting on whether her mother brought her up in the Tongan way at all Sulia says,

> She didn't consciously, but I think she did subconsciously. We were hit all the time; I was hit every day for just stupid things. I don't believe in hitting children, that's my personal view. But—pissed off with that. God, that pisses me off! I used to see them just lay into their kids. You can't do that, that's just disgusting. Um—and being very strict and demanding obedience, no talking back, I mean, I find you can get that in the Anglo-Saxon community too, but I find it can be at a very intense level with the Tongan community. Don't look a certain way, obey me, whatever I say.

Sulia's father never interfered with her mother's discipline of the children, and although he did not use physical punishment with his daughters, he did with his sons. Sulia's mother also insisted that Sulia and her sister maintain an appearance that conformed to Tongan norms, which meant plaiting their hair for school and not being allowed to wear makeup or earrings. However, her mother never explained these strictures as Tongan practice, but simply as "the way it is."

From Sulia's perspective, her parents did not really deal with the fact that they had different backgrounds. She recalls,

> They never had Tongan-Australian arguments. I think they are starting to now, as my mum is becoming more assertive, but I think the arguments, I think she just tried to be what a good wife was supposed to be and obey the husband. So the Tongan issue never came up, which really pisses me off, because you know, everything's just so bloody white! And it's almost like half of us kids were being denied that, so . . . just in favor of white, not in favor of color, you know! . . . I

wouldn't say my father was sensitive to her needs as a woman, as a human being, or even as a Tongan woman, whereas within our patriarchal family we tend to have to lean towards the Australian, Anglo-Saxon way of doing things. However, we kids are starting not to take that any more. We start to, I myself included, start to question and be a bit curious about the Tongan side of us as well.

Despite her mother's negative views of Tonga, Sulia's parents took her there for a year as a young child. She remembers being teased by other children as *fie pālangi,* but "I even noticed with relatives that we were given higher precedent than the others, just for the fact that I was half *pālangi,* so I always felt that I was not treated equally to my other Tongan cousins." Of the Tongans she has encountered in Melbourne, Sulia believes "massive allowances" have been made for her because it was known she did not speak Tongan or understand the Tongan way.

Any Tongan language she learned during her year in Tonga was quickly forgotten, and Sulia's mother did not encourage her to speak Tongan at home. Sulia explains that this was "to protect us from the culture. And I understand, I think she didn't want us to be in her situation when she was a kid, just stuck in poverty and nowhere to go." Now, she says, "I do wish she had taught me the language. I think that's a part of me that needs to be made whole. And I've tried to deny it for many years, but I think I do wish that. Whether I'll learn it or not is yet to be decided, but I do wish she had taught me the language. But I think she might have been scared that I'd have gone into the Tongan culture." Sulia says that the reason she did not want to learn Tongan until she was an adult was the "bad connotations" the language had, having been used by her mother only when she was in a rage with the children.

As a child in Australia, Sulia admits she sometimes felt embarrassed to be Tongan, partly because of her mother's negative attitudes. Seeing other Tongans "not doing Australian-Anglo things" also embarrassed her, and this feeling was exacerbated by the racism she experienced, with people often assuming she was aboriginal. The racism, she says, was "another reason why I think I had been so anti-Tongan, because it just brought me trouble the whole time, from either the Tongan community or the Anglo community."

As she grew older, Sulia's interest in her Tongan "side" fluctuated.

I would have to say for myself it's always been there, sometimes stronger, sometimes it's been stronger, sometimes it hasn't been stronger. . . . I was always interested, but also disinterested for various reasons, but I would say I am the most interested now, the most relaxed about it than I've ever been, at twenty-eight years of age. And interested actually to have a look. I don't think I will find a dramatic change [in myself], I don't think there will be a dramatic change, I think there will be a feeling of more wholeness, and I tend to think I'll be more *pālangi* than Tongan at the end of my search. . . . I always identify as half Tongan, half Australian Anglo-Saxon. Even with Tongans, they'll ask me "Oh, are you Tongan?" and I find myself saying "No, I'm half Tongan." I just like to make the distinction that I'm not one or the other, I'm both, and I'd like to be accepted as such. . . . I would say I look half Tongan and half Australian. If I didn't look Tongan . . . I would say I was just Australian.

For Sulia, with her lack of Tongan language and cultural knowledge, it is her appearance that ultimately determines her identification. "I go visually, because I'm not accepted as a white person."

In describing what she likes about Tongans, Sulia reveals her ongoing ambivalence.

I like the way they can just sit down and just laugh. I think that would probably be—just sit down and laugh. I mean, I know that there's some horrific gossip as well that can go on, I mean really bad, but when they don't do that, just having a great time, that's when I have a really good time with them. Laughing, teasing one another. Generosity to an extent, but I think there are a lot of expectations when you start getting into that arena, which I don't like, because then you get a lot of spongers. And I can be very Australian like that: pay for myself, independent, that sort of thing. I would have to say, probably the feeling like you are part of a community. Really feeling like you belong. Even though I don't belong, there are, still sort of that feeling, like when I do feel it, a certain part of me, it's like, oh yeah, I can really feel that, and that's really nice. But I think that comes with a lot of baggage.

As for what she does not like, she says, "I think it would have to be how rigid they can be. How incredibly strict, and no room for discussion. That's the way it is. . . . I think that really breaks people." She adds, "I find that I'm really tense being around Tongans. Even though I can enjoy them, I find that I'm just tense, like doing the wrong thing, saying the wrong thing, what have you." When she considers what her life might have been like if she had grown up in Tonga, Sulia says thoughtfully, "I think I would have had real problems there; I don't know how I would've turned out. I know that I would not have been happy, but as to the extent and intensity of my unhappiness I couldn't say. But what I don't like is that I find it incredibly rigid. I would have to say that that would probably be the worse component if I had lived my childhood in Tonga. Not only having to obey my parents, but having to obey the whole system."

Sulia has made a decision not to get involved in sending remittances to Tonga, having seen her mother send a great deal over the years. She also feels very negative about Tonga generally, as her previous comments indicate, but has been having telephone conversations with a cousin living in Tonga who is encouraging her to visit so she can see a more positive side.

Sulia's ideas about child rearing are strongly shaped by her unhappy childhood, and when asked what she would like to teach her own children, she immediately gives a long list of values such as self-love, self-acceptance, freedom, individuality, and so on, and says she would allow them to explore their Tongan heritage. "If I was advising other young parents of Tongan descent I would encourage them to allow themselves to be open and allow their children to be open to explore their individuality and their Tonganess, so I think that's what I would have liked."

On the topic of marriage, Sulia's mother told her much the same thing that many young Tongan women hear. "She was always, 'Oh, be careful marrying a Tongan,' so my message was never marry a Tongan, so that's how I perceived it. Because, you know, they'll hit you, you'll have to do all the work—basically because the woman would have to do so much. It would be a very uneven relationship." This advice affected Sulia's views of marriage. "I always vowed never to marry a Tongan . . . and I don't think I will, I just don't think it's in my cards. I may be wrong, but I really don't think I will. I'm ready to look at the Tongan thing, look at my [Tongan] side, then go on, on my own." Nevertheless, she laughs and admits, "I could never walk away from my Tonganness; I've tried, and I can't do it!"

7

Looking Ahead

At the beginning of the twenty-first century, what does it mean to be Tongan for the tens of thousands of Tongans living away from those tiny, scattered islands in the South Pacific? In terms of relationships with the wider societies in which they live, it means being part of a nonwhite ethnic minority group that frequently has its specific identity submerged under the broader grouping of "Polynesian" or "Pacific Islander." The stereotypes attached to these categories mean that Tongans experience racism and discrimination, or at least encounter preconceived notions of what Tongans or "Islanders" are like. Within the Tongan populations overseas, being "Tongan" goes far beyond such stereotypes and the recognizable markers of ethnicity, such as appearance, music, food, and so on. Yet as we have seen, defining just what "being Tongan" really means is impossible, since each individual creates his or her own understanding, which is inevitably influenced by the experience of living outside Tonga.

A Tongan wedding I attended late in the year 2000 exemplified the kind of blending of Tongan and non-Tongan elements that characterizes the lives of so many of these overseas Tongans. The ceremony itself was in a small church where a predominantly Tongan congregation worships every Sunday; on this occasion the only non-Tongans present, apart from myself and my two youngest children, were the spouses of Tongans. The bride and groom and their attendants wore Western-style wedding clothes: a white bridal gown, formal suits, and satin bridesmaid and flower girl dresses. The minister was an Australian woman and the service was in English, with several hymns sung in Tongan.

The bride's family has been in Australia since the mid-1980s and is part of a large extended family that has migrated to Australia over a period of over forty years. Her immediate family has been only moderately successful overseas, and while they could not afford a lavish reception with hundreds of guests, they ensured that six large pigs were spit-roasted and that the fifty or so guests had plenty to eat and drink. Their modest backyard had been transformed by the erection of a makeshift covering decorated with *ngatu* and pandanus mats. The gifts were a mixture of *koloa* and "traditional" Western wedding presents of household goods.

Some of the adults made emotional speeches in Tongan, interspersed with a Tongan string band and popular Western music played by a young Tongan man acting as disc jockey. The children, most of whom could not understand the speeches, chatted in English about their schools and friends and sundry other topics. Women in their Tongan clothing—*puletaha* and *kiekie*—laughed, clowned, and gossiped, while adolescents in the latest teen fashions hung about rather uncomfortably at the edges of the covered area or found places away from the adults to joke and flirt with one another.

Similar scenes are played out in every Tongan population throughout the diaspora, always a "mixing" of influences, with more or less emphasis on the Tongan elements. The generational differences that were so apparent at this wedding are found wherever there are Tongan migrants and their descendants, although as we have seen, the differences *within* generations can be almost as stark as those *between* them. At the heart of these differences lies the concept of *anga fakatonga*, which, together with the Tongan language, is viewed by many Tongans as *defining* Tongan identity—even to the point that some claim it is possible for someone with no Tongan "blood" to be accepted as Tongan if they are competent in these respects.

The relationship between identity and language is highly contested and has emerged as a central issue in broader debates about cultural identity. Language is often regarded as a crucial marker of "authentic" identity and can become a powerful means of asserting membership in a group, both to members of that group and to the wider society. Recognition of broader cultural competence can become dependent on knowledge of language: the idea of language as a "key" to culture and tradition. Ulf Hannerz has argued that while language has dominated the way people think of cultural boundaries, globalization is challenging this, with people increasingly communicating across languages (1996, 21). However, the reassertion of local identities in the context of globalization could act to curb this challenge, at least in terms of ideas of "authentic" group membership. All of the young people I spoke with said one of their priorities with their own children will be to teach them to speak Tongan fluently. Lusi said, "More than anything, I just want them to be able to speak Tongan fluently. This will pay off in the future. Speaking Tongan means having to think and feel like a Tongan, and if they could speak English too, then I would be more than happy." She added, "It's really disappointing that I can't speak the language enough to communicate with non-English-speaking Tongans. I feel as though I am so rude at times when I don't say anything to Tongans that don't speak English but I really want to."

Whether their determination to teach their children Tongan can overcome the obstacles Tongan parents overseas already face remains to be seen, and the extent to which the third and later generations of Tongans overseas speak Tongan is likely to have a significant impact on attitudes toward "authentic" Tonganness. Already, those who, for whatever reason, do not have the requisite language skills or cultural knowledge often wish to claim their own rights to "authenticity." Many young Tongans who know little or nothing of the Tongan language or "the Tongan way" claim a Tongan identity based on biological and, more important, emotional identification with what they see as essential "Tonganness."

These young Tongans are not in an unusual position, and many studies of the descendants of migrants have shown that it is possible for them to retain an identification with their parents' cultures and yet have little knowledge or understanding of those cultures as well as poor language skills. Like second-generation Mexicans in the United States (Keefe and Padilla 1987), many young Tongans emphasize generalized "cultural" values, such as the importance of involvement with the extended family, given their lack of more specific cultural knowledge. Thomas Fitzgerald argues in his study of second-generation Cook Islanders in New Zealand that "[i]dentity does not necessarily involve the maintenance of a separate culture, and social changes may not detract from self-conscious awareness; rather, such changes often enhance identifications" (1998, 255).

While this argument captures the perspective of many young people, it neglects the fact that they are perceived by many (both "insiders" and "outsiders") as inauthentic, thereby undermining their claims to identity. Many of the young people at the Tongan wedding described above still identify as Tongan, yet with their lack of language and cultural competence their location on the edges of the activities symbolizes the positions they often hold in Tongan "communities" overseas. They may claim to be Tongan, but they will not be fully accepted as such by those who define being Tongan in terms of *anga fakatonga* and language ability.

The Future of the Tongan Way

The struggles over authenticity and identity leave many young Tongans living overseas anxious about whether they can count as "real" Tongans. While it is common for them to shift between identities, with varying degrees of difficulty, most still feel that at least part of their cultural identity is Tongan. Even those for whom the struggle has been especially difficult tend to feel their Tongan identity is unshakable; as Sulia said, "I could never walk away from my Tonganness; I've tried, and I can't do it!" I frequently heard statements such as "a Tongan will always be a Tongan no matter what."

For some young people this sense of an intrinsic, immutable identity is not only a matter of an essential quality of Tonganness with which they are born, it is confirmed by the ethnic identity imposed on them by the wider society in which they live. Within migrant Tongan populations cultural and ethnic identities are becoming increasingly merged and mutually defining. Even so, for some Tongans, both young and old, Tongan identity is simply not as important in their lives as other aspects of their identities, or it is something that can be taken for granted rather than self-consciously asserted. Individuals' attitudes toward their cultural identities can also shift over their life span, and some of those young people who were so obviously uncomfortable at the Tongan wedding may well become more self-consciously "Tongan" at a later stage and proudly relocate themselves from the periphery to the center. Of course, even if they do so, "the Tongan way" they enact and embody will reflect the ongoing transformations of this concept and associated practices.

While many Tongans I have spoken with expressed faith in the essential and enduring quality of being Tongan, fewer were as certain of the future of *anga fakatonga*, despite its close association with identity. Only a minority of people believe *anga fakatonga* will be retained by Tongans living overseas, and even then most admit that it will be transformed—indeed, some acknowledge that such a broad, fluid concept is inherently amenable to constant transformation and redefinition. Those who see the concept as fixed and bounded do not acknowledge such transformations, and when seen in opposition to

Western cultures that are also perceived as unitary and static, it becomes something that can be "lost," particularly in the context of migration. As Mosese, twenty-seven, born in Tonga but raised in Australia from the age of five, commented, "The Western culture will eventually swallow up all other cultures it meets. That is its drawback . . . the Western culture is too strong." Some argue that young people are actively rejecting the Tongan way so that it will no longer be passed down through the generations. Still others blame intermarriage, and others see parents as the culprits for not teaching their children *anga fakatonga*. Not all want to place blame, however, and some older people, like 'Ana (Case Study 1), argue that migrants *should* let go of their "traditions." Losa contemplated the loss of *anga fakatonga* and said, "I don't think it worries me; I'm more Australian now, I've been here for twenty years!"

Despite the strong criticisms many younger Tongans have with regards to aspects of the Tongan way, few seem to want to abandon it altogether. They tend to accept that it should be transformed, saying, for example, that "good" elements such as respect should be kept, but altered to better suit life overseas. Lesieli, who identifies herself as being "in the middle" of Tongan and Australian identities, says she would like to combine Tongan and Western elements of parenting. Yet she fears that *anga fakatonga* will be lost altogether, saying, "I just think it's going to disappear sometime. That's what makes me think I want to bring my kids up the Tongan way."

Many Tongans now realize that maintaining Tongan values and practices can be an uphill battle for parents, given that their children's lives are filled with other influences. Increasingly, parents are having to compromise and maintain a flexible attitude toward the Tongan way. While they may worry that doing so risks "losing" *anga fakatonga*, it has become clear throughout this book that this flexibility is the most successful parenting strategy, reducing the likelihood of generational conflicts and enabling children to balance their identification as Tongan with those other influences.

Parents who are willing to accept that *anga fakatonga* often can be renegotiated and "adapted" tend to have higher levels of education, which is in turn frequently associated with higher socioeconomic status and an ability to mix comfortably with non-Tongans in the workplace and other contexts. It is the more strictly "traditional" parents who often find themselves clashing with their children. Fearful of losing the Tongan way, such parents often attempt to force their children to comply with their expectations, thus risking that the children rebel even further or even leave home. Yet as we have seen, parental strategies can be influenced by children's responses, and sometimes when there are conflicts with older children, parents become more willing to blend Tongan and non-Tongan elements in order to prevent similar problems with their later-born children. Many Tongans now promote two key changes to parenting: a reduction in the use of harsh physical punishment and the encouragement of open communication with children. Rather than insisting that their children be "Tongan" in every respect, the ideal for many parents today is that their children feel secure in their Tongan identities while also feeling at ease in the wider societies in which they live.

The extent to which Tongans are willing to critique the Tongan way is not simply determined along this "traditional" and "modern" axis. We have seen that many other intersecting elements contribute to individuals' attitudes, including gender, length of time overseas, education, religion, and particular life experiences. Age is a significant factor, with adolescents and young adults often the harshest critics of Tongan values and practices, although remarkably few turn away from their own Tongan identities on the basis of such criticisms.

A Computer-Mediated Future?

The desire of young people to feel that they "belong" as Tongans is apparent in their enthusiastic embracing of the Internet as a means of forging and maintaining connections with other Tongans throughout the world. Sites like the Kava Bowl have helped to engender a stronger sense of global "community" for participants. Such sites can become part of the process of identity construction by facilitating discussion of what it means to be Tongan overseas, by enabling participants to share their opinions, experiences, and problems, and by helping revitalize the Tongan language. The sites create new forms of transnational ties, and in doing so contribute to what Aihwa Ong describes as "the dynamic construction of new kinds of transnational ethnicized subjectivity" (1999, 243; see Morton 2002b).

This sense of belonging to a global community became apparent during a burst of enthusiasm about genealogies on the Tongan History Association forum in 1999. Tongans from many parts of the diaspora contributed information about their families and asked each other for assistance in tracing their family histories. The establishment of the

Mormon genealogical web site that same year created further interest in the possibilities of the Internet for setting up records of the information they collected. One participant wrote,

> The internet and globalisation are seen by many as a threat to culture into the future. However, by giving us free access to codifying our heritage, in many ways I think it is a lifeline to an increasingly dispersed peoples and culture. Imagine the benefit of future generations being able to log in and find—firstly information on their own heritage, but then to further that knowledge linked to the traditions, history, and wisdom of the greater Tongan population. Alongside that, the ability to find "identity" lost in the real world but signposted in cyberspace. (THA 16.8.99)

One of the enthusiastic participants in the THA discussion on genealogies said he believed if enough records could be collected, the kinship relationships between all Tongans the world over could be shown. Another responded, "I do share your dream and I'm sure that somehow all Tongans are connected" (THA 15.3.99).

Although it has been used primarily to forge and maintain links between Tongans across the diaspora, participation in the KB and similar sites also can enhance the affective ties of diasporic Tongans to their "homeland," even in the case of Tongans who have never been to the islands. A number of the young people I interviewed had little connection with Tonga as they grew up, leaving phone calls and other forms of contact with relatives to their parents. However, as adolescents and young adults they began to use Tonga Online and other Tongan-oriented sites to keep up with news from Tonga, communicate with relatives in Tonga, and search for information on topics such as mythology, dance, and history.

The Internet thus provides a means for young Tongans, many of whom are feeling alienated from their Tongan "heritage," to feel connected to Tonga. This in turn can strengthen their identification as Tongan. Joe, as we saw in chapter 5, admitted he had lost any sense of "bonds" with Tonga, even though his parents and some siblings are in Tonga. He commented, "Actually discovering the kavabowl on the internet has brought the biggest 'piece of something Tongan' back into my life." Before he began using the Internet he phoned his family in Tonga once or twice a month, but, he said, "soon they'll be on the net as well so we'll probably talk every day." Since I began my research in the mid-1990s the number of Tongans who are accessing Tongan-oriented sites has increased noticeably. Gerard Ward has warned for the Pacific more generally, "If contributions from the heartland do not remain strong, informative and numerous, the understanding and sense of identity to be gained by the expatriates will fade" (1999, 34). The Internet has the potential to be an important part of such contributions and thus to play a role in retaining Tongans' links to their homeland.

Within Tonga, there have been a number of moves to ensure that ties to the diaspora and the world are strengthened through computer-mediated communication (CMC). Stressing the importance of the Internet for overcoming problems of isolation, Taholo Kami has described the Internet as "God's gift to the islands" (*Tonga Chronicle* 1999e), and while many Tongans have never used a computer in their lives, the younger generations in Tonga are rapidly becoming familiar with this technology.[1] Already, there is increasing emphasis on computer studies and the use of the Internet in even the remote schools (*Matangi Tonga* 1998a), and Tongan churches and associations overseas are channelling their fund-raising efforts into the provision of computing equipment in schools. Distance learning is being promoted, with arrangements already in place to work with educational institutions in New Zealand and the United States (*Tonga Chronicle* 1998h, 1999c; *Matangi Tonga* 1998b).

Tonga's crown prince has a vision of Tonga as a more technologically sophisticated nation. "It's not only possible but, I think, highly desirable. It's not as if developed countries have an exclusive on computer training. It's such a new thing in the world that actually we can all start off at the same level" (P. Fonua 1998; see *Matangi Tonga* 2001b, 2001c). Tongans are being given a clear message—from their beloved royal family, the schools, the media, and their families in the diaspora—that computer technology has the potential to link them more closely than ever to the rest of the world. By mid-1999 advertisements were appearing in the *Tonga Chronicle* proclaiming "The Internet is the future" and inviting Tongans to learn how to produce and maintain their own web sites through courses held in the Royal School of Science. There are already Tongan-based Internet sites, such as Kalianet (see chapter 3), and the number of e-mail users is constantly growing within the government, business, and private sectors.

As well as its potential in areas such as tourism, education, and business, the use of the Internet to forge stronger links between the diaspora and Tonga can be seen as part of a broader process that George Marcus has identified in which Tonga's king is attempting "to retain the Tongan state as the center of a society in centrifugal motion" (1993, 32). In the case of the Internet, it is the king's children, including his heir, who have been most enthusiastic in their visions for Tonga's future. They are in effect continuing the king's efforts "to preserve Tonga's position as *both* the economic and symbolic center of an internationalizing culture" (Marcus 1993, 32, emphasis in original).

The widespread enthusiasm for the potential of CMC to connect Tonga with the diaspora does not entirely match the reality, however. Practical obstacles such as the high cost of computers and Internet connections, lack of necessary infrastructure, low rates of computer literacy, and difficulties with servers and power supplies impede those in Tonga who do wish to link into the global community. Even if these obstacles can be overcome, CMC offers only a particular kind of transnational connection, and to be effective as a link between Tonga and the diaspora it will need to be interrelated with, and further facilitate, the kind of ties that already exist.

Ties between Tonga and the Diaspora

The efforts being made to "wire-up" Tonga to create new links with the diaspora can be seen as part of the process that Linda Basch, Nina Glick Schiller, and Cristina Szanton Blanc have described as "deterritorialized nation-state building," in which a nation's people can live anywhere in the world yet retain their ties to the nation of origin (1994, 269; see Appadurai 1996). They describe the processes by which such "transnational" migrants and the political leaders from their country of origin construct an ideology in which the migrants are "loyal citizens of their ancestral nation-state" (Basch, Glick Schiller, and Szanton Blanc 1994, 3). Further, transnationalism challenges the very idea of the nation-state, given that many members of a nation-state such as Tonga now live beyond its geographic borders.

While it can be important for the governments of such nations to encourage continued ties between migrants and their homeland, these ties can also create a certain ambivalence toward the migrants. As Basch, Glick Schiller, and Szanton Blanc found for migrants from the Caribbean, a home government in the process of building a "deterritorialized nation" welcomes the remittances sent by migrants and welcomes them as visitors, but it may not be so welcoming if the migrants want to return home permanently and bring new ideas—about issues such as class, gender, and power—with them (1994). For example, with the rise of the Pro-Democracy Movement (PDM) in Tonga, the government became more wary of returning migrants (in some cases even as visitors), as it could not be sure of their level of support for the PDM or what influence they might have on Tongans at home.

There has been no need for the Tongan government to call on immigrant Tongans to support its policies or to lobby other governments, as was the case, for example, with the use of Filipinos in America to lobby the U.S. government on behalf of Corazon Aquino. For the most part, the organizations formed by Tongans overseas have had links with Tonga only on the basis of fund-raising and other support, and while this support needs to be recognized as part of the "nation-building" process, it does not entail direct involvement in Tongan political affairs.

Another important difference between the situation in Tonga and those in the Caribbean, the Philippines, and other cases where transnationals have involved themselves in the politics of their home nations is that Tongan politics have remained comparatively stable. Migrant Tongans have not felt the need to call on foreign governments to intervene in Tongan affairs. In addition, most Tongans are reluctant to appear disloyal to their home country, given the overarching pride they have in Tonga's independence and the role attributed to the monarchy in retaining this status (Morton 2001a).

Further discouraging the direct involvement of migrants in Tongan politics is the fact that they are unable to vote in Tongan elections. However, this issue was raised with the prime minister's office in 1999, and it is possible arrangements may be in place for the 2002 elections (P. Fonua 1999). Pesi Fonua states that if overseas Tongans over age twenty-one who have retained citizenship—cautiously estimated as 25,000—were allowed to vote, it could make a significant difference in the outcome of elections, given that in the 1996 elections 27,948 votes were cast (56.09 percent of potential votes).

The rights of long-term migrants to lease land in Tonga is another highly contentious issue and has been raised for some time without resolution. Tensions surrounding issues such as voting and land rights bring into question the role of overseas Tongans in their homeland: is it their role to participate in the process of nation building only indirectly, as through remittances, or, as some would argue, should they play a more direct role? Ward has said of the Pacific,

Those who live overseas and seek to hold to their emotional, social and potential economic links with the homeland, are likely to argue for continued recognition of rights. The whole question has the potential to create great rifts between the homeland and expatriate communities. In matters of rank and status it is possible that similar tensions might arise. (1997, 192)

Some migrants are attempting to play a more direct role in the affairs of their homeland; a recent example of these efforts is the establishment of the Tonga-USA Business Council (TUBC) in 2000 (*Matangi Tonga* 2000b). The first president of the council made this intended role explicit when he described the TUBC and its members as "nation builders." Even the desire expressed by some younger overseas Tongans to return to Tonga to work can be seen in this way, as they frequently envision their actions as a means of "helping" Tonga with its typically "Third World" problems.

Despite the commitment of some overseas Tongans to an involvement in the affairs of their "homeland," there is certainly the potential for development of the "great rifts" Ward described in relation to issues of migrants' rights. Already, other rifts are emerging—the growing tension regarding remittances and the practice of sending children and adolescents to Tonga, and the sometimes unwelcoming reception of migrants and their descendants who visit the kingdom—that are creating an increasingly ambivalent relationship between Tonga and the diaspora.

The "futurist scenario" that Marcus imagined in 1981 in which he suggested Tonga could lose its political and economic importance to migrants is rapidly becoming a reality for many Tongans overseas. He suggested that "Tonga might remain merely a struggling nation-state in the face of flourishing overseas concentrations in places like Hawaii and California, residents of which would continue to affect the overall conditions of Tongans at home by their selective participation and contributions in persisting family networks" (1981, 60). While some overseas Tongans are actively maintaining and even increasing their participation, not just in family networks but in other arenas, such as business, many more are reducing the level of such involvement. It is ties *across* the diaspora that are strengthening, and unless there is a resurgence of transnational ties (perhaps facilitated by information technologies), links with Tonga will weaken. As the young people who have been the focus of this book move into adulthood and have children of their own, the relationships between Tonga and the diaspora will undergo further transformations that are likely to diminish even more the significance of the Tongan nation in the hearts and minds of Tongans living outside its borders.

Panethnicity

One such challenge to Tonga's centrality to migrants is already becoming apparent: the adoption by some Tongans of broader, panethnic identities. In their study of the emergence of a pan-Carribean identity, Basch, Glick Schiller, and Szanton Blanc note that "transmigrants play significant roles in challenging the nationalism of their home countries by building regional identifications and movements" (1994, 276). Many young Tongans in the diaspora are identifying themselves as "Pacific Islanders" and "Polynesians." These terms were historically created by Europeans in the process of exploring and colonizing the Pacific and continue to be imposed at the level of government in the migrant receiving nations. Yet some young Tongans are now welcoming the opportunity to have a larger group with which to identify. One young man, son of a Tongan father and Australian mother and who grew up in Australia and another South Pacific country, explained that he had a "more pluralist view of being a Pacific Islander, as much as a Tongan" (e-mail 1.10.97). Makalesi said, "I am Polynesian by identity, race, color and roots. It is me! I am proud to identify myself as Polynesian. It is an exotic word. . . . I love the word and hearing it reconfirms my roots, identity, background and my uniqueness. Yes, please call me South Pacific Islander, call me Polynesian, call me Tongan. I am proud of it."

Of course, there are some who reject a broader Pacific identity, as with New Zealand-born Vika, now living in Melbourne. "Pacific Islander: that's a group, it's not who I am. No. Thinking about it now, it doesn't actually tell you who I am." Vika's attitude is influenced by her experiences in New Zealand and her resentment that people often assume she is Maori; being known as Tongan has become important to her. Sarah, eighteen, is also New Zealand born and is similarly influenced by externally imposed stereotypes. She distinguished between the terms "Polynesian" and "Pacific Islander": "I have no problem with being called Polynesian; however, I am not very fond of being called a Pacific Islander. Even though they are the same people, it is just that when someone says Pacific Islanders I picture them to be dirty, unorganized, big/large, and lazy, and with Polynesians I picture tanned, slim/fit, clean people."

A number of young people commented that they resented being confused with Maori, Samoans, or other Islanders and that this brought out their sense of pride in being Tongan. This pride is evident in the "100% Tongan" and "Tongan Warrior" T-shirts and the clothing printed with *ngatu* designs that are popular among teenagers. However, young people can also be seen wearing Maori bone necklaces and sporting tattoos based on other Pacific motifs: they want to be acknowledged as Tongan by others but have incorporated a broader "Islander" identity into their own self-representations.

Steven Francis has observed that for some Islanders, identifying with one another helps them to establish a sense of community.

> United by shared feelings of displacement and a perception of persecution—from sources ranging from other school students to symbols of authority such as police—but without the support of the extended family network, young Pacific Islanders seek each other out. . . . This community support network of other Islander teenagers allows them to differentiate themselves from their parents (whom they believe to not understand the difficulties of their lives in Australia) and their Anglo peers. (1995, 188)

In Melbourne some young people who do not have much to do with their own "ethnic" group, out of choice or because there are not many in their area, move into other Pacific groups. For example, they may go to another Island church or socialize with a group of friends from one or more of the other groups. Their identification tends to be an emotional rather than practical one in that they identify with other Islanders but dress and act primarily as Australians. These young people describe feeling a kind of bond with other Islanders and say it gives them a special status—even in mundane situations, such as knowing that an Islander doorman at a nightclub will let them in ahead of other patrons. Many young people who are becoming interested in Tongan dance are also learning other Pacific dance styles to include in their performances.

Identifying as an Islander or as Polynesian can also be more comfortable for young people—particularly the children of intermarriages—who feel they are not fully versed in the Tongan way and language and so feel somewhat insecure about their Tongan identity. An Australian youth worker who accompanied one Tongan group to a national church youth convention told me they had befriended members of a Samoan group from Sydney and one of the smaller Tongan groups, also from Sydney. She added that the group she accompanied from Melbourne disliked a larger Tongan group from Sydney "because they were more Tongan than the Tongans!" The smaller group, on the other hand, "operated a lot more in the Australian way, or appreciated the Australian way."

To some extent population size affects the level of interaction between Tongans and other Islanders, with smaller populations less likely to experience intergroup rivalry and more likely to develop panethnic identities. A Samoan in Adelaide, Australia, wrote on the KB that "the Tongans and Samoans here are TIGHT. I am Samoan and my best friend is Tongan. Maybe the reason us Polys stick together in this place is because there are not so many here. Can the problem [of gang rivalry] in SLC [Salt Lake City] be that there are too many polys that they have to fight each other for survival. . . . We need unity for survival y'all, especially in another man's land. Don't let jealousy and anger spoil it all for us" (KB 5.5.97). Yet even within larger Islander populations panethnic solidarity and identification occurs: a Tongan man from Salt Lake City claimed "us Tongans in SLC, we got the love for the Samoans and I'm sure they gotz it for us, but some don't!!! . . . My love for all Polynesians, because if we can't stay together then we're all sorry!! One love please!" (KB 2.5.97, original capitalized).

The formation of panethnic groups involves the creation of new ethnic boundaries and cooperation between groups previously seen as distinct by others and by themselves (Espiritu 1992). Panethnicity usually emerges as a result of externally imposed groupings—for example, in government classifications that determine the allocation of resources. This then encourages the ethnic groups to work within that panethnic categorization, and the panethnic group can also become "a political resource for insiders, a basis on which to mobilize diverse peoples and to force others to be more responsive to their grievances and agendas" (Espiritu 1992, 7). There can be disadvantages to panethnic identity, however, as when outsiders' hostility to any one of the subgroups becomes directed at all subgroups within a panethnic category (Espiritu 1992, 6). Internal divisions and conflicts also can create difficulties for individuals or particular subgroups; as Yen Le Espiritu points out, panethnicity involves both fusion and fission (1992, 14).

Individuals within a panethnic group may continue to operate within their distinct ethnic groups in many contexts, but at times may assume the panethnic identity for particular purposes, a process Espíritu calls "ethnic switching" and which can be a matter of choice or an external designation (1992, 15). However, over time, there can be a lessening of differences between the groups as they begin to borrow ideas and practices from one another, intermarry, and generally develop not only a shared identity but a shared culture. Increasingly, they may also draw their histories together to create a postcolonial awareness of shared disempowerment and discrimination; in the case of Pacific Islanders this includes both their history of colonization and "missionization" and their experiences in the diaspora.

In most countries where Pacific Islanders have settled they are, for political purposes, designated as belonging to the "Pacific Islander" category and must work within it to access resources and achieve any political participation. Given the comparatively low level of political activism among most Islanders, their panethnic identity is, more importantly, a means of achieving a sense of group solidarity, which extends beyond national borders. Identification within broader groupings such as "Polynesian" and "Pacific Islander" is a process that began long before large-scale migration commenced and that today has significance within the Pacific, both through regional organizations and institutions (e.g., the South Pacific Commission and the University of the South Pacific), and in the relationships between Pacific nations and the rest of the world. Tongan anthropologist and novelist Epeli Hau'ofa has, in recent years, promoted the notion of a "substantial regional identity" to protect the "collective interests" of Islanders, although he prefers the term "Oceanian" to "Pacific Islander" (1998, 392–393). Hau'ofa recognizes that this regional identity extends beyond the Pacific Ocean, given the process of "world enlargement" occurring through migration and international travel (1994, 156).

This panethnic identification is becoming increasingly apparent an Tongan and other Pacific-oriented Internet sites. Taholo Kami has described the KB as relevant to "the Global Pacific Island Community" (e-mail to author 12.11.98). This perception is shared by some who participate in the KB. "We as Pacific Islanders are at the verge of a New era, and it is through sites like the Kavabowl that we not only get an insight of what others think, but what our own understandings of the region we live in are. By clearly knowing who we are in the world, we are empowered to stand up to any group with the power to say 'We are *Pacific Islanders* and we have a place in this world no matter how small'" (KB 23.9.96, emphasis in original).

The more positive views of a pan-Pacific identity have been countered by criticisms of its homogenizing effects, which, Melani Anae argues, can encourage generalizing and stereotyping of migrants (1997). Anae describes labels such as "Polynesian" and "Pacific Islander" as having "a forced ethnic salience" and argues that the cultural, linguistic, historical, and other differences found between Pacific peoples "far outweigh the one commonality of shared New Zealand experiences" (1997, 128, 132). She notes that older migrants from the Pacific are more resistant to the use of these terms than younger ones. Those born in New Zealand often feel a sense of commonality that is encouraged by their designation as "Pacific Islanders" within schools and other institutions. This "PI identity" is, she claims, likely to be replaced by "a more ethnically defined one" as they become adults (1997, 132). Using the example of Samoans in New Zealand, Anae concludes that if young people develop a secure sense of their identities as "NZ-born Samoans"—rather than as Pacific Islanders—they can become "healthier" members of both the wider New Zealand society and their Samoan family, church, and community (1997, 136).

Anae has criticized the annual Pasifika Festival in Auckland as promoting a pan-Pacific identity, which is reduced in this context to outward displays of "culture" as found in music, dance, and fashion (1997, 131). She adds that given the situation of many Pacific migrants, who are facing poverty, unemployment, and discrimination, "What is there to celebrate? . . . [W]e need to critically examine and understand what culture, cultural identity and ethnicity means not for some kind of generic Pacific Islander, but for the different ethnic minority populations and people—caught within this pan-ethnic identity" (1997, 131).

While Anae's critique raises some salient issues, her account presents ethnospecific and panethnic identifications as mutually exclusive, whereas for many young people they are simply facets of their multiple identities. A post on the KB reads, "I'm straight up Tongan and dang proud of it. I love my people and everything we stand for but I also love my Samoan brothers and sisters cause in my eyes we all from the same neighborhood in that big old ocean, we just live in different houses. I love all my Poly people so its all about that 1love [i.e., "one love"]. Just remember, when you are at an unfamiliar place and you see another Poly then there is a bond there like no other (KB 12.3.98).

Anae also ignores the possibility that for some young "Islanders" living overseas, it may not be possible for them to establish secure identities within their specific "ethnic" groups, even as adults, if they lack the language and cultural competence that enables them to be acknowledged by others as authentic members of that group. The panethnic identities provide the sense of community and solidarity from which they feel excluded within their specific groups. Panethnic identities have also emerged in other migrant populations; for example, Suzanne Oboler's study of Latinos in the United States showed that many young Latinos try to fit into a Latino stereotype, minimizing their lack of language, historical knowledge, and cultural practices. This has led to the creation of an "ideal" Latino, and those who do not fit the stereotype then become marginalized and the community fractured. (1995, 172). A very similar process has been identified for the emergence of ideal "Chicano" traits (Keefe and Padilla 1987), and Oboler speculates that the homogenizing label of "Hispanic" may also be adopted by young people of Latin American and Spanish descent in the United States (1995, 170). Of course, the populations who take on these identities as Latinos, Chicanos, and Hispanics are much larger minority groups in the United States than Islanders, and they have very different histories of interaction with white Americans, but a similar process is already evident among Pacific Islanders in cities such as Auckland, Los Angeles, and Salt Lake City.

The Pacific Islander and Polynesian identities young people adopt vary at the local level, so that, for example, the Islander youth in New Zealand, who call themselves "PIs" or "Polys" or "NZ Borns" have developed "a new patois, new music, new fashion, new customs and practices which mark their distinctness" (Macpherson 1997, 95). These youth have incorporated influences from other sources (such as local Maori culture) that differ from those that have an impact on Islanders in other centers. Because of their smaller numbers, Islanders in centers like Melbourne have had less opportunity to develop new styles, but they borrow from the larger populations of Pacific youth in the United States and New Zealand.

Some external influences are more widespread, so that throughout the diaspora, Rastafarian influences are apparent—for example, in the dreadlocks sported by many young Islanders and in the reggae music that has been adapted to create a uniquely Islander sound. Another significant influence has been from African American youth culture.[2] Even in Tonga the influence can be seen in the young men who adopt the dress, slang, and body language of African American youth. In the village in which I lived and worked in 1988 there was a "gang" of youths who called themselves the Revenge of the Black Power. In the diaspora this identification is even more apparent, especially in the United States, where young Tongans and African Americans often live in the same neighborhoods and share a sense of marginalization. On the KB this influence is evident, with frequent use of "ebonic" slang and terms like "Bro" and "Sistah" when addressing other youth.

A KB post complaining of Polynesians behaving like African Americans and calling each other "niggas" (KB 25.3.98) received an angry response from a Tongan from California: "We peeps out in Killa Cali may act Black and dress like it but when it comes down to culture we REPRESENT our POLYNESIAN ROOTS so you betta chickty check yo self on that point" (KB 25.3.98). He angrily called the writer a "FOB" (fresh off the boat). Another wrote that "nigga" is used to mean friend, homey, or pal and claimed, "We proudly share our culture with our Black Brothers and vice versa. We most definitely know who we are and where our fathers and fore-fathers are from" (KB 25.3.98). However, for some young people identification with other minority groups, combined with internalization of negative stereotypes about Islanders, can lead them to feel a loss of their specific cultural identities. This sense of loss was expressed in a post on the KB.

> I went to a white school and a white church just because my mom doesn't want me to associate with those "BADD POLYNESIAN": Growing up as a Tongan in a community where there are many Tongans, I must admit I was told by relatives and friends to limit my socialization with Tongans. Of course being young and knowing all too very well the "stereotypes" I abided by this rule for most part of my life. I hung around African Americans and pretty much adapted to their way of life, style of speaking, and pretty much becoming ethnically an African American. Losing my identity of being a Tongan American was pretty hard to regain. I missed out on the beautiful culture that we are so very blessed with. (KB 19.3.98)

Constructing Identities

Adopting panethnic "Polynesian" and "Islander" identities and borrowing elements from other groups such as African Americans is part of the complex and often challenging process of constructing cultural identities for young Tongans living in the diaspora. Vijaya Joshi, writing of second-generation Indians in Australia, suggests that they occupy a "third space" that is neither Indian nor Australian. Arguing against assumptions that the children of migrants will experience culture conflict and have "a multiple, irreconcilable identity," she argues that their multiple identities "can be a liberating state" (1996, 1). Some young Tongans also find a sense of liberation in being able to move between identities in different contexts, experiencing what they so often describe as "the best of both worlds."

Another study—of Sikh teenagers growing up in England—describes these different contexts as "cultural fields" and points out that "[t]he shifts in the relations of power and culture from one cultural field to the next provide varying opportunities for second generations to 'play' with cultural identities. . . . As British-Sikhs participate within these different cultural fields, they create, not one unitary cultural identity, but rather multiple cultural identities that acquire situationally specific meanings and forms" (K. Hall 1995, 253). Kathleen Hall observes that the young people are sometimes Indian, sometimes British, and "there is a great deal of time for them to play with identities that lie somewhere in between" (1995, 254). Tongans also "play" with identity, as when they shift between the Tongan and English versions of their names, play with language to blend Tongan, English, and other vocabularies, or deliberately combine Tongan and other elements in their clothes and other aspects of their appearance. It is not all play, however, and we have seen that issues such as language use become critical to young people's identity constructions. Using Tongan becomes a claim of authenticity, and the variations of English they use—like ebonics—can become defiant assertions of other facets of identity.

Young Tongans, like young people in much of the world, are exposed to a vast array of possibilities as they create and recreate their identities. Writing about young Surinamese who have been brought up in the Netherlands, Livio Sansone describes Amsterdam, with its many different ethnic groups and subcultures, as a "symbol bank" from which youths could borrow elements in constructing "new, and more complicated, youth styles and ethnicities" (Sansone 1995, 135). The processes of globalization and transnationalism have meant that young Tongans both at home and overseas now have access to the "symbol banks" of the world. In some respects they are not confined to "Tongan," "Australian," or "American" identities if they do not wish to be and can experiment with different identities, shift between them, or blend and meld them in a process that for some is exciting and liberating but can also be confusing and can create considerable tension within their families. Other Tongans, including their kin, can pressure the young people to be "true" Tongans, and of course they must also deal with the imposition of ethnic identities upon them by the wider societies in which they live.

The diverse responses of young, overseas Tongans to the options available to them in constructing their identities illustrate the broader diversity I have described in this book. In examining Tongans' heterogenous experiences of migration and settlement, my aim has been to convey a sense of their struggles and successes as they deal with issues within their own families and in their interactions with others in the lands to which they have moved in search of "opportunities." Given the vastly differing experiences I have described, there is no neat conclusion to be made, either optimistic or pessimistic. Some face a lifetime of struggle; unemployed or in poorly paid jobs, dealing with racism and feeling alienated in the land that they believed offered so much hope. Some of the young people will leave school early, become involved with drugs, gangs, and crime, and move further and further away from their families and their sense of being Tongan. Others will find what their parents had hoped for them and more and will watch their own children succeed in their education and, later, employment, while cherishing their Tongan "roots" and asserting their identities with pride. Most, of course, lie somewhere in between. For now, at least, most are also "in between" in another sense, living in Australia, the United States, New Zealand, or elsewhere, yet maintaining ties to the islands of Tonga through remittances, visits and phone calls, Internet forums and chat rooms, or simply in their hearts.

APPENDIX A

The Tongans of Melbourne, Australia

Many of the voices heard throughout this book have been those of Tongans living in Melbourne. For readers who would like a more detailed description of this particular diasporic "community," this appendix presents a brief history of Tongan settlement in Melbourne and an analysis of statistics compiled from a survey of one hundred households spread across the metropolitan area.

Melbourne is the capital city of Victoria, Australia's smallest mainland state, which has the second largest population (after New South Wales) of all the states and territories. The 1996 census recorded a population of nearly 4.5 million, originating from 208 different countries, speaking 151 languages, and following more than 100 religious faiths (Victorian Multicultural Commission 1999). The five largest groups of migrants are from England, Italy, Greece, Vietnam, and New Zealand. Melbourne is home to a large proportion of the state's migrant population, with 87 percent of all overseas-born Victorians residing there (Maher and Caldow 1997, 1). A high proportion (69 percent) of the overseas-born migrants are from non-English-speaking countries; these migrants comprise approximately 20 percent of the total population of Victorians—the highest proportion for Australia. Parts of Melbourne have particularly high numbers of migrants, including some areas with around half their population born overseas, but the migrant population is also dispersed throughout the entire metropolitan area.

Within Victoria's migrant population, Pacific Islanders are a small group, but it is impossible to give accurate figures as to their numbers given various problems with the collection of statistics, discussed below. In the 1991 census 10,856 Pacific Islands–born individuals were recorded for the Melbourne metropolitan area, and in the 1996 census the number had risen to 12,416. At the end of the twentieth century, I estimate that there were approximately 14,000 Pacific Islands–born individuals in Melbourne, not allowing for overstayers, who may account for several thousand more.

Some groups of Pacific Islanders are quite substantial, including those from Tonga, Fiji, and Samoa, while others are very small groups, such as those from the islands of Kiribati, Vanuatu, Tokelau, and Tuvalu. The larger groups tend to have their own churches and often have formal associations such as the Samoan Advisory Council. Another large group is the New Zealand Maori, who are not included in the figures above. It is even more difficult to ascertain Maori numbers because usually they are not disaggregated from the figures for New Zealanders in Australia, but a recent estimation is that there were 5,606 Maori in Melbourne in the late 1990s (Maori and Pacific Islander Community Based Services 2000, 30).

Melbourne was the primary destination of migrants to Australia in the early post–World War II period, but by the time Tongans began to migrate in significant numbers, Sydney (in New South Wales) had taken over this position. The 1996 census records that 70 percent of the Tongan-born population in Australia lived in New South Wales, with considerably fewer in Victoria (14.4 percent) and Queensland (11.3 percent), and the remainder scattered through the other states and territories (statistics supplied by the Department of Immigration and Multicultural Affairs [DIMA]).

Over the years, Tongan-born settler migrants to Victoria have fluctuated in numbers, but the average number has remained small. In 1977–1978 there were only 10 new arrivals recorded; the number rose to 42 in 1997–1998, and the average over the 1977–1998 period was 21.2 per year, peaking at 62 in 1987–1988 (settler arrivals statistics supplied by DIMA). The number of new migrants arriving has been low, but with an increase of 52.7 percent between 1986–1991, the Tongan population has grown faster than other Oceania-born groups, which have increased by 31.9 percent.

Assessing the number of people in Melbourne who identify themselves as being of Tongan ancestry is difficult, particularly since the 1996 census recorded birthplace but not ethnicity. For Victoria as a whole, the 1996 census recorded just over 1,000 Tongan-born individuals,[1] with 748 for Melbourne. In my sample of 100 households, with 430 people of Tongan descent, 44.9 percent were born in Australia and a further 7.4 percent in New Zealand. If we apply this ratio to the 748 Tongan-born individuals recorded in the census (Australian Census 1996), we obtain a total of 1,140 Tongans in Melbourne. However, this figure is not very helpful, given the considerable underreporting in the census. My own estimation is that in the year 2000 there were approximately 3,000 people of Tongan descent in Melbourne.

The limitations of the official statistics for Tongans also make it difficult to ascertain accurate numbers for Tongans in Australia as a whole. One of the main problems is that they are, as in the United States, a relatively small population, so they are often placed in broader categories such as "Pacific Islanders," "Oceania," and, simply, "Other." When Tongans and other Pacific Islanders are combined with New Zealand in the broad category "Oceania," this grossly distorts the figures. Even when New Zealand is presented as a separate category, Pacific Islanders tend to be categorized as "Other Oceania and Antarctica," sometimes with separate figures for Fiji and Papua New Guinea (e.g., Bureau of Immigration and Population Research 1994b). A further problem is that the category "New Zealand born" used in some analyses is not disaggregated to reveal the different ethnic groups. Thus community profiles of the New Zealand born, which are based respectively on the 1991 and 1996 Australian censuses, discuss the history of immigration from New Zealand to Australia, yet make no mention of Pacific Islanders (Bureau of Immigration and Population Research 1994a; McMurray 2000).[2]

Official migration statistics are limited by their inability to reveal changes in individuals' status over time, or what Jean Louis Rallu calls "category jumping" (1994; see also Rallu 1993). For example, figures based on "settler" statistics are misleading, as they only show holders of migrant visas who have indicated their intention to settle in Australia, not the many who arrive on student, visitor, and other visas and later decide to settle more permanently. Thus Rallu's figure of 1,947 for net migration between 1986 and 1990 is well more than double the settler arrivals figure of 737 for this same period (Rallu 1993, 8).

Australian census statistics are also of little help, as in most of the data Tongans are again included in composite categories. Information on "ethnicity" is limited, and most censuses have asked for details of citizenship, country of birth, and parents' birthplace, but not self-identification. Only the 1986 census also included the question "What is each person's ancestry?" with space for individual responses. Census figures give numbers of Tongans primarily by birthplace and language, both of which are unreliable indicators of the number of people who identify themselves as Tongan. Using the criterion of respondent's birthplace, successive censuses have shown an increase in the number of Tongan-born individuals in

Australia from 448 in 1971 to 2,616 in 1981, then to 4,476 in 1986 (Connell, Harrison, and McCall 1991, table 1.3, 10). By the 1996 census the number had risen to 7,068 persons. The unreliability of such statistics was revealed in 'Osaiasi Faiva's 1988 survey of the Manly-Warringah area of Sydney, which found four times the number of Tongans that had been reported in the 1986 census; even for the Tongan born only, the figure was nearly 30 percent more (1989).[3]

The official statistics on Tongans in Melbourne, and in Australia more generally, are clearly problematic: not only do they give unreliable figures for the number of Tongan migrants, but they also tell us little about the circumstances of their lives in this country. The aim of my survey of households was to gain a detailed "snapshot" of a sample of the Tongan population in Melbourne—a population that has its own unique characteristics while also reflecting many of the general features of Tongan populations throughout the diaspora.

The History of Tongan Settlement in Melbourne

Few Tongans settled in Melbourne before the 1960s; however, a number of Tongans had visited and attended schools since the 1920s. Most notable was Queen Sālote's half sister, Fusipala, who attended the Methodist Ladies College (MLC) from 1926 to 1928.[4] The ties between Tonga and MLC have endured—for example, the queen herself laid the foundation stone of a new building in 1953; one of the early Tongan migrants to Melbourne was a teacher there; and a student exchange program between the college and Tonga's Queen Sālote College continues today.

In the late 1950s a few Tongan women arrived in Melbourne to study nursing at the hospitals there, including Epworth and the Royal Melbourne, and at regional hospitals such as Bendigo Base Hospital. These women were followed by a trickle of other Tongans, mainly young women and usually in groups of two or three, who came to attend nursing and secretarial classes. By the 1970s the Tongan students had begun to choose a more diverse range of courses, and some completed university degrees. Some students were church sponsored, but others whose families in Tonga could afford to support them traveled independently. A few married couples came to study, but many of the single students married Australians and settled in Melbourne, with a few gradually losing touch with the other Tongans. Another, much smaller, inflow of Tongan migrants in the 1970s were women who had married Australians in Tonga and came to settle in Melbourne and raise their families.

The number of Tongans in Melbourne began to grow more quickly in the 1970s as migrants had children and brought family members from Tonga to join them. By that time a sense of community had grown among the Tongans, who had begun by meeting socially and then in 1969 formed the Tongan Christian Fellowship (TCF) to meet for prayer, Bible study, and social interaction.[5] The Tongans also began to hold monthly services at the Wesley Church in the city, with the support of some ministers and others who had served as missionaries in Tonga and worked in Tongan secondary schools.[6] One of the members of the TCF later described in a church newsletter how the Fellowship began.

> At weekends they came together to sing hymns and share stories of the old country, and on occasions, to meet a new arrival who would bring greetings and messages of love from home. These gatherings were of a mixed nature, full of laughter and fun interwoven with tears of joy and sadness and always ended up with a determination not to miss the next gathering where there was always some Tongan food available. (*Austonga News* 1996)

In 1970 the TCF began holding weekly church services, which continued to be the focus of the Tongan community in Melbourne for several years, until the growth of the Tongan population and tensions within the group led to fissions, with several groups breaking away to form their own church communities catering to different denominations. The TCF nevertheless continued to grow, and in 1977 it became the first Tongan group to be listed in the Department of Social Security's *Directory of National Group Organisations in Australia* (1977, 48). By that time the group had around two hundred members and was already involved in fund-raising, sending money to help causes in Tonga (such as improvements to Vaiola Hospital), and the Pacific Cyclone Appeal. In 1986 the TCF became a Uniting Church parish, with a Tongan minister (Semisi Lātū) who had studied theology at Queens College in Melbourne and been granted permanent resident status in Australia. In 1991 the congregation moved to the Canterbury Uniting Church, in Melbourne's wealthy eastern suburbs, and today the church still has a predominantly Tongan membership.

Throughout the 1980s and 1990s further splits occurred in the Tongan population, and new church communities emerged as Tongan ministers from different denominations were brought to Melbourne and the rural areas of Victoria to which Tongans had moved in search of work. Another large Tongan congregation in Melbourne, which originated from one of the first groups to break away from the TCF, now is part of the Free Wesleyan Church of Tonga. This church is located in one of the western suburbs (a working-class area), where many of the more recent migrants have settled.

Although there are now Free Wesleyan churches in Melbourne, which have a close association with the Free Wesleyan Church in Tonga, the majority of Tongans in Australia belong to the Uniting Church. Since 1986 the Tongans of the Uniting Church in Australia have held an annual conference, now attended by over a thousand Tongan ministers and members. The conference was originally called by the Mission and Evangelism Committee to help Tongans in Australia settle into the Uniting Church and help non-Tongan parishes adjust to increasing Tongan membership. Known as the Tongan National Body, the representatives who attend the conferences are able to voice their opinions to the wider church about issues of concern to them—for example, recently the church proposed the ordination of homosexual ministers, something to which many Tongans were strenuously opposed. A member of the Tongan National Body was elected to the Ethnic Congregations Task Force in 1995, and other Tongans have been involved with Uniting Church bodies such as their Council of the Pacific (for Islanders in New South Wales), and the Synod Committee for Immigration and Ethnic Affairs. Tongans have also been members of the Victorian Inter-Church Immigration Council.

The major issue of concern at the 1994 Uniting Church conference was the relationship between the Uniting Church and the Wesleyan Church, an issue that had been causing tension within the Tongan population in Australia for some time. The Methodist Church in Australia, which most of the early migrants had joined, merged with the Congregationalists and some Presbyterians to form the Uniting Church in 1977. In its theology and social thinking it became "markedly less conservative," taking on a quite different view in many respects to the Wesleyan Christianity known by Tongans (Grainger 1998, 70). For instance, the Uniting Church encourages the congregation to be actively involved in services and in decision making about church business, hence for some special services, as on Mother's Day, the minister may play quite a minor role.

The tension between these churches was the cause of many of the splits within the Tongan population in Australia. As Gareth Grainger states, "The tendency amongst Wesleyan Tongans living in Australia has been since the 1970s to fragment into small family based independent church groups, whereas the Tongans of Catholic and other backgrounds have tended to adhere more closely to their original church loyalties" (1998, 71). Some potential tensions between the different churches in

Melbourne have been avoided by the institution of interfaith meetings, established in the mid-1980s and held several times each year. These meetings include most denominations (exceptions include the Mormon Church, one of the Wesleyan Methodist groups, and the Free Church of Tonga) and are attended by around three hundred to four hundred Tongans. The meetings rotate around the different churches, and their format varies from conventional services to presentations by youth groups, choir performances, and panels of ministers answering questions from the congregation. The aim, as one of the participating ministers commented, is to "pull the barriers down" between the different denominations.

The Melbourne Tongans in the Late 1990s

By the time I began my research with the Tongans of Melbourne in January 1995, they were a well-established but still relatively small migrant group, scattered across the metropolitan area and interacting with each other primarily through their churches and extended families. My research was completed in July 1999 and included a survey of 100 households, covering 479 individuals, using a detailed questionnaire eliciting a wide range of information, from basic demographic details (age, sex, number in household, etc.) to information on language use, social activities, and frequency of contact with relatives. In the analysis (see below) of these surveys, "Tongan household" is used to indicate the 60 households whose members were all Tongan or part-Tongan. A total of 321 persons lived in these homes. "Mixed households" are those 40 households where one or more members are non-Tongan, and they included 158 persons, 49 of them non-Tongans. A number of these households are essentially Tongan households, with one additional non-Tongan person, usually the partner of a Tongan member. Unless there are significant differences between the Tongan and mixed households, the analysis below does not differentiate between them.

Age and Sex

As the graph below indicates, the sample population is youthful, with the highest numbers in the zero to five age group and the majority (69.6 percent) under thirty.

Ethnicity and Country of Birth

Table 1 shows the ethnicity of the sample population, based on the ancestry of the parents of each individual, as well as country of birth.[7]

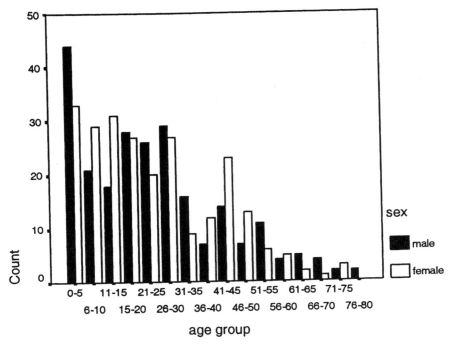

Graph 1: Age and sex of the total sample.

Table 1
Ethnicity and Country of Birth

	Country of Birth				TOTAL
	Tonga	Australia	New Zealand	Other	
Ethnicity					
Tongan	199	100	32	—	331
Tongan Australian	2	73	—	—	75
Other part-Tongan	3	20	—	1	24
Australian	—	38	—	—	38
Other non-Tongan	—	5	3	3	11
TOTAL	204	236	35	4	479

Within the forty mixed households, the Australians and other non-Tongans were primarily spouses of Tongan household members. Others included kin of non-Tongan wives, such as parents, siblings, and in one case children from a previous relationship. There were also two non-Tongan foster children in one household and a non-Tongan family friend in another.

Describing the "third generation" in this sample is not straightforward: only one Tongan couple who were both born in Australia had children. Of their six children, five were born in New Zealand and one in Australia, and their ages ranged from eight to twenty-four. Three other couples, two with one child and one with three, were Tongan Australians married to non-Tongans. There were also four couples in which one partner was born in Tonga and the other in Australia; three of the latter were Tongan Australian and one Tongan. Each of these couples had one child. Thus fifteen children could be counted as "third generation," at least on one parent's side. Apart from the family of six children, the other children were all under the age of six, including three newborns. The number in this generation is likely to grow rapidly in the near future, as there are a number of young married couples within the second generation who are planning to start their families soon. There was only one child in the study who is of the fourth generation: the grandchild of the couple with six children (above), whose father was born in Samoa.

As table 1 shows, nearly twice as many Tongans were born in Tonga as in Australia. However, if part-Tongans are included, the total of Australian-born individuals in the sample (193) is only slightly less than those born in Tonga (204). The four people in the category of "other" birthplace were born in England, Germany, and Samoa.

Birthplace in Tonga

Very few studies of Tongans overseas have included statistics on their origins within Tonga. Wendy Cowling's survey of 199 adults in Sydney found that 79 percent were from Tongatapu (41 percent of those were from Nuku'alofa, the capital), 13 percent from Vava'u, 6 percent from Ha'apai, and 2 percent from Niuatoputapu (1990, 195). My own sample showed a far greater proportion of migrants from Nuku'alofa living in Melbourne than in Sydney (89.8 percent of those from Tongatapu). These figures support the general perception held by Tongans in both cities that Melbourne Tongans are "town" Tongans (see chapter 3). For the whole sample of Tongan-born individuals, 81 percent were from Tongatapu, 17 percent from Vava'u, 13 percent from Ha'apai, 5 percent from the Niuas, and 2 percent from 'Eua.

Table 2
Length of Time in Australia by Birthplace

| | Time in Australia | | | |
	0–5 years	6–10 years	Over 10 years	TOTAL
Birthplace				
Australia	77	43	116	236
Tonga	55	25	124	204
New Zealand	21	1	13	35
Other	—	—	4	4
TOTAL	153	69	257	479

Length of Time in Australia

As shown in table 2, over half of the Melbourne sample had been in Australia for over ten years. The table shows the fluctuations in migration patterns, with fewer arriving in Australia in the late 1980s (six to ten years before the survey).

The significant number born in Australia and who have resided for over ten years (24.2 percent of the total) is an indication of the high proportion of second-generation Tongans in this population.

Marital Status

The youthful nature of the Tongan population in Melbourne is also reflected in the data for marital status, with 35.6 percent of individuals in the sample over age fifteen still unmarried. A further 55.8 percent were married (including de facto relationships), 3.3 percent separated, 3 percent divorced, and 2.3 percent widowed. In total there were eighty-seven currently married couples (including nine de facto couples) in the sample, including one male homosexual relationship (a Tongan and Australian couple).

Only six individuals over thirty had never been married, while in the sixteen to twenty age group none had been married and only two were in de facto marriages.[8] Six of the hundred households had two married couples (including de facto marriages), while seventy-four had one couple and twenty had none. The number of married couples is not necessarily an indication of how "extended" the family is within the household, as many households had extended family members who were unmarried, divorced, or widowed, often with their own children.

Household Size and Composition

The sample households ranged in size from one person to seventeen, with an average of 4.8 persons. The mixed households showed less variation in size, with twenty-nine of the forty households having between two and four persons. Only twenty-two of the hundred Melbourne households had seven or more people (five of which were mixed households), compared with 35 percent of Tongan households in New Zealand (Statistics New Zealand 1998, 22).

The inclusion of extended family members in many households means there is considerable variation in their composition. Table 3 reveals how diverse the family arrangements can be.[9]

The table shows that it is far more common for extended family members in the households to be related to the wife than the husband. In several of these households a Tongan husband or boyfriend has been brought into an existing non-Tongan household.

It is also clear that there was much less variation in household composition in the mixed families, although they were by no means confined to nuclear families. Many of the "mixed" households are basically Tongan households with one non-Tongan—for example, an older couple and their children, with one of the adult children's non-Tongan spouse. Of these mixed households, in ten cases the non-Tongan was the husband and in eight the wife.

Table 3
Household Composition

Household Type	Tongan	% of all Tongan	Mixed	% of all Mixed	TOTAL
Nuclear	21	35	22	55	43
Couple	3	5	8	20	11
Nuclear and wife's kin	8	13.3	6	15	14
Couple and wife's kin	—	—	1	2.5	1
Nuclear and husband's kin	4	6.6	1	2.5	5
Couple and husband's kin	1	1.7	—	—	1
Three generations	3	5	1	2.5	4
Four generations	1	1.7	—	—	1
Single parent	12	20	—	—	12
Single person	6	10	—	—	6
Family and friends	1	1.7	1	2.5	2
TOTAL	60		40		100

There were no single-parent families in the mixed households, but there were twelve in the Tongan households, five of which were comprised of just a mother and her child or children. In the remaining cases other kin are present; for example, in two cases women live with their adult brothers, and in another case a woman lives with her father, a female cousin, and the cousin's son (thus the household has two single parents). In the only case of a male single parent, he and his child live with two adult male cousins. One of the single parents is actually the grandmother of the child; she chose to be recorded as parent because she has informally adopted the child.[10]

Only one of the single parents has never married, four are widows, four are divorced, and three are separated but not divorced. Their children range in age from under one to twenty-seven. The 1996 New Zealand census, which defined a dependent child as under eighteen and not working full time, recorded 27 percent of Tongan dependent children as living in one-parent families (Statistics New Zealand 1998, 21). If we use the New Zealand census definition, the twenty-one children who fall in this category in my sample make up 10.8 percent of the total cohort of dependent children.[11]

Rather than try to describe all the different household types, the following are some examples of the more complex domestic arrangements in the sample households:

A Tongan man, his New Zealand–born Samoan wife, and their child; the husband's brother and his Tongan wife, and their two children

A couple and their children, as well as the man's father and sister, and the sister's children

A man, his de facto wife, his brother, and the brother's son

A couple and their child, the wife's sister and her husband and children, and two of the man's brothers

A couple and their children, the man's brother and two sisters and his male cousin, and the woman's brother

A couple with nine children, the man's adult niece and her three children, and two of the man's cousins' children

Location in Melbourne

Australia's 1996 census showed that Tongan speakers are scattered throughout most of the local government areas (LGAs) of Melbourne. It is difficult to ascertain from the census figures just how dispersed Tongans are because, as in the tables produced from census data, information is given only for LGAs with more than a hundred Pacific Islands-born people. My sample of households, covering forty-four different postal-code areas, is spread across the entire metropolitan area, providing a diverse sampling of Tongans throughout Melbourne.

A few areas of Melbourne have some clustering of Tongan households, including Ringwood in the northeast, Footscray in the west, and Frankston in the southeast, all of which are working-class areas. Unlike some other diasporic Tongan populations where geographical clustering has occurred due to employment patterns, these clusters have arisen partly due to members of large extended families choosing to live near one another, and partly due to proximity to Tongan churches.

The hundred households surveyed reported a variety of reasons for choosing to live in particular suburbs. Living near other family members was the main factor (given by thirty-three households), followed by liking the area (twenty-four), and being near the workplace of one or more household members (eighteen). The remaining households gave an assortment of other reasons: for example, some had little choice about their location, as they were in accommodations provided by a church or were in public housing; others had chosen to live close to the tertiary institution where one or more household members were studying; and others chose an area where housing was affordable.

Home Ownership

Seventy-two of the hundred households lived in houses, twenty-seven in flats (apartments), and one in a caravan (trailer). Most households lived in the standard three-bedroom (forty-one households) and four-bedroom (twenty-two households) homes of the suburbs. Five households lived in five-bedroom homes, and twenty-two households lived in two-bedroom homes. Nine households had only one bedroom, and one couple and one individual live in "bed-sits" (one-room apartments with no separate bedroom).

The majority (fifty-nine households) were in rented accommodations, while thirty-six owned (or were purchasing) their own home, and five did not pay rent (these lived in church houses and other accommodations linked to work or study). Of those who owned their own homes, equal numbers (eighteen each) were Tongan and mixed households, comprising 30 percent of the Tongan households and 45 percent of the mixed households. Sixty-five percent of the Tongan households were renting, compared with only 20 percent of the mixed households. For both household types, the rate of home ownership is significantly lower than that for the total population of Melbourne, where, according to the 1996 census, 64.6 percent of dwellings are owned or being purchased and only 22.8 percent are being rented (Australian Bureau of Statistics 1997, 17, table 2)

However, the rates of home ownership for Melbourne Tongans in the late 1990s are higher than those recorded in Faiva's study of Tongans in Sydney, where 90.8 percent of households rented and only 9.2 percent owned or were buying a home (1989, 21, table 4.6). Similarly, John Connell, Graham Harrison, and Grant McCall found that of Tongans recorded as residents in New South Wales in the 1986 census, only 5.2 percent stated that they owned their own homes outright, with a further 13.9 percent purchasing their home. This level of home ownership was one of the lowest in the state (1991, 108–112). The Sydney studies were conducted a decade before my own, and it is to be expected that the longer migrants have been in Australia, the more likely they are to buy their own homes. For the Melbourne Tongans, of the seventy-six households where at least one of the adults has been in Australia for over ten years, thirty-five owned or were buying their homes, whereas there was only one case in which recent migrants (resident for under five years) were buying a home. This accords with the situation in the United States, where only 29 percent of Tongans who migrated after 1980 owned their own homes. The rate increased with length of stay, so that 66.6 percent of those who migrated before 1965 owned their own homes (Small 1997, 66).

There may also be differences in the overall socioeconomic status of the Tongans in Sydney and Melbourne and the availability of housing loans; certainly the cost of housing is higher in Sydney. Yet another factor is that Australian-born Tongans are more likely to purchase homes than rent; in New Zealand over 40 percent of New Zealand-born Tongans live in homes that are owned or being purchased by a household member. Those born overseas are more likely to live in rented accommodation. (Statistics New Zealand 1998, 48).

Time in Suburb

The majority of people in the Melbourne survey (61.2 percent) had lived in their present suburb for five years and under. A further 14.8 percent had been in the suburb for six to ten years, and 24 percent for over ten years. If the length of time people have been in their suburb is compared with the length of their residence in Australia, we find that at least 37.2 percent have moved at least once within Australia since arriving, as they have been in Australia longer than in the suburb in which they now live.

Others may have moved within the same suburb, but this is likely to be a small number.

When the respondents were asked how long they intended to stay in the area in which they lived, just over half (fifty-one households) replied that they would stay for more than three years. Most of those who owned their homes indicated that they intended to stay for over three years, but many (twenty-one households) of those renting were also keen to stay for at least that long. A third of the respondents were unsure how long they would stay where they were currently living.

Education

Table 4 compares the education level of the sample group in Melbourne with their ethnicity, for those over the age of fifteen. There were no significant gender differences in educational levels.

In this table, "Tongan HLC" refers to the Tongan Higher Leaving Certificate; "NZ School Cert." is the New Zealand School Certificate; and "HSC/VCE" are, respectively, the Higher School Certificate and Victorian Certificate of Education. Each of these certificates marks the successful completion of high school education. Of those who had no formal qualifications, thirty-two were still attending an educational institution, and sixteen who had high school qualifications were continuing their education at the time of the survey.[12]

Also at the time of my survey, 303 (63.3 percent) of the 479 respondents did not attend any form of educational institution, 163 (34 percent) were full-time students, and 13 (2.7 percent) were part-time students. Of

Table 4
Education Level by Ethnicity (over Age Fifteen)

	Ethnicity					
Education Level	Tongan	Tongan Australian	Other part-Tongan	Australian	Other non-Tongan	TOTAL
None	128	21	5	20	5	179
Tongan HLC	36	—	—	—	—	36
NZ School Cert.	6	—	—	—	—	6
HSC/VCE	20	4	—	4	4	32
Trade certificate	5	3	—	2	—	10
Diploma	14	—	—	2	1	17
Degree	12	5	—	6	—	23
TOTAL	221	33	5	34	10	303

those who were students, the majority were in primary school (34.5 percent) or secondary school (33.9 percent). Preschool students accounted for only 7.2 percent of the group; most Tongan parents do not send their children to preschools (or kindergartens as they are known in Victoria). Tertiary students (23.3 percent) were at universities, technical colleges, and theological colleges. There were also two students at special schools for the intellectually disabled.

The school retention rate among young people is high in this sample. For the group aged between fifteen and seventeen, twenty-five of the twenty-eight (89.3 percent) were still at school, with only one person under seventeen not at school. By comparison, 83 percent of this age group within the total population of Victorian young people were still at school (Australian Bureau of Statistics 1993, 39). Of those in the sample aged eighteen and nineteen (the ages at which most have completed secondary school), 66.7 percent were still undertaking study, compared with 52 percent of Victorian young people in 1991. Even the group aged between twenty and twenty-five had a higher rate than the total: 25.8 percent compared with 23 percent. These higher rates can be largely attributed to the strong emphasis on education in many Tongan families, as discussed in chapter 3.

Employment

The employment status of all individuals in the sample, by gender, is shown in table 5.

For those who are employed, unskilled work is the most common occupation, as it is for diasporic Tongans generally. Table 6 shows that this is

Table 5
Work Status by Gender

Work Status	Male	Female	TOTAL (% of total sample)
Employed	90	62	152 (31.7)
Unemployed (benefits)	18	21	39 (8.2)
Unemployed (no benefits)	3	1	4 (0.8)
Pensioner	5	7	12 (2.5)
Home duties	7	39	46 (9.6)
Student	73	82	155 (32.4)
Not yet in school	42	29	71 (14.8)
TOTAL	238	241	479

Table 6
Type of Job by Gender

Type of Job	Male	Female	TOTAL (% of total employed)
Professional	8	11	19 (12.6)
Own business	3	3	6 (4.0)
Managerial	3	—	3 (2.0)
Clerical	1	5	6 (4.0)
Skilled trade	21	4	25 (16.6)
Laborer	31	16	47 (31.1)
Other unskilled	23	22	45 (29.8)
TOTAL	90	61	151

the case for both male and female workers. However, table 6 also reflects the trend for higher rates of professional employment; just over a decade earlier Faiva found only 0.6 percent of his sample were in professional positions (1989, 20).

Within the sample, Tongans have the highest rate of employment in unskilled jobs (35.7 percent), part-Tongans a significantly lower rate (18.4 percent), and non-Tongans the lowest rate (13.6 percent). As we have seen, most of the part-Tongans were born in Australia; as discussed in chapter 3, those born overseas are more upwardly mobile than were their parents.

Income Sources

Full-time work was the main source of income for 72 percent of households. Eighteen of the households had more than two people employed, and there were even two households with six people in employment. Table 7 shows the forms of income for all households, revealing that fifteen of the households rely on government benefits for their income. This rate is higher than that found by Faiva in his survey, where only 5.4 percent of the households relied on some form of government benefit (1989, 23). These benefits include unemployment, sickness, single-parent, and special benefits (the latter for people in need who do not fall into the former categories); the widow's and old-age pensions; and Austudy (payments to tertiary students). In the category of "Other" were six households, with five relying on scholarship funds and one on payments for caring for foster children.

Table 7
Main Form of Household Income

Type of Income	Tongan	% of all Tongan	Mixed	% of all Mixed	TOTAL
Full-time	39	65	33	82.5	72
Part-time	2	3.3	2	5	4
Unemployment benefits	8	13.3	—	—	8
Sickness benefits	1	1.7	—	—	1
Other government benefits	7	11.7	1	2.5	8
Family business	—	—	1	2.5	1
Other	3	5	3	7.5	6
TOTAL	60		40		100

Citizenship

The 1991 Australian census showed that after two to three years 22.7 percent of all migrants became citizens; after four to five years this figure was at 50 percent; and for migrants who had lived over twenty years in Australia, 73.1 percent had become citizens. (Goldlust 1996, 25). The rates are lower for the Melbourne Tongans, with only 29.9 percent of Tongan-born individuals holding Australian citizenship. Permanent-resident status (43.6 percent) is preferred over citizenship because it does not necessitate relinquishing Tongan citizenship.

Of the nearly 30 percent with Australian citizenship, 18 percent have been in Australia for zero to five years, 24 percent for six to ten years, and 36.3 percent for over ten years. Interestingly, for the New Zealand-born Tongans now living in Australia, 40 percent were Australian citizens, and a further 45.7 percent were Australian permanent residents. Only 9 of the 236 Australian born had taken out Tongan citizenship, and 4 had New Zealand citizenship.

Language Use

As stated in chapter 3, for those in the sample over age five with Tongan ancestry, 26.3 percent spoke only Tongan at home, 24.8 percent only English, and the rest a mixture of both languages. The proportion of Tongans who speak only English at home is likely to increase; while their numbers are not large enough to be statistically significant, nearly half of the children in the sample aged three to five spoke only English at home.[13]

Looking at levels of language competence, I found that 12.5 percent of Tongans could not speak Tongan very well or did not speak it at all, whereas of the Tongan Australians and other part-Tongans, 40.3 percent did not speak Tongan well and 35.8 percent not at all. Far fewer part-Tongans could read Tongan well: 17.9 percent did not read well and 76.1 percent not at all. Only two of the Australian and other non-Tongan group spoke Tongan very well, and both were Australians who had lived in Tonga and had married Tongans. Eighty-three percent of non-Tongans did not speak Tongan at all.

Religious Affiliations

Table 8 shows the four main religious denominations of survey respondents.

In the table, "Wesleyan" includes both the Free Wesleyan Church of Tonga and the Tongan Wesleyan Methodist Church, as most respondents simply stated that they were Wesleyan. Denominations not listed in the table were each identified by less than ten of the respondents and include (in order of frequency) Maama Foʻou or Tokaikolo, Bahaʻi, Church of Jesus Christ of Latter-Day Saints (Mormon), Baptist, Assembly of God, Church of England, and Seventh-Day Adventist.[14] Sixteen respondents—three part-Tongan and the rest non-Tongan—stated that they had no religious affiliation.

Family Ties

Although the majority of the households sampled lived more than five kilometers away from their relatives, more than half of the respondents visited family members at least once a week, as shown in table 9.

Women visit family more often than men, with 72.6 percent of women visiting weekly or more often, compared to 63.4 percent of men. Tongans and part-Tongans also were more likely to see their families frequently: 22 percent saw their families daily and another 27.4 percent saw them two to

Table 8
Religious Affiliation (Groups of over 20) by Ethnicity

Religion	Tongan	Tongan Australian	Part-Tongan	Australian	Other non-Tongan	Total (% of total sample)
Uniting Church	147	46	11	10	2	216 (45.1)
Catholic	58	3	8	12	2	83 (17.3)
Wesleyan	66	12	1	2	—	81 (16.9)
Free Church	33	—	1	—	—	34 (7.1)

(Ethnicity spans the columns Tongan, Tongan Australian, Part-Tongan, Australian, Other non-Tongan)

Table 9
Frequency of Visiting by Location of Extended Family

| | Location of Extended Family | | | | | |
Frequency of Visits	Up to 1 km	1 to 5 km	Elsewhere in Victoria	Other Australian state	None in Australia	TOTAL
Daily	23	42	34	—	—	99
2 to 3 times per week	6	49	72	—	—	127
Once per week	2	18	80	—	—	100
Once per fortnight	1	18	32	1	—	52
Once per month	—	1	12	1	—	14
Less than once per month	—	1	22	47	2	72
Never	4	—	1	5	5	15
TOTAL	36	129	253	54	7	479

three times a week; in comparison, 8 percent of Australians and other non-Tongans saw their famlies daily, and 18.4 percent saw them two to three times weekly. The figures for the latter group could be misleading in that many of them are the spouses of Tongans and thus included their Tongan affines as "family" in responding to this question. If only their natal family had been included, the frequency would be even lower.

Socializing

The time commitment involved in church life means many Tongans socialize mainly with others in the church, as well as with members of their extended families. Nearly 20 percent of the individuals in the total sample stated that they socialized only with Tongans, and nearly the same number socialized mostly with Tongans. Another 26.7 percent socialized equally with Tongans and Australians, nearly 20 percent mostly with Australians, and 12.1 percent only with Australians However, only 1.5 percent of Tongans socialized only with Australians, and only 1.9 percent of the total sample socialized mainly with other ethnic groups, usually those of a non-Tongan spouse.

Females were nearly twice as likely as males to socialize only with Tongans, whereas males were more likely than females to socialize with Australians. This occurrence is largely due to the gendered differences in social activities, with females more often staying close to home or visiting relatives. Even the young women who have been allowed to go out unchaperoned tend to do so with groups of Tongan friends and cousins.

Males are more likely to go out to public venues such as hotels and clubs, often with non-Tongans met through work or sports clubs.

Picturing an Overseas Tongan Population

This "snapshot" of one hundred households in Melbourne at the end of the twentieth century provides us with a picture of the diversity of Tongans' lives. Like most other populations of Tongans around the world, this group includes both the first wave of migrants, who arrived in the 1960s and 1970s, their descendants, and the more recent arrivals of the 1980s and 1990s. Also characteristic of these overseas populations is their youthfulness, and with the growing number of Tongans who have been born and raised overseas come various changes, including higher levels of education, some movement away from unskilled employment, an increasing rate of home ownership, and so on. These changes, very broadly speaking, indicate a tendency to take on many elements of the lifestyle of the wider society. However, other factors, such as continuing involvement with Tongan churches and the importance of the extended family, reveal that a sense of "community" persists, even in the geographically scattered population of Melbourne.

The data furnished by household questionnaires give us only a partial picture of Tongans' experiences overseas; to flesh out statistics such as those provided in this section it is vital to look more closely at those experiences and to explore the ways people perceive them. By focusing on issues surrounding the notion of cultural identity, this book has attempted to do just that. Concepts such as "assimilation" or "adaptation" are too simplistic to capture the range of ways in which Tongans adjust to their new circumstances overseas. For most Tongans living overseas, "the Tongan way" is still a concept that shapes their identities, no matter how contested and multiply interpreted it may be. It is a concept that is not easily or readily abandoned, and closely examining the ways in which it is negotiated, reconstructed, and challenged in the context of migration is crucial in understanding the internal dynamics of populations of Tongans as well as the impact of their interactions with the wider societies in which they live.

APPENDIX B

Profiles of Interviewees

Throughout this book many individuals have been mentioned and their interview responses quoted. To give a clearer sense of who these people are without divulging their identities, the following profiles are brief descriptions of the individuals and their households (not including people with whom I had only informal conversations). As some people are mentioned at various different points in the book, these profiles will make it easier to keep track of "who's who." They also offer a picture of the diversity of the circumstances of the Tongan population overseas.

Profiles are not provided for the Tongan ministers interviewed as they would be too readily identifiable. For this reason, when quoting the ministers I do not indicate which church they represent.

'Aisea

Male, age fifteen. Brother of Sela (below). Still in high school, 'Aisea was born in Australia and speaks both English and Tongan fluently. He is keen to live in Tonga for a year or two, as did three of his older brothers.

'Ana

Female, age thirty-eight. 'Ana migrated to Australia via New Zealand in the late 1970s and met her husband, Peni, in Melbourne. They now live with their two teenage children and two of 'Ana's nieces in a rented three-bedroom home in a working-class suburb. (See Case Study 1.)

Anapesi

Female, age fifteen. Anapesi lives with her parents and nine siblings in Melbourne and attends high school. Born in Tonga, she migrated with her mother and sister in 1985 to join her father, who was already working in Australia. The family has little contact with kin in Tonga, and she is discouraged from associating with other Tongans her age. Anapesi speaks English fluently and has some difficulty with Tongan, although she speaks to her parents in Tongan.

Anasela

Female, age nineteen. Born in Melbourne, Anasela's parents migrated in the early 1970s. She chose to return to Tonga and stay with kin for three years in her early teens, but now she has no contact with family in Tonga and does not keep up with Tongan news. In Melbourne she does not associate much with other Tongans and does not belong to a Tongan church, although her parents and two siblings still attend. She is more comfortable speaking English and prefers Western food, music, clothes, and so on.

Bianca

Female, age twenty-four. Bianca was born in California after her parents migrated there in 1972. They are a Mormon family, but she has now left the church. She speaks mainly English and feels uncomfortable speaking Tongan. Growing up, Bianca was closely involved with the other Tongans in the area, and her family also maintained close contact with relatives in Tonga, sometimes sending remittances in money and goods. Bianca's parents have now retired and returned to Tonga, and she contacts them almost daily. She also keeps up with Tongan news through the Internet and videos sent by her mother or other relatives. Bianca is working in an unskilled job while studying part-time at university. (Interviewed via e-mail.)

Feleti

Male, age twenty-nine. Brother of Haloti (below, and see Case Study 3). Born in Melbourne, Feleti is married with three young children. The family lives with three of his adult relatives in a five-bedroom home Feleti and his wife, Palu, are in the process of purchasing. Palu is Tongan born and has been in Australia for over ten years. They all speak English at home, as only Palu speaks Tongan well. None of the members of the household have educational qualifications beyond high school, although two are now studying at tertiary institutions. Four are working full-time. They all mix with both Tongans and non-Tongans and see their Tongan relatives frequently. All belong to the Uniting Church, but Feleti and Palu do not attend a Tongan church.

Fonua

Male, age eighteen. Born in Tonga, Fonua and his parents moved to Australia when he was two months old. His Tongan father and Australian mother separated when he was two years old, and he grew up with his mother and, after some years, an Australian stepfather and two half sisters. He has visited Tonga several times with his mother, most recently when he was sixteen, but he speaks no Tongan. Fonua has no contact with kin in Tonga or with Tongans in Melbourne, where his father and several half siblings live.

Fusi

Female, age thirty. Fusi's mother was born in Tonga and moved to Australia in the early 1960s, where she married an Australian and settled permanently. Fusi has now married an Australian, and they live in a tiny apartment in the inner suburbs of Melbourne. Neither have educational qualifications, and both work in their own business. They speak English, and Fusi does not know any Tongan, nor does she mix with Tongans outside her own family. They do not attend church. (Sister of Sue, below.)

Gillian

Female, age thirty-nine. An American married to a Tongan, Gillian has four children and lives in Utah. The family belongs to the Mormon church and formerly attended a Tongan ward but have now moved to a non-Tongan congregation. Both parents are well-educated professionals. At home, the family speaks English, and Gillian speaks Tongan only poorly. They keep in touch with other Tongans, and while the children have been raised as Americans, they are proud of their Tongan identity and have enjoyed holidays in Tonga with their parents. (Interviewed via e-mail.)

Haloti

Male, age nineteen. Haloti lives in Melbourne with his parents, two sisters, grandmother, and his father's sister and her two adult children. His parents moved to Australia in the late 1960s, and Haloti and his siblings were born in Melbourne. (See Case Study 3.)

Helenā

Female, age thirty-eight. Born in Tonga, Helenā moved to the United States in the 1962. She grew up in California but has moved to Utah with her American husband and their five children. She rarely contacts relatives in Tonga but keeps up with events in Tonga through newspapers and videos. The family mixes with the Tongans in their area and attends a Tongan ward of the Mormon Church. Although raised in a strictly Tongan home, she has not followed the Tongan way with her own children and would like to return to Tonga with them for a year or two so that they can learn about *anga fakatonga*. Helenā speaks little Tongan, and the family speaks English at home. (Interviewed via e-mail.)

Jane

Female, age fifty-one. The Australian partner of a Tongan man, Jane lives with her husband and two adult children in their own four-bedroom home. Jane married in the early 1970s, when her husband was at university in Melbourne. Jane's husband speaks some Tongan at home, but the rest of the family speaks only English. The family is well educated; Jane has a diploma, her husband a degree, and both of the children attend tertiary institutions. Both parents work in professional positions. The family has long been involved in a Tongan church (Uniting Church), and while the parents and daughter remain involved, the son has moved to a different, non-Tongan church and generally has much less to do with other Tongans than the others.

Jenny

Female, age twenty-nine. Married to Viliami (below). University-educated Jenny worked in Tonga for several years, where she met Viliami, and speaks fluent Tongan.

Joe

Male, age thirty. Joe lived in Tonga until he was sixteen, when he was sent to a boarding school in New Zealand. Until about six years ago, he returned to Tonga for the Christmas holidays to be with his family. Both of his parents are part-Tongan. During his time with his parents he was raised strictly, but many elements of the Tongan way were not followed, such as the *faka'apa'apa* between brothers and sisters. After school he stayed on in New Zealand, but he keeps up with news in Tonga through the Internet and friends and relatives in New Zealand. Still unmarried, he speaks both English and Tongan and belongs to the Mormon Church. (Interviewed via e-mail.)

Julie

Female, age forty-five. Julie, an Australian, met Samuela, her Tongan-born husband, through their membership in the Mormon Church. They recently married and moved into a home they are in the process of purchasing in a new estate on the outskirts of Melbourne. Her husband migrated in the 1980s; he completed high school in Tonga and now works in a factory. Julie has a degree and is in a professional position. They speak English at home, and although Julie is trying to learn Tongan, she speaks only poorly as yet. They mix with both Tongans and non-Tongans.

Kerry

Female, age twenty-two. Kerry and her Tongan-born husband, Lopeti, have a young daughter and live in a rented two-bedroom home. Lopeti moved to Australia in the late 1980s with his parents and siblings. Kerry's parents were also migrants, from Malta, and she was born in Australia. Lopeti has a tertiary education (diploma) and works full-time in a skilled position, while Kerry is currently studying part-time and has no paid employment. Kerry speaks Tongan poorly, so they speak English at home. Lopeti grew up attending a Tongan church (Uniting Church) and now takes his daughter with him, but Kerry is a Roman Catholic and so attends the Tongan church only for special services. They see their families frequently and also socialize with Tongans and non-Tongans.

Kylie

Female, age thirty-one. Australian wife of Sioeli (below). Kylie works at home, caring for their four children.

Langi

Male, age seventy. Langi, his Australian wife, and one adult son live in a four-bedroom house; Langi's two other children have married and left home. The couple lived in Tonga for some time, and their children were born there, but they have lived in Australia since the mid-1980s. Both Langi and his wife have degrees, and their son is currently at university. The couple both work full-time, but Langi plans to retire soon. They all speak English at home, although Langi and his wife both speak Tongan fluently. They socialize mainly with Australians, and Langi's relatives are either interstate or still in Tonga. They do not attend a Tongan church but belong to a Uniting Church congregation.

Lesieli

Female, age sixteen. Sister of Sela (below). Still in high school, Lesieli is fluent in both Tongan and English.

Lopeti

Male, age twenty-five. Husband of Kerry (above).

Lopini

Female, age fifteen. Daughter of 'Ana (above, and see Case Study 1). Lopini is still in high school. She speaks Tongan poorly but socializes mainly with young Tongans from the Uniting Church she attends with her family.

Losa

Female, age forty. Losa, a widow, lives with her three children, her mother, and her brother and his wife and their young child. All but the children were born in Tonga, and Losa moved to Melbourne in the mid 1970s with her husband. Her mother joined her in the late 1980s and her brother's family in 1990. She is in the process of purchasing her home, a three-bedroom house in an outer suburb of Melbourne, and the family relies on her widow's pension, as her brother and his wife are both studying. All speak both Tongan and English well, using mainly Tongan at home. They are all actively involved with a Tongan church (Uniting Church).

Lose

Female, age sixteen. Born in Australia, Lose's parents migrated in the late 1970s. She lives with her parents and three siblings and attends high school. She speaks a little Tongan but is more comfortable speaking English; she is determined that when she has children they will learn Tongan. She socializes with both Tongan and non-Tongan friends and sees other Tongans frequently through church and social events. She attends a Tongan church (Uniting Church).

Lucy

Female, age nineteen. Lucy's parents moved to American Samoa, where Lucy was born, in 1970, and stayed there until 1981, when they moved to the United States. The family now lives in Texas and belongs to a Tongan congregation of the Methodist Church. The children were raised in the Tongan way. Lucy, a college student, speaks English fluently and Tongan well, and at home she speaks Tongan with her parents and a mixture with her siblings. She has no contact with kin in Tonga but reads Tongan newspapers and watches videos of events in Tonga. (Interviewed via e-mail.)

Lusi

Female, age twenty-four. Sister of Haloti (below, and see Case Study 3). Lusi is a tertiary student. She speaks little Tongan but socializes with other young Tongans from the Uniting Church she and her family attend.

Makalesi

Female, age twenty-nine. Makalesi's grandfather migrated to the United States in the early 1960s, and all seven of his children followed him. Makalesi's family settled in California. (See Case Study 4.)

Malia

Female, age twenty. Malia's parents migrated to Australia in 1968, and she and her three siblings were was born in Melbourne. As well as her parents and siblings, her household includes her sister-in-law and brother-in-law, two nieces, and a nephew. She has completed high school and works as a shop assistant. Malia was not raised to follow *anga fakatonga*. Her Tongan is poor, and she would like to live and work in Tonga at some stage. Malia and her family attend a Tongan church (Uniting Church).

Manu

Male, age sixty-five. Manu and his wife live in a three-bedroom house provided by the church. They own another house in which one of their adult children lives with her husband. Their other children have also left home. The couple moved to Australia in the early 1970s while Manu undertook tertiary studies and stayed on permanently. They both speak English well but prefer to converse in Tongan at home, and they socialize almost exclusively with other Tongans. Both attend a Tongan church (Free Wesleyan).

Mary

Female, age twenty-five. Mary lives with her aunt, 'Ana (above, and see Case Study 1). Mary's parents went to Australia in 1976 while her father studied, with Mary (age six at the time) and her sister. Mary attended primary school in Australia, then they returned to Tonga so her father could work there (a condition of many scholarships). After seven years they migrated to Australia, bringing her grandparents with them. Mary and her sister have been living with their aunt, 'Ana, for over a year. Mary does not speak Tongan but has some involvement with other Tongans, mainly through the Tongan church (Uniting Church).

Megan

Female, age thirty-nine. An American now divorced from her Tongan husband of fifteen years, Megan lives with three of her five children and a foster son in Alaska. Megan married her husband soon after he migrated to the United States with his aunt, uncle, and cousins. During their marriage they lived in Tonga for two periods of several months, but she no longer keeps up with Tongan news or maintains contact with her husband's family in Tonga. Two of her daughters have married Tongans, and all of her children identify themselves mainly as Tongan and are involved with other Tongans through the Mormon Church. The family speak English, and Megan's Tongan is poor. (Interviewed via e-mail.)

Mele

Female, age forty. After moving to New Zealand in 1981, where she undertook tertiary studies, married, and had five children, Mele moved with her family to Melbourne in the early 1990s. They now rent a small, three-bedroom house in a working-class suburb. Mele is in a professional position, while her husband does semiskilled work, and all the children attend school. At home, the parents speak Tongan, and while they try to insist that their children do so as well, the children prefer to speak English with each other. Mele's husband's English is poor. The family is actively involved with a Tongan church (Uniting Church).

Mike

Male, age thirty-one. Married to Sālote (below, and see Case Study 5). Born in Australia to Maltese parents.

Mosese

Male, age twenty-seven. Now married to an Australian and with a young daughter, Mosese was born in Tonga and migrated to Melbourne with his family in 1976. His parents are, by his own description, "very traditional Tongan," and as a teenager he was sent to school in Tonga for four years. He speaks both Tongan and English fluently and works in security.

'Ofa

Female, age nineteen. Born in Australia in 1977 while her parents were visiting family, 'Ofa was raised in Tonga until the age of six. At that time her parents visited Australia again and left her to stay with her mother's brother's family. In her early teens she went to live in the United States with her parents and siblings, who had migrated there, and she lived with them until the age of seventeen, when she was sent back to live in Melbourne. She now lives in a rented four-bedroom home with her paternal grandmother and aunt and two cousins. All but 'Ofa were born in Tonga, and while her grandmother has lived in Australia for over twenty years, her aunt and cousins moved only in the 1990s. All members of the household speak Tongan and English fluently and speak mainly English at home. None have educational qualifications beyond high school. 'Ofa's two cousins work full-time in unskilled positions, and both older women in the household receive sickness benefits. All belong to a Tongan church (Uniting Church), and while 'Ofa, like her grandmother and aunt, socializes mainly with other Tongans, her cousins mix more with Australians.

Palu

Female, age thirty-two. Wife of Feleti (above), Palu moved to Australia in the 1980s and is fluent in both Tongan and English. She studies part-time and cares for their three young children.

Paula

Male, age fifty-one. Paula and his wife, Siu, and four children, ages six to twenty, live in a rented three-bedroom house in Melbourne. He migrated in 1975 and was followed by his wife and oldest child five years later. (See Case Study 2.)

Sālote

Female, age thirty. Sālote has lived in Tonga, New Zealand, and Australia. She now lives in Melbourne with her Maltese husband, Mike, and their one-year-old son. (See Case Study 5.)

Samuela

Male, age thirty. Married to Julie (above).

Sarah

Female, age eighteen. A university student, Sarah lives in New Zealand with her parents and sisters, having migrated in 1993. Her brother remains in Tonga. She visits Tonga at least once a year, usually for the Christmas holidays, and keeps in touch with Tongan news through the Internet. The children speak both English and Tongan fluently, but her parents did not keep to the Tongan way in raising them. She has many Tongan friends but seldom attends Tongan functions and does not attend a Tongan church. (Interviewed via e-mail.)

Seini

Female, age sixty. One of the first Tongans to settle in Melbourne, arriving in 1961, Seini lives with her Australian husband and adult son as well as her adult nephew (Tongan Australian) in a rented three-bedroom home. Her daughter has married and left home. Seini's husband and children do not speak Tongan, and apart from her involvement with a Tongan church (Uniting Church), they live a "Western" lifestyle. Her husband did not further his education beyond high school and works as a tradesman. Seini has a tertiary diploma and worked for many years but is now doing voluntary work. Their son also works as a tradesman, and their nephew does unskilled work. Seini sees her relatives weekly at church and sees some Tongans socially, but the others see them less often and socialize with non-Tongans.

Sela

Female, age twenty-six. Still single, Sela lives with her parents, six of her siblings (two others have married and left home), and her maternal grandmother. Also living with them in their four-bedroom home (owned by her parents) are two of her brother's children. All but her two youngest siblings were born in Tonga, and the family moved to Melbourne in the late 1970s. Sela's grandmother does not speak English well, but the other members of the household are fluent in both Tongan and English, speaking a mixture of both at home. Two of her siblings have tertiary diplomas, the highest educational level in the family, and Sela is studying for a degree. The rest either completed high school, have no qualifications, or, in the case of the younger members, are still in school. Five of the adults in the household are working, all in unskilled jobs. The family belongs to a Tongan church (Uniting Church) and frequently sees members of their large extended family in Melbourne.

Sioeli

Male, age thirty-six. Sioeli met his wife, Kylie, while studying in Australia. They now have four young children and rent a three-bedroom house in a new housing estate in the outer suburbs of Melbourne. Sioeli is working full-time in an unskilled job while studying part-time. He already has a tertiary degree but is studying in a new field. Kylie did not complete high school and has no paid employment. Sioeli is still fluent in Tongan, but Kylie and the children do not speak it at all. They all belong to a Tongan church (Free Wesleyan), they socialize with a mix of Tongan and non-Tongan friends and family, and they see Sioeli's family daily.

Sione

Male, age thirty-eight. Sione, his wife, and four children live in a rented apartment. The couple migrated to Melbourne in the early 1980s, and their children were all born in Australia. Sione is undertaking theological studies, and the family's only income is his student allowance. The children are all under the age of eight, and Sione and his wife are trying to teach them to be fluent in both English and Tongan. They are actively involved in a Tongan church (Free Wesleyan).

Sitiveni

Male, age thirty-four. Tongan-born Sitiveni is living in Europe, having moved to live in his wife's homeland several years ago. Now divorced, they have two young children. Sitiveni is trying to teach them to speak Tongan and to know something of the Tongan way, but with no other Tongans in the city where he lives, their lives are primarily European. He does not keep in contact with family in Tonga, but he uses the Internet to find news of Tonga and to communicate with other Tongans. (Interviewed via e-mail.)

Siu

Female, age forty. Wife of Paula (above, and see Case Study 2).

Solomone

Male, age thirty-one. Solomone's parents traveled to New Zealand for his birth, to access the better medical facilities, but returned to Tonga when he was a few months old. They migrated to the United States in 1971 and settled in Los Angeles. Still single, Solomone is highly educated and in a professional position. His parents speak Tongan to one another at times, but the family mainly speak English at home. Solomone's Tongan is poor, but he is trying to improve it. He and his siblings grew up in an area with no other Tongans, and while he and his sister have begun interacting with other Tongans as adults, his two brothers mix only with non-Tongans. However, the children were raised according to *anga fakatonga* in many ways. Solomone's parents maintain limited contact with kin in Tonga, but they keep up-to-date with events in Tonga through *The Tonga Chronicle* and relatives in other locations overseas. (Interviewed via e-mail.)

Sosefa

Male, age forty-four. Sosefa, his wife, and four children live in a large house provided by the church in a wealthy suburb of Melbourne. The couple came to Australia in the early 1980s with their first child, and the other children were born in Melbourne. They all speak English at home, and the children's Tongan is poor. Sosefa already has a university degree and is undertaking postgraduate studies part-time, and his oldest child is also at university and working part-time. His wife works full-time in a skilled position. Although the whole family is actively involved in a Tongan church (Uniting Church), the children all prefer to socialize with non-Tongans.

Sue

Female, age thirty-two. The child of a Tongan mother and Australian father, Sue lives with her Australian husband and their young daughter in a rented two-bedroom home in an inner-city suburb of Melbourne. Sue and her husband did not complete high school, and they own their own business. Sue speaks no Tongan, and they have little to do with the Tongans in Melbourne beyond her own family, although as a child she was more involved through her parents. They do not attend church. Sister of Fusi (above).

Sulia

Female, age twenty-eight. The daughter of a Tongan mother and Australian father, Sulia is unmarried and lives alone in a rented apartment close to her work. (See Case Study 6.)

Sulieta

Female, age twenty-four. Born in Tonga, Sulieta was sent to the United States as a young child to live with her grandparents in Utah. She returned to Tonga to attend high school for several years, then returned to Utah with her parents; like so many Tongan Mormons, the family settled in Utah. All of her eight siblings attended school both in the United States and Tonga. Still unmarried, she is now a university student. Sulieta is fluent in both Tongan and English and prefers to speak Tongan. With her siblings, she was raised to follow the Tongan way, with only minor adjustments to living in America. She and her family maintain close contact with kin in Tonga through letters and phone calls. Her immediate family sends remittances for special occasions, and the relatives in Tonga send them Tongan souvenirs such as T-shirts. Sulieta also keeps up with what is happening in Tonga by reading newspapers, seeking information on the Internet, and watching videos sent by kin. (Interviewed by e-mail)

Susana

Female, age nineteen. Susana lives with her parents and four siblings in a rented four-bedroom home. Her parents moved to Australia in the 1980s and lived in Queensland before moving to Melbourne in the early 1990s. Susana and her siblings were all born in Australia. At home, her parents speak both Tongan and English, but the children all speak English, and their Tongan is poor. The oldest child, Susana is now at university and working part-time; her siblings are still in school. Her father has a degree but is doing semiskilled work, while her mother works in an unskilled job; both work full-time. Most of their relatives live interstate, so they seldom see them, but the family is involved in a Tongan church (Uniting Church). Her parents socialize mainly with Tongans, and the children mostly with Australians.

Tavake

Male, age twenty-six. Tavake's parents migrated separately to the United States, where they met and married and had three children. The family lives in California, and Tavake has now left home. Still single, he speaks both Tongan and English fluently. Tavake and his siblings were not brought up in the Tongan way, but they did learn about Tongan culture and feel comfortable if they attend Tongan events. There are no Tongans where he lives, and he does not maintain contact with kin in Tonga, but he keeps up with Tongan news through newspapers. (Interviewed via e-mail.)

Thomas

Male, age forty. The son of a Tongan father and *pakeha* New Zealander, Thomas is divorced from a non-Tongan and lives in New Zealand. His father was sent to New Zealand to be educated and stayed on when he married. Thomas and his two siblings were not raised in the Tongan way, and he does not speak Tongan. He has visited Tonga several times and hopes to return to marry a Tongan woman and live there permanently. He keeps in close contact with an aunt there and sends money to his father, who now lives in Tonga. He keeps up with Tongan news through the Internet and letters from relatives. In New Zealand, however, he does not associate with other Tongans, nor does he belong to a Tongan church. (Interviewed via e-mail.)

Tupou

Male, age fifty-two. Tupou and his family live in a leafy suburb of Melbourne in a large, four-bedroom home. The household consists of Tupou and his wife, 'Alisi, three of their four children (one son has married), his mother, and his sister and her two children. Tupou and 'Alisi moved to Australia in the late 1960s, and their children were all born in Melbourne. His mother, sister, and nieces followed them some ten years later. All members of the household except the grandmother speak English fluently, and as all of the younger generation speak little Tongan, the main language used in the household is English. Both Tupou and 'Alisi have tertiary qualifications and work full-time; one of their children is at university, and the others are still in school. All belong to a Tongan church (Uniting Church). (Father of Haloti; see Case Study 3.)

Veisinia

Female, age nineteen. Born in Australia to parents who migrated in the late 1970s, Veisinia lives with her parents and three siblings, her grandmother, and her niece. She has finished high school and is currently unemployed. Her parents raised her in a "traditional" manner, and she speaks Tongan fluently. She attends a Tongan church (Uniting Church).

Vika

Female, age eighteen. Vika lives with her parents and brother in a rented apartment. Her parents migrated separately to New Zealand in the mid-1970s and married there and had two children. In 1995 the family moved to Melbourne because her parents felt the Australian education system was better than New Zealand's. The family all speak Tongan at home; her father speaks English well enough to get by, but her mother's English is poor. The children speak Tongan very well but have difficulty reading it. Vika is at university, and her brother is still in high school. Their parents have no educational qualifications and rely on the father's sickness benefit to get by. The family attends a Tongan Catholic Church, and while her parents see other Tongans socially, Vika and her brother socialize with Australians. They see little of their extended family, from whom her parents are estranged.

Viliami

Male, age twenty-six. Viliami married his Australian wife, Jenny, while she was working in Tonga. He moved to Australia with her in the early 1990s, and both are undertaking university studies and renting a small apartment. Jenny also works full-time. She speaks Tongan fluently, so they speak a mixture of Tongan and English together. Viliami has few relatives in Melbourne, so they tend to socialize mainly with Australians, but he does regularly attend a kava club, and they see Tongans occasionally at social events. They belonged to a Tongan church (Uniting Church) for some time but were unhappy with various aspects of this church and have now moved to an Australian congregation.

NOTES

Chapter 1: Introduction: Migration and Cultural Identity

1. Pseudonyms are used for all people interviewed and when quoting informal conversations. Interviewees' ages are in parentheses after the first mention of their name. 'Ana is the first of this book's six case studies, which offer detailed portraits of Tongan families living overseas.

2. I have chosen to use the term "non-Tongan" as it is a more inclusive term than "*pālangi*," which Tongans often use to mean foreigners in general but which more specifically refers to people of Anglo-European descent.

3. In an early paper on my research (Morton 1998a) I wrote of migrants "creating their own culture" to describe their diverse ways of coming to terms with being Tongan overseas.

4. Three of the people (ages twenty-eight, twenty-nine, and thirty) featured in the case studies are in between this older group and those under twenty. They were selected not on the basis of their ages but because they reflected deeply on their experiences and current situations. Their accounts offer insights into the long-term process of growing up Tongan overseas.

5. Within the literature on ethnic and cultural identity there is general agreement that it is difficult to precisely define such amorphous concepts. Yet they are important concepts, not least because people utilize them in their real-world interactions (Banks 1996). A whole range of elements has been described as components of ethnic identity, from emotional attachment and shared values and attitudes, to behavior and practices such as language, clothing, shared celebrations, and so on. A great deal of effort has gone into attempting to identify and quantify such elements and to relate them to aspects of individual psychology such as self-esteem.

6. The constructivist approach to ethnicity is influenced by recent work on self and identity that rejects any notion of a singular, fixed identity in favor of an emphasis on multiplicity, flexibility, and context and that acknowledges that aspects of a person's identity can at times be fragmented and conflicted. However, some of this work neglects the subjective *experience* of continuous identity that in most individuals overrides such fragmentation. As Henrietta Moore has observed, the facts of physical embodiment and historical continuity, together with this sense of an ever-present self, "[hold] these multiple subjectivities together so that they constitute agents in the world" (1994, 55).

7. I have avoided the use of terms such as acculturation and assimilation, as they have become so loaded with negative connotations as to have been rendered analytically useless.

8. There are interesting parallels between this process of reconstruction within ethnic populations and the similar processes occurring in their countries of origin as people deal with rapid social change. A substantial literature exists on the politics of tradition in the Pacific (see, e.g., Jolly 1992; Jolly and Thomas 1992; Lindstrom and White 1993; Turner 1997).

9. One strand of the constructivist, or situational, approach to ethnicity is the instrumentalist approach, which views ethnicity as essentially political, with the use of symbolism to manipulate collective identity and ethnic ties and to make political gains and obtain moral and material support (Tilley 1997). I would argue that while this can be one element of ethnicity, for most people it is certainly not the most crucial.

10. See Morton 2001a for a discussion of the cultural memories associated with Tonga's "independence," in which this visit of Tupou I to Sydney is an important element.

11. Details of the early travels of Tongans can be found in several chapters of Rutherford (1977) and in Wood-Ellem (1999).

12. In its early stages Tonga Online presented a typically romanticized image of Tonga for non-Tongans; in 1998 the introductory blurb read: "Never colonized, the Kingdom of Tonga is the last Polynesian kingdom featuring a unique culture, friendly people in an idyllic South Pacific island setting. Tonga Online attempts to bring you complete coverage of the Kingdom of Tonga." In 1998 the site began to include live coverage of important events in Tonga, such as the King's 80th birthday and the annual Heilala Festival, as well as live interviews with various personalities in Tonga.

13. The Kava Bowl is discussed in the present tense here, but the site has been "down" since late 1999 and is unlikely to be restored. Taholo Kami has now formed Kami Communications, a virtual publishing company, which recently established *iTonga*, "Tonga's First Online magazine" (http://www.itonga.net), linked to Tonga Online. Some former Kava Bowl participants have now turned to other discussion forums (see chap. 3).

14. All direct quotations from the Internet are reproduced as they appeared on screen, including the use of non-standard English, capitalization, misspellings, etc. Care has been taken not to reveal the identity of participants, and the posts are identified only by the date on which they were posted—presented here in day/month/year format.

15. Other interviewees were recruited through e-mail discussion lists (Tongan Cyber Network and Kau Ta'e'iloa) that were linked to Tonga Online but which no longer exist. Fifteen interviews were conducted via e-mail, including three with non-Tongan partners of Tongan migrants. The interviewees live in the United States, New Zealand, and Europe, and their ages range from eighteen to sixty-three.

16. Detailed, semistructured interviews were conducted with forty-five individuals ranging in age from fifteen to seventy. With a few exceptions these were drawn from the group covered by the household surveys. In some cases two or more members of one family were interviewed. Five ministers (all male) and four people

(two female, two male) who work with church youth groups were also interviewed. In addition, nineteen young people from a church youth group, aged twelve to nineteen (with one exception, who was twenty-seven), gave written answers to questions similar to those asked in interviews. I have included extracts of many of these interviews (oral and written) throughout the book, and in these cases profiles of the individuals and some background information on their households can be found at the end of the book.

17. This whole process is not without tensions between family members about who should be sponsored, who should support new arrivals with accommodations and expenses, who did the most to help people "get their papers," and so on.

18. The abbreviations are as follows: FZD = father's sister's daughter; MZD = mother's sister's daughter; M = mother; MZS = mother's sister's son; B = brother; ZS = sister's son.

19. The term "part-Tongan" is somewhat unsatisfactory as it implies that identity can be segmented in some way, but it is the most common term used by young people themselves apart from more problematic terms such as "mixed blood" or the Tongan term *"hafekasi"* (half caste). "Australian-born Tongan" is also used at some points, but it should be noted that "Australian-born" has not become a common identifier for young Pacific Islanders in Australia, in contrast to the commonly used "New Zealand-born" in New Zealand. I found there was considerable confusion about terminology, with some young Tongans calling themselves "Tongan Australian" because they had been brought up in Australia. This confusion also mars the literature on Tongan migrants; for example, Small (1997) uses the term "Tongan-American" to refer to any Tongan living in the United States.

Chapter 2: Leaving Tonga "For Our Future"

1. Throughout the book I use the Australian categories of education: "primary" encompasses ages five to eleven or twelve; "secondary," or high school, from around twelve to eighteen; and "tertiary" is any form of post-high school education, such as university or college.

2. Tonga's king, Tāufaʻāhau Tupou IV (then crown prince), was educated from 1933 to 1937 at the Methodist Church's Newington College, Sydney, where other chiefly young men had been students as early as 1896 (Wood-Ellem 1999, 42). All of Tonga's premiers and prime ministers from 1923 to 1992 were also educated at this college (Grainger 1998, 64). The king continued his education at Sydney University (1938–1942), becoming the first Tongan university graduate.

3. The Mormon Church (the Church of Jesus Christ of Latter-Day Saints) has had an important role in Pacific Islander migration; however, since the 1970s this role has diminished due to changing practices within the church as well as changing U.S. immigration policies (Stanton 1993). Nevertheless, the Mormon Church is one of the fastest growing in Tonga, and the 1996 census recorded 13.8 percent of the population as Mormon (*Tonga Chronicle* 1998f; see Gordon 1990).

4. Sudo, and George Marcus (1993, 27), both estimate the number of Tongans in the diaspora to be close to the number in Tonga. The 1996 census in Tonga counted a population of 97,784, of whom 98.2 percent were Tongan and part-Tongan (*Tonga Chronicle* 1998c, 1998e).

5. In 1997 new standards were put in place for federal data on race and ethnicity, and data now include the category "Native Hawaiian or Other Pacific Islander." This was used in the 2000 census, which also allowed respondents to identity as being of one or more races (U.S. Census Bureau 2000, 2001a).

6. Vincent Parillo has only one paragraph on "Other Asian Americans and Pacific Islanders" (1990, 336). Elliott Barkan's *Asian and Pacific Islander Migration to the United States* (1992) uses the "APAC" (Asian and Pacific Islander) category of the U.S. census, despite the fact that Pacific Islanders comprised only 2 percent of persons in the category. For example, in the figures given for APAC migration to the United States from 1972 to 1985, Tongans are only 0.28 percent of the total (Barkan 1992, 62, table 1).

7. The information I present on this case is compiled from discussions with Reverend Kioa, documents he kindly provided, and a number of newspaper articles: *The Sun* (24.6.84, 4.10.84, 17.11.84, 21.12.85), *The Age* (24.10.84, 17.11.84, 21.12.85), and *The National Times* (29.11.85).

8. Late in December 2000, Tongan overstayers were in the news in Australia when a fifty-three-year-old Tongan man being kept in Melbourne's Maribyrnong Detention Centre awaiting deportation killed himself. He had been arrested while picking fruit, a job he took up after many years of working in factories in Sydney, where his mother (a permanent resident) lived. The man climbed a pole topped by a basketball ring and stayed there for eight hours before jumping to his death. He had lived in Australia for about seventeen years and had seven children to support in Tonga. One of his sons, at the age of fifteen, had stowed away on a ship to join his father and was arrested with him and returned to Tonga. (Compiled from articles in *The Age*, 29.12.2000:1–2, 30.12.2000:5, 2.1.01:1–2, 3.1.01:4.)

9. There is a substantial literature on Pacific Islanders in New Zealand, although little of this focuses specifically on Tongans. For particularly useful collections of papers see Macpherson, Spoonley, and Anae 2001; Spoonley, Pearson, and Macpherson 1991; Spoonley, Macpherson, and Pearson 1996.

10. European landlords in New Zealand influenced the pattern of settlement of the early Polynesian migrants by offering only poor accommodations in particular areas, creating concentrations of migrants that were perpetuated as more migrants moved into the same areas (Macpherson 1997, 87).

11. The ministry maintains an Internet site with a range of information about its functions and structure, statistical and other information about the separate Islander groups, and news of relevant events (http://www.minpac.govt.nz).

12. Cathy Small's study of an extended Tongan family in California and their links to relatives remaining in Tonga was the first detailed ethnographic study of Tongans in the United States to be published (1997). Small's focus is primarily on the "first generation" of Tongans in America.

13. The New Immigrant series published by Allyn and Bacon in 1995 did not include any accounts of Pacific Islander migrants (see Glick Schiller 1997).

14. Since 1990 this has made 55,000 permanent resident visas available annually to international applicants, chosen by random selection through a visa lottery (U.S. Department of State 1998). Applicants can enter the lottery for no charge, and for the 2000 lottery, over eight million applications were received (all in October

1998). Of these, 110,000 were selected by the lottery, including 178 from Tongans; however, at the time of writing no figures were available about their success rate (U.S. Department of State 1999). Applicants are required to meet various criteria, including a high school education or its equivalent, or two years of on-the-job training or experience.

15. It is difficult to compare the statistics for Tongans and other Pacific Islanders across different U.S. censuses, given the changes to questions and the small size of the population, which increases the margin for inaccuracies (U.S. Census Bureau 2001b, 3). The 2000 figure is more than double the 17,606 reported for the 1990 census, and even if only those identifying solely as Tongan (27,713) are taken into account, this is still a substantial difference (U.S. Census Bureau 1999). The total number of Pacific Islanders in 1990 was 365,024, a 41 percent increase over the 1980 census (U.S. Department of Commerce 1993; for earlier data see Levin and Ahlburg 1993). For 2000, the Pacific Islander population alone, at 398,835, is an increase of 9.3 percent, while the population recorded as Pacific Islander alone and in combination with other races was 874,414—an increase of 140 percent (U.S. Census Bureau 2001b, 9).

16. Step migration through New Zealand is also difficult; the Trans-Tasman Agreement formerly allowed for free movement between Australia and New Zealand for citizens of those countries, but the Migration Reform Act of 1994 requires New Zealand citizens to obtain a new special category temporary residence visa (SCV) under which they are allowed to legally remain in Australia to work and study, then apply for citizenship after a minimum of two years (Finney 1999, 102).

17. Some of these changes include a surge in new building construction and the expansion of the media in Tonga (three television stations, six newspapers, two magazines, and three radio stations) and a strong push for improved telecommunications (P. Fonua 2001).

18. These discrepancies are difficult to explain and may be more a result of research design and methodology than any significant difference in the populations surveyed. The two researchers who discovered a decline in remittances were Tongan, but I am unsure if (or how) this would have influenced their results. My own study did not include the collection of data on remittances and relied instead on people's own descriptions of their patterns of remitting.

19. See Dennis Ahlburg's discussion of remittances and poverty among Pacific Islanders in the United States (2000).

20. Many of the studies of remittances do not take these kinds of variables into account. Both James (1997b), for Tongan migrants, and Macpherson (1994), for Samoans, look beyond the quantitative data to uncover the diverse and interrelated influences on migrants' remittance behavior.

21. This may be one way Tongans in Tonga are beginning to reciprocate the assistance that has been given to them by migrants, as Princess Pilolevu suggested they should in a 1996 interview.

> My main concern with Tongans abroad is because they send the remittances home to Tonga and I think it's our responsibility that we look after the Tongans abroad. We can't just leave them out there to fend for themselves and whenever we need $100,000 to build a church or school we go out there and get them to

give. I think that it is time that the Tongans in Tongatapu also looked after the Tongans abroad. (M. Fonua 1996, 17)

22. Occasionally, fund-raising tours are unsuccessful. One group that toured Australia in 1998 raised only enough to cover their airfares and left the Tongans they had stayed with considerably out of pocket.

23. Another large amount reported was A$390,000 spent in late 1996 on purchasing land in Sydney and constructing a new church; this money may have been collected over some time and so was not included in the 1996–1997 total. Other large amounts of money raised during the same period that were not included in the total were cases where Tongans in Australia contributed to a fund-raising effort that crossed several nations, usually the United States, Australia, and New Zealand.

Chapter 3: Life Overseas: Community and Conflict

1. Studies of Samoans in New Zealand have shown a similar reliance on these two key social institutions (Pitt and Macpherson 1974; Macpherson 1984, 1991, 1997). Leulu Va'a's description of the Samoan churches in Sydney reveals parallels with Tongan churches, particularly in terms of the internal conflicts between pastors and their congregations and between members of congregations (1995). Samoan churches in Sydney are also similar to Tongan churches in that their success can be largely attributed to the strong personalities, wide experience, and administrative skills of the founding ministers (Va'a 1995, 134).

2. Thanks to Niko Besnier for pointing out this distinction.

3. Like most Western nations, Australia has a range of services specifically targeting "ethnic" groups; however, since the late 1980s there has been a continuing decline in the provision of such services (Langfield 1995, 5), further diminishing the level of support available to Tongans.

4. Since this writing, DIMA has become the Department of Immigration and Multicultural and Indigenous Affairs, or DIMIA.

5. "Qualifications" refers to the successful completion of a course of education, such as a degree, diploma, certificate, and so on.

6. The more recent census, in 1996, is unhelpful, as 74 percent of Tongans in Melbourne and 86.5 percent in rural Victoria were recorded as a "not stated or inadequately described category" for the question on forms of employment.

7. Their brother, Reverend James Lātū, who has lived in Australia for over thirty years, kindly gave me access to his file of news clippings from the 1970s and 1980s. A number of articles appeared in 1974 and 1975 when Sanitesi's athletics club began lobbying the Australian government to allow him to stay in Australia; he was granted permanent residence but went on to represent Tonga in the Commonwealth Games in 1982 (Clarke 1974; *The Herald* 1971; *The Sun* 1975a, 1975b; *Tonga Chronicle* 1979; *Village Courier* 1982, 2).

8. Newspapers and other media around the world took great delight in reporting that with Wolfgramm's win Tonga had won the most medals per capita at the 1996 Olympics.

9. Several Tongans have played for the Australian Wallabies team in international competitions. The annual "Willy O Cup" that is part of the annual Sydney rugby competition is named after one of these players, Viliami (Willy) Ofahengaue.

10. Two recent television series, *Treasure Island* (aired in 2000) and *Shipwrecked 2* (aired in 2001), have been based on small, uninhabited Tongan islands.

11. Issues of "race" are more prominent in the United States than in Australia, where "ethnicity" has more currency. Pepi Leistyna coined the term "racenicity" to express the impact of constructions of race on perceptions of ethnic difference in the United States (1999; see Steinberg 2000).

12. The Tongan History Association (THA) forum was linked to the Kava Bowl and was the site of the kinds of discussions similar to those found on the KB. As with the KB, the site has been down for some time and is unlikely to be restored. The new Planet Tonga site has set up a THA forum, but as one of many forums it has not attracted many participants.

13. Newspapers and other forms of media in Australia are wary of using expressions such as "of Pacific Islander appearance" in crime reports, as a result of campaigns by panethnic associations to remove ethnic stereotyping from the media.

14. In Tonga itself there appears to be a rising anti-Chinese sentiment after the recent wave of Chinese immigrants, who have complained about a spate of crimes against them including assaults, arson, burglary, and housebreakings (*Tonga Chronicle* 1999a, 1999b). There is also anecdotal evidence to suggest that attitudes toward *pālangi* are becoming more negative in Tonga.

15. The effects of "social stress" on the health of Samoans in urban California have been studied by Craig Janes (1990), and his findings are relevant for many Tongan migrants.

16. The violence that can be fueled by alcohol consumption contributes to the negative stereotypes described earlier. To give just one example, in October 2001 three young Tongan men in Melbourne were jailed for assaulting a West Indian test cricketer after a night of drinking in the city (Gregory 2001).

17. Most initiatives attempt to deal directly with youth, but there have been some attempts to include parents, such as the seminar on family issues organized in Melbourne by the Canterbury Uniting Church (1993). The Tongan community parenting classes that have been run since 1991 in Salt Lake City, Utah, are another example.

18. It is regarded as a great shame to the family if young people are sent to juvenile detention centers or jails, and they are seldom visited by family members. Parents may even disown their children in such cases. However, some Tongan ministers, as well as this group, do visit and become the young people's only link with the Tongan community.

19. One of the oldest such groups is the Tongan Farmers' Co-operative Federation, established in Hawai'i in 1975 to lease land on O'ahu and Moloka'i for farming agricultural products for sale and organizing fairs to exhibit their produce and handicrafts (*Tonga Chronicle* 1997b).

20. The society aims to encourage Polynesian children in the United States to "know and take pride in their remarkable heritage" (Polynesia Polynesia Cultural Heritage Society 2001); a similar organization is the Literature and Arts Heritage Guild of Polynesia, based in Utah, which promotes interest in the "Polynesian Heritage" as a means of keeping youth away from gangs and crime.

21. There were thirteen non-Tongan presenters and eighteen Tongan, and very few non-Tongans were among the large audience. In addition, over four hundred Pacific Islander high school students attended the conference for a morning as part of their involvement in Pacific Islander Awareness Week..

22. Alan Howard raises the possibility of the emergence of "new global communities" of Pacific Islanders through the World Wide Web and discusses the case of the web site he established for Rotumans in 1996 (Howard 1999; see also Ogden 1999). In her fascinating doctoral thesis, Marianne Franklin examines the "postcolonial politics of representation" found on Pacific Islander discussion forums, including the Kava Bowl (2001).

23. Kalianet is named after the ancient *kalia,* the double-hulled, seagoing canoes once used to travel the vast Pacific ocean. Established in February 1997, the site proclaims, "The navigational skills required by these early travellers are again required by the modern Tongans using computers to navigate this satellite connection to the InterNET."

Chapter 4: Identity in the Diaspora: Perspectives of the First Generation

1. The prince and princess lived in Canberra from December 1995 to January 1998. The prince became the patron of the Tongan Association, and in June 1996, the princess formed and became president of Loto Taha (One Heart) Tongan Women's Association. Both were actively involved in the City Uniting Church and Tongan social activities (Finney 1999).

2. Small describes Tongans who "go home for two or three months each year," living in poor conditions in the United States yet owning "fine houses" and being regarded as "important figures in the village" (1997, 192). I did not encounter any Tongans who return annually like this, and given the expense involved, it seems this would be a small minority of migrants. It is certainly true that there can be a great disparity between people's socioeconomic status overseas and the perceptions held in Tonga of their "success" as migrants. In some cases this is due to their investment in homes and businesses in Tonga, but more often it is their ostentatious display of expensive clothing, generous gifting, and so on, during their visits to Tonga.

3. The issues impacting on Tongans' attitudes toward returning "home" are similar to those described by Cluny Macpherson for Samoan migrants (1985).

4. This is not a unique practice; for example, Colleen O'Neal notes that Koreans and Indians "attempt to preserve the integrity of their cultural practices" by sending children home for "culture training" (1999, 223).

5. The derogatory term "coconut" is often applied to Tongans (and other Islanders) who have taken on Western ways: they are said to be brown on the outside and white on the inside.

6. *"Tapu"* (taboo) is the term used to refer to the practices associated with *faka'apa'apa,* since they commonly involve restrictions on behavior.

7. The *fahu* is the person who has high status and the associated rights at life-crisis events and is most often a child of the *mehekitanga;* even in Tonga the importance of this role is diminishing (Morton 1996, 288n6).

8. Macpherson and Macpherson describe the "ceremonial inflation" that occurred among Samoans in New Zealand as extended families became "bigger and wealthier" (1999, 289). They report that during the 1980s and 1990s this trend has reversed, partly due to the economic downturn in that country.

9. I have explored the debates on the KB about language use in more detail elsewhere (Morton 2002a).

10. I am referring in this discussion only to English, as on the KB it is rare to encounter languages other than English or Tongan. However, there are Tongan migrants in non-English-speaking countries as well, and they have similar concerns about the loss of Tongan-language skills.

11. *"Tō'onga faka-Tonga"* means Tongan manners and behavior, thus is similar to *anga fakatonga*.

12. In their call for contemporary Pacific Islander artists to contribute to an exhibition titled "Lanuola" (The colors of life) in San Francisco in 2001, the organizers described the exhibition as an attempt "to reimagine and inaugurate a contemporary Pacific aesthetics that strongly contests the negative and monolithic representations of Pacific Islanders that are prevalent in the White mainstream media" (e-mail, 1.12.2000).

13. Tohi was raised by his grandmothers in Tonga, and they taught him the ancient stories of Tongan gods and heroes. Later he moved to New Zealand and became involved with gangs in the late 1970s before training at the Maori Art and Craft Centre and producing sculptures that are now displayed in many sites in New Zealand and elsewhere, including the United States, Japan, and Saudi Arabia (Tāmo'ua 1998).

Chapter 5: Diasporic Youth: "Stuck between Two Worlds"?

1. Jean Phinney and Mary Jane Rotheram use an approach based on developmental psychology that focuses on issues of self-concept and self-esteem. Their work is a valuable contribution to our understanding of the processes of ethnic identity formation, yet there is little attempt to locate these processes beyond the family and ethnic group. The contributors to their book also tend to ignore young people's agency in developing their own identities.

2. Micaela Di Leonardo has critized what she calls the "ethnic family culture" genre of studies, in which the family structures and values of ethnic groups were assumed to be transmitted to each successive generation, hindering the process of assimilation. Particular characteristics of ethnic groups were therefore seen as the source of any difficulties they experienced in their host societies, rather than other factors such as the broader structural features of those societies. As she points out, "all of daily life, not just family life, is part of the construction and reconstruction of ethnic identities (1984, 24).

3. The Tonga Visitor's Bureau estimated that up to five thousand expatriate Tongans visit each year, and while most stay with family, there are an increasing number who choose to stay at holiday resorts, particularly when they are accompanied by non-Tongan partners (*'Eva* 1998).

4. Niko Besnier reports for overseas-born Tongan men that "their awkwardness in performing Tongan maleness, including speaking Tongan as a preferred lan-

guage, frequently brands them as fakaleitī-like, regardless of whether they present any identifiable sign of effeminacy in their comportment" (forthcoming).

5. In fact, the KB can be seen as helping to promote literacy in both Tongan and English, and being text based it provides an opportunity for participants to express their opinions, describe experiences, engage in discussions, and otherwise practice their written-language skills.

6. Mark Warschauer has discussed the potential of the Internet to assist with language maintenance and revitalization, which he sees as a means of defending "community, autonomy, and power" (2000, 166). Using the example of Hawaiian sites, he argues that the Internet provides "opportunities for those who challenge English-language hegemony."

7. Ulf Hannerz has argued that while language has dominated the way people think of cultural boundaries, globalization is challenging this, with people increasingly communicating across languages (1996, 21). However, the reassertion of local identities in the context of globalization could act to curb this challenge, at least in terms of ideas of "authentic" group membership.

8. The research involved 120 young people from six different ethnic groups, all living in Melbourne, including twenty Pacific Islanders (two Tongan) from the Frankston area, in southeast Melbourne, where many young people are from low socioeconomic backgrounds, living in a disadvantaged area with few recreational activities available apart from hanging around in the shopping malls or on the streets. Although no evidence of American-style gangs of Pacific Islanders was found in Melbourne in the late 1990s, there were indications that some gang activity had occurred; for example, the Tongan Mafia, a gang with branches in several parts of the diaspora, had been active at times (White et al. 1999b, 29).

9. White et al. (1999b, 33) found that while some Pacific Islander youth claimed to belong to "gangs" because they experienced racism, they were also using this as an excuse for violent behavior and were often racist toward other groups, particularly Asians.

10. Rogelia Pe Pua (1996) surveyed a hundred street-frequenting youths in Sydney, of whom twenty-four were Pacific Islanders (two Tongan males and four females).

11. White et al. (1999a) point out that the term "gang" has no fixed meaning and is often used to refer to any group of young people who frequently socialize together. The term is often used by the media to sensationalize the activities of such groups, creating and reinforcing stereotypes of young people, particularly those from recognizable ethnic groups.

12. White et al. conducted their research in Melbourne, and it is misleading to generalize their findings to Australia. For example, Sydney has a much larger Pacific Islander population, and it is well known that gangs are present, including rival Tongan and Samoan gangs.

Chapter 6: Intermarriage: "A Two-Way Life"

1. Various other terms could be used to describe the couples' relationships, including "outmarriage," "mixed marriage," or "interracial marriage." In discussing marriage here I also include de facto marriages. The latter are far less common, as

older Tongans generally strongly disapprove of such relationships and the pressure on young people to marry legally is still strong.

2. While 389,612 people identified themselves as from one Pacific Islander group, another 9,223 were from more than one Pacific Islander group, and a further 475,579 were from one or more Pacific Islander groups in combination with one or more other races (U.S. Census Bureau 2001b, 9).

3. I have not included here nine marriages between Tongans and Tongan Australians. Also not included are the ten Tongan and part-Tongan single parents who were previously intermarried and who have between them eighteen children.

4. I surveyed thirty-six single Tongans and part-Tongans about their marriage preferences: nineteen of the females (70.3 percent) said they would prefer to marry Tongans, whereas only three of the males (33.3 percent) said the same. Fewer were adamant that they would not marry a Tongan—only eight females and one male. Two males said it would not matter as long as the marriage was happy, and four females and three males were unsure of their preferences. The higher number of female responses is due to only a few of the males answering this question on the written questionnaires given to the church youth group.

5. Alice is one of a small number of overseas-born Tongans who are over forty. Her mother was taken to New Zealand during World War II by her *pakeha* New Zealander relatives.

Chapter 7: Looking Ahead

1. In the context of the Asia Pacific Economic Summit 2000 it was reported that Asia-Pacific Internet use is "growing at a compound rate of about 45 per cent. Within three years, it will be more than 25 per cent of the entire world's online population" (*The Age* 2000).

2. Interestingly, young Tongans in the United States were unanimous in their refusal to accept being placed in the category "Asian and Pacific Islander," and this externally imposed identification has not had any apparent effect on constructions of Islander or Polynesian identity.

Appendix A: The Tongans of Melbourne, Australia

1. Even obtaining an accurate figure from the census is difficult: the C-LIB 96 CD-ROM of the 1996 census data gives a figure of 1,014 Tongan-born individuals in Victoria, and two separate sets of statistics supplied by DIMA, based on census figures, show 1,023 and 1,018.

2. More surprisingly, these community profiles barely mention New Zealand Maori.

3. The Australian census has collected information on the birthplace of individuals' parents in 1921; from 1971 onward, however, Tonga has usually been in the category of "Other." Citizenship figures were collected until 1986, when the question was changed to ask simply whether or not the person was an Australian citizen. Questions on language use have also changed over time: in 1976 respondents were asked to list all languages regularly used; in 1981 they were asked about their ability to speak English; in 1986 the questions covered the language they used and

their English ability; and in 1996 the census recorded the language used at home and English ability.

4. Fusipala had lived in New Zealand between late 1920 and late 1925, living with a *pālangi* family and later attending an Anglican school (Wood-Ellem 1999, 143). In mid-1926 some Australians attended the celebrations of the centennial of Christianity's arrival in Tonga, and Fusipala returned with them to enrol in MLC (Wood-Ellem 1999, 143). While she was in Melbourne, a Tongan choir from Tupou College toured Victoria and New South Wales, and she participated in some of their Melbourne concerts (Wood-Ellem 1999, 144).

5. The first president of the TCF was a woman who had come to Melbourne to train as a nurse, then married a *pālangi* and settled permanently in Australia.

6. These supporters included Reverend Dr. Harold Wood, former principal of Tupou College and later principal of the MLC in Melbourne, and Reverends Fred Mackay, Ron Woodgate, George Harris, and Howard Secomb. Other strong supporters were Dilys Rowlands, former principal of Queen Sālote College (1945–1968) and Mary Thompson, another former principal of the same college (1934–1944) and principal of Siu'ilikutapu College in Vava'u. These *pālangi* who had connections with Tonga were also supportive of the Tongans in Melbourne in many other ways, for example, by providing accommodations for students and short-term visitors. Thanks to Elizabeth Wood-Ellem for this information.

7. The eleven non-Tongans other than Australians are: Indian (one), Maltese (two), English (one), Greek German (one), German (two), white New Zealander (two), and Samoan (two).

8. One is an eighteen-year-old woman living with an older man (both Tongan), and the other is a twenty-year-old Tongan Australian man living with an older Tongan woman.

9. The ages of the six people living alone ranged from twenty-seven to forty-two; three were female and three male (two were of mixed descent). The seventeen two-person households were mainly young couples who chose to live independently rather than with extended family members, as would be the norm in Tonga.

10. Within the total sample of households there are three other households with single parents; however, these are part of larger extended family households, as in the case of a widow and her children who have been incorporated into her brother's household.

11. New Zealand's 1996 census also recorded that 22 percent of Tongans lived in one-parent families, compared to 16 percent for the total population. In the United States, 19 percent of Pacific Islander families had a female head of household, with no spouse present (U.S. Department of Commerce 1993, 4; no separate figures for Tongans).

12. A few tertiary students were studying on scholarships and living away from their families. These students can find studying at this level difficult when English is their second language and they do not have family support; consequently, they have a poor completion rate. A report on scholarship students in New Zealand showed that between 1995 and 1997, 21 percent of Tongan students failed to graduate (Mangisi 1999, 5).

13. In the United States, the 1990 census showed that 45 percent of second-generation Tongans over the age of five spoke Tongan at home (Small 1997, 233n42).

14. The 1996 census in Tonga recorded that 41.3 percent of the population belonged to the Free Wesleyan Church of Tonga. Members of this church who migrate to Australia usually join either the Uniting Church, the Free Wesleyan Church, or the Wesleyan Methodist Church. In Tonga, 16 percent of the population were Roman Catholics, 13.8 percent were Mormons, 11.7 percent belonged to the Free Church of Tonga, and the remainder were members of the Tokaikolo Church of Christ, Seventh-Day Adventists, Assembly of God, Anglican, and "non-Christian religions" (*Tonga Chronicle* 1998f).

REFERENCES

Age, The. 1999. "Migrant parent program slashed." 2 April, 4.
———. 2000. "The Net widens." 12 September, 9.
Ahlburg, Dennis. 1991. *Remittances and their impact: A study of Tonga and Western Samoa.* Pacific Policy Papers no. 7. Canberra: National Centre for Development Studies, Australian National University.
———. 2000. "Poverty among Pacific Islanders in the United States: Incidence, change, and correlates." *Pacific Studies* 23(1–2):51–74.
Ahlburg, Dennis, and Michael Levin. 1990. *The North East passage: A study of Pacific Islander migration to American Samoa and the United States.* Canberra: National Centre for Development Studies, Australian National University.
Alba, Richard. 2000. "Assimilation's quiet tide." In *Race and ethnicity in the United States: Issues and debates,* ed. Stephen Steinberg. Oxford: Blackwell, 211–222.
Amit-Talai, Vered, and Helena Wulff, eds. 1995. *Youth cultures: A cross-cultural perspective.* London: Routledge.
Anae, Melani. 1997. "Towards a NZ-born Samoan identity: Some reflections on 'labels.'" *Pacific Health Dialog* 4(2):128–137.
Appadurai, Arjun. 1996. *Modernity at large: Cultural dimensions of globalization.* Minneapolis: University of Minnesota Press.
Appleyard, R. T., and Charles Stahl. 1995. *South Pacific migration: New Zealand experience and implications for Australia.* Canberra: AusAID.
Austonga News. 1996. 21, 2.
Australian Bureau of Statistics. 1997. *1996 Census of population and housing: Selected social and housing characteristics for statistical local areas: Victoria.* Canberra: Australian Bureau of Statistics.
Australian Census. 1996. C-Lib 96 CD-ROM.
Banks, Marcus. 1996. *Ethnicity: Anthropological constructions.* London: Routledge.
Barkan, Elliott. 1992. *Asian and Pacific Islander migration to the United States: A model of new global patterns.* Contributions in Ethnic Studies no. 30. Westport, Conn.: Greenwood Press.
Barrier, N. Gerald, and Verne Dusenbury, eds. *1989. The Sikh diaspora:*

Migration and the experience beyond Punjab. Delhi: Chanakya Press.

Basch, Linda, Nina Glick Schiller, and Cristina Szanton Blanc. 1994. *Nations unbound: Transnational projects, postcolonial predicaments, and deterritorialized nation-states.* Langhorne, Pa.: Gordon and Breach.

Bedford, Richard. 1984. "The Polynesian connection: Migration and social change in New Zealand and the South Pacific." In *Essays on urbanisation in Southeast Asia and the Pacific,* ed. R. Bedford. Christchurch: Department of Geography, University of Canterbury, 113–141.

Benguigui, Georges. 1989. "The middle class in Tonga." *Journal of the Polynesian Society* 98(4):451–463.

Benson, Susan. 1981. *Ambiguous ethnicity: Interracial families in London.* Cambridge: Cambridge University Press.

Bernal, Martha, and George Knight. 1993. "Introduction." In *Ethnic identity: Formation and transmission among Hispanics and other minorities,* ed. Martha Bernal and George Knight. Albany, N.Y.: State University of New York, 1–7.

Bertram, Geoffrey. 1986. " 'Sustainable development' in Pacific micro-economies." *World Development* 14(7):809–822.

———. 1999. "The MIRAB model twelve years on." *The Contemporary Pacific* 11(1):105–138.

Bertram, Geoffrey, and Ray Watters. 1985. "The MIRAB economy in Pacific microstates." *Pacific Viewpoint* 26(3):479–519.

Besnier, Niko. Forthcoming. "Transgenderism, locality, and the Miss Galaxy beauty pageant in Tonga." Forthcoming in *American Ethnologist.*

Bott, Elizabeth. 1981. "Rank and power in the kingdom of Tonga." *Journal of the Polynesian Society* 90(1):7–81.

Bottomley, Gillian. 1992. *From another place: Migration and the politics of culture.* Cambridge: Cambridge University Press.

Breger, Rosemary, and Rosanna Hill. 1998a. *Cross-cultural marriage: Identity and choice.* Oxford: Berg.

———. 1998b. "Introducing mixed marriages." In *Cross-cultural marriage: Identity and choice,* ed. Rosemary Breger and Rosanna Hill. Oxford: Berg, 1–32.

Brown, Richard. 1998. "Do migrants' remittances decline over time? Evidence from Tongans and Western Samoans in Australia." *The Contemporary Pacific* 10(1):107–151.

Brown, Richard, and John Connell. 1993. "The global flea market: Migration, remittances and the informal economy in Tonga." *Development and Change* 24:611–647.

Brown, Richard, and John Foster. 1995. "Some common fallacies about migrants' remittances in the South Pacific: Lessons from Tongan and Western research." *Pacific Viewpoint* 36(1):29–45.

Brown, Richard, and Adrian Walker. 1995. *Migrants and their remittances: Results of a household survey of Tongans and Western Samoans in Sydney.* Pacific Studies Monograph no. 17. Sydney: The University of New South Wales.

Bull, Vika, and Linda Bull. 1996. *Princess Tabu* compact disc. Melbourne: Mushroom Records International.

Bureau of Immigration and Population Research. 1994a. *Community profiles 1991 census, New Zealand born.* Canberra: Australian Government Publishing Service.

———. 1994b. *Immigrant families: A statistical profile.* Statistical Report no. 12. Canberra: Australian Government Publishing Service.

Campbell, Ian. 1992. "The emergence of parliamentary politics in Tonga." *Pacific Studies* 15(1):77–97.

———. 1994. "The doctrine of accountability and the unchanging locus of power in Tonga." *Journal of Pacific History* 29(1):81–94.

Canberra Times. 1999. "'First' light to fall on soldier's grave." 31 December, 5.

Canterbury Uniting Church. 1993. "Seminar of Tongan-Australian families." Unpublished report in author's possession.

Chan, Janet. 1996. "Police racisms: Experiences and reforms." In *The teeth are smiling: The persistence of racism in multicultural Australia,* ed. Ellie Vasta and Stephen Castles. Sydney: Allen and Unwin, 160–172.

Clark, Andrew. 2000. "Mix and match." *The Age,* 12 February, 4.

Clarke, Ron. 1974. "Give this guy an even break." *The Sun,* 28 January, 34.

Clifford, James. 1994. "Diasporas." *Cultural Anthropology* 9(3):302–338.

Connell, John. 1987. "Paradise left? Pacific Island voyagers in the modern world." In *Pacific bridges: The new immigration from Asia and the Pacific Islands,* ed. James Fawcett and Benjamin Cariño. New York: Center for Migration Studies, 375–404.

———. 1990. "Modernity and its discontents: Migration and change in the South Pacific." In *Migration and development in the South Pacific,* ed. John Connell. Canberra: National Centre for Development Studies, Australian National University, 1–28.

Connell, John, and Richard Brown. 1995. "Migration and remittances in the South Pacific: Towards new perspectives." *Asian and Pacific Migration Journal* 4(1):1–34.

Connell, John, Graham Harrison, and Grant McCall. 1991. South Pacific Islanders in Australia. Background report to conference on Pacific Island migration to Australia.

Connell, John, and John Lea. 1995. *Pacific 2010: Urbanisation in Polynesia.* Canberra: National Centre for Development Studies, Australian National University.

Connell, John, and Grant McCall. 1989. South Pacific Islanders in Australia. Research Institute for Asia and the Pacific. Occasional Paper no. 9. Sydney: University of Sydney.

Conniff, Michael. 1994. *Africans in the Americas: History of the black diaspora.* New York: St. Martin's Press.

Cornwall, Grant, and Eve Stoddard, eds. 2001. *Global multiculturalism: Comparative perspectives on ethnicity, race, and nation.* Lanham, Md.: Rowman and Littlefield.

Cowling, Wendy. 1990. "Motivations for contemporary Tongan migration." In *Tongan culture and history,* ed. Phyllis Herda, Jennifer Terrell, and Niel Gunson. Canberra: Department of Pacific and Southeast Asian History, Research School of Pacific Studies, Australian National University, 187–205.

Cox, D., and M. Low. 1985. *Migration from the South Pacific: A welfare perspective.* Melbourne: International Social Service and Department of Social Studies, University of Melbourne.

Cunneen, Chris. 1995. "Ethnic minority youth and juvenile justice: Beyond the stereotype of ethnic gangs." *Current Issues in Criminal Justice* 6(3):387–394.

Cuthbertson, S., and R. Cole. 1995. *Population growth in the South Pacific Island States–Implications for Australia.* Bureau of Immigration, Multiculturalism, and Population Research. Canberra: Australian Government Publishing Service.

Daniel, G. Reginald. 1992. "Beyond black and white: The new multiracial consciousness." In *Racially mixed people in America,* ed. Maria Root. Newbury Park, Calif.: Sage, 333–341.

Davies, Judy. 1978. "Latu keeps title." *The Sun,* 31 January, 66.

Department of Immigration and Multicultural Affairs. 1996. *Annual Report 1995–6.* Canberra: Australian Government Publishing Service.

———. 2001. *2002–2003 Migration and Humanitarian Programs: A discussion paper.* Canberra: DIMA.

Department of Social Security. 1977. *Directory of National Group Organisations in Australia 1977.* Canberra: DSS.

De Vos, George. 1990. "Conflict and accommodation in ethnic interaction." In *Status inequality: The self in culture,* ed. George De Vos and Marcelo Suarez-Orozco. Newbury Park, Calif.: Sage, 204–245.

Di Leonardo, Micaela. 1984. *The varieties of ethnic experience: Kinship, class, and gender among California Italian-Americans.* New York: Cornell University Press.

Ecumenical Migration Centre. N.d. "Pacific Island Forum: EMC's work in relation to Pacific Island Communities." Unpublished document.

Eller, Jack, and Reed Coughlan. 1993. "The poverty of primordialism: The demystification of ethnic attachments." *Ethnic and Racial Studies* 16(2):183–201.

Espiritu, Yen Le. 1992. *Asian American panethnicity: Bridging institutions and identities.* Philadelphia: Temple University Press.

'Eva. 1998. "Homecoming holidays" 40:4–5.

Fabrier, Nicolle, and Ken Cruikshank. 1993. "Students from the Pacific Islands and education." In *A world perspective on Pacific Islander migration: Australia, New Zealand and the USA,* ed. Grant McCall and John Connell. Pacific Studies Monograph no. 6. Sydney: Centre for South Pacific Studies, University of New South Wales, 53–57.

Faeamani, Sione. 1995. "The impact of remittances on rural development in Tongan villages." *Asia and Pacific Migration Journal* 4(1):139–155.

Faiva, 'Osaiasi. 1989. *The Tongans in Manly-Warringah: A community survey.*

Manly, New South Wales: Health Promotion Unit, Manly Hospital and Community Services.

Fenton, Steve. 1999. *Ethnicity: Racism, class and culture.* London: Macmillan.

Finney, Frances. 1999. "'I thought it would be heaven': Migration, gender, and community amongst overseas Tongans." M.A. thesis, Australian National University.

Fitzgerald, Thomas. 1998. "Metaphors, media and social change: Second-generation Cook Islanders in New Zealand." In *Pacific answers to western hegemony: Cultural practices of identity construction,* ed. Jurg Wassmann. Oxford: Berg, 253–267.

Foliaki, Siale. 1999. "Mental health among Tongan migrants." *Pacific Health Dialog* 6(2):288–294.

Fonua, Mary. 1996. "Pilolevu takes Tongan values into the international business arena."*Matangi Tonga* 11(1):14–18.

Fonua, Pesi. 1991. "'Ana Taufe'ulungaki's up-hill battle to save the Tongan language." *Matangi Tonga* 6(2):10–11.

———. 1998. "It's a bit too late to be married, says Tonga's bachelor Crown Prince." *'Eva* 41:6–11.

———. 1999. "Too late for overseas Tongans to vote." *Matangi Tonga* 14(1):3–4.

———. 2001. "Wiring up Nuku'alofa." *Matangi Tonga* 16(1):12–15.

Forté, Geraldine. 1994. *Appropriating old cultures into new futures: From the Kingdom of Tonga to California.* San Jose, Calif.: Pacific Rim Resources.

Francis, Steven. 1995. "Pacific Islander young people: Issues of juvenile justice and cultural dislocation." In *Ethnic minority youth in Australia,* ed. Carmel Guerra and Rob White. Hobart, Tasmania: National Clearing House for Youth Studies, 179–192.

Franco, Robert. 1997. "The kingly-populist divergence in Tongan and Western Samoan chiefly systems." In *Chiefs today: Traditional leadership and the postcolonial state,* ed. Geoffrey White and Lamont Lindstrom. Stanford, Calif.: Stanford University Press, 71–83.

Franklin, Marianne. 2001. "The Internet and postcolonial politics of representation: Pacific traversals." Ph.D. dissertation, University of Amsterdam.

Gailey, Christine Ward. 1992. "A good man is hard to find: Overseas migration and the decentered family in the Tongan Islands." *Critique of Anthropology* 12(1):47–74.

Gans, Herbert. 1997. "Toward a reconciliation of 'assimilation' and 'pluralism': The interplay of acculturation and ethnic retention." *International Migration Review* 31(4):875–892.

Gilmore, Robert. 1973. "Don't worry, they won't eat us." *The Herald,* 13 March, 4.

Glick Schiller, Nina. 1997. "U.S. immigrants and the global narrative." *American Anthropologist* 99(2):404–408.

Goldlust, John. 1996. *Understanding citizenship in Australia.* Bureau of Immigration, Multicultural and Population Research. Canberra: Australian Government Publishing Service.

Gordon, Tamar. 1990. "Inventing the Mormon Tongan family." In *Christianity in Oceania: Ethnographic perspectives*, ed. John Barker. Lanham, Md.: University Press of America, 197–219.

Grainger, Gareth. 1997. "Tonga and Australia since the end of World War II." Paper presented to the Tongan History Association Conference, Canberra.

———. 1998. "Tonga and Australia since World War II." In *Echoes of Pacific war*, ed. Deryck Scarr, Niel Gunson, and Jennifer Terrell. Canberra: Target Oceania, 64–75.

Gregory, Peter. 2001. "Three jailed for 'vicious' attack on cricketer." *The Age*, 18 October, 7.

Grijp, Paul van der. 1993. "After the vanilla harvest: Stains in the Tongan land tenure system." *Journal of the Polynesian Society* 102(3):233–253.

———. 1997. "Leaders in squash export: Entrepreneurship and the introduction of a new cash crop in Tonga." *Pacific Studies* 20(1):29–62.

Hage, Ghassan. 1998. *White nation: Fantasies of white supremacy in a multicultural society.* Sydney: Pluto Press.

Hall, Kathleen. 1995. " 'There's a time to act English and a time to act Indian': The politics of identity among British-Sikh teenagers." In *Children and the politics of culture*, ed. Sharon Stephens. Princeton, N.J.: Princeton University Press, 243–264.

Hall, Stuart. 1990. "Cultural identity and diaspora." In *Identity: Community, culture, difference*, ed. Jonathan Rutherford. London: Lawrence and Wishart, 222–237.

Hamilton, Kendall, Daniel Glick, and Jeff Rice. 1996. "The Crips and Bloods of promised land: Gangs of Pacific Islanders in Mormon country." *Newsweek*, 13 May, 72–73.

Hannerz, Ulf. 1996. *Transnational connections: Culture, people, places.* London: Routledge.

Hao'uli, Sefita. 1995. "Radio *faikakai* after midnight." *Matangi Tonga* 10(2):10.

Hau'ofa, Epeli. 1994. "Our sea of islands." *The Contemporary Pacific* 6(1):148–161.

———. 1998. "The ocean in us." *The Contemporary Pacific* 10(2):392–410.

Herald, The. 1971. "It's able Albert." 23 December, 15.

Holton, Robert. 1994. "Social aspects of migration." In *Australian Immigration: A survey of the issues*, ed. Mark Wooden, Robert Holton, Graeme Hugo, and Judith Sloan. Bureau of Immigration and Population Research. Canberra: Australian Government Publishing Service, 158–213.

Howard, Alan. 1999. "Pacific-based virtual communities: Rotuma on the World Wide Web." *The Contemporary Pacific* 11(1):160–175.

Jakubowicz, Andrew, Michael Morrisey, and Joanne Palser. 1984. *Ethnicity, class and social policy in Australia.* Sydney: Social Welfare Research Centre, University of New South Wales.

James, Kerry. 1991. "Migration and remittances: A Tongan village perspective." *Pacific Viewpoint* 32(1):1–23.

———. 1993. "Cash and kin. Aspects of migration and remittance from the perspective of a fishing village in Vava'u, Tonga." In *A world perspective on Pacific Islander migration: Australia, New Zealand and the USA*, ed. Grant McCall and John Connell. Pacific Studies Monograph no. 6. Sydney: Centre for South Pacific Studies, University of New South Wales, 359–373.

———. 1994. "Tonga's pro-democracy movement." *Pacific Affairs* 67(2):242–263.

———. 1997a. "Rank and leadership in Tonga." In *Chiefs today: Traditional leadership and the postcolonial state,* ed. Geoffrey White and Lamont Lindstrom. Stanford, Calif.: Stanford University Press, 49–70.

———. 1997b. "Reading the leaves: The role of women's traditional wealth and other 'contraflows' in the process of modern migration and remittance." *Pacific Studies* 20(1):1–27.

Janes, Craig. 1990. *Migrations, social change, and health: A Samoan community in urban California.* Stanford: Stanford University Press.

Jenkins, Richard. 1997. *Rethinking ethnicity: Arguments and explorations.* London: Sage.

Jensen, Leif. 1989. *The new immigration: Implications for poverty and public assistance utilization.* New York: Greenwood.

Jolly, Margaret. 1992. "Specters of inauthenticity." *The Contemporary Pacific* 4(1):49–72.

Jolly, Margaret, and Nicholas Thomas, eds. 1992. *The politics of tradition in the Pacific.* Special Issue of *Oceania* 64(4).

Jones, Alison. 1989. "The cultural production of classroom practice." *British Journal of Sociology of Education* 10(1):19–31.

———. 1991. *"At school I've got a chance." Culture/privilege: Pacific Islanders and Pakeha girls at school.* Palmerston North, New Zealand: Dunmore Press.

Joshi, Vijaya. 1996. "You mean there's a positive side?!: Identity issues for second generation migrant women." Paper presented to the Second Women in Migration Conference, Bureau of Immigration, Multicultural and Population Research, Sydney, 3–4 June.

Jupp, James. 1996. *Understanding Australian multiculturalism.* Bureau of Immigration, Multicultural and Population Research. Canberra: Australian Government Publishing Service.

Kaeppler, Adrienne. 1978. "Exchange patterns in goods and spouses: Fiji, Tonga, and Samoa." *Mankind* 11(3):246–252.

Ka'ili, David, and 'Anapesi Ka'ili. 1999. "Can we become Tongan without speaking Tongan?" *Moana* 2:15.

Ka'ili, Tevita. 1997. *"Ala 'i sia, ala 'i kolonga* (Skillful at *sia,* skillful at *kolonga*): An indigenous Tongan proverb for contemporary Pacific Islanders." *Moana* 1:7.

Kalantzis, Mary, Robyn Gurney, and Bill Cope. 1992. *The parent-school partnership: Issues of parent participation in culturally diverse schools.*

Working papers on Multiculturalism no. 18. Wollongong, New South Wales: The Centre for Multicultural Studies, University of Wollongong.

Kallen, Evelyn. 1982. *The Western Samoan kinship bridge: A study in migration, social change and the new ethnicity.* Leiden: E. J. Brill.

Kalonikali Tonga. 1996. "*Fakatāpui senitā Pule La'ā 'i Senē*" 33(38) (Sept. 19):14.

Kearney, M. 1995. "The local and the global: The anthropology of globalization and transnationalism." *Annual Review of Anthropology* 24:547–565.

Keefe, Susan, and Amado Padilla. 1987. *Chicano ethnicity.* Albuquerque: University of New Mexico Press.

Kibria, Nazli. 1997. "The construction of 'Asian American': Reflections on intermarriage and ethnic identity among second-generation Chinese and Korean Americans" *Ethnic and Racial Studies* 20(3):523–544.

Krishnan, Vasantha, Penelope Schoeffel, and Julie Warren. 1994. *The challenge of change: Pacific Island communities in New Zealand, 1986–1993.* Wellington: New Zealand Institute for Social Research and Development.

Lafitani, Siosiua. 1992. "Tongan diaspora: Perceptions, values and behaviour of Tongans in Canberra." M. Letters thesis, Australian National University.

Langfield, Michele. 1995. "A thirty-year history of the Ecumenical Migration Centre." *Migration Action* 17(2):3–7.

Larner, Wendy, and Richard Bedford. 1993. "Island-born and New Zealand-born Pacific Islanders in the workforce: A perspective." In *A world perspective on Pacific Islander migration: Australia, New Zealand and the USA*, ed. Grant McCall and John Connell. Pacific Studies Monograph no. 6. Sydney: Centre for South Pacific Studies, University of New South Wales, 187–201.

Lawson, Stephanie. 1994. *Tradition versus democracy in the kingdom of Tonga.* Regime change and regime maintenance in Asia and the Pacific discussion paper no. 13. Canberra: Department of Political and Social Change, Australian National University.

Lee, Helen Morton. 2002a. "Debating language and identity online: Tongans on the net." In *Going native on the net: Indigenous cyber-activism and virtual diasporas over the World Wide Web*, ed. Kyra Landzelius. London: Routledge.

———. 2002b. "All Tongans are connected: Tongan transnationalism." In *Pacific Island societies in a global world*, ed. Victoria Lockwood. Englewood Cliffs, N.J.: Prentice Hall.

Leistyna, Pepi. 1999. "Racenicity: The relationship between racism and ethnicity." In *Critical ethnicity: Countering the waves of identity politics*, ed. Robert Tai and Mary Kenyatta. Lanham, Md.: Rowman and Littlefield, 133–171.

Levin, Michael, and Dennis Ahlburg. 1993. "Pacific Islanders in the

United States census data." In *A world perspective on Pacific Islander migration: Australia, New Zealand and the USA*, ed. Grant McCall and John Connell. Pacific Studies Monograph no. 6. Sydney: Centre for South Pacific Studies, University of New South Wales, 95–144.

Lindstrom, Monty, and Geoffrey White, eds. 1993. *Custom today*. Special Issue of *Anthropological Forum* 6.

Literature and Arts Heritage Guild of Polynesia. 2001. http://polynesia 2000.bizhosting.com

Macpherson, Cluny. 1984. "On the future of Samoan ethnicity in New Zealand." In Tauiwi: *Racism and ethnicity in New Zealand*, ed. Paul Spoonley, Cluny Macpherson, David Pearson, and Charles Sedgewick. Palmerston North, New Zealand: The Dunmore Press, 107–127.

———. 1985. "Public and private views of home: Will Western Samoan migrants return?" *Mobility and identity in the South Pacific*. Special Issue of *Pacific Viewpoint* 26(1):242–262.

———. 1990. "Stolen dreams: Some consequences of dependency for Western Samoan youth." In *Migration and development in the South Pacific*, ed. John Connell. Canberra: National Centre for Development Studies, Australian National University, 107–119.

———. 1991. "The changing contours of Samoan ethnicity." In Nga Take: *Ethnic relations and racism in Aotearoa/New Zealand*, ed. Paul Spoonley, David Pearson, and Cluny Macpherson. Palmerston North: Dunmore Press, 68–83.

———. 1994. "Changing patterns of commitment to island homelands: A case study of Western Samoa." *Pacific Studies* 17(3):83–116.

———. 1997. "The Polynesian diaspora: New communities and new questions." In *Contemporary migration to Oceania: Diaspora and network*, ed. Ken'ichi Sudo and Shuji Yoshida. JCAS Symposium series 3. Osaka: The Japan Center for Area Studies, National Museum of Ethnology, 77–100.

Macpherson, Cluny, and La'avasa Macpherson. 1999. "The changing contours of migrant Samoan kinship." In *Small worlds, global lives: Islands and migration*, ed. Russell King and John Connell. London: Pinter, 277–295.

Macpherson, Cluny, Bradd Shore, and Robert Franco, eds. 1978. *New neighbors . . . Islanders in adaptation*. Santa Cruz, Calif.: Center for South Pacific Studies, University of California, Santa Cruz.

Macpherson, Cluny, Paul Spoonley, and Melani Anae, eds. 2001. Tangata o te moana nui: *The evolving identities of Pacific peoples in Aotearoa/New Zealand*. Palmerston North, New Zealand: Dunmore Press.

Maher, Chris, and Wayne Caldow. 1997. *Atlas of the Australian people— 1991 census: Victoria*. Canberra: Australian Government Publishing Service.

Mahler, Sarah. 1998. "Theoretical and empirical contributions toward a research agenda for transnationalism." In *Transnationalism from below,* ed. Michael Smith and Luis Guarnizo. New Brunswick, N.J.: Transaction Publishers, 64–100.

Maingay, Samantha. 1995. "The social mobility, identity, and community networks of second generation Pacific Islanders in Auckland." Ph.D. dissertation, University of Auckland.

Mamak, Alexander. 1993. "Becoming a competent migrant community: The case of American Samoans in California." In *A world perspective on Pacific Islander migration: Australia, New Zealand and the USA,* ed. Grant McCall and John Connell. Pacific Studies Monograph No. 6. Sydney: Centre for South Pacific Studies, University of New South Wales, 149–159.

Mangisi, Sione. 1999. "Letter to the editor: Where does Tonga stand academically?" *Tonga Chronicle,* 29 July, 5.

Maori and Pacific Islander Community Based Services. 2000. Oceanic peoples in Victoria: Report on the Maori and Pacific Islander Community of Victoria.

Marcus, George. 1974. "A hidden dimension of family development in the modern kingdom of Tonga." *Journal of Comparative Family Studies* 5(1):87–102.

———. 1981. "Power on the extreme periphery: The perspective of Tongan elites in the modern world system." *Pacific Viewpoint* 22(1):48–64.

———. 1993. "Tonga's contemporary globalizing strategies: Trading on sovereignty amidst international migration." In *Contemporary Pacific societies: Studies in development and change,* ed. Victoria Lockwood, Thomas Harding, and Ben Wallace. Englewood Cliffs, N.J.: Prentice Hall, 21–33.

Martin, Jean. 1978. *The migrant presence: Australian responses 1947–1977.* Sydney: George Allen and Unwin.

Matangi Tonga. 1994. "Awoken by memories of Tonga" 9(3):35.

———. 1998a. "High tech for Niuatoputapu" 13(1):17.

———. 1998b. "Royal School of Science: Overseas studies on-line, a dream come true" 13(2):3–4.

———. 2000a. "Australia demands tough bonds" 15(3):22.

———. 2000b. "Flag of nation builders" 15(3):3.

———. 2001a. "Editorial: A peaceful revolution" 16(1):5.

———. 2001b. "HRH wants to put Tonga in the forefront of information technology" 16(1):16–17.

———. 2001c. "Cutting edge communications will liberate the common man" 16(1):18–19.

McCall, Grant, and John Connell, eds. 1993. *A world perspective on Pacific Islander migration: Australia, New Zealand and the USA.* Pacific Studies Monograph no. 6. Sydney: Centre for South Pacific Studies, University of New South Wales.

McMurray, Christine. 2000. *Community profiles 1996 census: New Zealand born.* Canberra: Department of Immigration and Multicultural Affairs.

Mindel, Charles, Robert Habenstein, and Roosevelt White, Jr., eds. 1988.

Ethnic families in America: Patterns and variations. 3d. ed. New York: Elsevier.

Moala, Meleane. 1986. "Tongan workers in Sydney." In *Why don't they ask us? We're not dumb!: A study of the experiences of specific target groups in Australia,* ed. Peter Shergold and Loucas Nicolaou. Canberra: Department of Immigration and Ethnic Affairs, 219–229.

Moore, Henrietta. 1994. *A passion for difference: Essays in anthropology and gender.* Cambridge, U.K.: Polity Press.

Morton, Helen. 1996. *Becoming Tongan: An ethnography of childhood.* Honolulu: University of Hawai'i Press.

———. 1998a. "Creating their own culture: Diasporic Tongans." *The Contemporary Pacific* 10(1):1–30.

———. 1998b. "How Tongan is a Tongan? In *Echoes of Pacific war,* ed. Deryck Scarr, Niel Gunson, and Jennifer Terrell. Canberra: Target Oceania, 149–166.

———. 1999. "Islanders in space: Tongans online." In *Small worlds, global lives: Islands and migration,* ed. Russell King and John Connell. London: Pinter, 235–253.

———. 2001a. "Remembering freedom and the freedom to remember: Tongan memories of independence." In *Cultural memory: Reconfiguring history and identity in the postcolonial Pacific,* ed. Jeannette Mageo. Honolulu: University of Hawai'i Press, 37–57.

———. 2001b. "'I' is for identity: What's in a name?" In *Computer-mediated communication in Australian anthropology and sociology.* Special issue of *Social Analysis,* ed. Helen Morton, 45(1):67–80.

Multicultural Affairs Unit. 1996. "Pacific Islands-born Victorians: Labour force status, 1991 census." Table provided by Multicultural Affairs Unit, Department of Premier and Cabinet, Victoria.

Murphy, B. 1993. *The other Australia: Experiences of migration.* Cambridge: Cambridge University Press.

Nagel, Joanne. 1994. "Constructing ethnicity: Creating and recreating ethnic identity and culture." *Social Problems* 41(1):152–176.

Niumeitolu, Fuifuilupe. 1997. "Editorial." *Moana* 1:2.

Niumeitolu, 'Ofo. 1993. "Tongan health: A personal view." In *A world perspective on Pacific Islander migration: Australia, New Zealand and the USA,* ed. Grant McCall and John Connell. Pacific Studies Monograph no. 6. Sydney: Centre for South Pacific Studies, University of New South Wales, 71–81.

Oboler, Suzanne. 1995. *Ethnic labels, Latino lives: Identity and the politics of (re)presentation in the United States.* Minneapolis: University of Minnesota Press.

Ogden, Michael. 1999. "Islands on the Internet." *The Contemporary Pacific* 11(2):452–465.

Olson, Lisa. 1996. "Boxer's silver medal a knockout performance in Tonga." *The Age,* 6 August, C6.

O'Neal, Colleen. 1999. "Possibilities for migration and anthropology." *American Ethnologist* 26(1):221–225.

Ong, Aihwa. 1999. *Flexible citizenship: The cultural logics of transnationality.* Durham, N.C.: Duke University Press.

Parillo, Vincent. 1990. *Strangers to these shores: Race and ethnic relations in the U.S.* 3d. ed. New York: Macmillan.

Pedraza, Silvia. 1994. "Introduction from the Special Issue editor: The sociology of immigration, race, and ethnicity in America." *Social Problems* 41(1):1–8.

Peltz, Rakhmiel. 1995. "Children of immigrants remember: The evolution of ethnic culture." In *The labyrinth of memory: Ethnographic journeys,* ed. Marea Teski and Jacob Climo. Westport, Conn.: Bergin and Garvey, 27–48.

Penny, Janet, and Siew-Ean Khoo. 1996. *Intermarriage: A study of migration and integration.* Bureau of Immigration, Multiculturalism and Population Research. Canberra: Australian Government Publishing Service.

Pe Pua, Rogelia. 1996. *'We're just like other kids!': Street-frequenting youth of non-English speaking background.* Bureau of Immigration, Multicultural and Population Research. Canberra: Australian Government Publishing Service.

Perminow, Arne. 1993. *The long way home: Dilemmas of everyday life in a Tongan village.* Oslo: Scandinavian University Press and the Institute for Comparative Research in Human Culture.

Phinney, Jean, and Mary Jane Rotheram, eds. 1987. *Children's ethnic socialization.* Newbury Park, Calif.: Sage.

Pitt, David, and Cluny Macpherson. 1974. *Emerging pluralism: The Samoan community in New Zealand.* Auckland: Longman Paul.

Poirine, Bernard. 1998. "Should we hate or love MIRAB?" *The Contemporary Pacific* 10(1):65–105.

Polynesia Polynesia Cultural Heritage Society. 2001. http://www.punawelewele.com/polynesia2/cultural.htm

Portes, Alejandro. 1997. "Immigration theory for a new century: Some problems and opportunities." International Migration Review 31(4):799–825.

Price, Charles. 1987. "The Asian and Pacific Islands peoples of Australia." In *Pacific bridges: The new immigration from Asia and the Pacific Islands,* ed. James Fawcett and Benjamin Cariño. New York: Center for Migration Studies, 175–197.

Rallu, Jean Louis. 1993. "Arrivals and departures of Pacific Islands-born in Australia." Paper presented to the Bureau of Immigration and Population Research Conference, Asia-Pacific Migration Affecting Australia: Temporary, Long-Term and Permanent Movements of People. Darwin, September.

———. 1994. "Australia and Pacific Islander migration." *Australian Population and Migration Journal* 3(2–3):431–443.

Reitz, Jeffrey. 1980. *The survival of ethnic groups.* Toronto: McGraw-Hill Ryerson.

Root, Maria, ed. 1992. *Racially mixed people in America.* Newbury Park, Calif.: Sage.

Rosenblatt, Paul, Terri Karis, and Richard Powell. 1995. *Multiracial couples: Black and white voices.* Thousand Oaks, Calif.: Sage.

Rosenthal, Doreen, and Anthony Cichello. 1986. "The meeting of two cultures: Ethnic identity and psychosocial adjustment of Italian-Australian adolescents." *International Journal of Psychology* 21:487–501.

Rosenthal, Doreen, and S. Shirley Feldman. 1992. "The relationship between parenting behaviour and ethnic identity in Chinese-American and Chinese-Australian adolescents." *International Journal of Psychology* 27(1):19–31.

Rosenthal, Doreen, and Christine Hrynevich. 1985. "Ethnicity and ethnic identity: A comparative study of Greek-, Italian-, and Anglo-Australian adolescents." *International Journal of Psychology* 20:723–742.

Rotheram-Borus, Mary Jane. 1993. "Biculturalism among adolescents." In *Ethnic identity: Formation and transmission among Hispanics and other minorities,* ed. Martha Bernal and George Knight. Albany, N.Y.: State University of New York, 81–102.

Roy, Parimal, and Ian Hamilton. 1997. "Interethnic marriage: Identifying the second generation in Australia." *International Migration Review* 21(1):128–142.

Rumbaut, Ruben. 1994. "The crucible within: Ethnic identity, self-esteem, and segmented assimilation among children of immigrants." *International Migration Review* 28(4):748–793.

Rutherford, Noel, ed. 1977. *Friendly Islands: A history of Tonga.* Melbourne: Oxford University Press.

Sansone, Livio. 1995. "The making of a black youth culture: Lower-class young men of Surinamese origin in Amsterdam." In *Youth cultures: A cross-cultural perspective,* ed. Vered Amit-Talai and Helena Wulff. London: Routledge, 114–143.

Sassen, Saskia. 1998. *Globalization and its discontents.* New York: The New Press.

Scarr, Deryck, Niel Gunson, and Jennifer Terrell, eds. 1998. *Echoes of Pacific war.* Canberra: Target Oceania.

Schoeffel, Penelope, and Malama Meleisea. N.d. "Spare the rod? Conflicting cultural models of the family and approaches to child socialisation in New Zealand." Draft Research Report. Centre of Pacific Studies, University of Auckland.

Segal, Ronald. 1995. *The black diaspora.* London: Faber.

Singh, Pashaura, and N. Gerald Barrier, eds. 1996. *The transmission of Sikh heritage in the diaspora.* New Delhi: Manohar Publishers.

Small, Cathy. 1997. *Voyages: From Tongan villages to American suburbs.* Ithaca, N.Y.: Cornell University Press.

Spickard, Paul. 1989. *Mixed blood: Intermarriage and ethnic identity in twentieth century America.* Madison: University of Wisconsin Press.

Spoonley, Paul, Cluny Macpherson, and David Pearson, eds. 1996. Nga Patai: *Racism and ethnic relations in Aotearoa/New Zealand.* Palmerston North, New Zealand: Dunmore Press.

Spoonley, Paul, David Pearson, and Cluny Macpherson, eds. 1991. Nga Take: *Ethnic relations and racism in Aotearoa/New Zealand.* Palmerston North: Dunmore Press.

Stanton, Max. 1993. "A gathering of saints: The role of the Church of Jesus Christ of Latter-Day Saints in Pacific Islander migration." In *A world perspective on Pacific Islander migration: Australia, New Zealand and the USA,* ed. Grant McCall and John Connell. Pacific Studies Monograph no. 6. Sydney: Centre for South Pacific Studies, University of New South Wales, 23–37.

Statistics New Zealand. 1995. *Tongan people in New Zealand: A statistical profile.* Wellington: Pacific Islands Profiles.

———. 1998. *Tongan people in New Zealand: Pacific Islands profiles.* Wellington: Pacific Islands Profiles.

Steinberg, Stephen, ed. 2000. *Race and ethnicity in the United States: Issues and debates.* Oxford: Lanham.

Sudo, Ken'ichi. 1997a. "Introduction: Contemporary migration in Oceania." In *Contemporary migration to Oceania: Diaspora and network,* ed. Ken'ichi Sudo and Shuji Yoshida. JCAS Symposium series 3. Osaka: The Japan Center for Area Studies, National Museum of Ethnology, 1–10.

———. 1997b. "Expanding international migration by the Tongan people: Strategies and socio-cultural effects on the homeland." In *Contemporary migration to Oceania: Diaspora and network,* ed. Ken'ichi Sudo and Shuji Yoshida. JCAS Symposium series 3. Osaka: The Japan Center for Area Studies, National Museum of Ethnology, 101–111.

Sun, The. 1975a. "Sportsman fights to stay." 20 February, 3.

———. 1975b. "Chance for Tongan star—all smiles." 21 February, 3.

Szeps, Josh. 1997. "Cultured? Me? Fat chance!" *The Sydney Morning Herald,* 8 February.

Tai, Robert, and Mary Kenyatta, eds. 1999. *Critical ethnicity: Countering the waves of identity politics.* Lanham, Md.: Rowman and Littlefield.

Tāmo'ua, Pilimisolo. 1998. "Sculptor seeking in work and life to preserve, strengthen traditional cultural values." *Tonga Chronicle,* 26 November, 5.

Tedlock, Barbara. 1996. "Diasporas." In *Encyclopedia of cultural anthropology.* Vol. 1, ed. David Levinson and Melvin Ember. New York: Henry Holt and Company, 341–342.

Tiatia, Jemaima. 1998. *Caught between cultures: A New Zealand-born Pacific Island perspective.* Auckland: Christian Research Association.

Tilley, Virginia. 1997. "The terms of the debate: Untangling language about ethnicity and ethnic movements." *Ethnic and Racial Studies* 20(3):497–522.

Tizard, Barbara, and Ann Phoenix. 1993. *Black, white or mixed race? Race and racism in the lives of young people with mixed parentage.* London: Routledge.

Toafa, Viliami, Losa Moata'ane, and Barbara Guthrie. 1999. "Belief and trust: Health caring for migrant Tongan healers and patients in New Zealand." *Pacific Health Dialog* 6(2):160–167.

Tonga Chronicle. 1979. "Sanitesi disqualified." 7 September, 8.

———. 1996a. "Ha'apai college gains multi-purpose hall." 2 May, 1.

———. 1996b. "Utah's Tongan community celebrates success." 3 July, 2.

———. 1996c. "1,500 in N.Z. attend youth rally." 26 September, 8.

———. 1996d. "Language classes at Oz school helping kids retain heritage." 14 November, 5.

———. 1997a. "Pacific islanders start U.S. centre to teach reading, traditional culture." 31 July, 3.

———. 1997b. "Tongan farmers' group in Hawai'i to stage fairs." 11 September, 1.

———. 1998a. "King urges health, life-style concerns." 5 February, 3.

———. 1998b. "Funds for 'Apifo'ou raised in Australia, New Zealand." 5 February, 8.

———. 1998c. "1996 census data revealed." 12 February, 5.

———. 1998d. "Census shows Kingdom to be a young country." 19 February, 1.

———. 1998e. "Census reveals marital status, ethnicity." 26 February, 5.

———. 1998f. "Census reveals religious preferences, Wesleyan Church still Kingdom's largest." 5 March, 4.

———. 1998g. "1996 Census reveals 98.5 pct literacy." 19 March, 1.

———. 1998h. "Royal School of Science for Distance Learning providing worldwide university courses." 4 April, 1.

———. 1998i. "Hawai'i Christian youth seek funds here." 23 July, 2.

———. 1998j. "Hawai'i youths raise T$42,988." 6 August, 3.

———. 1999a. "Chinese community report crime wave, carry concerns to Minister, Commander of Police." 14 January, 3.

———. 1999b. "Community seeks understanding, equality of treatment." 14 January, 3.

———. 1999c. "T$500,000 business, computer centre opened for Tupou High School." 6 May, 3.

———. 1999d. "More Tongans overstay in Australia than any other group, contributing to world's highest rate." 27 May, 4.

———. 1999e. " 'God's gift to the islands' says Ha'apai director of U.N. project." 2 September, 1.

Tonga Council of Churches. 1975. *Land and migration*. Papers presented at seminar. Nuku'alofa, 22–26 September.

Tonga Today. 1988. "Me no can speak Tongan no more." 2(9):13, 40.

Tongan Herald. 1998. "Seeds of hope: Tongan Youth Council." 16 October, 20.

Tsolidis, Georgina. 1995. "Greek-Australian families." In *Families and cultural diversity*, ed. Robyn Hartley. Sydney: Allen and Unwin, 121–143.

Tucker, Jim. 1999. "Kefu keeps faith." *The Daily Telegraph*, 5 November, 78.

Tu'inauvai, Meleane. 1995. "Young people and communication." *Austonga News* 17:2.

Tu'inukuafe, Edgar. 1990. "Tongans in New Zealand—A brief study." In *Tongan culture and history,* ed. Phyllis Herda, Jennifer Terrell, and Niel Gunson. Canberra: Department of Pacific and Southeast Asian History, Research School of Pacific Studies, Australian National University, 206–214.

Turner, James West. 1997. "Continuity and constraint: Reconstructing the concept of tradition from a Pacific perspective." *The Contemporary Pacific* 9(2):345–381.

Urciuoli, Bonnie. 1995. "Language and borders." *Annual Review of Anthropology* 24:525–546.

U.S. Census Bureau. 1999. Database C90STFIC. http://www.census.gov.

———. 2000. Racial and ethnic classifications used in Census 2000 and beyond. http://www.census.gov/population/www/socdemo/race/racefactcb.html.

———. 2001a. Census 2000 brief: Overview of race and Hispanic origin. http://www.census.gov/population/www/cen2000/briefs.html.

———. 2001b. Census 2000 brief: The Native Hawaiian and other Pacific Islander population: 2000. http://www.census.gov/population/www/cen2000/briefs.html.

U.S. Department of Commerce. 1993. *We the Americans: Pacific Islanders.* Washington, D.C.: Bureau of the Census, Economics and Statistics Administration.

U.S. Department of State. 1998. Office of the spokesman press statement: Diversity Immigration Visa Program (DV-2000). http://secretary.state.gov/www/briefings/statements/1998/ps980803.html.

———. 1999. Office of the spokesman press statement: Results of the Diversity Immigration Visa Program (DV-2000). http://secretary.state.gov/www/briefings/statements/1999/ps990524b.html.

Va'a, Leulu Felise. 1995. "*Fa'a Samoa*: Continuities and change. A study of Samoan migrants in Australia" Ph.D. dissertation, Australian National University.

Vasta, Ellie. 1995. "The Italian-Australian family: Transformations and continuities." In *Families and cultural diversity,* ed. Robyn Hartley. Sydney: Allen and Unwin, 144–166.

Vasta, Ellie, and Stephen Castles, eds. 1996. *The teeth are smiling: The persistence of racism in multicultural Australia.* Sydney: Allen and Unwin.

Vertovec, Steven. 2001. "Transnationalism and identity." *Journal of Ethnic and Migration Studies* 27(4):573–582.

Vete, Mele Fuka. 1995. "The determinants of remittances among Tongans in Auckland." *Asia and Pacific Migration Journal* 4(1):55–68.

Victorian Multicultural Commission. 1999. Annual Report 1998/1999. Melbourne: VMC.

Village Courier. 1982. "Tongan brothers." 1 October, 2

Ward, Gerald. 1997. "Expanding worlds of Oceania: Implications of migration." In *Contemporary migration to Oceania: Diaspora and network,* ed. Ken'ichi Sudo and Shuji Yoshida. JCAS Symposium Series

3. Osaka: The Japan Center for Area Studies, National Museum of Ethnology, 179–196.

———. 1999. "Widening worlds, shrinking worlds? The reshaping of Oceania." Pacific Distinguished Lecture 1999. Canberra: Centre for the Contemporary Pacific, Australian National University.

Warschauer, Mark. 2000. "Language, identity and the internet." In *Race in cyberspace,* ed. B. Kolko, L. Nakamura, and G. Rodman. New York: Routledge, 151–170.

Wentworth, William. 1980. *Context and understanding: An inquiry into socialization theory.* New York: Elsevier.

Westwood, Sallie, and Annie Phizacklea. 2000. *Transnationalism and the politics of belonging.* London: Routledge.

White, Rob, Santina Perrone, Carmel Guerra, and Rosario Lampugnani. 1999a. *Ethnic youth gangs in Australia: Do they exist? Overview Report.* Melbourne: Australian Multicultural Foundation.

———. 1999b. *Ethnic youth gangs in Australia: Do they exist? Pacific Islander young people.* Report no. 3. Melbourne: Australian Multicultural Foundation.

Wilkins, Jenny, and Nilufer Yaman. 1994. The Multicultural Juvenile Justice Project: Report for the Department of Health and Community Services and the Department of Justice. Unpublished report.

Wilson, Bruce. 1999. "What ever happened to . . ." *The Daily Telegraph,* 5 November, 80.

Wolfgramm, Robert. 1994. "Kai Viti: On being Fijian without being 'a Fijian.'" Ph.D. dissertation, La Trobe University, Melbourne.

Wood-Ellem, Elizabeth. 1999. *Queen Sālote of Tonga: The story of an era 1900–1965.* Auckland: Auckland University Press.

Wooden, Mark, Robert Holton, Graeme Hugo, and Judith Sloan. 1994. *Australian immigration: A survey of the issues.* Bureau of Immigration and Population Research. Canberra: Australian Government Publishing Service.

Zack, Naomi, ed. 1995. *American mixed race: The culture of microdiversity.* Lanham, Md.: Rowman and Littlefield.

INDEX

adoption. *See* fostering
African Americans: and intermarriage, 194–195; and Tongan youth, 250–251
Ahlburg, Dennis, 32, 58, 295n.19
Anae, Melani, 151, 249
anga fakatonga. See Tongan way, the
artists overseas, 119
associations. *See* organizations
Australia: education in, 55–56, 269–270; employment in, 56–59, 270–271; home ownership in, 267–268; immigration policies in, 20–21, 24–27, 62; Pacific Islanders in, 51–52, 177, 255–256; remittances from, 31, 32, 34–35, 38–39; Tongan population of, 24–27, 256–258. *See also* Melbourne; churches, Tongan

birthplace of migrants, 47–48, 263–264
Brown, Richard, 8, 35; and John Connell, 32; and John Foster, 32, 33, 35; and Adrian Walker, 22, 25–26, 30–35, 56–57
Bull, Vika and Linda, 118, 178

chain migration, 10, 17, 23
child care, 41
Christianity. *See* churches, Tongan
churches, Tongan, 41–45, 70–71, 296n.1; in Australia, 11, 42, 43, 259–261, 273; criticism of, 44, 161; and intermarriage, 210; and migration to Australia, 24; and racism, 64; in Tonga, 28–29, 303n.14; and youth, 43–44, 75,

104–105, 160–163, 180. *See also* Mormon Church
citizenship, 93–94, 272
Connell, John, 8, 19, 28; and Graham Harrison and Grant McCall, 57, 258, 268; and Grant McCall, 19, 29
crime, 61, 67, 73, 297n.16. *See also* gangs
cultural identity, 1–5, 8, 13, 81, 95, 136–140, 172–173, 235–237, 251–253; and citizenship, 93–95; and family, 91, 94–95; and intermarried parents, 206–209; and part-Tongans, 214–221, 229, 231–232. *See also* language; Tongan way, the

dance, Tongan, 101–102, 121–122, 173
diaspora, 6. *See also* transnationalism
discrimination. *See* racism

education, 52–56, 123, 164, 269–270; and cultural change, 106, 115; and remittances, 33; travel overseas for, 7–8, 16, 25, 52–53
elderly migrants, 40
employment, 56–60; in Australia, 56–57, 270–272; in New Zealand, 21–22, 56, 57, 58; in the United States, 56, 57–58
English language, 43, 49–50
ethnic identity, 3–5, 172, 237, 299n.2. *See also* cultural identity; pan-ethnic identity
ethnicity. *See* ethnic identity
"ethnic socialization," 136

ex-students' associations, 37, 38, 42, 45, 83

Faeamani, Sione, 32–33
Faiva, 'Osaiasi, 41, 71, 258, 268, 271
faka'apa'apa (respect), 95–99, 105, 147, 160, 165; and Christianity, 96; and cross-siblings, 87, 98–99, 121, 124, 178, 203; and fathers, 97, 121, 124; and *mehekitanga* (father's sisters), 97–98, 121, 157; and Mormons, 116
family. *See* kinship
fatongia (obligations). See *kavenga*
Finney, Frances, 5, 19, 48, 100, 189, 295n.16, 298n.1
Foliaki, Siale, 71–72
fostering, 41, 75, 89, 204
friendships, 123, 133–134, 168–169, 274–275; disapproval of, 46, 73, 87–88, 92
fund-raising, 37–39, 43

Gailey, Christine, 85
gangs, 61, 166–169
gender, 101; and changing roles, 45, 102–103, 113–115, 121, 157–160, 179; and intermarriage, 103, 196–198, 208, 229. See also *faka'apa'apa*
gossip, 116, 156–157, 178
Grainger, Gareth, 20, 25, 76–77, 260, 293n.2

health problems, 71–73
history of migration, 7–8; to Australia, 10, 24–25, 258–259; to New Zealand, 21–22; to the United States, 23
household composition, 40, 261, 264–266

identity. *See* cultural identity; ethnic identity
illegal immigrants. *See* overstayers
immigration policies: in Australia, 24–25, 26, 65, 93; in New Zealand, 21–22; in the United States, 23
Internet, 79–80, 150, 202, 239–242. *See also* Kava Bowl
Islanders. *See* Pacific Islanders

James, Kerry, 28, 29, 31, 37, 90, 295n.20

Ka'ili, David (Tevita), 170; and 'Anapesi Ka'ili, 149–150
Kami, Taholo, 9, 91, 170, 241, 248, 292n.13
Kava Bowl, 1, 8–10, 92, 152, 170–171, 248, 292n.13; and language, 111, 149
kavenga (obligations, "burdens"), 30, 155–156; and intermarried couples, 191–192, 203, 225–226
kinship, 99–100, 163; as motive for migration, 15, 17, 132; networks overseas, 7, 15, 28, 40, 83, 91–92, 239–240, 273–274. *See also* remittances
Kioa case, 20
koloa (ceremonial wealth), 37, 100, 101, 156, 235

Lafitani, Siosiua, 20, 30, 42, 46–48
language, 48, 110, 235, 272–273. *See also* English language; Tongan language
Latter Day Saints, Church of Jesus Christ of. *See* Mormon Church
leisure activities, 43–44, 45–46. *See also* sports

Marcus, George, 27, 29, 241–242, 293n.4
marriage: and advice to youth, 181–182, 191–192, 233; choice of spouse, 185–186, 187–188, 190, 193–194, 198–199
Macpherson, Cluny, 29, 188, 192, 250, 294n.10, 295n.20, 296n.1, 298n.3; and La'avasa Macpherson, 299n.8
Maingay, Samantha, 58
McCall, Grant; and John Connell, 8
media, 78–79; representations in, 60–62, 66–67
mehekitanga (father's sisters). See *faka'apa'apa*
Melbourne, 10, 255; population of Tongans in, 10–13, 47, 256–257; Tongan churches in, 11, 42–43
MIRAB, 30
Moala, Meleane, 41, 59

monarchy. *See* royal family
Mormon Church, 44, 162–163; and education, 16, 54; and migration, 16, 23; and the Tongan way, 116
multiculturalism, 5, 63, 188
multiple identities, 219, 252–253
music, 118, 173

New Zealand: education in, 55, 56, 75, 112, 302n.12; employment in, 56–58; home ownership in, 268; immigration policies in, 21–22; and intermarriage, 188–189; one-parent families in, 265; overstayers in, 19; and step-migration, 25–26; Tongan population of, 3, 21–22. *See also* Pacific Islanders
nobility, 28, 46–47, 153, 156

Organizations, formal, 52, 76–78, 112–113, 259; youth, 171–172
overstayers, 19–20, 25, 48, 61, 72

Pacific Islanders: in Australia, 51–52, 177, 255–256; education and, 55, 56; employment and, 56–59; and intermarriage, 188–189; and media, 79; and migration, 8, 18; in New Zealand, 19, 21–23, 52, 57, 58, 73, 119, 151, 160–161; and organizations, 52, 77–78; and pan-ethnic identities, 245–250; in the United States, 18, 23–24, 52, 56, 57–58, 295n.19
panethnic identity, 6, 245–250; and intermarriage, 195–196
part-Tongans, 12, 190, 214–224, 225, 228–229, 230–233
physical punishment, 89–90, 105–109, 164–166, 184; and intermarried couples, 212–213, 229, 230
Planet Tonga, 79–80, 150
Poirine, Bernard, 33
Polynesian. *See* Pacific Islanders
postcolonial issues, 6, 170, 248, 298n.22
Pro-Democracy Movement, 28, 243

racism, 60–69, 135, 139, 177; and intermarried couples, 191,

194–195; and part-Tongans, 231; and police, 75–76
remittances, 27–28, 29–39, 242; and second generation, 34, 39, 155. *See also* fund-raising
respect. See *faka'apa'apa*
royal family, 28, 241–242; and cultural change, 117–118; and overseas travel, 7, 60, 71, 83–84, 258, 293n.2

Samoans, 99, 100, 296n.1, 298n.3, 299n.8; and employment, 57–58; and health, 297n.15; and intermarriage, 188, 192; and remittances, 31, 32, 295n.20; and youth, 29, 151–152, 249. *See also* Pacific Islanders
siblings. See *faka'apa'apa*, gender
Small, Cathy, 18, 23, 29, 31, 69, 100, 188, 293n.19, 298n.2, 303n.13
Spickard, Paul, 187, 193–194
sports, 45, 60–61, 104, 173–174
step migration, 18, 23, 25–26
Sudo, Ken'ichi, 18, 32, 293n.4

tala ova. See overstayers
Tiatia, Jemima, 151, 161
Tohi, Filipe, 119
Tonga, 27–29, 102; churches in, 28–29, 303n.14; "contraflows" from, 37, 83; and English language, 49, 110–111; and intermarriage, 189–196; and Internet, 80, 240–242; migrants' ties to, 6–7, 81–83, 240–245; migrants' views of, 120, 152–154; migrants visiting, 84–85, 145–148, 180–181, 183; motives for migration from, 15–18, 132; part-Tongans visiting, 219–221, 231; population of, 3, 28, 293n.4; returning to, 84–86; sending children to, 86–90, 121, 122, 142–145, 180, 184–185, 210–212, 229; and tensions with migrants, 31, 90–91, 243–244. *See also* history of migration; remittances; transnationalism
Tongan Christian Fellowship, 10, 259

Tongan language, 51, 59, 87,
111–113, 148–151, 175–176,
235–236, 303n.13; and non-Tongan
spouses, 201–202, 223, 227;
and part-Tongans, 221–223, 228,
231
Tongan way, the, 1–2, 90, 95, 124, 138,
235, 275; changes in, 113, 117–
119, 120, 154–155, 237–238; and
Christianity, 104, 116; and
churches, 44; criticism of, 120–
121, 139–140, 152, 155, 179, 227,
239; loss of, 2, 90, 101, 238; and
pālangi way, 109–110, 115, 141–
142, 156, 174, 178, 227, 238–239;
youth's understanding of, 122,
138, 172, 184. See also
faka'apa'apa; gender
Tonga Online, 9. *See also* Kava Bowl

transnationalism, 6–7, 14, 29–30, 31,
81, 83, 239, 242–244, 252

United States of America: and education,
53–54, 56; and employment,
56; home ownership in, 268; immigration
policies in, 23; and intermarriage,
189, 193–195; one-parent
families in, 302n.11; and racism,
66–67, 69; Tongan population of,
18, 23–24. *See also* Pacific Islanders

Vete, Mele Fuka, 30, 35

White Australia policy, 24–25, 65, 93,
190
Wolfgramm, Robert, 219
Wood-Ellem, Elizabeth, 292n.11,
293n.2